CHINA MISSION

Also by Audrey Ronning Topping

The New York Times Report from Red China (with Tillman
Durdin, James Restin, and Seymour Topping) (1971)
A Day on a Chinese Commune (1972)
Holiday in Peking (1972)
Dawn Wakes in the East (1973)
The Splendors of Tibet (1980)
*Charlie's World: The Improbable Adventures of a Hong Kong
Cockatoo and His American Family* (2000)

LOUISIANA STATE UNIVERSITY PRESS)|(BATON ROUGE

Audrey Ronning Topping

CHINA MISSION

A PERSONAL
HISTORY
from the
LAST
IMPERIAL
DYNASTY
to the
PEOPLE'S
REPUBLIC

Published by Louisiana State University Press
Copyright © 2013 by Louisiana State University Press
All rights reserved
Manufactured in the United States of America
FIRST PRINTING

DESIGNER: *Mandy McDonald Scallan*
TYPEFACE: *Whitman*
PRINTER AND BINDER: *Maple Press*

Library of Congress Cataloging-in-Publication Data

Topping, Audrey.
  China mission : a personal history from the last imperial dynasty to the people's republic / Audrey Ronning
Topping.
    pages cm.
  Includes bibliographical references and index.
  ISBN 978-0-8071-5278-2 (cloth : alk. paper) — ISBN
978-0-8071-5279-9 (pdf) — ISBN 978-0-8071-5280-5
(epub) — ISBN 978-0-8071-5281-2 (mobi) 1. Missionaries—China—Biography. 2. Ronning family. 3. Topping, Audrey—Childhood and youth. 4. China—History—1861–1912. I. Title.
  BV3427.A1T66 2013
  266.0092'2—dc23
  [B]

                                              2013008352

*With eternal love and respect
for my grandparents Halvor N. Ronning
and Hannah Rorem Ronning,*

*whose courageous service as missionaries
and educators in Imperial China has
inspired generations of their descendants.*

Time present and time past
Are both perhaps present in time future,
And time future contained in time past.
If all time is eternally present
All time is unredeemable.
—FROM "BURNT NORTON" (1936),
   BY T. S. ELIOT

CONTENTS

ILLUSTRATIONS

FOREWORD

Like any great novel or movie, *China Mission*, by Audrey Ronning Topping, tells a compelling story filled with drama and a wonderful, if somewhat extraordinary, cast of characters. China from the late nineteenth to the early twentieth century confronted a series of domestic and international crises that would ultimately end the Qing Dynasty (1644–1911) and launch the ailing society into a decades-long struggle of revolution and violent transformation. Into this maelstrom would come the Ronning family and friends, arriving in the early 1890s as devout Christian missionaries who, with personal grit, unending hard work, and enormous courage, would survive and even thrive. Led by the indefatigable Halvor Ronning and his new bride, Hannah—Audrey's grandparents—the Ronnings would take on the Herculean task of setting up a Christian mission in the central Chinese city of Fancheng. There they would experience exhilarating successes from extending medical care to the indigent, including abandoned female newborns, to breaking the boundaries of outmoded traditions by offering "modern" education to young men and especially women. Yet with every success and cultural breakthrough came personal tragedy, including the early death of Halvor's missionary sister, Thea, while the entire young family would have a series of close calls at the hands of growing antiforeign violence—the "Boxers United in Righteousness"—spreading like wildfire throughout the Chinese countryside.

Most families on surviving such an ordeal would have thanked their lucky stars and never returned from their new sanctuary back in the United States, where the Ronnings resided from 1899 to 1901. But as Audrey's eloquent narrative makes crystal clear, the Ronnings were not your everyday, self-interested clan but from a hardy Norwegian stock that, like their Viking ancestors, could not resist taking on any and all challenges no matter what the risks. Once the savagery of the Boxers was subdued by the equal savagery of the interventionist eight Allied Powers that relieved the Siege of Peking in 1901, Halvor loaded up his wife and brood and returned to Fancheng, picking up where they had left off, offering to any and all willing Chinese spiritual and medical care along with the educational opportunity that defined the Ronnings' mission. While local resistance of Chinese elders to his efforts, especially the education of young women, would gradually subside, antiforeignism among the still-suffering Chinese people remained a constant threat, especially when, in 1905, much of the region was hit by a devastating famine that rekindled such sentiments. The source of Halvor's persistent trials was not, however, exclusively Chinese: his respect for China's traditions and beliefs, especially its ancient philosophies of Confucianism, Daoism, and Mohism, collided with the narrow and often petty views of colleagues within the China Inland Mission. "Not westerners," Halvor reminded his newly arrived and untested critics, "but the Chinese themselves must bring the gospel of Christ to China under the conditions that already exist or not at all." Unfortunately for Halvor, such noble thoughts would largely be ignored, to the detriment of the future Christian mission.

Assisting Halvor and Hannah were two of their equally tough and often entertaining sons, Audrey's father, Chester, and her uncle Nelius, who were born and raised in China. Considering themselves no different from their Chinese brethren, the young and often irreverent boys spent much of their childhood steeped in local Chinese folklore and tales of the Celestial Kingdom, especially as recounted by the wily Teacher Sen Li-fu, who had befriended the Ronnings upon their arrival in Shanghai in December 1891. While both sons would share in the trials and tribulations of the family, Nelius and Chester would, like their father, often respond to the enormous personal risks of their time in China and later in the Canadian wilderness with mirth and a cavalier attitude that offers a contrast to today's standards of youthful angst that is nothing less than inspiring. In what is perhaps one of the most revealing lines in the book, Chester remarked, "While my parents were out Christianizing the Chinese, I was in the kitchen being heathenized by the cook." Indeed, upon their brief return in 1899 to the family's native Norway after fleeing the Boxers, both brothers would feel like "foreign devils" among their own extended family, and later, in Iowa, they would yearn for a return to Fancheng, where they were treated as equals by friends and the family amah alike.

The Ronnings experienced still more personal tragedy after their return to China in 1901 as Hannah, like her lovely sister-in-law, succumbed to one of the mysterious diseases that afflicted so many missionaries, especially women. But even this would not derail the infinitely resilient Halvor (who, in Audrey's words, would die "in action" at the ripe old age of eighty-eight) from his unwavering commitment to his Chinese mission as the Fancheng school prospered and grew into today's largest middle and high school in Hubei Province.

Years later, Chester would display the same grit and determination during yet another family run-in with local antiforeign anger. Speaking in his native Hubei dialect to the great surprise of his Chinese attackers, who wanted to "kill the foreign devil," Chester coolly responded, "I am just a lump of mud [a phrase identifying himself with the locals] like you are," and then casually walked away, saving himself and his young family. This coolness under fire would serve Audrey's father well over the years, from his early adventures with his brother Nelius in traversing the wilds of the Canadian Northwest to reach their father's Valhalla settlement in the Peace River District of Alberta to his decades of work as Canada's ambassador to India and other world hotspots where a lesser man might have mishandled delicate situations. This was especially apparent when in the late 1960s Ambassador Ronning served as a key intermediary between the North Vietnamese and the Americans in setting the stage for the end of the Vietnam War.

In recounting the many adventures and tragedies her family confronted both in China and Canada, where they had become citizens in 1908 and where her uncle Nelius would tragically disappear in the Great Slave Lake of the Northwest Territories, Audrey relies on a mother lode of personal letters, memoirs, and stunning photos. But *China Mission* is no mere family story: the narrative covers key moments and characters in the rich tapestry of China's ancient and contemporary history. Perhaps no character is more enticing—and maddening—than the infamous Empress Dowager Cixi, concubine to the Qing Emperor Xianfeng (reign 1850–61). Following the emperor's death, the dowager executed his ministers and became regent (acting ruler) behind the Dragon Throne of her underage son, the Emperor Tongzhi (reign 1861–75), who died mysteriously shortly after his coronation. To assure her regency, Cixi murdered her sister and installed her four-year-old nephew as Emperor Guangxu. When he came of age, she relied on Machiavellian skills of deceit to frustrate the young emperor's doomed efforts at reforming China's morbid political and education system while almost single-handedly driving out the foreign presence through her skillful manipulation of the Boxers. After their ignominious defeat at foreign hands, Cixi turned on her erstwhile Boxer allies to ensure her own survival. She died in 1908, leaving a political vacuum in China that neither Sun Yat-sen nor other aspiring revolutionaries could fill.

Like her grandparents, parents, and Uncle Talbert, Audrey could not resist the lure of returning to China. Spending time as a student and radio commentator in Nanking during the Chinese Civil War in the 1940s, she would meet her future husband and journalist ally, Seymour Topping, before fleeing the country in November 1948 with her mother and siblings as Chinese Communist forces advanced on the Nationalist capital. A Canadian citizen, Audrey returned to the People's Republic of Mao Zedong's Chinese Communist Party, though often with mixed results. An accomplished photojournalist and reporter, she witnessed the chaos of Mao's Cultural Revolution (1966–76) only to be driven out—again—this time by rabid Red Guards who denounced her as a "Ronning dog of Imperialism." Once such madness had subsided, Audrey returned on multiple occasions, often in the company of her peripatetic father, who with typical diplomatic skill had befriended China's Premier Zhou Enlai in 1954 at the Geneva Conference ending the first Vietnam War. With the premier's personal assistance, Audrey gained early access to closed historic sites and produced riveting reportage, some reproduced in this volume, on her exclusive visits to the remains of ancient Buddhist cities and the newly excavated Terracotta Army of China's first emperor, Qin Shihuang, outside the western city of Xi'an, while also producing memorable television documentaries including *The Forbidden City* for NBC. The most compelling of her visits recounted here came in 1984, when she accompanied her father on his ninetieth birthday to his Fancheng birthplace. There the Ronning entourage of family, friends, and local Chinese admirers visited Hannah's preserved gravestone, the Ronning schools, and Halvor's historic church, which since the Cultural Revolution had functioned as a carpentry shop. Unperturbed, Chester—who like his father believed that foreigners must accommodate themselves to China's rich traditions but also its often difficult realities—responded with his usual aplomb: "Don't worry about the church. It doesn't matter. It is being put to good use. Remember Jesus Christ was once a carpenter's son!" To this, an elderly Fancheng resident respectfully replied: "Lao Fuzi [venerable teacher] talks reason." The church was later restored. For Audrey and her extraordinary family, this is their true legacy, which to this day brings everlasting benefits to Chinese and "foreign devils" alike.

Lawrence R. Sullivan
Long Beach, New York

PREFACE and ACKNOWLEDGMENTS

Within the common destiny is the individual destiny. That destiny is fixed by heaven, by the stars in their courses. Only as one lives does the pattern of one's life show forth.
—IDA PRUITT, *A Daughter of Han*

It had been raining that night, and the streets of Fancheng were muddy. A Chinese woman who had been following us took the arm of my father. "Please, Lao Fuzi, let me help you along."

He thanked her profusely in Chinese and politely asked her "propitious" age.

"Oh, I am a mere seventy-five," she said, "and how old are you?"

"Only a humble ninety years," he replied.

She stopped to look at him closely. He stood six foot three, with a full thatch of gray hair. Her gray topknot barely reached the Order of Canada pin on his lapel.

"But how is it you speak such good Chinese?" she asked.

"Because I am Chinese."

"No, that can't be," she said, looking into his blue eyes.

"Oh, yes, I was born right here in this town," he said, tapping his cane on the earth.

"Is that so? Well, why don't you look Chinese?"

"Well, you see," he said in a conspiratorial tone, "I have lived so long in Canada that I am beginning to look like one of them."

The woman's mouth dropped open and a silver cackle rang out. "Aiya! Lao Fuzi! You are a character," she said as she slapped his arm. Then she loudly repeated the conversation to the dozens of other Chinese who had gathered to look at this family of tall, blond foreigners who had journeyed for thousands of Chinese li from beyond the seas to pay respects to their ancestor's grave and to celebrate their father's ninetieth birthday.

"He may look like a foreigner," said an onlooker, "but he sounds like a true lump of mud," a term natives of the area jokingly apply to themselves.

"Right," said Dad, "I'm just an old lump of mud, like the rest of you."

They all laughed merrily and wished us favorable winds.

The title of my book, *China Mission*, has two meanings. Historically, it refers to the missionary efforts of my grandparents Halvor and Hannah Ronning and later their son Talbert, who sought to bring their Christian faith, their compassion, and their devotion to humanity to China. My father's true mission, however, was to convey to the West, through diplomacy, a deeper knowledge and understanding of the vast, complex, ancient Chinese civilization and of modern China. As a child he had identified with his Chinese playmates. His curiosity about things Chinese was endless. As a teacher and diplomat, he associated with China's top intellectuals, artists, and political leaders, but he once spent a week walking across the Chinese countryside with a peasant pushing a wheelbarrow, learning about the man's life and becoming his fast friend.

We are all the sum of our ancestors but products of our own time. A person's life in the present begins with one's forefathers and is continued with one's descendants. Almost every Buddhist temple cherishes a Buddha of the Past, a Buddha of the Present, and a Buddha of the Future, representing the continuity of life and the invisible Golden Cord that connects us all to the cosmos.

My Norwegian American grandparents, the Reverend Halvor N. Ronning and his wife, Hannah Rorem Ronning, unknowingly formed a family pattern when they served in Imperial China as Lutheran missionaries with the China Inland Mission from 1891 to 1908. My father, Chester, one of their seven children, was the first foreign child born in Fancheng, Hubei Province. He spent a half century in China as a student, teacher, and diplomat.

During the past century, members of the Ronning family have witnessed most of the major events in China that culminated in the Chinese Civil War (1946–49) between the ruling Nationalists led by Generalissimo Chiang Kai-shek and the insurgent Communists led by Chairman Mao Zedong. My grandparents were involved with the Sino-Japanese War in 1894–95, the Hundred Days of Reform in 1898, the subsequent Palace Coup, the violent Boxer Uprising in 1898–1901, the legendary Siege of Peking, and, finally, the death of the last emperor, Guangxu, and the empress dowager in 1908, resulting in the collapse of the last Imperial dynasty, the Manchu Qing Dynasty (1644–1911). My parents, Chester and Inga Ronning, were teachers in China during the Warlord Period in the 1920s and were witness to the emergence of student revolutionaries in the missionary schools. I first went to China in 1946 during the outbreak of the Civil War, where I met my husband, Seymour Topping. I have since returned to the People's Republic over a dozen times as a journalist. The destinies of my ancestors, like my own, were inextricably interwoven with the history of China.

Since my grandparents' time, members of our family have returned to China as diplomats, teachers, students, journalists, and in business. Nine members of our family were born in China, and three have died there. Most of the events recounted in this book happened before I was born, but as a child I was entranced by the exciting tales so vividly told by my grandfather and father about their adventures in China that in my flights of fancy, I imagined I was there as well.

My first trip to China was actually a figment of my childhood imagination. At the age of four, urged on by my two older siblings, I climbed into the forbidden attic in Grandpa's log cabin in northern Alberta, where he stored mysterious treasures brought back from seventeen years as a Christian missionary in China. The trapdoor had been beckoning us kids ever since we arrived for our summer visit to Grandpa's homestead in the Peace River District in northwestern Alberta. My sister Meme, then six, and brother Alton, eight, were both born in China. As toddlers, they were evacuated along with our older sister Sylvia and our parents, who had been teachers in Grandfather's high school for Chinese students. When antiforeign uprisings became dangerously hostile during the Great Revolution in 1927, they were ordered out of the country. Nevertheless, like many "old China hands," my siblings posed as "experts" on China, since they had actually been there. When Alton told me he was digging a hole to China, and Meme said the Chinese walked backwards and upside down, I believed them. After they shoved me up to explore the attic and were sure I was still alive, they followed me up the ladder. As our eyes became accustomed to the darkness, we found ourselves surrounded by wicked idols staring at us with bulging glass eyes, snarling lacquer dragons slithering under the sloping eaves, and fat laughing Buddhas. Trembling in fear, I asked the experts, "Is this China?" "Yeah!" said Alton, glaring at the dragons, "but don't you dare tell anyone we've been here." We ran for our lives, but the memory remained forever. We were not alone in our childhood misconceptions and fear of the "mysterious" pagan China. At the turn of the nineteenth century, Western adults knew little about China, and the Chinese in the "Middle Kingdom" knew even less about the outside world. Dangerous misunderstandings arising through prejudice, greed, arrogance, and ignorance on both sides led to tragic conflicts, which my ancestors witnessed on the ground.

My hectic escape from the mythical beasts in Grandpa's attic was not the first time members of our family "ran for our lives." Our family has the dubious distinction of having been kicked out of China six times. By a series of miracles, my grandparents survived the Boxer Uprising (1898–1901); my parents fled China during the Great Revolution in 1927. During World War II, my missionary uncle Talbert escaped by riding his bicycle before the advancing Japanese troops. I first traveled to China in 1946 and lived for two years in the Nationalist capital of Nanking with my mother and siblings during the Chinese Civil War. In November 1948, I was evacuated from Nanking. My future husband, the journalist Seymour Topping, was held captive twice by Chinese Communist troops in 1949 while covering the Battle of the Huai-Hai, the decisive conflict of the Civil War. In 1951, my father ran a dangerous gauntlet to get out of Communist China during the Korean War. As a photojournalist covering the beginning of the Great Proletarian Cultural Revolution in 1966, I was hastily escorted out of the People's Republic by the Red Guards, who thought it was fun to call me a "Ronning dog of Imperialism." What amazes me is that we kept coming back.

The China of my ancestors, "Old Cathay," and the northwestern wilderness of Alberta that I write about in this family history no longer exist except in books, old photographs, and cherished memories. This is a story about the lives of my missionary and diplomatic forebears and how they related and reacted to the unique events and personalities of their own time. It is a story of, as my father expressed it, "the way it was and is no more." My missionary grandparents went eagerly to China to convert the "heathen," but over time they learned more from the Chinese than was learned by those they would proselytize.

The experiences of my ancestors caused a major shift in the way I, as a Westerner, was taught to think. My hope is that this book will open meaningful and new dimensions to the lives of my descendants, now and forever.

❊

I am deeply indebted to the wise and generous people who contributed to the creation of this book. Foremost, I am grateful to my devoted husband and journalistic partner, Seymour Topping, who shared his vision and insights acquired during his distinguished career as a war correspondent and an editor. My profound thanks go also to Professor Lawrence R. Sullivan, China specialist with the Weatherhead East Asia Institute at Columbia University, for his meticulous editing, preparation of the index, and sharing of his time and Chinese cultural expertise. A special thanks to my dear friend Dr. Judith Economos, for her sympathetic support and edifying suggestions. I am grateful also to John Maxwell Hamilton and Andrew Burstein for their encouraging early read of my manuscript. I am most appreciative that the distinguished Louisiana State University Press, directed by MaryKatherine Callaway, elected to publish my book and provide the valued services of Catherine L. Kadair, senior editor, and the skillful line-editing of Susan Murray. Not the least, heartfelt thanks to my computer wizards, Sonal Vaidya and Dwight C. Douglas, for their indispensable technical assistance.

MILESTONES in the LIVES of the RONNING FAMILY

March 3, 1862	Halvor N. Ronning is born in the parish of Bo, Telemark, Norway.
May 18, 1865	Thea Ronning, his sister, is born in Telemark.
November 6, 1871	Hannah Rorem is born in Illinois to Togrim and Anna Rorem, originally from Stavenger, Norway.
Spring 1883	Halvor and his sister Thea travel to America to attend school.
1887	Halvor Ronning is ordained in the ministry at the Red Wing Lutheran Seminary in Red Wing, Minnesota. Brother Nils Ronning arrives in America.
1890	Halvor Ronning and Hannah Rorem meet in Radcliff, Iowa.
November 1891	Halvor, Thea, and Hannah travel to China to become the first Lutheran missionaries with the China Inland Mission in China's interior.
December 24, 1891	Halvor and Hannah are married in Hankow.
1893–99	The Ronnings live in Wuch'ang and Fancheng, Hubei Province.
1893	First son Nelius Ronning is born in Hankow.
1894	Chester Ronning is born in Fancheng; mission schools and Mercy Institute open.
1894–95	Sino-Japanese War.
1898	Thea Ronning dies suddenly in Fancheng; Hundred Days of Reform.
1899	Palace coup in Peking against Emperor Guangxu; reformers executed. The Ronnings narrowly escape during the Boxer Uprising.
1899–90	The Ronnings return to Telemark, Norway, and to Iowa.
1900	Siege of Peking by Allied Powers; Empress Dowager Cixi and Royal Court flee to Sian (Xi'an).

1901   The Ronning family is welcomed back to China; the empress dowager returns to Peking.

1905   Famine breaks out in central China.

February 9, 1907   Hannah Ronning dies in Fancheng at age thirty-six, leaving seven children.

1907   Chester and Nelius leave for school in America.

1908   Emperor Guangxu is apparently murdered by the empress dowager, who dies the next day. Reverend Halvor Ronning and his five younger children flee a China in turmoil and settle in Bardo, Alberta; the Ronnings become Canadian citizens.

June 11, 1911   Halvor marries Gunhilde Horte; Chester Ronning meets Inga Horte.

1913   Halvor takes the Athabasca Ice Trail to the Peace River District in Alberta, Canada, and founds a Norwegian settlement called Valhalla; Chester and Nelius follow by way of the Edson Trail.

1918   Chester and Nelius join the Canadian armed forces during World War I; Chester and Inga are married while Chester is on home leave from the Canadian Air Force.

August 20, 1920   Nelius Ronning is reported missing in the Great Slave Lake, Northwest Territories, Canada. He is assumed drowned.

1921–22   Chester, Inga, and five-year-old Sylvia travel to Peking.

1923   Chester returns to Fancheng to become headmaster in his father's Hung Wen Middle School.

May 13, 1924   Son Alton Nelius is born in Fancheng.

September 16, 1926   Daughter Bernice Ingrid (Meme) Ronning is born.

1927   Chester and family are ordered to leave China during the Great Revolution; they return to Canada, where Chester becomes president of Camrose Lutheran College.

1928   Audrey is born in Camrose, Alberta.

1930s   Kjeryn and Harmon are born.

1942–45   In World War II, Chester becomes director of Canadian air force intelligence and assists in breaking the Japanese military code.

1943   Chester's brother Talbert Ronning goes to China as a missionary during the Japanese occupation in World War II.

1944   Talbert escapes advancing Japanese troops and returns to the United States.

1945   Chester returns to China as a Canadian diplomat in Chungking and Nanking.

1946   Audrey, mother, and siblings join Chester in China.

1947   Audrey studies at Nanking University and becomes engaged to Seymour Topping, an American foreign correspondent.

November 23, 1948   Audrey and family are evacuated by air shortly before Communist troops enter Nanking.

April 1949   Chester and Top witness the fall of Nanking to the Communists.

October 1, 1949   Mao Zedong announces the establishment of the People's Republic of China.

November 1949   Audrey and Top marry in Alberta, Canada. They are stationed in Saigon to cover the French Indochina War.

1951   Halvor Ronning dies in Valhalla at age eighty-eight.

June 1966   Chester makes a secret mission to Hanoi to negotiate peace between the United States and North Vietnam. Audrey returns to China to report on the Cultural Revolution for the *New York Times Magazine.*

1967   Inga Ronning dies in Camrose at age seventy-two.

1971   Chester and Audrey return to China on invitation of Premier Zhou Enlai, the first of many trips to the mainland.

1976   Death of Zhou Enlai and Mao Zedong.

1983   Chester and family return to China to pay respect to mother Hannah's grave and to celebrate Chester's ninetieth birthday in his birthplace, Fancheng.

December 31, 1984   Chester Ronning dies in Camrose.

AUTHOR'S NOTE on SOURCES and CHINESE ROMANIZATION

The primary source and inspiration for *China Mission* are the personal letters hand-written to loved ones by three generations of the Ronning family recording their experiences in China and Canada. The letters serve as narrative threads woven into a vivid tapestry entwining the history of our family with the history of China. This book begins with family letters and eyewitness accounts of historical events by my grandparents Halvor Ronning and his beloved wife Hannah when they served as Hauge Synod Lutheran missionaries in Imperial China and, after Hannah's death, with the adventures of Grandfather and his seven children exploring northern Canada. The story continues with letters from my father, Chester Ronning, after his return to China as a teacher during the turbulent Warlord Period in the 1920s and later includes his personal and official correspondence as a senior Canadian diplomat during the Chinese Civil War (1946–1949) and the American war in Vietnam. I have also drawn on letters and reminiscences of my own as a student at Nanking University in Nationalist China and later as a journalist in the People's Republic. The letters, indicated in italics, were written in days of gladness and in days of strife and sorrow. They were composed in greater freedom, intimacy, and spontaneity than they would have been if intended for the public.

Other on-the-ground accounts of historical events are from my family members' own books: *The Gospel at Work*, by Halvor and his brother N. N. Ronning; *The Boy from Telemark*, by Nils Ronning; and *A Memoir of China in Revolution: From the Boxer Rebellion to the People's Republic*, by Chester Ronning, as well as from my own books and articles for the *New York Times*, *National Geographic Magazine*, and other publications. Additional historical sources include an unpublished typescript, "A Study of Chinese History," by the Chinese historian Mike Peng. Most useful was the memoir *On the Front Lines of the Cold War: An American Correspondent's Journal from the Chinese Civil War to the Cuban Missile Crisis and Vietnam*, by my husband, Seymour Topping. Details of these and other sources can be found in the bibliography; note citations have been kept to a minimum. All descriptions of historical events are as accurate as my research and family stories (written and oral) can make them. Chinese poems appearing in translation at the beginning of many chapters are from the third edition of the excellent work by Henry H. Hart, *Poems of the Hundred Names.*

Wade-Giles and/or the Chinese Postal Map Romanization (e.g., Peking, Nanking) systems, which came into use in the late Qing Dynasty, are used for references to Chinese terms, place names, and individual names, including leaders of the Nationalist Party, that figured prominently in the lives of my grandparents and parents in order to retain the flavor of the historical period. Otherwise, names of provinces, major place names, and individuals prominent in Chinese history both before and after 1949 are rendered in Hanyu Pinyin, which, initially developed in Moscow, became standard in the PRC in the 1950s and in Western newspapers and books since the 1970s. The only exception is the spelling of Chester Ronning's hometown of Fancheng in Hubei Province, which in Wade-Giles should be spelled "Fanch'eng" but is for purposes of simplicity rendered throughout the volume, especially in the letters produced by the Ronning family, in Pinyin as "Fancheng."

CHINA MISSION

Prologue
China's Incredible Find

China's twentieth-century diplomacy or its twenty-first-century world role must begin—even at the cost of oversimplification—with a basic appreciation of the traditional context and history.

—HENRY KISSINGER, *On China*

THE GARMENT OF MORTALITY

Today
I sit in the halls of state.
Tomorrow?
Tomorrow I shall sleep
In the silence of the grave
For my span of life
Now nears its latter end

But when, or how,
Or in what form
I shall return
It is not granted unto mortal man
To know.

—SHI LINGYU,
JIN DYNASTY (AD 265–420)

Up from the Grave: Discovery of the First Emperor's Army

Once upon a time in the Kingdom of Qin, there dwelt a prince who wanted to live forever and spent his life searching for the fountain of youth. He inherited the throne at age thirteen and spent the next twenty-one years in battle until, in the words of China's Han Dynasty historian Sima Qian, he conquered the six other Warring States "like a silk worm devouring a mulberry leaf." The king then took the words *huang* and *di*, meaning "divine ruler," and in 221 BC anointed himself Qin Shihuangdi, First Sovereign Emperor of Zhongguo, the Middle

Kingdom. The emperor declared that his dynasty would rule for ten thousand years, but his ruthless rule lasted a mere fourteen years, the shortest in the history of China. In that brief time, however, he created an Imperial dynastic system with an absolute monarchy that lasted for two thousand years.

The emperor, a cruel despot who lived in constant fear of assassination, boasted 270 luxurious palaces that were copies of royal residences in the conquered states. But his life was so secret that he slept in a different palace each night. When he died mysteriously at age forty-nine during a journey in pursuit of the Elixir of Immortality, his Chancellor Li Si and Chief Eunuch Zhao Gao, fearing rebellion, hid his death from everyone in the Imperial cortège. The mile-long procession of golden horse-drawn chariots returned to the capital with the dead emperor incognito. It was midsummer. The eunuch piled rotting fish on a cart following the Imperial chariot to hide the odor of the decomposing corpse. In 210 BC, China's First Emperor's putrefying body was entombed with ostentatious pomp and ceremony in a dragon-shaped copper sarcophagus floating on a sea of mercury, in a spectacular subterranean palace inside a fifteen-story-high tumulus constructed according to cosmic principles, called Mt. Li.

A century later the tumulus in Mt. Li was described by the historian Sima Qian:

> As soon as the First Emperor became king of Qin, excavations and building had been started at Mt. Li, while after he won the empire, more than 700,000 conscripts from all parts of the empire worked there for 36 years. They dug through three subterranean streams and poured molten copper for the outer coffin, and the tomb was filled with models of palaces, pavilions, and offices, as well as fine vessels, precious stones, and rarities. Artisans were ordered to fix up crossbows so that any thief breaking in would be shot. All the country's streams, the Yellow River, and the Yangtze were produced in quicksilver and by some mechanical means made to flow into a miniature ocean. The heavenly constellations were above and the regions of the earth below. The candles were made of whale oil to ensure their burning for the longest possible time.*

The First Emperor's legendary tumulus is now in the process of being excavated. In December 2012, Chinese archaeologists discovered the ruins of a

---

*Sima Qian, *Records of the Grand Historian*, cited in Audrey Ronning Topping, "China's Incredible Find," *National Geographic Magazine*, April 1978, 448.

massive palace complex under the tumulus that may confirm the two-thousand-year-old description of historian Sima Qian. Xinhua news agency reported that the finding included a main building overlooking eighteen courtyard-structured houses. Sun Weigang, a researcher with the Shaanxi Provincial Institute of Archaeology, says the palace is about a quarter of the size of Beijing's Forbidden City and is a clear predecessor to Beijing's Imperial Palaces. Mt. Li may hold the greatest Imperial secrets and the richest treasures in the history of China.

Twenty-two centuries after the first emperor joined his ancestors, I was an eyewitness to his virtual resurrection. It was the summer of 1975. I had the privilege of being the first Western journalist to report for *National Geographic Magazine* and the *New York Times* on the spectacular discovery of the emperor's life-size pottery Honor Guard, which had been entombed with him. I was accompanied by my father, Chester Ronning; my daughter, film-producer Lesley (who received the unique gift of visiting the site on her twentieth birthday); my sister Meme Westlein; and her son, a cinematographer, Richard Westlein. Our family group was given special permission to view the excavation site because Chester was a close friend of Chinese Premier Zhou Enlai.

From Xi'an, we drove in a caravan of black limos with the mayor of Xi'an and two archaeologists. A mile east of the emperor's tumulus we parked in a peaceful millet field edged with persimmon trees. The rich, red soil of the Yellow River Valley had been slashed open and rolled back like an old Chinese scroll to reveal the first of seven thousand life-size terracotta warriors, horses, and war chariots arrayed in battle formation to safeguard the emperor in eternity. Standing in a downpour viewing these ancient warriors reaching out from the wet earth after 2,200 years of burial, we were moved almost to tears. Here and there a lifelike hand and a booted foot stuck out from the cold turf-prison. Proud heads fallen from broken bodies looked up from their ancient grave with haunted eyes brought glisteningly alive by the rain. Some of the figures were upright, intact, and poised as if waiting for a command to attack. Others lay smashed and scattered; their bronze swords had been taken when soldiers of the succeeding Han Dynasty (206 BC–AD 220) looted and burned this part of the Qin emperor's mausoleum.

Perhaps it was because of my personal connection to China that I found this surrealistic tableau of the Terracotta Army profoundly moving. I was witnessing the first archaeological evidence of China's first dynasty, in all its struggles and glory, being unfolded before my eyes. Right then I determined to write this memoir about my ancestors who, two millennia after the collapse of the Qin, had experienced the fall of China's last Imperial dynasty.

Like many great archaeological finds, the discovery was accidental. In 1974, some peasants from the village of Xiyan, near Xi'an, while digging a well unearthed a life-size clay head and notified the State Bureau of Cultural Relics. The find marked an iconic moment that would bring the First Emperor of China to world attention.

Archaeologists soon discovered the huge, subterranean vault harboring brigades of pottery soldiers guarding the emperor's tomb. In some respects, the site was even more important than Tutankhamen's tomb, for the young pharaoh—however magnificent his treasures—was not a figure of great historical significance, whereas Qin Shihuang changed the course of Chinese history, like his latter-day successor Chairman Mao Zedong, who often compared himself to Emperor Qin. History knows Emperor Qin as the man who unified China and ordered construction of the Great Wall as a defense against nomadic tribesmen of the Central Asian steppes. Seven hundred thousand conscripts and prisoners of war linked older walls across mountain passes into that single stone wall, which at 3,800 miles in length is still the longest fortification on earth. Thousands of forced laborers perished during its construction. Their bones were crushed and buried beneath the massive gray rocks, earning the Great Wall the grim sobriquet of "the longest cemetery in the world." When I first walked on the Great Wall in 1966, I sensed their spirits still howling in the sharp perpetual wind, haunting the thousands of grim watchtowers standing stark and foursquare along the parapets.

History records that Qin was a tyrant who sacrificed untold numbers of slave laborers and prisoners of war on such megalomaniacal projects as his splendiferous tomb complex, the Afang Palace, which accommodated ten thousand people, and 270 lesser Imperial palaces connected by covered roads and filled with beautiful gardens, exotic animals, and sensuous women. He also attempted to build a bridge across the ocean. But his reign, for good or evil, became one of the greatest turning points in Chinese history, rivaled only, two millennia later, by Mao Zedong and the establishment in 1949 of the People's Republic of China.

After the first Qin Dynasty in 221–206 BC, China passed through many periods of Imperial splendor. There were eleven major dynasties and many lesser ones, but the first two empires, the Qin and Han Dynasties, could be said to represent the Imperial Age because they laid out the basic dynastic system: a unified and centralized imperial state that, with few interruptions, lasted until my grandparents witnessed the fall of the Qing Dynasty, China's last.

PART I

ARRIVING
in the
MIDDLE
KINGDOM

Imperial China during the Qing Dynasty
Map by Mary Lee Eggart

1

Destination Shanghai

The outbreak against foreigners in China at the close of the Century, like most human events, and all things Chinese, has its roots in the remote past, without some knowledge of which it can by no possibility be understood.

—A. H. SMITH, *China in Convulsion* (1901)

December 1, 1891, the Year of the Dragon

Three American missionaries braced themselves on the deck of the *SS Oceanic* as the rising sun exploded across the horizon like a hallelujah chorus lighting up the distant shores of the Celestial Kingdom. The morning sunbeams turned the rough ocean waters into molten gold and reflected off the massive, full-blown sails of the ocean liner as it crossed from the Pacific into the East China Sea on its maiden voyage—half steam, half sail—to China via Japan.

Three weeks earlier, Reverend Halvor N. Ronning, his sister Thea Ronning, and Miss Hannah Rorem had boarded the ship in San Francisco. They were the first missionaries from the Hauge Synod of the Norwegian Evangelical Lutheran Church of America to be assigned to the China Inland Mission. On this auspicious day they had risen early, eager to capture the first sight of Shanghai, notorious in the West as "the wickedest port in the Orient." Their mission: to spread the Gospel of Jesus Christ to the "heathen" Chinese. Halvor looked forward to the challenge with confidence and complete faith in his mission. To Hannah the experience seemed surreal. She later wrote the first of many letters to her mother, in beautifully formed schoolteacher penmanship, using a fine-point feathered quill dipped in black India ink: *When we approached the coastline of China I could feel my heart beating wildly but nothing else seemed real. I still can't believe we are here. For the occasion Thea and I wore the stylish outfits we purchased in San Francisco. Dear Mama, pray for us.*

My grandmother died twenty years before I was born, but because I heard so much about her as a child, I have always felt that I knew her well. When I read her letter a half century later, I imagined her looking at her new suit admiringly and hoping my grandfather, Halvor, whom she still addressed as

"Reverend Ronning," would like it. Before dawn, Hannah had slipped from her bunk and dressed quickly in her brand-new navy-blue serge traveling suit. Shivering from the morning chill, she stepped into the long, discreetly bustled skirt and smoothed it over her white muslin petticoat, leaving just a hint of the lace flounce around the bottom. She hastily pulled the silk lavender blouse over her broad shoulders and tucked it into the narrow waistband. The fitted jacket had fashionably puffed sleeves and a large velvet collar. She swirled her long, auburn hair into a peacock twist on the crown of her head and hurried on deck. Halvor and Thea were waiting for her. "Hurry, hurry!" called Halvor, who was given to drama: "The Celestial Kingdom is rising on the horizon!" He threw his arms wide and shouted to the heavens. "Hallelujah! We are here at last!"

Even if Hannah had wanted to hug him, she would have restrained herself. Norwegians didn't do things like that, and she did not want to reveal the frightening fact that she was falling in love. Instead, she grasped the ship's railing with both hands and let the salty wind sting her cheeks. The nearness of Halvor's strong, tall frame must have given her a much-needed sense of security. My father kept the only photo taken of his parents on the *Oceanic* on his desk in our house in Camrose, Alberta. The missionaries had posed for the ship's photographer on the occasion of Hannah's twentieth birthday, November 6, 1891. Their Nordic ancestry is clearly visible. I thought my grandfather Halvor looked more like a Viking warrior than an ordained minister. He was twenty-nine years old, stood six foot two, straight as a Norway spruce, but he appeared a bit stiff in the white, starched collar he had first put on in honor of Hannah's birthday. His Prince Albert suit coat with velvet lapels fit neatly over his athletic frame, but his thick wavy hair, not barbered since they left America, was whipping wildly in the wind. There was something clearly contradictory about his appearance that captured an integral aspect of his character. Even in black-and-white photos, his strange blue eyes, set into strong, aesthetic features, sparked with a fervor that was both a strength and a weakness. Even then, his roguish grin and strong cleft chin seemed rather incongruous to the image of piety he aspired to portray. His sister Thea, then twenty-five, had a soft dimple in her chin. Her braided blond hair was coiled twice around her head. A few tresses, dislodged by the wind, floated around her head, forming a halo of silken threads. Her widely spaced turquoise eyes reflected innocence and amazement.

Although I never met my great-aunt Thea, in the photo she appeared too delicate to be a pioneer missionary in such a mysterious and troubled land. Hannah, a bit taller and slimmer than Thea, stood between the two Ronnings. When

I was a child, various relatives commented that I looked like my grandmother. This pleased me and stirred my curiosity. I had the same high forehead and a dimple in my chin, but beyond that I could not claim any resemblance. Her deep-set blue eyes had an intense look that conveyed an inner strength and an aura of confidence. To me, the three missionaries looked so pure and noble, so wonderfully young and strong, so painfully innocent. I have always felt sad about the fact that I never met my great-aunt Thea or my grandmother Hannah, but grandfather Halvor lived to be eighty-eight, and I knew him well and loved him deeply. Like all of his seven children and ten other grandchildren, I was fascinated by Grandpa. We all thought he was the greatest storyteller who ever lived—but his stories were not fairy tales.

In Nagasaki the missionaries had transferred to a small steamer called the *Kobe Maru* to continue their journey to the pilot station of Shanghai, where the rusty waters of the Huangpu River clash with the blue waters of the East China Sea. They lay anchor under the shadow of the mighty Woosung Forts, built by the Chinese to guard this main entrance to China. Armed warships from Britain, France, Russia, Japan, Germany, Belgium, and the United States, all flying their own flags, had been stationed at this gateway to China to provide security for the foreign concessions in Shanghai and other Chinese ports that had been forcibly opened by the Allied Powers after the British triumphed in the First Opium War (1839–42).

Halvor surveyed the harbor. This was the site of the famous Battle of Woosung on June 16, 1842, that was waged between the United Kingdom and the Chinese forces of the Manchu Qing Dynasty. Fourteen British steamships armed with cannons mounted on swivels blew nineteen Chinese war junks, with their patched, bamboo-rigged sails, out of the water. While the British suffered two sailors killed and twenty-five wounded, hundreds of Chinese were killed or wounded, and 250 guns, left over from the Ming Dynasty (1368–1644), were captured. This inglorious British victory was to have lasting repercussions on world trade and China's relations with the West as the Chinese Empire was forced through a series of humiliating "unequal treaties" to allow the lucrative opium trade, even though the emperor had banned the "foreign mud" in the late eighteenth century. In the infamous Treaty of Nanking (1842), Britain arrogantly imposed severe financial penalties on the Qing, opened five coastal ports to trade, and forced the ceding in perpetuity of Hong Kong island to the British Empire. This was followed by the 1859 Treaty of Tientsin ending the Second Opium War (1856–60), which legalized opium in China and opened up eleven additional "treaty ports," including the inland city of Wuhan to which the missionaries were heading. Western residents demanded the right to live in their own protected "concessions" that were not subject to local Chinese law but to the laws of their own countries. The missionaries would soon learn that this principle of "extraterritoriality" was a major infringement of Chinese sovereignty that would become a leading cause of the antiforeign sentiment that culminated in the infamous Siege of Peking and the eventual fall of the Qing Dynasty.

I am amazed by the scene spread before us. This entrance to China looks like a war zone with battleships armed with guns on the decks. We counted flags from seven countries. Fleets of Chinese sailing junks, with high-pooped sterns and bulging eyes mounted on the prows, are flapping their orange sails like wounded monarch butterflies as they maneuver precariously close to the foreign ships. Native crafts are plying busily among the multitude of old tugs and overloaded dredgers. From the moment the Empress *dropped anchor she was surrounded by hawkers in sampans advertising their wares in high singsong voices, selling all kinds of goods and curios. The decks are hung with laundry, stacked with crates of squawking chickens and overloaded with cargo and people. I wonder how the boats can stay afloat. Hannah waved to some children who were tied to the decks with rope but the boat people glared back at her grim faced. Some shook their fists and shouted oaths that fortunately Hannah could not understand but she was upset. She is a very sensitive and compassionate woman and is a great comfort to me and Thea. She did not realize that the hostility was directed towards the ships, not us, for a whole generation of Shanghai boatmen are being gradually reduced to stark poverty because the foreign ships are taking their livelihood away by transporting the goods and passengers that had been theirs for centuries.*

It was not until they were nearing Shanghai that Hannah began to have doubts about her mission. *Dear Mama: . . . Sailing up the Huangpu to Shanghai we saw miles and miles of grave mounds on the river banks. At first I thought they were haystacks. I can't believe that all those countless Chinese have died without being saved. But think of all the millions of living souls who have not yet seen the light. It fills me with despair. How I envy Rev. Ronning's unshakable confidence in his noble vision. Oh Mama, I wonder if I am up to the task. Pray for me.*

She had a right to wonder. Hannah had graduated from a Teacher's Normal School and taught school for three years in Radcliff, Iowa, but she had never received any training to qualify her as a missionary in China. Thea had studied in the Red Wing Lutheran Seminary in Red Wing, Minnesota, but had no training in Chinese studies. Halvor, after graduating from Oslo University in Norway, had studied for four years at the Red Wing Lutheran Seminary and graduated as an ordained minister. While Halvor had received some instruction in Chinese history and philosophy as well as in the basics of the Chinese language, Hannah and Thea had not been required to learn a word of Chinese or study Chinese customs or culture. In fact, the only Chinese person they had ever met was a waiter at a San Francisco restaurant. To be sure, Lutheran Minister Hogland in Radcliff had tried to encourage Hannah, advising her to keep perfect control of herself at all times and to "be kind and considerate in all circumstances and have sweet and gentle manners towards your fellow missionaries as well as towards the Chinese, who are keen judges of character." The minister, whose knowledge of China was based on his contact with the local Chinese laundryman, seemed satisfied with his words of wisdom, but Hannah felt that his advice hardly qualified her for the tremendous challenge she had undertaken. But at the time she didn't really care. She was in love and having an exciting adventure.

Through his field glasses, Halvor spotted a wrecked locomotive on the remains of China's first railway, built by the British fifteen years earlier, in 1876, at a very high cost. It had been meant to carry passengers and freight from Woosung to Shanghai, but the railroad operated for only a short period before Chinese officials purchased the line with plans to dismantle it because they believed it was disrupting local trade while the smoke and noise of the train was disturbing the spirits of the "wind and water" (*fengshui*). A crafty official had sabotaged the railroad by offering a destitute coolie 100 silver dollars to kill himself by running into the path of the train. The sum would be paid to his family after the deed was done. When his mangled body was finally discovered, an angry mob tore up the tracks, as the official knew they would.

Shanghai

The steam launch carried the missionaries up the Huangpu River, through the turbulent white waters of the "Heaven-sent Barrier" and past the dreaded quicksands of the Woosung, where hundreds of ships had been grounded and swallowed whole. Finally, they reached the delta where the golden waters of the mighty Yangtze poured into the Huangpu, mixing the silt of the two rivers. Over millennia this silting had formed the land where the city of Shanghai was built. The sounds of the waterfront grew louder as the Americans sailed into the harbor: firecrackers, drums, screeching chickens, squealing pigs, horns, soldiers marching, strange chanting, and hundreds of other unfamiliar sounds. Within the pandemonium was gathered the greatest concentration of wealth and misery that any city on earth would know.

The naïve American missionaries were unaware that they had arrived in China during the decline of the Manchu Qing Dynasty. In 1891, 80 percent of the people were illiterate peasants on the verge of starvation while the corrupt and fossilized Imperial Court with the mandarin aristocracy was wallowing in political intrigue and decadent luxury. The notorious Empress Dowager Cixi ruled behind the figurehead of her sickly son, Emperor Tongzhi, who would soon be replaced by her nephew. At this point, the missionaries, like most foreigners, had never heard of a secret society that would become known as the Yihequan, or "Boxers United in Righteousness," comprised mainly of gangs of youthful rabble-rousers and superstitious peasants. The members excelled in martial arts and claimed to possess magical powers that made them invulnerable to swords and bullets. Their predecessors, the White Lotus, had led a rebellion against the Manchu court beginning in the 1790s, but were defeated and forced underground, only to rise again as the Boxers. By the time the Ronnings arrived in 1891, antiforeign sentiment was spreading throughout the Chinese countryside that would ultimately lead to the horrific Boxer Uprising.*

Hannah was both thrilled and terrified by the vista of Shanghai. It looked as if all of the 400 million people in China were on the Shanghai docks that morning. Small boats immediately surrounded their ship. Through the mass of floating humanity her eyes focused on a rickety sampan being maneuvered by a ragged woman wielding one long oar on the stern. Hannah wrote to her mother: *Two naked children looked up at me with pleading eyes. They had bloated bellies and were leashed, like dogs, to the deck to keep them from falling overboard. A small girl . . . reached up to beg for anything she could get. I threw some American coins as I had nothing else but as the children scrambled for them they were splashed in the waves from the launch. The mother shook her fist and swore at me. I turned to Rev. Ronning but he said that nothing in his power could be done to help those children. We must first establish our mission, he said, and then perhaps we can help them. I have never felt so helpless. May God give us strength!*

Among the Chinese on the dock were two foreigners, easily distinguishable by their height, foreign suits, and black top hats. They were Sigvald Netland and Johannes Brantzaeg of the China Inland Mission Society of Norway, who had come from Hankow to welcome the new missionaries. They tipped their hats and introduced their friend and translator Teacher Sen Li-fu, a Chinese scholar and fellow mission worker. Sen wore a teacher's long, blue silk gown and a black

---

*Joseph W. Esherick, *The Origins of the Boxer Uprising* (Berkeley: University of California Press, 1987), xiii.

satin skullcap. His smile was genuinely warm. Hannah told her mother that she liked him immediately. A long, braided queue hung down his back. His smooth, bronzed skin stretched tightly over his high cheekbones. Hannah had never seen a man without a trace of whiskers. He was taller than most Chinese but seemed almost frail beside the sturdy, bewhiskered Norwegians. Halvor shook hands with Netland and Brantzaeg and bowed to Sen with his fists together in Chinese fashion. "*Ni hao bu hao?*" (How are you?), he said in Chinese with a Norwegian accent. Teacher Sen smiled politely and held out his hand. "Oh, you speak Chinese very well," he said in perfect English. "I am fine, thank you, and how are you?" Sen enunciated every word clearly. Then he turned to the ladies and bowed. "Welcome, welcome. It is indeed a pleasure and honor to welcome you to my country."

The travelers were soon engulfed in the dockside confusion. Workers were throwing large sacks of rice onto the dock from a barge nearby. Mr. Netland guided the new arrivals to a sheltered corner to make way for the swarm of coolies stampeding onto the dock to carry the sacks for a few pennies. As the Americans coughed and struggled to breathe, a strange new noise rose above the cacophony of city sounds: a high buzz, like the plaintive humming of a thousand bumblebees. It was the song of a thousand coolies. As each man hoisted a sack onto his shoulders and jogged away he joined the chorus: "*Hunga dee yodee yodee, yodee hodro hunga*"—a meaningless melody of notes in a minor key. It was a sad, resigned, haunting wail, a pathetic lament that rang of drudgery.

When the dust settled, the missionaries brushed themselves off and got on with their unloading. Hannah's throat constricted in apprehension as she watched her precious organ, their steamer trunks, and carpetbags being lowered by bamboo braided ropes over the side of the launch. As soon as the baggage touched the dock, a great squabble of shouts and shoving broke out among the porters over who should carry the bags. The coolie-master cracked a long whip over their naked backs to keep them in check. Even in the cold December weather, the men wore only loose cotton pants and straw sandals. An ugly red welt rose on the back of a young coolie standing near Hannah. He could not have been more than thirteen years old. The boy's face remained stoic, but Hannah screamed and implored Halvor to stop the whipping. He raised his arms and shouted, "Stop! Stop! This is not necessary!" The coolie-master paid no attention to Halvor but obeyed when Teacher Sen objected and said he would choose the bearers himself. The coolies tied their burdens onto each end of their yo-sticks and hoisted them across their calloused shoulders to a waiting donkey cart Netland had hired.

Mr. Netland guided the new missionaries to a nearby teahouse from where they could watch the unloading while he informed them about conditions in China. Halvor took notes in his diary: *Sigvald Netland informed me of some serious anti-foreign uprisings. He said we are heading straight into the heart of the anti-Christian movement spreading rapidly throughout the Yangtze River Valley. I did not tell the women. Netland said that the Imperial Court has become corrupt and is bogged down in political intrigue and decadence. There is a great deal of unrest because peasants in the countryside are starving and illiterate. Revolution is in the air. The intellectuals and students are aware that after two and one half centuries of Manchu rule the Qing Dynasty is shaking in its boots. The greedy European nations are slavering like hungry wolves to get their share of the kill. Netland thinks that the Qing Dynasty is on its last legs but the Manchus won't go down without a fight. Netland is afraid there will be a blood bath, but I have complete faith that God will protect us so we can do His will.*

Their baggage was loaded into two donkey carts and the missionaries got into rickshaws pulled by coolies. They proceeded up Bubbling Well Road toward the China Inland Mission in the British Concession. The wide streets were filled with more people than Hannah had seen in her whole life in Iowa. She later wrote to her sister Rebecca: *Thea and I felt a thousand eyes staring at us. They must have found us even stranger than we found them. Many of the men were wearing long robes and cloth shoes while the women were in pants and tunics. Can you imagine? Many of the women were leaning on walking sticks and mincing along on bound feet. How painful it must be for them hobbling along like that. Worst of all were the beggars who followed us, some with open sores. They pointed and laughed at our blue eyes and bustled skirts. I was sorry I wore my new suit. Halvor got out of his rickshaw to walk beside us. When the beggars got too close he waved his arms and roared fiercely. The beggars scattered for a minute but were soon back to enjoy the show. Thea and I began to laugh when Halvor roared but Netland cringed in embarrassment. It was Mr. Sen who rescued us. He ordered the beggars to show more respect. We have nothing to give! He shouted in Chinese. Clear the way!*

The missionaries found Shanghai even more imposing than San Francisco. The soldiers of seven nations paraded under their flags flying atop the tall buildings that lined the waterfront. For security, the Foreign Powers had created a protected International Settlement in Shanghai that occupied a choice area, roughly 7.5 miles long and 2.3 miles wide. The perimeter was lined with strong concrete blockhouses topped with steel observation turrets and guarded by security forces from each nationality. Within the International Settlement, each country had its own "concession" with full powers of self-government. This gave the foreigners complete privileges over Chinese trade, commerce, and customs, but the Chinese government was held responsible for protecting foreign residents and was forced to grant "extraterritoriality" to all foreign-occupied land.

The Americans rode along the Bund self-consciously in their caravan of rickshaws and donkey carts, past the Hong Kong & Shanghai Bank (where Halvor changed money), the Princely House of Jardine, Matheson & Co., the English-language *North China Daily News,* the Glen Line, and other establishments. But Hannah could not stop thinking about the coolies struggling to pull their heavy loads: *I could not believe it. We were actually being pulled by human beasts of burden treated far worse than we ever treated our horses. Thea and I were horrified but what could we do. The poor men were even fighting over the privilege of hauling us.*

The coolies' desperate scrabbling was a telling indication of the squalor behind the impressive façade of the foreign concessions. If Halvor had been aware of the misery that underlay the apparent prosperity, he might not have been so confident of his future as a missionary. Here in the Chinese inner city, beyond the walls of the foreign concessions, lay one of the greatest concentrations of human suffering and despair in the world. More than two hundred thousand people were living cheek by jowl, rotting alive in the foulest of slums. It was the home of thieves and murderers, scavengers, and hired killers. Here prostitutes too old or diseased to ply their trade elsewhere trafficked in kidnapped girls. Here the hopeless opium sots came to die and madmen came to feel at home. Corrupt politicians came to hire willing assassins and cruel slave masters. Young boys and drunken sailors were "Shanghaied" to work on condemned ships.

As they passed the Customs House, the sun reflected off a huge portrait of Queen Victoria hanging just below the clock tower. One hundred and fifty years later it would be replaced by a portrait of Mao Zedong, and the clock that rang like London's Big Ben would be changed to chime the melody of the first line of the revolutionary ballad "The East Is Red." On Nanking Road the missionaries ran into a great mass of workers pouring out of the factories manufacturing silk, thread, matches, fireworks, and a variety of other products, on foot, bicycles, rickshaws, sedan chairs, donkey carts, and horse-drawn carriages, all pushing and shoving and competing for the right of way.

Meeting a Roman Catholic

Passing through the French Concession, just beyond the International Settlement, the Lutherans experienced firsthand a symbol of the gap between the Catholic and Protestant missionaries, which was indicative of the line between the officials and the ordinary people in China. They were startled by two loud cannon blasts, and suddenly two armed French soldiers ordered them roughly off the road to let a "governor" pass. They watched as a tasseled and curtained sedan chair carried by eight bearers—the number appropriate to the highest-ranked Chinese official—came out the gate of a walled-in compound, with outriders and attendants on foot. A large golden cross under an umbrella of honor was borne in front. Netland explained that the passenger was a Roman Catholic bishop who was also the spiritual ruler of the whole province. Like all Catholic bishops in the Middle Kingdom, he had adopted—under the principle of the *imperium in imperio*—the rank of a Chinese governor and wore a huge coral button on his elaborate hat to prove his official rank. He smiled tolerantly as he passed the Americans, giving them a royal wave and flashing a large Vatican ring.

At the northern end of the Bund, the missionaries came to the Garden Bridge, which rose like a half moon to span Soochow Creek. The coolie pulling the two women could not keep pace, and, seeing this, Halvor jumped out of his rickshaw, removed his Prince Albert suit coat, and began pushing their rickshaw from behind. His hair tumbled over his eyes. Hannah later wrote to her sister Rebecca that she had never seen him looking so handsome: *An Englishman sitting in a sedan chair carried by two bearers passed us. He looked at us with a shocked expression, and said, "I say there, Yank! Don't you know that in China no gentleman does hard labor?" Halvor just waved at him: "Yah well Sir," he said, "I guess I am no gentleman." Thea and I burst out laughing but Mr. Netland recognized the British Consul and hid his face behind his fan so the Englishman would not recognize him, but he could not hide his smile.*

They stopped at an iron gate guarding the entrance to the British Concession, where Mr. Netland showed the guard a pass. The crowds of Chinese who had been following them suddenly disappeared. No Chinese were allowed in the International Settlement except servants. Teacher Sen wished them Godspeed and took his leave.

In the British Concession, the missionaries proceeded along the wide streets where Englishmen in white gabardine suits and pith helmets were riding in sedan chairs carried on the shoulders of two or four bearers. The only Chinese in the street were the coolies and Chinese amahs in white tunics and black pants pushing pink-cheeked blond babies in high-wheeled perambulators. Here and there a pigtailed cook was hauling a cartload of food supplies for his master. The British homes were enclosed in gated compounds protected by high stone walls spiked on top with jagged glass and barbed wire. Black-bearded Sikhs, recruited from British India, stood guard in blue uniforms with brass buttons and yellow turbans, one hand on their curved cutlasses. They saluted smartly as the Americans rode by. Halvor returned the salutes. Hannah and Thea strained to catch glimpses of the great white mansions behind the walls where English ladies and gentlemen were sipping their noonday gin and tonics under yellow umbrellas on spacious green lawns while teams of coolies plucked Chinese weeds from the English grass.

The rickshaw caravan of lowly Lutherans turned north into Seward Road, where they arrived at the walled-in compound of the China Inland Mission. It was a welcome sanctuary for the rejoicing messengers of Christ, who were too weary to worry about the future. In 1891, no one could possibly have imagined that this complicated city of iniquities would evolve, in the next century, from a treaty port to a multinational hub of finance, a global city with influence over the world's commerce, fashion, and culture.

The Qing Dynasty (1644–1911)

The missionaries had arrived in a China that was about to change forever.

In the twelfth century, the Manchus, from the nomadic Jurchen tribe who lived by hunting and fishing in the forest clearings, had appeared from nowhere and conquered North Manchuria. In the beginning of the seventeenth century, the strongest Manchu chieftain, Nurhaci, invented the ingenious military and social organization called the "Banner System," which enabled him to conquer and unite Manchuria and eventually all of China. In this system, warriors were organized in companies identified by colored banners. More than a military force, however, the Banner System reached into every level of society. Everyone belonged to a banner, and taxation, conscription, and all administration were managed by the banner organization. In peacetime, the Bannermen and their families were farmers and craftsmen, but in wartime, each banner formed its own highly disciplined regiment in a most effective war machine. By this means, Nurhaci united the tribes, founded the Manchu kingdom, and established his capital at Mukden (today's Shenyang) in 1621. In 1626, leading an attack on the city of Ningyuan, he was defeated by the defending Ming Dynasty general Yuan Chonghuan, who was the first in China to use cannons made by Portuguese Jesuit missionaries. It was Nurhaci's first and only defeat. He died of his wounds seven months later.

His eighth son, Hong Taiji, renamed the Jurchen people as "Manchu" and named his dynasty the Qing (meaning "pure"). He organized the Eight Banner

System, and in two years sacked more than sixty cities in North China. When the Manchu Bannermen succeeded in capturing Peking under the leadership of the commander Dorgon in 1644, Hong Taiji's ninth son, a seven-year-old boy named Fulin, was installed as the first emperor of the Manchu Qing Dynasty, under the regency of Dorgon. Seeing no other way out, the last Ming emperor attempted to "save face" by hanging himself from a pine tree on Radiant Hill, overlooking Peking. The now historic tree, with one branch just high enough for a man to reach while standing on a rock, is still pointed out to visitors.

As time passed, the Manchus, like the Mongols, developed a deep respect for Chinese philosophy and literature. The "Forbidden City," which had been burned down during the fall of the Ming Dynasty in 1644, was restored to its original condition, and it remains the same today.* The Qing emperors and their court lived in the Imperial palaces and adopted the customs and manners of the Chinese so completely that they almost ceased to appear alien. Kangxi (Abundant Prosperity) ruled from 1661 to 1722 as one of China's most dynamic emperors, followed soon after by his grandson Qianlong (Heavenly Greatness), whose reign extended from 1736 to 1796. A benevolent and cultured ruler, Qianlong is best remembered in the West for his Imperial kilns that produced the most elegant porcelain and cloisonné the world has ever known. Qianlong was also a painter and a poet who compiled an immense Chinese anthology (known as the *Four Treasuries*) of some thirty-six thousand volumes of all the serious Chinese books and manuscripts. However, he censored all books that displayed any criticism of the Manchus and executed anyone found in possession of the prohibited books. Seventy writers were killed for their part in composing *History of the Ming Dynasty,* which included an account of the Manchu invasion.

From the social and economic point of view, the Manchus did their best to improve the lot of the peasants, who, during the Ming Dynasty, had become

---

*The main difference is the color of the ceramic roof tiles and the mythical beasts that guard the curved-up eaves on the corners of the roofs. When the Qing artists proved unable to reproduce the exact pigments of the Ming Yellow tiles, they removed them all and stored them in the four towers that mark the corners of the Imperial City wall. The Ming tiles were then replaced with a darker yellow, known as Qing Yellow. I learned this in 1972, when I spent two months with Lucy Jarvis producing the first documentary film for NBC television called *The Forbidden City.* I rode around the fabulous location on the back of the caretaker's bicycle. We became friends, and when I picked up a broken tile as a souvenir, he told me the story of the tiles and went into one of the towers by the moat to rescue a Ming Yellow chimera lion that once adorned the Temple of Supreme Harmony, which he presented to me. The cherished treasure now stands in a place of honor in my living room.

little more than serfs who worked the land and had no legal recourse against the abuses of the wealthy landowners. The Qing, however, returned part of the land belonging to the Imperial family to the state and confiscated the land of the privileged rich to distribute among the peasants as their own property—reforms that in the eighteenth century produced a rural standard of living in areas such as the lower Yangtze valley on a par with the most productive regions of Europe.

It is one of the ironies of history that this act of compassion by the Manchus may have caused the ultimate downfall of the Qing Dynasty, for the peasants flourished and multiplied beyond the capacity of the land. For the great masses of Chinese, life was lived on the thin edge of subsistence, with famine a constant threat. The Chinese population had always expanded to the limits of the food supply, and each time that supply had been reduced through war, floods, or other natural catastrophe, hundreds of thousands starved to death. China's population more than doubled in the period from 1650 to 1800, going from 123 million to 260 million, but the arable land increased by only 50 percent.

The Chinese, ordered to wear their hair in pigtails as the mark of Manchu dominance, waited for the Manchus to show signs of weakness to start the inevitable revolution. The first revolt occurred in the Yangtze River Valley in 1796, organized by a secret society called the White Lotus, which in the fourteenth century had emerged in support of the crumpling Ming. It raged intermittently for eight years before it was ruthlessly crushed by the Imperial Bannermen. This was only a prelude to the approaching civil wars that broke out again in 1813 and finally culminated in the Taiping Rebellion, which raged largely in southern China from 1850 to 1864 and may have cost as many as 20 million lives. But before that, China was forced to cope with "the devils from across the ocean." Contact with foreign traders resulted in the First Opium War (1839–42), waged against the British Empire. China's defeat brought Chinese prestige to a new low and initiated a century of foreign invasion and humiliation.

By the time my grandparents arrived in China in 1891, there were 430 million mouths to feed. Many peasants, dispossessed of their arable land, without employment, and unable to pay taxes, joined the ranks of political dissidents in secret societies and became revolutionaries. This was the genesis of the Boxer movement.

2

Crossing the Pacific

You are about to look upon the fascinating but frightening, once beautiful but now ravaged, face of the ancient and dying Imperial Empire of China; it is a sight that stuns the senses and defies imagination! Only through constant prayer and implicit belief in God will you have the strength to survive.

—DR. KEVIN W. MATSON, 1891

It was barely six months since Hannah had first seen Halvor and Thea on the stage of the Lutheran church in Radcliff, Iowa. When she shook hands with Halvor, she felt an immediate sense of predestination. The meeting changed her life beyond her wildest imagination. It was the spring of 1891, and Halvor and Thea Ronning had been appointed missionaries by the Hauge Synod of the China Mission Society and had come to the Lutheran church in Radcliff to raise funds. The attitude toward missionaries was far different at that time than it is today. The members of the congregation were hardworking, God-fearing farmers who thought of themselves as guardians and transmitters of the Christian heritage and culture. They were proud to contribute to a higher cause.

The Ronnings and all their ancestors had originally come from Telemark, Norway. In 1883, Halvor and Thea became the first members of their family, in the six hundred years of their recorded history, to leave Norway. Hannah's ancestors also came from Norway, and she was the first of the Rorem family to be born in the United States. She grew up on her father's cattle ranch in Iowa and, after graduating from Teacher's Normal School, became the local teacher in the Radcliff School and the church organist. On that fateful day she had come early to the church. The hall was already brimming over with eager parishioners.

The local pastor, Reverend C. C. Holter, introduced the missionaries: "We are thankful," he said, "and honored that the missionaries have chosen Radcliff to come and bring us the God-given opportunity to participate in a task that American Christians were preserved for: the spiritual awakening of the largest heathendom in the world—the Empire of China!" His attitude, which now seems rather shocking, was typical of the times.

The Reverend Ronning spoke with all the passionate eloquence the congregation expected of their messenger of Christ. He had a strong voice with a lilting Norwegian accent. Thea sat quietly on the platform looking at her brother in amazement as he paced dramatically back and forth, alternately waving his arms in the air and clasping his hands behind his back while he told his rapt audience about the history of missionary work in China. He began with a straightforward question that made everyone feel rather uneasy: *Where is China anyway? Some 50 years ago the Norwegian Lutherans in America did not take much interest in foreign missions. They were still pioneers too busy establishing a church of their own. We knew very little about China—many of us scarcely knew where China was—and we cared less. Very few knew that China was half the size of the whole North American continent with a population of over 400 million [sic] people. Very few knew that the recorded history of Chinese civilization, older than any other country, goes back over 4,000 years. None guessed that someday it would have a brilliant future.*

He concluded with an urgent plea: *Millions of Chinese are now dying every year from starvation, disease, war, and pestilence. My heart is crushed when I contemplate the great physical and temporal need of these poor Chinese but their eternal need is far greater. I will remind you of Jesus' words to his disciples: "Lift up your eyes, and look on the fields; for they are ripe already to harvest."* Halvor threw his arms to the heavens. *Now let us go forth. As yet it is still a hard time for sowing the seed, but there are many signs that there will be a glorious harvest. Let us sow, if need be, with tears and blood; we shall reap with rejoicing. China for Jesus must be our aim; China for Jesus.*

Hannah insisted on driving the carriage home from church and whipped the horses into a gallop. Hannah's younger sister Rebecca never stopped raving about the handsome young preacher, and her mother remarked on his divine smile. "You know he isn't married yet," she called to Hannah, who had let her long hair fly loose in the wind. Hannah laughed and replied—and here the family lore may verge into the apocryphal—"I'm not surprised. He's homely as a mud fence."

That night she prayed for guidance, and toward morning her father, who had died the year before, appeared to her in a dream: "It's all right, Hannah," he said. She snapped awake and made a decision that would not only change her life but the lives of her descendants for generations to come. At breakfast she told her family that she had received the "call" from God to go to China with the Ronnings as a Bible Woman. Her mother was not surprised. She asked her determined daughter what a Bible Woman was, and Hannah explained that because she wasn't trained as a missionary, she could assist Reverend Ronning as a Bible Woman. Rebecca urged her not to be so impulsive, but Hannah was irrepressible; she sent an urgent telegram to the China Mission Society Board, informing them that she desired to accompany Miss Thea Ronning and the Reverend Halvor Ronning to China as a Bible Woman.

The answer was: "Regrettably we have no funds for a third missionary." Hannah was not discouraged. She jumped on her horse and galloped full speed to Radcliff, where her three older brothers owned the general store. They were no match for their sister. Before the day was out, they had promised to help her raise the money. She cabled back that she would pay her own expenses to China and mailed them a sketch of her life:

I was born in La Salle County, Illinois, November 6, 1871. My parents were Torgrim and Anna Rorem. I was baptized by Rev. Elling Eielsen. When I was one year old, my parents moved to Hamilton County Iowa, where they established a good home on a farm, where I grew up . . . I was sent to a Teacher's Normal School at Dexter, Iowa. Satan tried to lull to sleep all my good intentions. I began to take part in worldly amusements and hastened forth on the broad way, but not without conscientious scruples. The admonitions of parents and other Christians made a deep and disturbing impression on my poor heart.

After graduation I taught common school for three terms. On January 9, 1890, my dear father died. His death caused me deeper concern about my soul than I had ever felt before. After a brief but hard struggle, I was won for Jesus and received the light and the power of truth.

I now began to feel an inner call to go to the heathen and tell them about Jesus as the Savior of all men. I have felt and feel how weak I am and how unfit for such a great mission, but the Lord has strengthened me so that I have been given the confidence to offer myself, body and soul, for Jesus and His cause, and now I stand ready to go to China as a Bible Woman. Christianity is not only a doctrine to me but a life, the life, the abundant life.

When the mission board agreed to her plan, Hannah was ecstatic. She was nineteen and had an unusually radiant and winsome personality. Her brothers called public meetings at which Hannah appealed for funds. She told congregations that she would be their personal messenger to spread the word to save the Chinese who had never had the opportunity to hear the gospel of Jesus Christ. She needed their support. She gave concerts, playing the organ and singing hymns in her full-throated voice, while her older brothers passed the hat. No one could refuse them. At the last meeting, held in the Rorem schoolhouse that her father, Torgrim Rorem, had built, there was standing room only. The Lutheran congregation had a local celebrity. That night she sang as never before; the audience deeply stirred, joined in the singing.

> Onward Christian soldiers,
> Marching as to war.
> With the cross of Jesus
> Going on before.

When the good folks ran out of money, they contributed their watches and rings. Everyone cheered when her brothers announced that they were contributing a portable Mason and Hamlin organ. A month later, with four steamer trunks and her precious organ, Hannah Rorem set out by train to join the Ronnings on their mission to China. The whole town was at the station to wish their young heroine Godspeed.

Miss Hannah Rorem was welcomed at mission headquarters in Faribault, Minnesota. Halvor and Thea, with their eighteen-year-old brother Nils, who had come from Norway to attend his first year at the Red Wing Lutheran Seminary, met her. During the next two weeks, Nils joined the three missionaries while they visited many congregations in the Hauge Synod—whose basic theological doctrine de-emphasized formal worship while stressing personal faith—to raise funds. They were treated like celebrities, with large crowds meeting them everywhere. The mission society recorded that "liberal offerings were received, people were mightily stirred and many were won for Christ and His cause."

The departure of the missionaries from Faribault caused a sensation. A farewell fest held at the largest hall in the city was crowded to capacity. To Nils's embarrassment, he was asked to sit on the platform with all the church dignitaries to listen to the farewell tributes. Reverend Ronning spoke on behalf of Hannah and Thea, as women missionaries were seldom expected to speak for themselves. At the dock, Nils hugged them all and then grasped Hannah's two hands. She could see he was struggling with his emotions. "Take care of them for me, dear Hannah," he said. "I will be so lonely. Write to me. God bless all of you." His voice choked, and he walked away quickly, without turning back, lest they see his tears.

As a child listening to my grandfather tell about the crossing, I imagined my grandmother standing on deck sailing toward China. On windy days, the sails were unfurled and the engines were silent. She would let her long hair fly with the wind as she gazed over the vast, heaving waters, bounded by nothing but the distant, trembling horizon. Thea wrote to Nils: *The stars look so close, I feel as if I could reach out and touch them. Remember Nils, Mama used to tell us that on a clear night in Telemark she could hear the stars sing. Listen, now I think I know what she meant.*

The *Oceanic* was the first ship of the White Star Line to carry passengers from San Francisco to China. The Norwegian-American missionaries were among 169 first-class passengers who were seated at round tables in the mid-ship dining room away from the noise and vibrations of the steam furnaces. One thousand less fortunate passengers were crowded into steerage, with single men in the bow and women and children in the stern. On the third day out, they hit a terrible storm. Thea spent the next few days in bed with seasickness. Hannah was one of the few who were not sick. Halvor wrote Nils that Hannah was "frisk som en fisk," a Norwegian rhyme meaning "healthy as a fish."

In his diary, Halvor noted that on November 11 Hannah came running to him screaming in horror. A Chinese man in steerage had died, and the Chinese had taken him on deck to burn his flesh in order to drive away evil spirits. Halvor explained that this was also for sanitary reasons. The next day Halvor went down to steerage to visit the Chinese and was shocked by the filth and cramped quarters. He discussed the wretched situation with a number of other missionaries on board, including a Methodist medical missionary, Dr. Robert Swallow, who had served in China for nineteen years, and the elderly Reverend Dr. Kevin W. Matson, whose early work was well known by scholar evangelists. They could do nothing more than pray for the Chinese.

Halvor took the opportunity afforded him by the voyage to learn from these veteran missionaries. Dr. Swallow told him the best way to learn Chinese was to talk with the people. He also advised Halvor not to wear Chinese clothes as there was no way a brown-haired man six foot three inches tall with blue eyes could show solidarity with the Chinese or disguise the fact that he was a foreigner. Matson agreed.

Nearly thirty years earlier Matson had sailed to China by way of Cape Horn. His ship was on the high seas for 167 days before reaching Shanghai. Halvor had read his books and remembered that the old gentleman had predicted, thirty years prior, that his "bones would be buried in a heathen land but would rise in a Christian one."

After dinner and evening devotion, the missionaries retired to the ship's salon, where Matson hoisted his short, rotund body into an upholstered chair and sat in the lotus position like a Chinese Buddha. He always waited until the others had settled before he held forth. Years later Halvor wrote about the enlightening talks with the old scholar who helped him see another side to Chinese culture. Halvor found him a fascinating blend of saint and sinner. A full gray beard and coarse features made him look like a pirate, but his hazel eyes were as clear and innocent as a child's. When Matson told of his first long voyage to China in 1863, he looked like the ancient mariner, but when he spoke of Chinese civilization and the need for Christianity, he appeared almost saintly. The old man's sonorous voice carried easily over the whine of the wind. Knowledgeable about the history and culture of China, Matson was alarmed by the ignorance of Western missionaries about the land and people they wanted to reach.

Halvor took notes in his journal: *You are about to look upon the fascinating but frightening, once beautiful but now ravaged, face of the ancient and dying Imperial Empire of China. It is a sight that stuns the senses and defies imagination! Only through constant prayer and implicit belief in God will you have the strength to survive. Whether in the service of God, country or in search of fortune, few have the slightest idea of China's politics or the quality and roots of their ancient civilization. China's coastal cities are now being turned into privileged sanctuaries for foreigners who speak not a word of Chinese nor care a whit about Chinese traditions. How many Christian missionaries have ever read the Confucian classics?* he asked indignantly. *Most missionaries have no idea of the rules of "etiquette" that regulate Chinese society or know anything about the four schools of Chinese philosophy.* The new missionaries must have felt intimidated but were eager to learn, and the veteran theologian was delighted to have an audience. They often talked late into the night.

Dr. Matson started with the Han Dynasty (206 BC–AD 220), which, in the reign of the Martial Emperor Wudi, was a time of philosophical synthesis. Confucianism, salvaged from the charred ruins of the Qin Dynasty, was placed above the other schools of thought as the basis of society and state. An examination system was developed for the selection, by scholastic merit, of government officials. Thus the Confucian criterion of "worth over birth" was adopted. It led to the scholar-official, or mandarin, class, which was to play a dominant role in China for the next two thousand years.

Although Han philosophy was largely Confucian in its ethical doctrines, it was Legalist in its economic theories and also contained the mystical thought of Yin-Yang and its five agents, which consists of metaphysical and cosmological speculation. While dating from early times, the Yin-Yang concept did not become a major element in Chinese thought until the Han Dynasty, when it was incorporated into Daoism. Dr. Matson claimed that Daoism was so entwined with Chinese thinking that it was impossible to have an appreciation of Chinese paintings or sculpture, their classical or unique rock gardens, nature poems, literature, or even politics without some understanding of it. *Yang symbolizes the male aspect in the universe: sun, fire, heat, Heaven, creation, dominance, spring, and summer. Yin symbolizes the female aspect in the universe: the moon, water, cold, earth, nourishing, autumn, and winter. Each force in its extreme produces its opposite and the two continue to succeed and balance each other, like a metronome, in a never-ending cycle.*

One evening he read from a translation of the *Yi Jing*, the *Book of Changes:*

The successive movement of Yin and Yang is called the Way (Dao). What issues from it is good, and that which brings it to completion is the individual nature. The man of humanity recognizes it and calls it humanity; the wise man recognizes it and calls it wisdom.

The people use it daily, but are not aware of it, for the Way of the gentleman is but rarely recognized. The constant reaction of the two forces on the physical and metaphysical planes has been used in Chinese philosophy to explain all processes of growth and change in the natural world. Yin and Yang became the father and mother of all creation. The doctrine that extremes produce opposites cautioned the scholars to always try to choose a central course, a "Golden Mean" between extremes. If you forget everything else I have spoken of, just remember the Golden Mean.

Japan was their first port of call, with stops in Yokahama, Nagasaki, and Kobe. They learned that Japan was recovering from one of the world's most devastating earthquakes, the Mino-Owari, which hit on October 28, 1891, and was the probably the cause of their rough crossing. The ship remained in Nagasaki long enough for the missionaries to take a tour of the city. Many of the passengers disembarked, and the Ronning party transferred to a smaller steamer, the *Kobe Maru*, with all their belongings. As they sailed out of the harbor toward China, Dr. Swallow pointed out a precipitous rock where in an anti-Christian outburst sanctioned by Japanese rulers in the sixteenth century, a large number of Catholic missionaries had been hurled to a miserable death. A flaring saffron sun was setting behind the cliff. The sky reminded Hannah of a fiery inferno. That evening she wrote: *Dear Mama: We came at last to our first stop, a pagan country which lies at the very door of China. We stopped in Japan to learn of the glorious things the Lord has wrought there the last few years. Thousands and thousands have destroyed their idols and have received Jesus Christ as their Savior. The history of missions has scarcely a more glorious chapter than what Christianity has accomplished during the last ten years. Here in Japan we learned that one sows, another reaps. In the city of*

Nagasaki is a large imposing church where we saw a large painting showing that in January, 1597, on the very spot where the church stands, twenty-six Christian Japanese were cruelly crucified in one day. I miss each and every one of you and pray that we meet again soon. Your beloved daughter Hannah.

The last evening on board, the travelers wished each other Godspeed. Dr. Swallow told the young missionaries that their most important task was to stay healthy. He pointed out that a sick missionary was nothing but a drain on everybody and their resources. They soon found this out for themselves. Dr. Matson was very serious in his final admonitions to the young missionaries: *"You must all understand that, like revolutionaries our lives are not our own, when you face the valley of the shadow of death, when you see the awful reality of pagan China it will be your challenge, your strength, your pride. The unbelievers cannot match our sacrifice or faith. They are powerless to stop our beliefs, so Christianity will win. We may not see it in our life time, but we must take the long view and sow our seeds now, while we can."* He leaned forward and spoke gently: *"Remember you are only God's humble messengers. The treaty ports of Shanghai, Ningpo, and Canton with their foreign concessions have been forced open by Western countries by acts of war for reasons of trade. We are going to China uninvited and unwelcome. Even though we have protection of extraterritoriality we must not enter China as conquerors but as spiritual messengers who treat the Chinese with respect. You are about to experience the most difficult but perhaps most rewarding challenge a Christian soul can have. Remember the Golden Mean."*

In Shanghai they bid a sad farewell to the old missionary.

3

Sailing up the Yangtze River to Hankow

Back in the mists of time, when the gods were maneuvering for power over the Celestial Kingdom, Emperor Yu Wang seized control of the rivers.

—SEN LI-FU, FROM THE CHINESE MYTH "SON OF THE OCEAN"

Protect us oh Lord from the wrath of the Norseman.

—ENGLISH BOOK OF PRAYER

The stay in Shanghai was short. The following evening at dusk the three American missionaries, along with the Norwegian missionary Sigvald Netland and the Chinese evangelist Sen Li-fu, set off from the China Inland Mission compound to Foochow wharf, where they boarded a wobbly tender to reach the *Ta-tung*, a British steamboat anchored in the Huangpu River. The squat double-decker was due to sail at dawn from the Huangpu River to where it joined the chocolate waters at the mouth of the Yangtze and proceed seven hundred miles up the great river to Hankow, in Hubei Province, where Reverend Ronning planned to open his mission.

The December air was cold and bitter. The missionaries were obliged to outmaneuver hundreds of agile Chinese passengers scrambling up a rickety wooden gangplank. But when they stood exhausted on deck looking at the dazzling array of lantern lights glittering from the streets of Shanghai, they forgot everything except the wonder of the Orient. Hannah looked expectantly upriver toward their unknown destiny but saw only a wide expanse of purple mystery. The Yangtze rises from the perpetual melting snows of the Tibetan Mountains and cascades downward through awesome canyons of its own carving. It twists and brawls its way through deep valleys until it finally spreads wings and gracefully sweeps across the alluvial plains of central China to the sprawling city of Shanghai, which is built entirely on the silt brought down over the centuries by the Huangpu and Yangtze and deposited at the mouth of the river.

Sen Li-fu had paid in advance for reserved comfortable cabins near the observation saloon. When they arrived on the top deck and tried to claim their cabins, however, the British captain told them that all the first-class cabins, indeed, the whole upper deck, had been commandeered by a pompous Manchu magistrate from Peking. When Halvor objected, the British captain apologized, saying he had orders from Peking, and suggested the missionaries take another steamer next week. Mr. Netland was outraged. The captain pointed out that foreigners did not have extraterritorial privileges at sea and offered them two cabins on the lower deck.

Their protests were interrupted by the figure of the Manchu magistrate walking toward them leading a full entourage. Hannah and Thea were fascinated by the procession. The Manchu's portly body was draped in a dark-blue, padded silk gown, and on his head perched a black satin cap with a wide, turned-up brim, crowned with a red button of rank. Directly behind him marched his two Manchu wives and six Manchu concubines looking like wax dolls in long satin robes and short brocade jackets. On their puffed, lacquered hair they wore the Manchu headdress, an enormous butterfly of black stiffened gauze anchored with pins of gold inlaid with a mix of jade, lapis lazuli, kingfisher feathers, cinnabar, and pearls. Their faces, except for bright red circles on their high cheekbones, had been painted and powdered stark white with rice flour. Their embroidered shoes with thick cloth soles were raised by a square wooden heel in the middle of the sole. The Manchu women were not crippled by bound feet like the upper-class Chinese women. Behind the women came some Chinese servant girls with natural feet and then a retinue of Chinese eunuchs with long pigtails wearing flashy robes embroidered with gold dragons. The Manchus had ruled that all servants and eunuchs must be Chinese and all concubines Manchu. They were followed by aides, sycophants, and small slave girls. The Chinese men were easily distinguished from the Manchus by their long queues and semi-shaven heads.

When the magistrate saw the foreigners, he put his hands together in the Chinese greeting. The Americans did the same. At the sight of the fair-haired, blue-eyed ladies in Western clothing, the Manchu women erupted into giggles and high-pitched chatter. The captain bowed to the Manchu and ushered him into the main cabin. His entourage occupied all the other first-class cabins. Two massive eunuchs, with sabers hanging from their satin girdles, hung the gold seal of the magistrate on the doors of the staterooms for which Halvor had paid hard-earned mission money. When the seals were attached, the eunuchs stood before the doors with their arms crossed and glared at the missionaries.

As the missionaries turned to leave, the doors of the women's cabins opened, and young slave girls came out and curled up like dogs on the floor in front of their mistresses' doors. Hannah and Thea were appalled. A Chinese steward led the missionaries to the lower deck, where he gruffly ordered a half dozen sullen passengers to leave two smoke-filled cabins and then ushered in the foreigners with a grand sweep of his arm. The small, dark cabins reeked of rancid cooking oil. Each had a bare double-decker bunk. The toilet was down the passageway, but they could smell the stench of urine from their cabins. Hannah heard rats scramble under the bunk and was certain she saw a flurry of long tails disappear into the holes in the wall. Fortunately, the missionaries had brought their own bedrolls, and they did their best to make themselves comfortable. As soon as they blew out the candles, the rats came out and began to run over the bunks. Hannah and Thea took their bedrolls out on deck. Halvor and Sigvald pulled the covers over their heads so they could not feel the rats walking over them. Halvor's feet stuck out over the end of his bunk.

"Good night, everyone. God bless and sleep well," he called in a muffled voice. "Just think, in the morning we shall be on our way to the very heart of this Celestial Kingdom."

In the saloon, the sharp clatter of ivory mahjong pieces and bamboo dominoes mixed with raucous talk and the clink of glasses. At dawn the steamer chugged out of the harbor and began the journey up the wide, swirling expanse of the great Yangtze River. The missionaries ate their breakfast of steaming rice on deck while looking in wonder at the legendary golden river and listening to Sen Li-fu tell an old Chinese myth about the "Son of the Ocean":

Back in the mists of time, when the gods were maneuvering for power over the Celestial Kingdom, Emperor Yu Wang seized control of the rivers. After meditating on Tusan Mountain and studying the markings on nine tortoise shells, he determined that the "River to Heaven" should run eastwards, through the mountains to the sea—but the spirits of the mountains refused to budge. The Emperor appealed to the Wizard Wu Tzu. She appeared to him as a great ape and with one mighty blow from her nostrils blasted a gorge halfway through the reluctant mountains. Exhausted, she retired in a cave where she lives to this very day. The new canyon enabled the river, now furious about the holdup, to rage through Wind Box Gorge and halfway through Witches Gorge before the mountains blocked it again. Modern geologists claim that the gorges were excavated during the past 250 million years or so by the impact of the hurtling waters, but the ancients relate that Emperor Yu himself hacked out the rest of the gorges with a cosmic ax and unleashed the torrents that now coil and hiss like mischievous dragons through the heartland of China into the Pacific Ocean.

This was only one of hundreds of legends known to the river people. No other river in the world has touched so many lives. Millions have perished in its

deadly rapids and periodic floods, but it has given life's sustenance to millions
more. Not only has the river nourished centuries of good harvests, provided a
granary for almost half of China's food products, offered unequaled adventure
to travelers and inspiration to poets and painters, but the mysterious rock formations and scenic beauty in the Three Gorges have given rise to folklore and
legends of the supernatural that have fascinated thousands of generations of
peasants as well as scholars, mandarins, aristocrats, and emperors. The lore of
the river itself embodies the mythic image of Old Cathay—the celestial, five-
clawed dragon—symbol of the emperors since Qin Shihuang unified China in
221 BC. Long Wang, the four-clawed Dragon King and chief of the gods of water
and rain, is alleged to have resided in a castle under Goose Tail Rock in Wind
Box Gorge.

The river, navigable for almost four thousand miles, was so wide at this point
that it looked to Hannah more like the sea. The banks on either side were distant
smudges of green. By noon, the river had curved and narrowed until the smudges
came alive with people and animals. Now the missionaries could see caravans
of donkeys and mules pulling their heavily laden carts along the stratified banks
that had been built up by layers of sediment deposited from year to year. The
lower banks were gracefully terraced by stone pebbled walls supporting the earth
that nourished the emerald-green rice paddies sparkling in the sun. Every few
miles, close to the water, stood a red-brick or white stucco temple where the
river people could worship the river gods. The tiled roof corners tipped up to
divert any evil spirits that might fall from the sky back up again as the spirits
can only travel in straight lines. Rivercraft of all types plowed back and forth
near the shoreline while haughty little steamers puffed through midchannel.
In the calmer waters close to shore, fishermen in wide conical hats squatted pa-
tiently on flat rocks lowering huge fishnets from a triangle of bamboo poles. The
steamer made slow headway against the swift current. It was relatively peaceful
on deck, and Teacher Sen used the time to teach the missionaries the basics of
Mandarin Chinese. At sunset on the second day, they sat on deck while Reverend
Ronning read aloud from the Bible and led the group in prayer. A large crowd of
curious Chinese stood watching them. Then something happened that Halvor
never talked about because he deplored violence. Years later, however, my father,
Chester Ronning, heard about it from his Auntie Thea and told it to his children
when Grandpa wasn't around. He was obviously proud of his father.

As Chester tells the story, it happened one evening during devotion. His father, Reverend Ronning, was reading the Bible aloud when he was interrupted

by a rough English voice yelling, "What the hell is goin' on here?" Halvor looked up to see the first mate, a bear of a man who had rampaged up and down China's coast for almost two decades before retiring to riverboats. His skin was scorched brown and his nose was as red as his grizzled beard from the dark rum he found to be the best way to kill the boredom of river travel. He was obviously drunk.

"I am the Reverend Ronning of the China Inland Mission, and these are my fellow missionaries. We are having our evening prayers and would be pleased to have you join us."

Ronning's hospitality seemed to enrage the sailor. "Well, I am Mr. Sanford and I'm 'ere to tell you that you can keep your dirty book to yourselves and stop trying to corrupt the 'eathen Chinese on this ship. You're only causin' trouble." He turned to the crowd of Chinese spectators and yelled, "Now get back to your cabins."

Ronning faced the smirking Englishman. "There is absolutely no need to speak to anyone in such a manner," he said too softly, eyes like steel. "We are causing no trouble here." His anger made his Norwegian accent more pronounced.

The first mate had underestimated the size of Halvor, who was probably one of the few men he had ever had to look up to. They stared at each other fiercely for a full minute before the sailor backed off. With the safety of a few yards and a few Chinese sailors between himself and the missionary, he began to laugh coarsely.

"So, you're goin' to preach to these Chinamen when you can't even speak decent English yourself, are you? You dumb Norwegian! Hah!" He leered at the women. "Watch out, ladies! That book your boyfriend is reading to you is the filthiest book I know. Aye, Preacher, you can't deny that now, can you?"

The Reverend Ronning grabbed the old sailor by the scruff of his neck and told the drunk that the Bible tells us about life as it is. It gives us examples of sinful men and women and tells us how God punished them. Each of us can interpret God's word in his own way. Some can learn from the sins of others and be saved. But some judge others by themselves and read to their own eternal damnation. "Now apologize to the ladies," he ordered.

At this point in the story, my father would stand up, march around the room, wave his arms in the air, and speak in a Norwegian accent in imitation of his father:

"Apologize, you dummkopf, or so help me aye vill pitch you into the Yangtze." Auntie Thea pleaded with him to stop until she saw that her brother had a wild grin on his face. He dropped Sanford in disgust. The sailor sagged to the deck. The Chinese were howling with delight, enjoying the diversion of a fight between foreigners, when the captain appeared. He ordered his first mate to go below. But Sanford was suddenly on his feet, his eyes bulging and his body swaying recklessly. He charged head down like a mad bull. Papa, at the last second, sprang aside. Sanford smashed blindly into the outer wall of the saloon in a crash that would have finished most men, but the rugged seaman let out a furious roar and was up and charging again. This time Papa spun around and lashed out with his right foot. It connected with the sailor's chin, stopped him cold, and sent him sprawling on his back. You can imagine the surprised look on Sanford's face. He wiped some blood from his mouth with his sleeve and shook his head. He was dead sober now. "W'ot 'appened?" he asked.

Reverend Ronning stood over him. "On your knees," he ordered. Sanford obeyed. "Now fold your hands and repeat after me," he said roughly. Then Halvor knelt beside Sanford and looked to the heavens defiantly. "Our Father, which art in Heaven," he roared, "hallowed be Thy name, Thy Kingdom come, Thy will be done"—he stopped and waited for the sailor. "Repeat after me!" he commanded. Sanford mumbled, "Our Father, which art in Heaven."

"Louder!" ordered Halvor. "Hallowed be Thy name!"

"Hallowed be Thy name!"

"That's better . . . Thy Kingdom come."

"Thy Kingdom come . . ."

"Thy will be done . . ."

"Thy will be done . . ."

"Good, good! Once more."

Sanford repeated the Lord's Prayer like a penitent child, and when they were finished, Halvor pulled him to his feet and slapped him hard on the back.

"Well done, Mr. Sanford! I am so glad you could join us this evening."

Sanford stuck out his hand. "You're in the wrong business," he said. "You should 'ave been a bloody sailor." Although neither of the men knew it then, they were destined to meet again under even stranger circumstances. The missionaries calmly returned to their prayers as if nothing had happened. Teacher Sen must have wondered if this new missionary was a man of God or a barbarian.

As darkness crept over the great river, greedy gamblers ringed the coin-stacked tables in the saloons, mahjong chips clattered, and cards slapped sharply. Strains of British battle songs rang from somewhere belowdecks, where the rough British crewmen were guzzling gin and exchanging bawdy tales of pirates and prostitutes. In the rat-infested cabins, euphoric figures lolled on floors and bunks sucking deeply on opium, or "foreign mud." The noxious fumes slunk stealthily along the narrow hall and up the ladders to the upper deck, where monotonous minor-key music was being played by the magistrate's musicians. The opium smoke rose and hovered in a greenish cloud above the *Ta-tung* as she belched and zigzagged her way up the Yangtze River to the center of the Celestial Kingdom, carrying her passionate Christian missionaries.

After their awkward first encounter, first mate Sanford avoided the missionaries for several days. Shortly after midday rice on the fourth day, however, he joined Reverend Ronning, who was alone on deck watching a commotion on shore. The boat had just dropped anchor off the treaty port of Nanking so the cook could transfer to a sampan and paddle ashore to replenish the food supplies. Neither man mentioned their previous encounter. Halvor was horrified to see two men locked together by a heavy wooden collar around their necks. Posted to the collar was a strip of thin paper giving their names and an account of their crimes, which he couldn't read. Sanford speculated that they had been caught stealing food.

The fact that Sanford was there showed friendly intentions. Halvor was grateful that he had no hard feelings. He wrote about their friendship to his brother Nils: *The old sailor told me he had sailed the rivers of China for the past ten years and seen things that no one would believe. He pointed to a small pool of water along the bank and said that last year he saw a crowd of people looking at two human heads floating around. Then he learned that a Chinese had killed his wife and his own cousin for committing adultery. For some inexplicable reason he cut their heads off and brought them to the Magistrate. To test the truth, the so-called wise Magistrate put the bloody heads in the pool. If they turned face to face, he said, it would prove they were guilty. But they turned back to back which proved they were innocent. The poor guy that killed them was seized, chained and dragged off to prison. This old sailor has seen many things that show that we must hurry to spread the Gospel and build churches and schools to help educate the ordinary Chinese who have no chance to learn to read. Today only the top one percent of Chinese have the chance to be educated. I pray for them all, especially Mr. Sanford.*

Between Kui Kang and Wuhan, the Yangtze was divided into six laps of thirty miles each. At the end of each stage was a large town where the steamer would stop to pick up supplies. On the seventh day, December 8, they could see the three cities that made up Greater Hankow, called Wuhan, spread out on both sides of the river. Wuhan was the capital of both Hubei and Hunan Provinces, with a combined population of 1.5 million. It was the commercial center of central China mainly because it had water communication with ten of China's eighteen provinces and a postal center. The large metropolis consisted of three cities: Hankow on the east side; Hanyang, which lies just across the Han River that joins the Yangtze at this point; and Wuch'ang on the west side. Along the banks, thousands of boat people lived on houseboats. Greater Hankow, like Shanghai, was a treaty port, and the Americans, English, Russians, French, and Germans all had their own concessions there, where they were above Chinese law and the Chinese were not allowed to enter. As the *Ta-tung* neared shore, the missionaries were overwhelmed by the scenes of poverty. Thousands of people were crowded into squat mud huts on the riverbank. Others were packed like sardines on boats anchored so close together that the water was not visible between them.

On shore, Reverend Daniel Nelson waited expectantly. He had waited almost a year for the new missionaries to arrive. Now he could see the smoke from their steamer as it passed the junction where the blue waters of the Han River flowed into the yellowish waters of the Yangtze, causing a dark-green circle of churning water. Nelson prayed that this time the missionaries would really be aboard and thanked God aloud when he saw the tall figure of Halvor waving his hat. Thea and Hannah stood on either side of him waving their handkerchiefs. Then he saw Teacher Sen and Sigvald Netland, who had left Hankow three weeks earlier to meet them in Shanghai. From the upper deck, the magistrate, surrounded by his colorful entourage, watched in amusement while Mr. Sanford helped the Americans supervise the unloading of their goods. Sanford bid a respectful good-bye to the ladies and slapped Halvor on the back. "Yer all right, preacher," he said gruffly. "Good luck to ya."

"God bless you, Mr. Sanford, and good luck to you, too." Eight years would pass before they would meet again.

Halvor and Daniel Nelson embraced warmly. Nelson was just over forty, but his brown beard was already frosted with gray, matching his thick, straight eyebrows that almost hid his intense, deep-set eyes. The missionaries piled into rickshaws and waved to the magistrate, who was leading his followers toward a long line of decorated sedan chairs. The Americans proceeded to the mission house in the British Concession. Sigvald Netland introduced his wife, Bertine. Hannah and Thea liked her immediately. She had been baking Norwegian cookies for the occasion. Neither Nelson nor his wife Anna seemed to notice their four wild children, who were racing around the room knocking things over and making Hannah laugh with delight.

Halvor was especially happy to meet the Reverends Hans Wikholm and Lars Johanson, pioneers of the Swedish mission who had arrived in Hankow a few months earlier. The Swedes had much in common and were eager to cooperate with the Norwegian Americans. They scheduled a series of planning sessions.

It was soon decided that Halvor, Thea, and Hannah, with the Netlands, would stay across the Yangtze River in Wuch'ang, where Nelson had secured a house. Here they would live while they studied the language in preparation for establishing a permanent mission somewhere in the interior of China. The Nelsons would remain with the mission in Hankow.

The next morning, the Wuch'ang contingent crossed the Yangtze in small sampans. They were to live in a house on the "Street of Saluting Dragons" that Nelson had acquired rather cheaply because it was believed to be haunted and no Chinese wanted to live in it. The house was enclosed, like most houses, within high stone walls. It stood lonely and dilapidated in the middle of a large, unkempt courtyard once studded with goldfish ponds and flower gardens. Halvor wrote to Nils: *Wuch'ang, December 1891: I am sitting here writing in a Chinese house in the very center of this walled-in heavenly kingdom. It is a large Mandarin house that no one has dared to live in since a Chinese hanged himself from a beam. The spirits are said to be very noisy in here. The name of the house is Tao-fo-di, Blessedness on Earth . . . It was terribly dirty when we came and now we have worked night and day to get it in somewhat decent shape. My carpenter tools stood me in good stead but my new Chinese friends were surprised to see a foreign scholar use his hands. All the scholars here grow long nails, sometimes almost two inches, on their little fingers to show that they never indulge in manual labor. However, I like to work hard and am not inhibited by old traditions. Praise the Lord! I am in splendid health. We are happy as never before.*

Halvor was obviously in love. Shortly after they arrived in Wuch'ang he proposed to Hannah, and she did not hesitate to say yes. They were married Christmas Eve, December 24, 1891, in the mission house in Hankow. The venerable missionary Reverend Griffith John performed the ceremony before the candlelit Christmas tree, which Halvor had cut down and dragged from the woods near East Lake. Thea had decorated it with painted eggshells and crowned it with a cross of silver paper. Hannah was a vision in a gown of creamy taffeta and lace that she had carefully packed in her steamer trunk, making Thea suspect that perhaps Hannah had planned the whole thing in Radcliff. Hannah wore a golden locket enclosing pictures of her parents, and a carved ivory comb held her hair in a twisted topknot. Halvor had managed to slick down his hair; he looked rather uncomfortable in his high-starched collar and white bow tie, but his eyes shone with pride. After a modest wedding feast they crossed the river in sampans, and their new servants welcomed the newlyweds to "Blessedness on Earth" with strings of firecrackers to blast away the evil spirits.

Hannah wrote home: *You will be surprised to hear that the two of us have exchanged the unmarried estate for the married one, namely Ronning and myself . . . Pray for us that God's blessing will rest upon us so we can continue our journey to heaven and try to win souls for Jesus. I am full of love and joy, and the glory of God.*

While the newlyweds were joyfully fixing up their new home, Thea felt she was losing her beloved brother to Hannah. The main reason she had come to China was to accompany Halvor. The mission society had a rule against sending unmarried men into the mission field; they had made an exception for Halvor because he was going with his sister. Christmas Eve and the wedding festival were occasions of rejoicing for everyone but Thea. In her despair, she wrote a confidential letter to Parson Osten Hanson, president of the Hauge Synod, whom the Ronnings had known in Telemark. She did not mention the wedding. Instead, she wrote that she was having spiritual problems with her own soul. She prayed that God would bless her so that she could rejoice on Christmas Day at the birth of Jesus. Suspecting the cause of her unhappiness, Sigvald Netland talked with Thea and attempted to ease her mind.

4

Culture Shock

HOMESICK

The waters of Wei
Flow to the east
Toward home!
Two tears
From my eyes
Fall into the stream,
And are borne away
—CEN CAN,
   TANG DYNASTY (AD 618–907)

Hankow, January 15, 1892. Dear Mama: We have arrived at our new mission at last! I can tell you that the Chinese live in a world beyond the imagination of our friends in Iowa. Halvor and Thea and I often walk on the ancient stone wall that surrounds the city. Here we have a splendid view of the surrounding country and the air is fresher than in the dirty streets. The wall stands 15 feet high and stretches fifteen miles around the city. It has eight iron gates. They are closed at sunset and open at sunrise. One evening Halvor was on the point of being left outside, which would have been extremely dangerous as the countryside is full of robbers. He prayed to God for help and as by a miracle he got it.

Mama dear, I am sorry to tell you that my heart is almost crushed when I take such a trip. Every day, from the wall we see small girls creeping along the ground. They can scarcely walk as the bones of their feet have been deliberately broken and bound in rags to keep them from growing. Why? Because some Chinese men think that small feet are beautiful and they won't marry big-footed girls. But I believe it is to keep the women from running away. What a cruel and terrible custom! The poor little girls' feet are only two to three inches long and will remain that way until death. Why are they creeping? With a small knife they are cutting grass to eat to still their hunger. At such a sight I become very depressed. I feel their pain and pray daily that God will help me learn Chinese quickly. God bless you Mama, I miss you so very much . . . so very much. Halvor and I have only been married for a week. My love for him is boundless but I have to tell you that China is more of a challenge than I expected. Your beloved daughter Hannah.

Hannah tried to catch the teardrops in her lace handkerchief, but they had already smudged the black ink so she drew flower petals over tears.

The Ronnings soon began to comprehend how enormous was their chosen task, but Hannah and Thea were not prepared emotionally for the suffering of China. How could they be?

On January 26, 1892, Halvor wrote to Nils from Wuch'ang: *Dear Brother: The problem of the missionaries in China is not only how to save the souls but also how to save their bodies from perishing from hunger and disease. If China could receive the light of education, science and technology it could become one of the most powerful nations on earth. But alas, this will not happen in my life time. We missionaries can only sow the seeds and pray for Heavenly rain. Last week Hannah and Thea and I took a walk on the wall surrounding the city. Before I could shelter the ladies from see-ing it we saw three Chinese being beheaded near the gate. It was a terrible sight. Each was forced to kneel and while one executioner held his head up by his hair, another sheared it off with one terrible swing of a curved sword. The dripping heads with their long pigtails were stuck on poles as a warning to other criminals. The headless bodies were then dragged outside the wall. There they were left, half naked, with their hands tied behind their backs for several days for people to look at. Brother it was heart-rending to see it . . . At the thought of their souls I paled with horror. I walked slowly, quietly, through the crowd and dipped my pen in their blood to send a message to my brethren at Red Wing Seminary. I shall soon with Chinese blood write an appeal to the church at home calling on God's children to hurry up with the gospel to the Chinese.*

Such misery depressed but did not dishearten Halvor. Rather, it spurred him to write the mission society, soliciting aid and support. On February 4, 1892, he used his considerable dramatic flair to vivify the scene and deliberately rouse the passions of those with authority to help. *Dear Brethren of the Mission Society: We now find ourselves in the heart of the remarkable kingdom. Let us take a trip into the city. How I wish it could be a reality. Crowds in the narrow streets. Low, tumble-down houses stand side by side as if steadying one another. Here stands a Chinese on the street cooking his food. At his side one is being shaved. Here some are butchering and close by one is repairing shoes. One the other side is a beggar who is busy doing away with insects in his shirt. Even more disgusting scenes present themselves. "Clear the way! Clear the way!" the carriers cry. They scream as if they were carrying the whole* world on their shoulders, though they have only empty sacks. Where is that smoke coming from? I'll tell you. No Chinese house has a chimney. The smoke finds its way out where best it can.

"Out of the way! Out of the way!" sound the cries again. This time some government official is being carried in a sedan chair by four men. Curtains prevent him from seeing the common people in their misery. Behind him and in front of him run a flock of dogs, pigs and children, barking, squealing and shouting. To get out of the way for such a procession we must step into a store. Wagons are not used in the streets. Everything, including stones and logs, is carried on the shoulders. Sometimes up to forty and fifty men carry a log.

In such a noisy and congested crowd, one soon gets tired. Add to all this, the intolerable smell because of the terrible filth which is thrown in the streets. But brethren, let us not go past the suffering as the priest and the Levite did. Am I not my brother's keeper?

Let us continue our work. On account of the uncleanliness there is much eye and skin disease. Look at these sad individuals. They are half naked, with open sores. Look at that old man, if you can! Only holes left where the eyes used to be. Further down are men and women left there half dead or dying. No, we cannot stand this anymore. Let us go down to the gate. I don't know if you can stand to look at these cut-off heads.

Let me tell you that a few days ago I dipped my pen in their blood to send you, my brethren, this message: REMEMBER THE CHINA MISSION. HURRY WITH THE GOSPEL TO THE CHINESE. LET NOT THEIR BLOOD COME UPON YOU!

Hannah and Thea needed all their inner strength to adjust to China. Unable to speak the language, they felt woefully inadequate to spread the Gospel. But ready or not, they were soon faced with their first challenge. Their innocence and frustration was expressed in a letter after eight neighborhood ladies, dressed in their finery, had come to call. Hannah wrote to her sister Rebecca: Seeing so many Chinese ladies coming we thought perhaps they had been sent by someone as reconnoiterers. We tried to treat them as well as possible. We invited them to tea and we set some bread and sugar before them. They did not want to sit down until they had looked all over the house as if they were unsure about the spirit of the hanged man. Finally they sat with us. Their faces were gleaming with joy. They would not eat anything but one took a serviette and put in it four slices of bread, very likely she had a hungry child at home. After tea they remained seated. We had no interpreter so we said everything we had learned in Chinese several times over but they just laughed and repeated it back to us. At first they stood quietly gazing at us and then began conversing with each other. When we stood up one came over to me and said something *tender and patted my cheek. Oh, how I wished I could have spoken to her. They all had bandaged feet no larger than a child's. How little we know of their suffering. My wish and prayer is that the Lord will help us to untiring study so we may be of some use out here.*

One can only speculate as to what went on in the minds of the Chinese women who undoubtedly came to visit as much out of curiosity as neighborliness. The pat on the cheek indicated that they must have felt equally as sorry for the well-meaning American women as the missionaries felt for them, and certainly the lady who put the strange-looking food in her serviette was only trying to be polite for she would never feed foreign food to her child. But it was a beginning.

With their new home in order and their mission field selected, the Ronnings devoted themselves to their Chinese studies and prepared for the trip to Fancheng. They hired two teachers, Mr. Ma Ho-ta, who came for two hours each morning and afternoon to teach the language, and Mr. Wu Te-ping, whom they called Lao Fuzi (venerable teacher), who came in the evening to teach them traditional Chinese customs and the Confucian classics, or at least the basic ideas. They all preferred the evening studies. Their language books consisted of a copy of the New Testament in Chinese and a huge sheaf of lesson sheets on which Teacher Ma, a man of pleasant and refined countenance, had written common sentences and plotted the sounds of the Hubei dialect. The first day it seemed almost hopeless. To Halvor's irritation, Hannah and Thea could not refrain from giggling at the strange singsong sounds. Hannah, who already spoke Norwegian and English fluently, soon showed an amazing facility for the spoken language. Her musical ear helped with the new tones, and her lack of self-consciousness in using the language at every opportunity proved to be a great asset. She talked to the cook, who could hardly keep a straight face, while the number-one boy laughed and corrected her. She just kept talking to everyone; the wash amah, the servant's children, the local merchants—anyone who would listen. When she made a mistake, she would be the first to laugh for she was too fun-loving for false dignity. Learning the language became a game for Hannah, and before long she had any number of Chinese eager to teach her new words and phrases. Her ready smile and alert, understanding eyes transmitted her inner warmth to the Chinese, and it was immediately reciprocated. She discovered that the Chinese were eager to talk. They often overestimated her knowledge and talked too fast, but she nodded sympathetically, knowing that listening was often a stronger message than words. When the story was over, they seemed satisfied to have expressed themselves. Hannah was soon speaking enough "kitchen Chinese" to run the household.

Thea was more restrained; she studied alone in her room, pronouncing the words quietly to herself over and over until she felt she could say something correctly. Halvor, too, was a bit shy about practicing on anyone except the teacher, but when he had learned enough Chinese to realize that Netland and other missionaries who had been in China longer than he had were not much better, he lost his inhibitions—but he never lost his Norwegian accent that the Chinese found interesting.

The English-speaking teacher of the Chinese classics, Mr. Wu, was a wizened and emaciated old scholar notable for the shockingly long, curved nails on his little fingers—at least three inches. The cultivation of these lethal-looking points proved to everyone that the only manual labor he had ever indulged in was to wield a calligraphy brush, which he did with great dexterity. His students also noticed that the nails came in handy for nose and ear picking as well as scalp scratching and other activities, but always in a most discreet manner. On the first day he brought the missionaries a porcelain spittoon as a house present, and they soon learned to place it near his chair during lessons. Mr. Wu had infinite patience and obviously relished his role as teacher. It gave him great face with his peers, and he was as zealous in his desire to enlighten these ignorant foreigners to ways Chinese as Halvor was to explain the Gospel to the heathens. Teacher Wu was eager to pass on the neighborhood gossip as well as the scandalous stories about the foreign diplomats in Peking. If Mr. Wu was reminded that time was up, he studiously ignored the hint by opening a new subject. However, when the accounting came at the end of each week, he charged only for precisely one hour each evening.

On the first evening, he appeared in an elaborate but tattered robe and a scholar's cap. Red yarn was braided into his sparse queue to make it appear thicker. He solemnly distributed little notebooks and asked his students to take notes for future consultation. He spoke clearly as if he was talking to children. Halvor dutifully wrote it all down: *Foreign missionaries in China sometimes speak contemptuously of Chinese customs, art and literature as if they were unworthy of serious consideration. Many disregard cherished traditions and are deliberately indifferent to established ethics and social courtesies. This attitude often produces deplorable results, unfortunate blunders and much mutual misunderstanding between the missionaries and the Chinese. Now the question is: What do we Chinese expect of the foreign missionaries who pretend to be a civilization equal, if not superior to the Mid-*

dle Kingdom? That is a big question for Christian propagandists, like yourselves, who wish to communicate new ideas and beliefs to the Chinese. Does your conduct and attitude appear to the Chinese worthy of a civilized people? If you appear to act like barbarians in the eyes of the Chinese you can hardly expect to induce them to accept your religion or even find favor with them. Do you agree with this, Reverend Ronning?

Halvor must have swallowed hard. "There is truth in what you say, Mr. Wu," he said in a controlled tone of respect. "We are eager to learn." When Teacher Wu felt that his pupils were suitably humiliated by their ignorance, he began to explain a few Chinese canons of politeness. "The position of a teacher must be carefully remembered," he told them, "for it is one of the highest in China, and he takes a place in the list of the 'Great Five,' that is, Heaven, Earth, Prince, Parent, and Teacher. In the household a teacher takes precedence over all that are below the master. According to the *Book of Rites* the scholar should never be tempted to 'go out' as teacher but insist in the pupils coming to his own residence; but in the case of foreigners, like yourselves, studying Chinese, where the teacher is invited to come to the learners' home, he should be treated as a friend and not as an employee or servant. The pupils should rise slightly from their chairs to salute him on arrival, and also to take leave of him on departing." He rose a bit and sat down. The three missionaries dutifully returned his salute.

"Very good," he smiled. "Now, you should know that the 'salary' of a teacher is distinguished from the 'pay' of a servant, and the terms must not be interchanged. The former is called a 'bundle of dried meat,' referring to the ancient practice of payment in kind, the latter means 'bitter labor.'" He fluttered his little fingernails significantly.

"In paying me my allowance, the polite method is to enclose the amount in a piece of red paper and place it, with both hands, on the table where I can see it. Remember that Chinese are very particular as to the method of presenting things, so it is well to keep these words of Mencius in mind: 'passers-by will not accept that which is rudely offered them, and even a starving beggar will not accept that which is thrown to him and indicated by the foot of the donor.'"

On and on he went, night after night, filling the eager missionaries with advice and information which they soaked up like sponges. They began with the *Doctrine of the Mean*, one of the four books of the Chinese classics which emphasizes the importance of right relations between the ideal scholar gentleman, who was obviously Mr. Wu himself, and those above and below him in the pecking order. He first advised them how to conduct themselves on social occasions.

"Now with respect to attitudes towards persons of various ages," he began, "all people of the older generation should be treated as fathers, those ten years older as elder brothers, and those five years older or younger as an equal. A respectful salutation must be made to all elders by holding the hands together at the chest and moving them up and down while bowing.

"Spectacles, if worn, should be removed because they are the equivalent of a bandage over the eyes, worn to shut the image of the person from his view as if to overlook the fact of his presence. While walking together the younger person should walk a pace or so behind and offer assistance to the elder where necessary. When meeting children of friends, it is proper to smile pleasantly. Avoid all appearance of boredom or sternness. The forbidding appearance of many foreigners is a distinct barrier to friendly relations, whereas a sympathetic expression is sure to create a good impression."

When the rules of Chinese etiquette had been drilled into his students and formal lessons were over, Teacher Wu often lingered on so he could talk about history and philosophy with Halvor. He liked to point out that at the same time that ancient Greece reached its highest degree of intellectual achievement, a cultural explosion was also taking place in China. It began toward the end of the Zhou Dynasty in the Spring and Autumn Period (722–481 BC) and continued through the period of the Hundred Schools of Thought (551–233 BC). During that time, a hundred new and different philosophies emerged and free debates about the relation of man to the universe and man to society abounded. Halvor was amazed to learn that these basic philosophic debates had been going on in China for more than two thousand years and the Norwegians had never heard about it.

When the House of Zhou was crumpling and the country was in anarchy, something fascinating happened that was to set a pattern throughout Chinese history: the most tumultuous political and social upheavals gave birth to the greatest thinkers, poets, and painters. During the Warring States Period (475–221 BC), China was experiencing one of its worst times. The number of warring states, by elimination of the weak by the strong, dwindled from 1,800 to seven. Times were so chaotic that the philosophers, scholars, and poets took to the hills rather than face man's inhumanity to man. The disgust and despair felt by these sensitive men at the corruption of worldly affairs sent them to seek solace in nature and to look within themselves to find new ways to grapple with social injustices. Amid the confusion of wars and cruelties, these ancient men of excellence displayed an originality and profundity of ideas that to this day has never been surpassed in China.

Of the Hundred Schools of Thought, at least four basic philosophies came to light and are still being discussed today by thinkers in both China and the West: Confucianism, Legalism, Daoism, and Mohism. Halvor discovered that it was impossible to understand China without some understanding of how these four philosophic theories have influenced China's politics, thought, and the character of its people. Volumes of translations and interpretations by scholars have been written about these philosophies, and, at the risk of oversimplification, I would like to touch on the basic thought of each philosophy.

The House of Zhou had passed its peak long before Confucius (551–479 BC) was born, but he looked back to it as the Golden Age and sought to sanction and refine the existing feudal system by looking into the past for guidance. Confucius was a humanist and idealist who advocated a return to government by virtue and merit. He believed that unless men individually embraced the ideal of *ren*—humanity, benevolence, or perfect virtue—there was no hope that society could be spared the evil, cruelty, and violence that was destroying it. To promote his philosophy, he taught three thousand pupils and chose seventy-two for advanced training. He traveled for fourteen years peddling his philosophies but failed to interest any kings or officials in his Golden Age. Finally, he decided to devote his remaining years to reflection and writing. He immersed himself in ancient studies and compiled the most important body of literature of ancient times, known today as the Five Confucian Classics: the *Yi Jing* (*Book of Changes*), the *Shu Jing* (*Book of History*), the *Shi Jing* (*Book of Odes*), the *Li Ji* (*Book of Rites*), and the *Chunqiu* (*Spring and Autumn Annals*). Like the works of many great geniuses, his books generated little interest in his own time. When Confucius died in 479 BC at seventy-three years of age, he was a broken man, unaware that his volumes would rank as the greatest classics in China, or that his *Book of Rites,* which gave detailed rules for the conduct of everyday life, would become the Confucian Bible. Confucius became the main molder of the Chinese mind and character, and over the next two centuries his philosophies touched every man, woman, and child in China, as well as vast numbers of people in the Western world.

Confucian teachings are detailed and complex. At the core of his teachings was the concept of "filial piety": one must first serve one's parents reverently and obediently and then one may fulfill the other duties to emperor and society. The key to the Confucian code is respect. This was true in terms of lineage, class, and position. Respect for everyone in a higher position: woman respects man, concubines and second wife respect first wife, children respect parents, younger brothers respect older brothers, sons respect their fathers, illiterate respects scholar, and so on up the pyramid until the ministers respect the mandarins and all kowtow before the emperor, who must kowtow only before Heaven, which has bestowed upon him the "Mandate" to rule. Filial piety became the cornerstone of all morality, but women were at the bottom of every scale. The amelioration of this ancient attitude toward women is perhaps the biggest change that has taken place in China since the People's Republic took power, enabling women to claim "half the sky."

In the twilight of the Warring States Period, Mencius (372–289 BC) carried the humanist standard of Confucianism. He advocated "government by personal virtue" and believed the nature of man to be basically good. The purpose of learning, he said, was simply to "seek the lost heart" of childhood innocence. As a political philosophy, it stood in middle ground between two extremes: Legalism and Mohism.

Legalism was the first philosophical totalitarianism. This school was strongly influenced by the First Emperor Qin Shihuang, who used it as a rationale for ruthless dictatorship. Its spokesman was Han Feizi (ca. 280–233 BC), pupil of Xunzi. Han Feizi's theory of human nature was the direct opposite of that of Confucius. He declared that man's nature was evil and that all goodness was a result of artificial training and discipline. His followers believed in strict adherence to the law and the shaping of man's character by means of generous rewards and severe punishments. "If you wait to find a naturally straight arrow-shaft you will have no arrow for a hundred generations," wrote Han Feizi. "If you wait to find a naturally round piece of wood, you will have no wheel for a thousand generations . . . But all the world over, men drive chariots and shoot game: how is it? Because they have the tools to force them into shape."

The Legalists advocated war as a means of strengthening the power of the ruler, expanding the state, and making the people submissive by harsh discipline. They put the state and its interests ahead of all human and moral concerns and conceived of a political order where authority would reside in a central administration and an absolute monarch.

Han Feizi was the teacher of Lord Shang Yang of the Qin and the organizing genius behind the first emperor's drive to imperial power. The old teacher Han Fei was rewarded for his contribution to the Qin State in the same manner he had advocated for others. He was cast into the dungeon and rather than being made to die the "death of a thousand cuts," he was allowed to commit suicide by poison.

On the other extreme was Mozi (ca. 470–391 BC), originally known as Mo

Ti. He was a pacifist who offered all-embracing, universal love as the prime governmental force in the world. He advocated disarmament and preached peace, utilitarianism, and uniformity. "What is the will of Heaven that we should all obey?" he wrote. "It is to love all men universally. How do we know it is to love all men universally? Because Heaven accepts sacrifice from all." His was a lonely voice among Chinese thinkers. In a land where family loyalty stood above all, he (like Krishnamurti in India) insisted that love for one's fellow men be universal, without favor or prejudice. Halvor believed this philosophy to be the closest one to his teaching of Christianity.

Next to Confucianism, the most influential Chinese philosophy has been the Daoist school, whose founder was Laozi ("venerable gentleman"), who lived sometime in the sixth century BC. Halvor's teacher often read passages from Laozi's book the *Dao Dejing* to his students. Laozi's philosophy is based on the mystic principle called the Dao, or the Way: the eternal and changeless cosmic force believed to be the essence of life and the source of all being. The whole source of unhappiness, he believed, lay in man's effort to control his destiny, thus impeding the flow of natural events. Life and death are only phases in the great cosmic circle of life: the visible world consists of phantoms that will pass; only the Dao remains eternal. Daoism was often the philosophy of the gentleman in retirement, of the political failure, the recluse and the scholar who abandoned human society in search of mystic harmony with the world of nature. Politically, Daoism stood for a minimum of organization or regulation in all public affairs and urged a do-nothing approach to all the problems of the world. By the time the Ronnings had arrived in China, many frustrated officials of the empress dowager's court had retreated into this philosophy, mainly because they had no other choice.

While Halvor was intensely involved in the study of the great philosophies, Hannah and Thea were being taught Chinese etiquette and customs, which they complained in letters home was "useless and stupid." Among other things, they were told that they should never go out alone but always in the company of a man or an amah. They learned that special cards, hand-printed on red paper, folded neatly, and bearing the inscription "The wife or sister of Reverend Halvor Ronning makes respectful prostrations" should always be carried. Ladies greet each other with the right hand holding the left sleeve while the hands are moved up and down and the head is bowed. Silver rings and bracelets should not be worn because white is the color of mourning. When meeting with a gentleman, the chairs should not be placed close together or face to face, and when tea is brought in, the lady does not drink or even lift the cup to her lips, but replies "please" to the guest's invitation to drink.

The missionary women had little patience or time for the fine points of Chinese courtesies. They were too busy learning the language and sending reports to mission headquarters. Accustomed to Scandinavian cleanliness, Thea was shocked by the sanitary conditions in China. *It is just like we have been told,* she wrote to the mission board, *out in the street shoemakers, tailors, barbers and all sorts of traders sit and ply their trades. One does not need to be hungry in China: one meets on the street people carrying stoves, and the grills are cooking warm food, running after us to see if we will have some. They have chopsticks and cups, naturally, with them: but only the greatest need would tempt us to eat at such a table. Sometimes in the streets one has to hold one's nose. Right beside the houses lie stacks of coffins with half rotten corpses in them. All they do is cover them with a little straw. It is enough to make one very discouraged.*

Thea wrote to a girls' society in Minnesota: *You would be amazed. The streets are narrow and crowded. We must walk single file. Many are blind or crippled. . . . On the way home from a prayer meeting people began to scream, "foreign devils, foreign devils!" but we thought of Jesus. . . . It is a work of patience to sit and learn Chinese all day. We live in a Chinese house with high walls around us. We have been invited to visit a couple of families here. It is strange to see women with bound feet limping back and forth on the earth floors. They gave us hot tea but the house was very dirty for it is common to have farm animals live in the house.*

Toward the end of 1892, Halvor and Hannah adopted the first of a number of Chinese children. *Dear Brother: I must tell you that we have adopted a Chinese boy named Wang Tang, aged ten. Yesterday, a brother of my teacher, Mr. Wu, was conscripted into the army. The soldier, who felt he would never be able to come home again, begged me with tears in his eyes to receive his son, who has no mother . . . I was glad to promise him to receive his son, a fine lad. Hannah is teaching him English. Soon he will be able to write you a letter . . . See what you can do about persuading some bright young men to become medical missionaries. I plan to leave in one week for Fancheng where we will start building our own mission which will include a school and a hospital.*

5

The New Mission Field

SEPARATION

Though the river still flows seaward
As before,
And the spring still bubbles
From the mossy ground,
Life has never been the same to me
Since you left home.
Yesterday I climbed the high hill,
As though again I saw
The white sail of your boat,
Fading swiftly in the distance
Like a dream.

—WU ZONG'AI, QING DYNASTY (1644–1911)

The missionaries from Norway and the Norwegian American missionaries decided to work together but maintain separate organizations. They agreed to build a new mission home in Hankow together and select a new mission field in an area where there would be room for all the Lutheran missions to help establish an independent Chinese Lutheran Church. Reverend Ronning was appointed superintendent of this large undertaking.

The new mission field was selected in a peculiar way that illustrated another side to Halvor's character and the amazing faith the missionaries had in the divine guidance of God as well as in Dr. Griffith John, a veteran missionary who had a scholarly interest in Chinese philosophy, especially Daoism.

Halvor, with Sigvald Netland and Daniel Nelson, met in the office of the venerable doctor to decide on a suitable mission field. Halvor had been introduced to Dr. John by an English Baptist missionary, the Reverend Timothy Richard. Both men were fluent in the spoken and written Chinese language. Richard had translated many books into Chinese including Robert Mackenzie's *The 19th*

Century, which had been read by some Chinese scholars and educated officials. He had published some proclamations favorable to missionaries that stressed the good deeds they had done in famine relief and medical work. Halvor was familiar with Richard's writings and the paper he had presented at a missionary conference in 1890, when he had prophesized that the missionaries "were on the brink of a volcano ready at any time to burst forth." Richard proposed that a memorial be drawn up to send to the empress dowager calling attention to the atrocities against the Christian Church, explaining the true aim of Christian missionaries, and requesting religious liberty. It was drawn up by seven missionaries, including Dr. John, in the hope that it would help stop the growing antiforeign sentiment. No reply came, however, and the persecution of the missionaries continued in the Yangtze Valley and elsewhere.

Dr. Griffith John was a Welsh Congregational missionary and a pioneer evangelist with the London Missionary Society. He was one of the first missionaries in Hubei Province and had been in China for thirty-five years when the Ronnings arrived. In appearance he was an impressive character, noted for his droopy black mustache contrasting with his white frizzy beard. He always dressed in fine Chinese robes and spoke classical Mandarin like a scholar. He befriended the new missionaries and took them to his own tailor to have them fitted with Chinese clothing, which, he explained, was less expensive and more practical than Western clothing. They ordered gowns and padded jackets. Halvor had a long, black silk scholar's robe with a red lining made for himself and ordered some bright brocade vests. On the advice of the respected Dr. John, he also purchased a Chinese cap with a false black queue attached to it. He told his brother Nils that he looked ridiculous in it but thought, for reasons I could never fathom, that it would make him look less conspicuous and show the Chinese he was sympathetic to their culture.

Ronning wrote the following about his meeting in *The Gospel at Work* (1943), which he coauthored with his brother Nils:

In regard to choice of a mission field, we realized that it was important to find a place as yet unoccupied and large enough in the future for all the Lutheran missions and thus make it possible to establish a Chinese Lutheran Church.

I called on Dr. John and asked for an opportunity for us to consult him in regard to a suitable mission field. He was glad to do this. The time was set and we met in his office. Kneeling down, we began the meeting with prayer. Then Dr. John hung a large map on the wall. With his cane in one hand he began to study the map, talking at the same time with God. First, he thanked God for these young and courageous Viking

THE NEW MISSION FIELD ❋ 51

sons He had sent to China. "Now, dear Lord," he went on, "Thou must, through Thy Holy Spirit, point out to me where these brethren ought to find their own field."

He stopped for a while and stood as if listening.

"Yes, this is surely the place. It will suit splendidly these Norwegians."

We felt that the place was holy. I shall never forget that time nor the man who stood there as a channel for God's Spirit, pointing out our future mission field. Then, with his cane he pointed to the northern part of Hubei and the southern part of Hunan. "Look here," he said, "here is a large mountainous region. Here is Hsiangyang and right on the other side of the Han River is Fancheng. Northeast of Fancheng lie large fertile plains with many millions of Chinese who have never heard of the Gospel of Christ and without a single missionary."

We accepted Dr. Griffith John's advice as a direct sign from God.

Halvor Ronning, Daniel Nelson, Johannes Brantzaeg, Teacher Tang, and a fellow missionary, P. Matson of the Swedish Covenant Mission of the United States, rented a junk with a bamboo-rigged patched white sail to journey six hundred winding miles up the Han River to the Fancheng area. There Halvor got his first taste of the growing antiforeignism. A letter to Nils, after returning to Wuch'ang, described their journey and gives us a unique look into the conditions of the countryside at that time. *1892: In Chinese clothes we left Hankow on May 11. With trust in God we began our first missionary journey in China . . . On the way to the boat I bought a few things and fell behind the others. Suddenly a large stone hit me in the head and I stumbled down on my knees. Fortunately, I had a thick cork hat on my head. It was the first of seven times I was stoned . . . It is quite dangerous to travel through an unknown country for people who are not familiar with conditions or the language. We journeyed partly by boat and partly riding on donkeys. Most of the country we passed through consisted of large tracts of level and beautiful land. It was strange for us to see the people busy with the harvest . . . There were many things that reminded us of Palestine in the time of Christ. We also saw threshing done by oxen . . .The people were exceedingly curious, hundreds of them came rushing to look at us. We sold many books and tracts and got a favorable impression of this field. At some places the people were very unfriendly and threw stones at us.*

It took two more trips before Halvor was able to secure permission from the civil mandarin in Hsiangyang (Fancheng's twin city and the civic center) to buy land to build a mission. The deal was negotiated with the help of Teacher Sen Li-fu and a middleman, Lao Ting. They paid six hundred silver dollars for a stretch of land along the banks of the Han River on the Fancheng side. Sen Li-fu was a Confucian scholar who had been converted to Christianity by Dr.

John shortly after he had failed the first official examination for entrance into officialdom. His family had depended upon him to become a mandarin and his father disowned him when he gave up his Confucian studies to study Christian theology. He helped the missionaries with the building plans and found a shop in Hankow where they could have doors, flooring, and windows made for the mission buildings and transported to Fancheng. Workers were hired, and the first story of a house for the missionaries was almost completed by the end of the year. No one realized that their problems were just beginning.

At this time, Dr. Thorstein Himle, a medical missionary, arrived from Norway and for a time joined Halvor in Fancheng. What Himle later wrote about the building of the mission indicated that Halvor's philosophical studies had paid off: *It is remarkable how much Ronning, despite all the hindrances the Chinese officials put in his way, was able to do in the first years on this mission field, unfamiliar as he was with people, conditions and language. He would not sit down and study the language, but by the daily association with the laborers, he not only learned the common language, but also the character of the people, their way of thinking and being, which became very valuable to him in the mission work. But it would take much more understanding and perseverance before it was over.*

Halvor returned to Hankow in time for the New Year, 1893, and the birth of his first son, Nelius Theodore, on January 22. Halvor was just getting used to being a father when, to Hannah's dismay, he was urgently called back to Fancheng. Teacher Sen Li-fu and Middleman Ting had been arrested, and all work on the mission had stopped. Halvor left immediately. He went alone because Nelson was sick. Two days later, while Halvor was sailing upriver, a typhoon hit the area. Hannah and Thea were frantic with worry when no word from Halvor was forthcoming. Once a week, mail came by post boat from Fancheng, and Hannah would go down to the river to meet the swift but frail craft that was propelled by one man, the mailman, who sat on the stern and dexterously plied a short, broad oar with his feet while he directed the course with the other oar, the handle of which he tucked under his arm. Hannah thought it was almost miraculous that the mail boat could traverse seventy miles between the rising and setting of the sun and could reach Hankow in five days. It was three weeks before a letter finally arrived from Halvor relating, almost as an afterthought, that he had been shipwrecked and narrowly escaped disaster.

Hannah delivered her reply personally to the mail boat the next morning. The mailman assured her that it would reach her husband in five days: *My dearest husband: I was worrying about you and thinking that in such bad weather you surely had met with disaster. After reading and re-reading your letter I thanked the Lord for being so merciful to you. I am ashamed of myself when I think how little confidence I really place in the Lord.*

In Fancheng, Halvor learned that just after the bamboo scaffolding for the second story of the house had gone up, the mandarin who governed the twin cities suddenly stopped all construction and threw Sen and the six workers into jail. Middleman Ting was sentenced to four hundred blows of the bamboo cane and a prison term. What Halvor was not aware of at the time was that when the mandarin saw the rising scaffolding he realized that the home of the foreigners would be higher than his own residence and the "Lamp of Heaven" that stood on a high pole before the mandarin's gate and was lit by torch every night to appease the spirits. Anything rising higher than the Lamp of Heaven would jeopardize the fragile geomancy balance of *fengshui*, thereby angering the spirits of the wind and water and bringing untold catastrophes to the area.

Unwilling to lose face by admitting the real reason for the arrests, the city magistrate, who was in cahoots with the mandarin, accused Sen of buying land in his own name with the intent to cheat the foreigners. Nelson came to assist Halvor. They tried repeatedly to see the mandarin but were forcefully stopped and warned to get out of Fancheng. Knowing that prison conditions were terrible, they stayed for over a month unsuccessfully attempting to negotiate the prisoners' release.

August 1893: In Hankow, Hannah and Thea were terrified by the ugly antiforeign hostility that was beginning to surface very close to home. Halvor, in Fancheng, received a letter from Thea written in wobbly handwriting with tear-smudged ink with shocking news. Two friends, Hans Wikholm and Lars Johanson, of the Swedish Mission in Sungpu, not far from Hankow, had been chased from their home and murdered by a Chinese mob. When found nine days later, their mutilated bodies could hardly be recognized. *We know that such a riot may start at any time. We have committed our souls and bodies into the hands of God. We need you, Halvor. Please come home! Hannah needs you.*

The corpses were brought to Hankow under military escort and laid to rest in the foreigners' cemetery, which later became known as Martyrs' Cemetery. Later, in his book *Forty-Five Years in China*, Timothy Richard reported the sordid details: "The missionaries climbed to the top of their house and tried to escape over the roofs of other houses, but they were pursued like rats, and when caught were brutally murdered. When the crime was reported to the Viceroy, he expressed no horror of the deed but he uttered the following memorable words:

'We do not want these missionaries. We oppose them, we raise riots against them, we destroy their churches, we kill their converts, we murder the foreigners themselves. Yet the astonishing thing is that the more we kill them, the more anxious they seem to come.'"

Hannah wrote a letter to Halvor that revealed her inner strength. Reading it a half century later, I was amazed at the courage and unselfish attitude of this young girl of twenty-one, in the midst of deadly turmoil in a strange country with her first baby and without her husband: *Since the murders I have dreamt unpleasant dreams and been awake in the night and prayed to the Lord to hold His strong and Mighty Hand over you and all the others. I presume you have by this time received the telegram I sent asking you to return. I know you have good reason to stay and I do not know that I have any reason for feeling as I do but for the last days my heart has been filled with anxiety. Netland has placed some ropes and ladders by the back garden wall in case we have to make a hasty retreat but we pray it will never come to that. My dear Halvor I should be very happy to have you come home now, that is if you do not think you can gain much by staying. I feel my strength is diminishing. Still not after my wish—but your own. Do what is right for the Lord.*

Caring for her first baby and running a household was becoming a huge strain on Hannah: *We are having some trouble with the servants. My Amah, Su-yin is having a terrible time, her husband gets drunk and threatens to kill her unless she gives him more money for brandy. I told her I would protect her and her three little children but the husband is fierce and unruly. The Netlands are a comfort and Nelson's daughter Norah comes to play with the children, she is a wonderful girl . . . Last night we were on the bund. It was a fair evening and all seemed to enjoy themselves so well. But I could not possibly do so for my thoughts were not here at all but they were where you are . . . Rec'd mail this week but still no letter from home. It all tends to make me feel—don't say more!* Before her letter reached Halvor, Mr. Johnson, who had only arrived a month earlier, died of the mysterious fever that killed so many missionaries at that time.

It was three months before Halvor gave up his attempt to free Ting and the other Chinese workers who were in jail. Before returning to Hankow, he sent a message to Sen Li-fu telling him to have courage and that he was going back to Hankow to refer the matter to the American consul and the American legation in Peking. *Hankow, September 1, 1893. Dear Brother: After a trip to Fancheng, lasting three months and being among the Chinese all the time, it was refreshing for body and soul to come home to my dear ones. Hannah is as beautiful as ever. Nelius did not know me when I returned. He was afraid of me with my long beard and wild hair, but we soon became good friends again. He is very cute and pulls his auntie's hair several times a day amidst great shouts. He laughs and talks so we can hear him throughout our whole apartments . . . The murder of the two Swedish brethren will result in a victory. The Norwegian consul has now more courage, and Germany, England and America have promised to help. The people of China are congenial but the government is afraid that the foreigners will take power away from them . . . We have adopted or given homes to several small Chinese boys and have begun a school here for them.*

It seemed there was no peace for the young missionaries. Sigvald Netland's wife, Bertine, who had always been hearty and strong, caught the fever of unknown causes that killed so many Westerners in those times. She died within a few days in delirium. Halvor, in a state of shock, administered holy communion to his friend Netland and his dying wife. Hannah and Thea prayed for a miracle, but it was not to be. She died on December 8, 1893, and was laid to rest the next day in the expanding Martyrs' Cemetery. Everyone wondered who would be next. On December 11, Sigvald wrote an anguished letter to the mission board: *We have sorrow upon sorrow out here. One witness after another is laid in the ground until Resurrection morn. Just think! He did not spare my beloved wife but took her from me. Oh God, how your ways are unsearchable! Teach me thy way, and let my soul once more have peace and rest.*

The year 1894 began auspiciously. In January, Halvor got word that the chief magistrate in Fancheng had released Sen Li-fu and the workers from prison. Middleman Ting, however, was still being held. Halvor and Netland returned to Fancheng with letters from the American consul in Hankow imploring the mandarin to let the building proceed. Sen met them at the dock. He had lost weight, but his spirit was undaunted. He embraced his friends warmly and informed them that the concerns about *fengshui* had been the real reason for the building stoppage. When they met with the mandarin, Halvor immediately agreed to build the mission only two stories high instead of three, and the mandarin, in response, issued a proclamation that the foreigners in the twin cities should be treated with respect. Halvor wrote to Hannah: *We have begun again. I am well and happy as only a child of God can be. Have not shaved since I left so you can imagine how I look. Expect to be back home by Easter.*

Halvor and Netland returned to Wuch'ang in April with the news that everything was ready for the opening of the mission in Fancheng. Two single women missionaries, Miss Oline Hermanson, a nurse who had earned her degree at Deaconess Hospital in Minneapolis, and Miss Olive Hodenfield, who had just graduated from the Breckenridge Institute in Decorah, Iowa, had arrived while they were away. Netland, who had been filled with loneliness since the death of his wife, was immediately taken with Miss Hermanson, and the other missionaries encouraged the relationship. Strangely, the conventional attitudes about widowhood and mourning did not apply in missionary circles in China. It was an accepted fact that Western women did not live very long in China, and so it was not unusual for a widowed missionary to marry within months of his wife's death. Many men remarried several times during their terms as missionaries. The "cause" took priority. There was a surplus of single missionary women, and marriage with them curtailed the temptation to seek out the company of Chinese women. Before the month was out, Sigvald and Oline were married and planning to go to Fancheng with the Ronnings. It was decided that the Nelsons, with their large family, would stay in Hankow to run the school and the children's home. The next weeks were spent in preparation.

6

Journey up the Han River

MOONLIGHT ON THE HAN RIVER

The clouds of sunset
Gather in the western sky,
And over the silent silvery Han
Rises a white jade moon.
Not often does life
Bring such beauty.
Where shall I see the moon
Next year?
—SU TONGPO, SONG DYNASTY (960–1278)

At dawn on May 1, 1894, the Ronnings arrived on the banks of the Han River to board the passenger junk *Man-Kan* and sail six hundred miles up the Han as it winds in innumerable S-bends to the walled-in twin cities of Hsiangyang and Fancheng, known today as Xiangfan. Halvor was eager to show Hannah the new mission station he had established in the commercial city of Fancheng directly across the Han from the official city of Hsiangyang. Hannah had become accustomed to the chaos of Chinese waterfronts, but when the morning sun rose over the scene she became as excited as a child watching a parade. Before her lay a colorful panorama of swaying masts from a variety of vessels that navigated the rivers, creeks, and canals of China. Fruit and vegetable boats were piled high with yellow melons and green winter cabbages. Close to shore, hawkers on the tea boats with shining stained-glass windows were selling hot brews. Billows of steam and appetizing odors rose from the floating kitchens sculling between the rows of houseboats that never moved from their anchorages. Boat people, considered inferior, were not allowed to live on shore. Faded blue laundry hung from bamboo poles on the decks of their floating homes. Hannah sympathized with these humble folk who were born, married, and died on their boats. Saffron-robed Buddhist monks floating around on canopied chamber-boats (*Lou-Shan*) with shimmering shrines were always ready, for a small donation, to solemnize weddings or say a prayer for the repose of the spirits of those unfortunates who had perished in the river rapids unwept, unsung, and uncounted.

Sigvald Netland and his new wife had a boat to themselves while the three Ronnings with baby Nelius; their adopted Chinese son, Wang; and Miss Hodenfield boarded a larger junk, the *Good Success*. The name was painted in Chinese characters on the high-pooped stern behind the open toilet holes. Fierce bulging eyes to espy the underwater rocks and dragons defended the prow. Hannah carried Nelius piggyback over the rickety gangplank extending from the bank over the water to the deck while Halvor carried Wang, who was terrified of the water. The mainmast, one solid piece of wood rising from midship, was topped with fluttering strips of red paper bearing propitious exhortations such as: *May this vessel scorn tempests from whatever quarter of the heavens they may come,* and *From every side of the compass may fair winds blow.* The patched, bamboo-rigged sails were still furled on the boom. Two rough wooden pavilions on the stern, painted black with a green border to indicate that Hankow was home port, were to serve as their living quarters for the next two weeks. The cabin was so low that Halvor could barely stand up. The foredeck was piled with rope, poles, and sculling oars. The hold served as the kitchen and living quarters for the cook and the eight-man crew. Trackers could be hired near the rapids to pull the junks upstream.

After the mooring taxes were paid, the captain beheaded two chickens as sacrifices to the river deities. As the boats cast off, everyone on shore bashed gongs and beat drums. Firecrackers exploded to propitiate the spirits of the wind and water (*fengshui*). By the time they unfurled the sails, Nelius, who was just learning to walk, was in such a state of excitement that he skidded across the deck and was caught by his father only seconds before he would have plunged into the water. Hannah harnessed a rope around his waist as she had seen the Chinese mothers do. At last, they were on their way to open the first China Inland Mission in the interior of China.

The next day the junks were slowed by the failing wind as they rounded a bend in the river. To prevent the boat from being swept downriver with the current, trackers were hired to pull the boat upriver. Hannah and Thea watched in wonder as a slight barefoot coolie shimmied up the mainmast to attach the bamboo cable running from the trackers' harnesses to the top of the mast. It had to be high enough to allow other boats to pass under it if necessary. Hannah screamed in protest when she saw Halvor jump into the water and wade ashore to join the trackers. This was a new experience he could not resist. The trackers each slipped a harness over one shoulder. Halvor did the same. The captain steered the rudder while the head tracker squatted on the bow of the junk in his black robes, like a vulture, screaming out orders to the coolies trekking up the tow path on the riverbank. Three sailors stood on the deck with long bamboo poles with metal points to prevent the boat from beaching or colliding with other rivercraft.

Then, on command, the men pulled together, straining against the swift current, every muscle taut, grunting in unison and lying almost flat against the harness. Hannah held her breath until the boat started to move. One slip and they would all be carried back to Hankow in the swift currents. Slowly the boat began to move forward. Two hours later, when they had rounded the bend, the wind from the south picked up and they were able to sail north again. Halvor climbed on board drenched with sweat, aching in every limb and grinning at Hannah. His sister Thea knew he was showing off again. The Chinese must have wondered what kind of a man he was.

In spite of the dockside ceremony to placate the spirits, tragedy struck on the ninth day out. A sudden squall erupted at a point where the river was too wide for the boats to make shore. The junk lurched from side to side. Halvor was herding everyone below deck when he realized that his ten-year-old son Wang was missing. Oh, Lord! He had seen the child heading for the toilets on the stern. He searched frantically. Fearing the worst, Halvor lowered a sloop over the side and rowed across the white-capped waters calling for his son. In a desperate attempt to rescue Wang, Halvor tossed off his shoes and dove under the dark waters until his lungs were bursting. He was carried downstream and was on the verge of being sucked into a whirlpool when he was pulled from the river by rescue workers in one of the red lifeboats that patrol the rapids. Wang's body was never found. Hannah helped Halvor climb back on deck. They were devastated. Halvor raised his fists to the heavens and thundered: "Why? My God. Why him? Why hast thou forsaken me?"

Halvor to Nils: *On the 9th of May we had the misfortune that our dear son, Wang Tang, drowned. It was a stunning blow . . . I had great expectations for him, perhaps too great. He was the first fruit of our labor. Why him? Why? What does it mean? We searched through the Bible for comfort and found little. Isaiah 57:1 helped a bit: "The righteous perisheth and no man layeth it to heart, and merciful men are taken away, none considering that the righteous is taken away from the evil to come." Brother! God works in mysterious ways. I have been so consumed with my own suffering and not of my son Wang. Forgive me. Wang is in Glory! But I wonder what is meant by the evil to come.*

The grief-stricken missionaries continued their journey. At the city of Sha-yang, about halfway to Fancheng, they stopped for supplies and ran into another unexpected situation later recorded by Halvor: *Dear Nils: This is May 17, Nor-wegian National Day. The day brings memories of Norway, the old home and of you, brother . . . It is two weeks since we left Hankow and we are only half way . . . We had great excitement yesterday. We had to remain here two days on account of lack of wind. When the people in the surrounding country heard that foreigners were on board they came in great crowds to look at us. In the afternoon the wind had risen and our men began to pull the boat. Now things began to happen. An eight-year-old boy had disappeared, and the father and mother claimed we had stolen him. The crowd grew furious and stopped the boat and wanted to come on board and look for the boy. We were struck with fear, because almost all riots begin with wild rumors which people believe. The parents kept crying aloud. The situation became tense. We suggested that two men might come on board to see for themselves. This they would not or dared not to do; all of them wanted to come. Our captain made a speech saying that he was Chinese and had with him twenty other Chinese who could testify that we had not stolen the boy. Fortunately we heard that the local mandarin lived nearby. We sent a messenger to him. He came and soon they all left and we had a peaceful night . . . except for thoughts of my son who was swept away from us so quickly I still cannot believe it. Who knows what is in store for the rest of us.*

As they approached Fancheng, the countryside became hilly and greener. Soon the Dabie Mountains were visible in the distance. Lush weeping willows hung low over the streams where women in conical hats were beating laundry on flat rocks. The villagers lived in clusters of thatched-roof mud huts surrounded by high mud walls; surmounted on each of the four corners were watchtowers manned with sentries keeping constant vigil for roving bandits. The missionaries were entranced by the constantly changing scenes on shore. Snatches of eternal China unrolled like traditional Chinese scrolls as the junk slowly sailed toward Fancheng.

Terraced, emerald-green rice paddies separated by mud ridges stretched to the horizon. The peasants, wading knee-deep in water, plowed the fields with wooden ploughs pulled by hump-necked oxen. Arched willow and bamboo trees edged the winding paths leading to distant pagodas. Fat-bellied children in round straw hats drove flocks of waddling white ducks and squealing black pigs along the riverbanks, while other small children lolled on the backs of long-horned water buffalo wallowing in the ponds amid pink lotus blossoms and scarlet water lilies that dotted the muddy water like drops of bright paint.

It was late afternoon on May 27 when the missionaries approached their destination. Massive city walls of Babylonian aspect loomed darkly. The dilapidated bastions, speaking of past glories, had surrounded the twin cities of Fancheng and Hsiangyang, astride the mighty Han, for some twenty centuries. At intervals along the top were crenellated fortresses of gigantic proportions. Ravens saluted them with mournful caws from the top of each bastion. Halvor reminded Hannah and Thea that it was within these walls that the famous scholar Zhuge Liang had been born and received the education that prepared him to be the chancellor of one of China's ancient kingdoms. It was also where Halvor's son Chester, my father, would be born.

The junks docked in the shadows at the foot of the wall. Halvor's colleague Sen Li-fu greeted them with tears in his eyes. Halvor fell to his knees and thanked God that they had finally reached their new mission field. That evening Hannah wrote home: *We followed the welcoming committee through a mysterious stone gate, so thick and black that it seemed more like an entrance to a cavern. I saw two rows of little wooden cages hanging from hooks on both sides of the gate. A flurry of flies buzzed around them. Mama dear I hate to tell you but I slowed down to get a better look. Horror of horrors! Each cage contained a human head with the long queue uncoiled to dangle in dusty degradation. Mr. Sen said they were thieves who had been caught trying to enter the city through a hole in the wall. Halvor was striding ahead talking with the others and didn't seem to notice. When we were inside the gate the people lined the roadway, pressing against each other to watch us pass. They stared open mouthed and climbed on top of each other to see us. Women with little pointed feet peered from the gates of the walled-in courtyards . . . Fancheng seems to be made of walls within walls all falling into dust and decay. Tonight I am feeling very, very far away from home, dear Mama, and from my brothers and sisters in America. I feel separated from you not only by distance but by centuries of time.*

From Halvor: *Dear brother Nils: We arrived in this walled-in kingdom yesterday. I am sitting in our new home and have it quite comfortable. The people are friendly. The mandarin sent a welcoming committee.*

Fancheng

On their first Sunday in Fancheng, Halvor and Hannah and Thea went for a walk on the city wall of Hsiangyang. Except for Peking and Nanking, Hsiangyang had the largest city wall and widest moat in China. The huge parapets, standing about forty feet high, were pierced with embrasures for artillery and loop holes for musketry. It was wide enough on top for several horses to gallop abreast. Inside the wall were barracks for troops. Stones were piled on the ramparts ready to be heaved upon the heads of strangers. On all four sides were massive archways with double gates that closed at sunset. The south entrance was the gate of honor set aside for mandarins and officials, and later Roman Catholic missionaries. Funeral processions, night soil bearers, or anything considered unclean was forbidden at the South Gate.

When the Ronnings descended the steep, crumbling stone steps to walk along the banks of the moat, they heard a piteous cry and saw a mangy dog sniffing at a pile of red rags near the water's edge. Halvor ran ahead and kicked away the snarling mongrel. He opened the bundle and was appalled to see the blue, contorted face of a naked baby girl, not yet a day old. Infanticide for girls was an accepted custom in China, and she had obviously been left to die. Hannah picked up the baby and they rushed back to the mission, where Hannah and Thea bathed and clothed her. A nursing amah agreed, for a price, to share her breast milk with the abandoned baby. Halvor christened her Lydia. She was the first of dozens of abandoned babies to be rescued by the missionaries. Hannah and Thea started a foundling home; the word spread quickly, and baby girls were often left outside the mission gate.

The Chief Magistrate and Middleman Ting

Foremost in Halvor's mind was the release of Middleman Ting and the six workers who had been arrested when construction of the mission was halted. Ting was not a Christian, so extraterritorial rights did not apply. Halvor and Netland made an appointment to call on the new chief magistrate. At the Yamen gate, two guards with bayonets stood at attention as the missionaries, in Chinese clothes, were ushered to the audience chamber. The new magistrate, wearing the official robe of a military magistrate of the second rank, a square breastplate embroidered with a golden lion, and a skullcap topped with the official coral button of rank, sat on an ornate throne on a raised platform. All ordinary mortals were required to kowtow three times and bang their heads on the floor nine times before approaching him. The missionaries, however, were not required to kowtow since foreigners had recently been exempted from this ritual by the emperor's decree granted on the advice of Wu Kedu, a well-known advisor to the Imperial Court. The edict gives a unique insight into the attitude of the Manchu Imperial Court. It stated: "Since the foreigners have no knowledge of correct ethical behavior and seek only material profit from their actions, there is no point in requesting them to follow ritual observances based on Confucian moral premises; to do so would make no more sense than assembling a group of sheep and pigs and requiring them to dance to music."

The two missionaries bowed respectfully to the magistrate, who motioned them to be seated on two chairs at a lower level. After tea and watermelon seeds, they were informed that arrangements had already been made to release Ting and the workers. Two bearers brought in a gold-gilt box and placed it on the right of the magistrate. He extracted the official seal and affixed it to a release paper.

The prison was a great shock to the compassionate missionaries. *When the gates to "The Tiger's Mouth" clanked shut behind us we stood facing a pebbled courtyard surrounded by low wooden sheds. There were no windows but we could see through small slits. The sheds were crowded with men. Our hearts were crushed. They could not stand straight for the ceilings were not more than three feet high. The stench was staggering and their cries, like wounded animals, were piteous. We were helpless to ease their agony but could only pray for God's mercy. Even worse was the sight of a dozen poor wretches in the middle of the yard, barefoot in the cold, with their ankles chained in shackles and heavy wooden collars padlocked around their necks. They were held in place by more chains which cut into their bleeding flesh. We were led to an inner courtyard to a row of cells holding manacled prisoners. In one of these sat Mr. Ting. It was the only cell with a chair in it and had obviously been recently cleaned, no doubt for our arrival. I could hardly recognize poor Mr. Ting; he was gaunt and bent. Netland and I put our arms around him and practically carried him out of his miserable cell. The six workers were in better shape.*

On the way out of the prison they came upon a dirty, wretched boy, not more than ten years old, the same age Wang had been. He was chained to a wooden block. The boy cried out to them, and Halvor could not pass him by. The jailer said that the boy had been caught stealing food. The two missionaries pooled their money to pay his fine and bribed the jailer to release him.

Halvor and Netland brought Ting to his home, where his wife was waiting. The mission had supported his family during his imprisonment and continued to do so until he recovered even though they were in serious need of funds. When the boy had been bathed and deloused, Halvor christened him Peter. He became the first student in Reverend Ronning's boys' school and, twelve years later, a teacher in the mission school.

7

Opening the Ronning School

Education of the common man is of prime importance to the modernization of China.
— HALVOR RONNING, 1894

If women take to learning, what will men do?
— OLD CHINESE SAYING

As supervisor of the mission, Halvor felt strongly that all Chinese children should be enlightened intellectually as well as spiritually. With Netland and a dozen workmen, he built a two-room schoolhouse, one for boys, whom he would teach himself, and one for girls, to be taught by Hannah and Thea. During June and July, they hung posters on the town bulletin boards announcing the opening of the schools and visited families in the area, urging them to send their children to the school, which was to open on August 1, 1894. Books and materials would be furnished by the mission. Reverend Ronning explained that the schools would be open to all children regardless of social standing, and that reading and writing would be taught first in Chinese and then in English for those who showed an aptitude for learning. He pointed out that the merit system established by Confucius was to be highly recommended but that it usually allowed for only one boy in a family or one boy in a whole village to be educated. There was no chance for the girls. In the mission schools, the average boy or girl could at least learn to read and write.

The response to educating the common child was cool, if not hostile. In an attempt to overcome this, Halvor personally invited the important men in Fancheng for tea and talk at the mission. Hannah wanted to invite their wives, but custom would not permit it. All the Chinese gentlemen accepted graciously, but at the appointed hour, not one arrived. Instead, a crimson paper with black characters was delivered to "The Rev. H. N. Ronning." It was a note, in flowery language, to the effect that if the honorable lady missionaries were not present the humble guests would respectfully accept a cup of tea with the Reverend Ronning. The ladies agreed to leave but only on the condition that they could, in Chinese fashion, stand behind the curtained doorway and listen from the next room. Halvor agreed reluctantly and sent a return note accepting his guests' condition.

The gatekeeper ushered in two officials, three Confucian scholars, and a handful of businessmen. After bowing and dispensing with the polite preliminaries, Halvor approached the subject. According to custom, tea could not be served until the business was over. Halvor spoke in Chinese with the aid of Teacher Tang. "As you know, Mrs. Ronning and Miss Ronning would like to open a school for girls and I will open one for boys. The mission will supply the books and school material and we will accept any children regardless of their social or educational background. We beg your cooperation and support. Think of the opportunity to educate your young."

The group had selected Mr. Tao Fu-ling, a well-known local scholar, as spokesman. His whole demeanor was one of arrogance thinly disguised by pretentious humility. His graying mustache drooped, and his eyes were cold, calculating slits behind thick glasses. As he spoke, his bony fingers played with his necklace of jade marbles: "Honorable missionary, we appreciate your lustrous gesture and know your intentions are lofty, but we have our own ways to educate our young people. In our system all have equal opportunity to compete for the official, even imperial examinations."

"All?" questioned Halvor. "Forgive me, Venerable Teacher, but usually only one boy in every family has the chance for education. We would like to educate all those who cannot compete for lack of funds or have failed the entrance exams. This includes boys and girls. We would like to give girls back the educational opportunities they once enjoyed centuries ago but are now deprived of."

A hurried, mumbled conference ensued from which Mr. Tao emerged smiling and sucking air through his yellowed teeth. "May I humbly suggest that you don't understand our problems, Honorable Missionary? You see, it is precisely because of our difficult experience of keeping educated women under control that led our forefathers to limit their schooling."

"Then you would forbid them to go to school?"

The scholar's smile widened. "Oh, no, we would not do that. We are progressive men. You could teach them how to read."

"Is that all?"

"Perhaps your lady missionaries could teach household arts, embroidery work, and ethics so they will be more aware of their filial and wifely duties. But their education, of course, should be quite different from the boys'." The group nodded in agreement.

"Would you then consent to the girls learning their rights as well as their duties?" asked Halvor.

"Oh, no!" answered the scholar without consulting his colleagues. He fluttered his long fingernails. "That is not at all necessary."

"But why should women be so subordinated?" asked Halvor boldly.

The scholar rubbed his hands together and assumed a patronizing tone. "You see, it is not that men selfishly rule women or that one sex has deliberately brought the other into subjection but because men are the Yang principle of the species while women are the Yin. The Yang is warmth, light, strength, wisdom. Yin is darkness, wetness, cold. The earth spirits are the Yin while the heavenly spirits are the Yang; therefore man is naturally superior in both wisdom and virtue. We are obligated to do what is fit and proper not only for ourselves but for women too. Women are necessary—but inferior. They must be kept under firm control. The sages stress the danger of educating women or letting them go about freely, for they may gain the upper hand and wreck society. Women are very hard to control," continued the scholar. "You can never tell where education will lead to. You are asking for trouble, Honorable Missionary. At the bottom of every trouble there is a woman."

The others mumbled, "True, true, wisely spoken." One official, fat as the Laughing Buddha, clasped his pudgy hands over his bulging belly and squeaked: "Open your boys' school if you must, but open a girls' school! Unthinkable! Why, if women take to reading, what will there be for men to do?"

Halvor coughed loudly and asked the number-one boy to pour the tea.

Halvor and Hannah used the example of the Tang Dynasty (AD 618–907) at its peak to persuade the town officials to allow the girls to attend their schools. That period represented a high point in Chinese civilization, but it is perhaps most remembered for the freedom that women enjoyed. Halvor explained that they wanted to restore the educational opportunities females once enjoyed but were now deprived of. The elite group, as Halvor recalled later, *listened with an air of apathetic indifference which seems to veil the inner feelings of most polished Chinese gentlemen.* He was soon to discover their real feelings.

At 6:00 a.m. on August 1, 1894, Reverend Ronning, in his black mandarin scholar's robe, set out for his new schoolhouse with long, purposeful strides. He held his adopted son, Peter, firmly by the hand and was full of fervor for his new project. But his enthusiasm was short-lived. Later he confided to Nils: *It was not a very auspicious beginning. When I came to the school house I found one small ragged urchin sitting on the steps. That was all. Yesterday there were two bedraggled boys plus Peter. We carried on classes as if we had a full house and they seemed to enjoy it greatly. I taught them how to count. The boys spread the good word. Today there were five. That's what we call progress, isn't it? They come here between six and seven in the morning. Spend some time at home at noon, then come back and read until it is dark. All the children read aloud at the same time, just as in Norway in days of old. It is a deafening noise, so it is almost impossible to be near the classroom. After a while we shall introduce more modern methods.*

While Halvor was joyfully making progress, Hannah and Thea were despondent. Theirs was to be the first girls' school in the interior of China, but in spite of their earnest campaigning, not a single girl had appeared on the first day. Obviously the citizens of Fancheng had been shocked at the very thought of educating girls, which was at that time a revolutionary and frightening idea. The scholars of the male-dominated society had, for centuries, used the ancient Yin-Yang theory to rationalize their attitude of superiority toward women and distorted it into a justification for keeping women under tyrannical control. A poem from the ancient *Book of Odes* also reveals the Chinese attitude toward women that, except for a few enlightened periods, persisted until the fall of the Manchu Dynasty in 1911 and in some areas until the establishment of the People's Republic in 1949:

> Sons shall be born to him, they will sleep on couches;
> They will be clothed in robes; have scepters to play with;
> Their cry will be loud.
> They will be resplendent with red knee covers,
> The (future) kings, the princes of the land.
> Daughters will be born to him.
> They will sleep on the ground;
> They will be clothed in wrappers; have tiles to play with.
> It will be theirs neither to do wrong nor good.
> Only of the spirits and food will they have to think.
> And to cause no sorrow to their parents.

Little wonder, then, that my grandparents had a difficult time getting the people in Fancheng to allow their girls to be educated. Customs regarding women were even more restrictive in China's interior than in the coastal cities. If a woman was not a beggar, servant, or low-class peasant, it was considered cause for divorce if she dared to venture out alone on the streets. She was allowed to stand in her gateway only in the evenings to look about. If called upon to go on an errand without her husband, she must ride a mule or travel in a curtained sedan chair. However, she could never do so during a new or full moon, when she could only wear black with a small veil over her face. If she did go out with her husband, she was obliged to walk three paces behind. In Fancheng, women could not lean against the frame of a door when visiting or even touch the door-step in crossing for fear she would gain power over the family in the house.

As it happened, the first girl student in the Ronning School was not a member of the gentry, but a ten-year-old girl whom Hannah and Thea bought at the slave market. It was unusual to find a girl for sale who had bound feet, for only the privileged classes perpetrated that horror upon their little girls. The servant class and peasants let the girls' feet grow normally so the crippling effect would not interfere with the work expected of them. The girl was in a state of shock and crying from fear and the pain in her tightly bound feet. She must have been orphaned or kidnapped. For a few strings of cash, she was rescued from her misery.

When they arrived back at the mission, Hannah and Thea unwrapped the two layers of filthy rags that had bound the child's feet. She screamed in agony as the blood suddenly rushed to her toes. They lowered her feet into a bucket of warm water with soothing oils. The child sighed in relief, but Hannah and Thea were horrified. *We saw with our own eyes what the Chinese call "killing the feet,"* wrote Thea in a letter to mission headquarters in Minnesota, imploring them to send funds for a hospital: *The smell was quite revolting but we tried not to notice. Her poor feet had been forced into line with the leg and the toes doubled under the soles of the feet. The big toes had been forced crooked to overlap the others. The bandages had been applied with a cruel amount of pressure. The child's feet were blue and the skin cracked and indented where the circulation had been completely cut off. Fortunately she was not yet permanently crippled as her young bones are still soft. It must be the cruelest custom ever inflicted by man. Mothers sleep with sticks which they use to beat the child if she disturbs the household with her wails and if that doesn't work they sometimes lock her in an outhouse. The little girls are often in such pain that their mothers give them opium to stifle the pain. We are told that the pain lets up after three years but many of the girls die of gangrene or shock before that. Some go mad and others become opium addicts. When they grow up they are crippled for life. They get no exercise because they can only walk on their heels with the knees stiff. The muscles of the calf never develop and the lower legs are like broomsticks with drooping folds of skin. But, thank God, our little girl will not suffer this. She will recover in time and we will do everything we can to give her a good education in our girls' school. Brother Halvor baptized her and we have named her Sarah, but her Chinese name is Hsiao Lin.*

Both Hannah and Thea wrote often about the cruelties of foot binding: *What induces a mother to impose such suffering upon a daughter?* agonized Hannah. *How my heart aches for all these little girls. When I think of myself at the glorious age of ten, running and leaping on my horse and galloping over the fields and jumping the creeks, and these poor children have no freedom at all and can barely walk. I cannot imagine that the Chinese men find it attractive but they say it is so. They call these hideously crippled feet "golden lilies." The ultimate disgrace for a middle class family is for their daughter not to get a husband and no man will marry a girl with natural feet . . . Now I see that we must first unbind the minds before we can unbind the feet.*

Three days after Sarah was sent to school, another ten-year-old girl was brought to the mission by her father, Chou Fu-yen, a well-off gentleman in the salt trade. He was a Christian who had been converted by Halvor but suffered because of it. His father, a tyrannical patriarch, had disowned him and compelled him to walk through the streets of Fancheng with a wooden placard on his back saying, "I am a Christian." Many people had mocked him, but he had held his head high. Later he told Halvor: "I did it for the Lord; my heart is at peace."

The salt merchant set an example by bringing his daughter to school, and gradually other girls came. The only criterion for entrance was that they did not have bound feet, and if they did, they were required to unbind them. Two weeks after the opening, Halvor wrote to Nils: *I have 11 small boys and the ladies have five girls. We must not be discouraged. Building has begun on the dormitories and the mission work is expanding rapidly.*

But between the lines of Hannah's letters a sense of her despondency began to surface. She was heartsick at the cruelties they witnessed daily. *How can God let these things happen to innocent children?* she kept asking. She began having nightmares.

8

The Sino-Japanese War, 1894–1895

Ah, many a home this day
In vain
Mourns for its fallen son,
And a wailing that rises to Heaven
Goes forth,
And bitter tears flow
Like the icy rains
Of winter.
—DU FU, TANG DYNASTY (AD 618–907)

August 27, 1894. Dear Nils: War! War! That is the topic here now. The gigantic Imperial Empire is in the throes of a war with the small island nation of Japan over Korea. China claims suzerainty over Korea, and Japan claims it to be an independent State under their protection. God alone knows what the end shall be. China is adamant, claiming that Korea has been their tributary for two hundred years. The young Emperor, whom everyone knows is but a tool of the Empress Dowager [Cixi], has publicly declared war and expressed contempt for the Japanese by referring to them as "Woren" [dwarfs]. 1,500 boys and men from our area have already been conscripted into the army. There is great weeping and consternation in the streets when the armed Manchu Bannermen storm through the town on horseback and forcibly drag the conscripts from their homes. None ever expect to see their family again. Tomorrow the Manchus and their reluctant Chinese recruits are going to leave on horseback for Peking. It will take a month before they reach their destination. The Chinese begin to see the need for railroads. Perhaps the war will be of value that way. It is rumored that the Commanding General, Li Hongzhang, has an impressive fleet of 65 warships while Japan has only 32. But the Japanese have steam engines and modern weapons. We wish the war may be sharp and brief with good results for the progress of the Gospel.

The *North China Daily News* printed and circulated the declaration of war, which was composed in flowery, self-righteous language. It ended with a severe warning to all who might think of dissenting. It read, in part:

> As Japan has violated the treaties and not observed international laws, and is now running rampant with her false and treacherous actions commencing hostilities herself, and laying herself open to condemnation by the various powers at large, we therefore desire to make it known to the world that we have always followed the paths of philanthropy and perfect justice throughout the whole complications, while the *Woren,* on the other hand, have broken all the laws of nations and treaties which it passes our patience to bear with. Hence we commanded Li Hongzhang to give strict orders to our various armies to hasten with all speed to root the *Woren* out of their lairs. He is to send successive armies of valiant men to Korea in order to save the Koreans from the dust of bondage. We also command the Manchu generals, viceroys, and governors of the maritime provinces . . . to prepare for war and make every effort to fire on the *Woren* ships and utterly destroy them. We exhort our generals to refrain from the least laxity in obeying our commands in order to avoid severe punishment at our hands. Let all know this edict as if addressed to themselves individually. RESPECT THIS!

The turmoil of war had an unexpected effect on the Ronnings' mission. The Manchu Bannermen, who had become dissipated and lost their will to fight, periodically swept through Fancheng and other interior cities to pick up conscripts to do their fighting for them. By rights of extraterritoriality, they were forbidden to enter the American mission compound. When the watchmen at the city gates sounded the gongs to signal the approach of the horsemen, the mission was suddenly filled with eligible young men who professed an urgent need to become Christians. Reverend Ronning accepted it as a God-given opportunity. He immediately began to exploit the situation and reveled in the chance to convert these heathens in spite of themselves. A church service was hurriedly arranged and continued for as long as the Manchus were combing the town for new conscripts.

When the Manchu Bannermen pounded on the mission gate, Hannah played the organ loudly and Halvor led the singing. Hannah later noted with amusement: *When the soldiers heard the music they stopped their pounding to listen. Every-*

one took part in the singing, but there was a lack of decision as to which tune should be sung. I played as best I could with one foot on the loud pedal but everyone sang his own song, the timing being only conspicuous by its absence. But there was one heart if not one tune . . .

> *It is the secret sympathy,*
> *The silver link, the silken tie*
> *Which Heart to Heart and mind to mind*
> *In body and in soul can bind . . .*

When the watchmen sounded the "all clear," our church service was over for the day. But we strongly urged them all to come back on Sunday.

In October 1894, Halvor wrote to Nils, expressing, for the first time, some apprehension about the role of Christianity in China: *Many people attend the church meetings now. The reasons may vary but I accept them all and try to do what I can. It is difficult for us to speak to the heathen about our God. I have come to the conclusion that if the Lord himself with His Divine power does not convert people, the Chinese will never be saved. I feel an eager desire to work and teach. God will give the growth. The townspeople are beginning to send their girls to our school. This is real progress . . . I don't know which will come first, education for all and then reform or reform and then education. I fear the latter will bring more violence. Just think of it, the noble and beautiful Norah Nelson, 15 years old, died when she was away from home. Mrs. Nelson has gone to Chefoo to visit her daughter's grave. Death is so terrible, but for Christians it is an entrance to eternal life. Nelius is enlarging his vocabulary. He points to your photograph and says "O-kel."*

October 26: Bad news for China. The Japanese are winning on land and sea. The fighting continues even though it seems hopeless. The North China Daily News says that the Japanese will be in China by November 30th with 100,000 men and capture Peking. The Japanese seem to be boiling over with hate and with lust to conquer China. With so many young men in the army the families who had depended on them were reduced to starvation. Many people were forced to beg or steal in order to survive. At 2:30 a.m. one morning the missionaries watched helplessly as half a hundred men stormed the home of Sen Li-fu and carried away all his belongings. The missionaries began to live in constant fear of robbers and the undisciplined soldiers roaming the streets: *We, too, shall undoubtedly receive a visit from such uninvited guests, but it's no use to worry.* Halvor and Netland began carrying loaded revolvers and slept with knives under their pillows and their hunting rifles at hand.

On December 13, 1894, in the middle of this chaos, my father was born. His father gave him the Norwegian name of Kjersten Alvin (later changed to Chester). He was the first American child to be born in Fancheng, a distinction he was proud of all his life. Blue-eyed and towheaded like his brother, he spent the first weeks snuggled beside his mother while she made Christmas presents and cardboard stars to adorn the large cypress tree that his father had chopped down and installed in the church hall. His mother was unable to breast-feed him and cow's milk was not available so, according to local custom, a Chinese wet nurse was employed to suckle the baby. Chester always felt a deep gratitude for this Chinese woman who saved his life.

On Christmas Day, Halvor wrote to Nils: *Merry Christmas brother! We have a special present for you. Another son, Kjersten Alvin! At Christmas we had a festival for the children; one hundred children present. We joined hands and danced around the tree singing and playing games. Good things are happening in our mission in spite of the war. Last month an important official set a fine example by sending his daughter to our school . . . Other gentry followed his lead. Now we have three schools going, the new one is for older boys. We have 50 children: 35 boys and 15 girls. First girls' school ever conducted in Hubei province. Some opposition noted. Only 2 girls rejected because their parents refused to unbind their feet. We are hoping they will soon have a change of heart. We are well and working with all our might. The war goes on. We pray daily for peace.*

Hannah wrote to her mother: *How I miss you all, especially now, when conditions are so difficult . . . It is hard for me to think of you so far away without shedding a few tears. Do forgive me. The war is still going on here. I do feel a bit nervous and unstrung sometimes. Thousands of soldiers pass through here on their way to Peking. The streets are full of them so we are sometimes afraid to go out because soldiers . . . are without conscience when they are away from home but this is probably true of every army . . . One evening last week we heard a dreadful commotion and . . . in the moonlight we saw a mob of soldiers pushing at the mission gate and climbing over the wall. They threw our faithful gatekeeper, Da-sen, to the ground. He began to scream. Netland and Ronning ran to help him and the soldiers stopped and stared at them like they had descended from the moon. Halvor began telling them that as soldiers they should act in a respectable manner. He said there were only women inside and it was not proper for them to go in. The Chinese are very particular about such things. They pushed him out of the way. Halvor could do nothing but try and keep them in a good humor. Thea and I saw them running towards the house. We were afraid they had come to plunder and perhaps worse so we blew out the lights and tried to hide. But Halvor called to us to come to the windows and show ourselves. We lit the lanterns again so they could see us. Thea carried Chester, who was sleeping, and I took Nelius and we sat in front of the windows with the babies on our laps. They did not try the doors but came to look at us. They stared at us and pointed to our hair and eyes. We were in our white night gowns so we must have looked very strange to them. Nelius was surprised to see so many faces looking at him. He began to laugh and wave at them. They seemed delighted and began to laugh and wave back. They looked like nice, young country bumpkins and I felt sorry for them because I knew they had been conscripted into the army by the Manchus and had little chance of ever seeing their families again. Eventually their curiosity was satisfied and they suddenly seemed embarrassed by their bold behavior. They left peacefully, talking to Halvor in a friendly manner. After they left, Halvor went to the river bank with some cash to ask the "King of Thieves" to protect us. This man was once a thief himself but Halvor has made friends with him. Now the King makes a great racket at our gate every night and throws fire crackers to warn the soldiers and robbers to stay away.*

In early 1895, China was still at war with Japan. The lumbering and poorly commanded Chinese fleet met the Japanese armada at the mouth of the Yalu River near the border with Korea, and a decisive naval battle ensued. Although the Chinese fleet outnumbered the Japanese two to one and consisted of some of the world's most powerful battleships constructed at great expense in Germany, it was completely destroyed, and the Imperial Empire suffered a humiliating defeat. The Middle Kingdom, center of the tribute system, was humbled before the tiny "island of dwarfs," a former vassal state that had borrowed China's own culture. The defeat was an incredible shock to the corrupt Manchu rulers and the Chinese mandarins, whose illusions of grandeur had long blinded them to the power of modern technology.

The war was terminated by the Treaty of Shimonoseki, the worst in a series of humiliations for China. The Russians had imposed control over Manchuria, the French had seized Indochina, and the Western powers had imposed their influence in the main seaports. But none of these moves was resented as much as the Japanese victory. China was obliged to renounce suzerainty over Korea and cede territories to Japan, including the Pescadores (Penghu) island group off Taiwan and the Liaodong Peninsula with Port Arthur (today's Lüshun), a critical base commanding entrance to the Yellow River and key to the defense of Peking. To add insult to injury, the emperor was forced to agree to pay indemnity to Japan, to open four more ports, and to give Japan the privilege of extraterritoriality and most-favored-nation status. All this at a time when China was attempting to rid itself of the unfair privileges already granted to Westerners in its own domain. *Now,* wrote Halvor, *perhaps the defeat by Japan will make China see the need for reform!*

As the months passed, the continual tension and overwork began to take their toll on Halvor. *June 4, 1895. Dear Brother: I have been sick with malaria and in bed for four weeks; my strength is almost gone and have shrunk in so there is nothing left but skin and bones, hair and whiskers. This is the first time I have ever been sick as far as I can remember. It has been hard on Hannah and Thea who have been watching each night. Netland has also been a great help. I have been cheered by many gifts to the mission from the Mandarin in thanksgiving for medical help that Netland and I gave him.*

July 10, 1895. The situation in China is very tense and increasingly so. There have been terrible riots. Many mission stations have been destroyed and the missionaries are being cruelly persecuted. Some have escaped to Hankow; others are in jail or missing. We are informed that the rioters are also here in Fancheng . . . I am up again and giving some time to the supervision of the work, but I am so weak you would hardly know me.

Hannah and Nelius have been sick. The climate is oppressive. It would be fine to make a visit to the mountains of Norway. The mission continues to expand and we pray daily for new missionaries. I have 40 to 50 men working everyday on new buildings. They are lazy and dumb, so it is hard on my patience. How paganism is depressing.

The antiforeign sentiment in China was growing rapidly. On August 19, 1895, Thea wrote to the mission that there had been horrible antiforeign riots against English missionaries in southern China: three children, eight women, and one man had been killed. "There appears to be a secret organization all over China. They want to kill all foreigners." She added that it was not as dangerous where they were in northern China.

9

Carving up the Chinese Melon

This is her story. She had been staying with her intended mother-in-law for many years. It is the custom here for poor families to send their small daughters to the home of their future husband where she is virtually a slave in the family until she is married. Even afterward she is a slave, but she must also bear as many children as possible.

—HANNAH RONNING, 1896

The missionaries had long realized the need for medical personnel. Sigvald Netland, who had a store of medical supplies and had acquired some knowledge of medicine in his youth, helped as best he could, but he was overwhelmed by the growing numbers who came to the mission for care. Once a week he rode on horseback into the countryside to proselytize and aid the sick. The two nurses opened a small clinic to help mothers care for newborn babies, but they were overrun by distraught young mothers seeking help, many not more than fifteen or sixteen years old. Hannah and Thea were dismayed by how many infants died in the first weeks of life and more because of ignorance than poverty. Cow's or goat's milk was never used, so the babies that could not be suckled were doomed to starvation. Untold numbers of infants had choked from indigestible foods that their misguided mothers had stuffed into their mouths. Hannah wrote about one woman in her early thirties who had borne twelve children; only two survived. Another had borne eight, and all died.

In October 1895 Halvor received word that the Hauge Synod was sending Dr. Thorstein Himle with his wife, four children, and another nurse, Marietta Horvik, to work with the Ronnings. They would be accompanied by a handsome young missionary, Carl W. Landahl, who was destined to play a major role in Thea's life. Thea, who through experience had become more confident in herself and competent in the language, volunteered to meet the new arrivals in Hankow and bring them to Fancheng. Glad to get away from her tedious studies, Thea boarded a houseboat for the journey and enjoyed the picturesque views of eternal China that she had learned looked much better from a distance. Daniel and Anna Nelson met her in Hankow but had no news of the new missionaries. Thea was worried. She had known the Himles in Faribault, Minnesota, and was looking forward to greeting their twin girls, whom she loved and had helped care for. After two weeks, only Carl Landahl arrived. He looked stricken and had terrible news. The Himles' two oldest children had contracted scarlet fever and diphtheria and had been hospitalized in Shanghai. Soon after they recovered, Mrs. Gidske Himle came down with typhus. Then the worst happened: the Himles' twin daughters contracted smallpox and died within the week. After their funerals, Mrs. Himle, understandably, collapsed again. Thea was devastated. She could not understand how God could be so cruel.

Thea and Carl, along with the Swedish missionary Sjoquist, left Hankow on November 26 and arrived back in Fancheng a week before Christmas. During the 400-mile journey, Thea and Carl comforted each other in their sorrow over the besieged Himles. She helped him learn Chinese, and a romance soon developed.

Back in Fancheng, the Ronnings were shocked to hear the tragic news. *How my heart goes out to the poor mother and father!* wrote Hannah. *They have passed through terrible days and nights. One thing to be thankful for is that Mrs. Himle, who was also very ill with it, recovered as if by a miracle.*

When the Himles finally arrived in the latter part of March 1896, Halvor went to meet them in Hankow: *You may believe it was great to see my friend Himle again. We stood and looked at each other a long time before we could speak. Himle with the loving face that was always smiling now stood gaunt and full of sorrow . . . He has suffered such a terrible blow. I hardly recognized him. After a while I saw it was the same Himle. We could only embrace each other. Mrs. Himle smiled bravely but her eyes were full of untold pain. They knew I understood.*

They returned to Fancheng, and in spite of the adversities, the missionaries continued to make plans and expand their work. Dr. Himle opened a dispensary. He set to work like a driven man. He was a rough, stocky man but had a look in his blue eyes that inspired complete trust. The mission bought a house with several small adjoining buildings for five hundred dollars. There were twenty rooms in all. They called it Mercy Institute. None of the missionaries imagined that ninety years later it would be the main hospital in Fancheng.

The first morning a distraught woman came running in and threw herself at Himle's feet, imploring him to save her only son, a fifteen-year-old, who had swallowed a dangerous amount of opium. He was unconscious in an oxcart outside, pale and looking like a corpse. The street was full of suspicious spectators, many of whom had warned the woman not to trust the foreign doctor. It was a critical moment. Himle knew that if the boy died, the mission would suffer a drastic setback and their lives might be in danger. There was no time to consider the consequences. He ordered four men to carry the boy into the clinic. The people followed, crowding into the small room, and watched in silence as Dr. Himle began artificial respiration and Hannah prepared the stomach pump. It was a hot, humid day, and the sweat poured down the doctor's brow. When he began to use the pump, the mother became hysterical and had to be restrained by Sen Li-fu, who spoke gently to her. Finally, the boy's stomach was washed out and an antidote given, but he lapsed into unconsciousness. The people began talking angrily among themselves. Himle asked the mother her son's name. "Wu Ying," she said, and Himle put his mouth close to the boy's ear. "Wu Ying!" he shouted. The boy sat up and opened his eyes in alarm. The onlookers cheered. Some ran into the streets shouting: "The boy that was dead is alive, come and see the *xiqi* (wonder)!"

The woman kowtowed before the doctor and banged her head on the floor until he pulled her to her feet. Then he raised his hands to still the crowd and preached to the mother: "If God had not sent us to Fancheng your son would have died. God created everything and gave us a Savior, Jesus. He loves you, dear friends, and sent us here to tell you about His love. You must all learn to know Him and serve Him and then you will have eternal peace."

The story of the American doctor bringing Wu Ying back to life spread quickly, and soon the clinic was crowded with patients. Hannah and Thea learned to lance carbuncles, treat gangrenous bound feet, and cure common skin and eye infections. They worked in the clinic almost every day after school and enlisted the help of the older children. In the evening, when Halvor was out preaching in the villages, Hannah and Thea wrote letters of appeal to mission headquarters pleading for more money for the hospital. Hannah included true stories that were painfully revealing about the poor and backward families that made up the vast majority of the Chinese at that time. *One day last week we had a very sad case. It was a 19 year old girl but because of starvation and abuse she was not larger than a child of 10 or 12 . . . She had been staying with her intended mother-in-law for many years. It is the custom here for poor families to send their small daughters to the home of their future husband where she is virtually a slave in the family until she is married. Even afterward she is a slave, but she must also bear as many children as possible. During five years she had never heard a kind word—and was ill-treated and starved, tho' within limit, so as not to let her die. Last winter was unusually cold and as she was not allowed quilts to keep warm, she froze her feet. Consequently, they commenced to pain, and as no one cared to help her they grew from bad to worse till at last she was unable to move around. When she could no longer work she was driven out in the cold to beg her bread. For three long weary months she crept from door to door suffering untold agony. Then she came to our Mercy Institute. You will hardly believe me when I tell you that her whole body externally and internally was full of worms . . . The girl is still in the hospital but an entirely different looking girl now. Her sores are nearly healed. She has clean clothes on, enough food to eat and a smiling face. We plan to give her a home, teach her to read and let her help us in the hospital.*

In the summer of 1896, a terrible cholera epidemic was spreading in Hankow. Nevertheless, Sigvald Netland volunteered to sail down the Han River to meet another new missionary, K. S. Stokke, in Hankow. Without warning, Netland fell victim to the dread disease. He was taken to a Catholic hospital, where his friend Dr. Gillison of the London Missionary Society struggled vainly to save him. In a few hours he died, leaving his wife, Oline, and two little daughters, Freda and Amanda, in Fancheng. He was only twenty-eight years old. He was buried in Martyrs' Cemetery beside his first wife and his two martyred Swedish friends. In August 1896, Halvor wrote: *Brother Netland's death shocked us terribly. When we heard the news all we could do was kneel and pray; Oh Eternity, Eternity, may we always have Thee in mind and live and act in the light thereof! Death has indeed become a constant companion. I could not help wonder: Who will be next?*

Halvor's answer came from an unexpected source. Nils wrote that their dear mother had died in Norway. Halvor replied: *How can it be that at my age I suddenly feel like a lost orphan? Though Mother had finished her work toward me, the message concerning her death came unexpected and hard especially as I had had such pleasure in the thought of going home to express my gratitude.* Thea was overwhelmed with grief, and Carl Landahl was a great comfort to her. In the evenings, Hannah invited Carl and Thea to songfests. Carl never approached the subject of marriage directly, but when it came time for him to go with Halvor to Taipingtien to prepare the way for a new mission, he asked Hannah to speak to Thea about marrying him.

Hannah suspected that Halvor had timed his departure so he would be away when her third baby was born, but she said nothing. She was secretly glad to be rid of him. He always made her nervous with his pacing back and forth until she felt the only way to stop him was to give birth. With Thea and Dr. Himle there to help, she could just relax and let it happen. Halvor and Carl loaded their bedrolls and a change of clothing onto the houseboat to sail up the Han to Taipingtien.

The baby girl was two weeks old when her father arrived home. He immediately sent a message to Nils: *Hurrah! We have been blessed with a baby girl, Almah . . . She was joyously welcomed by all! Hope to launch a new mission in Taipingtien next month. Have heard that a railroad is going to be built from Hankow to Peking. Just think—progress in old China at last.*

Thea knew she was in love when she saw Carl climbing out of the houseboat, all sunburned with long hair and whiskers. She embraced her brother and then, on impulse, kissed Carl on the cheek. Halvor told Hannah that Carl fairly danced back to the mission. The cook prepared a welcome-home feast with several river carp and a dozen geese they had bagged on the way home.

Thea cried when she accepted Carl's proposal. Halvor could not, as planned, perform the ceremony because as American citizens they were required to get married in the presence of the American consul, Charles Denby, in Hankow. The couple sailed down the Han and were met by Daniel Nelson in Hankow, who greeted them with the grim news that a dreaded cholera epidemic was raging through the city and his wife, Anne, had contracted it. The Chinese were dying by the hundreds, their unclaimed bodies lying rotting in the hot sun. To Thea's horror, just before the wedding, Carl was stricken with malaria. The fever lasted ten weeks, and Thea, who tended him lovingly, reported that he was near death several times. While Carl was recovering, Thea came down with cholera. What more could happen to the young couple? The pain was unbearable. Thea prayed for mercy and cried out, "Is God dead that he does not hear me?" The next morning, the doctor was amazed to find her alive. That both Carl and Thea recovered was regarded by the missionaries as a miracle.

Carl and Thea were married on October 2, 1896, and immediately sailed down the Yangtze to Kiukiang for their honeymoon. According to Carl, Thea, in a lacey beige blouse and long skirt, had never looked so beautiful. A beribboned pith helmet protected her blond braids and flawless complexion from the harsh sun.

On the way back to Fancheng they were joined by the Swedish missionary Reverend Matson. The journey up the Han was another test of courage. It took four long weeks. Robbers stopped the boat, and after a fierce struggle on board, breaking tables and stools, they took two crew members hostage and demanded ransom. Matson warned Landahl not to give their tormentors anything and stalled them by trying to talk reason. Meanwhile, Carl gave his safe-conduct pass to the captain, who showed it to the town officials witnessing the action. An official representative, Mr. Wang, soon appeared with a signed paper. He bowed three times, and his apprentice notarized the pass by killing a chicken and dripping its blood on the paper. The robbers returned the hostages. The Chinese crew drank wine, ate the chicken, and smoked pipes as they sailed back to Fancheng.*

*Gracia Grindal, *Thea Ronning, Young Woman on a Mission* (Minneapolis: Lutheran University Press, 2012).

Three weeks after their return, the Landahls left to establish the new mission in Taipingtien. Taipingtien was on higher ground than Fancheng, with fewer mosquitos and thousands of people who had never heard about Jesus. The station flourished under the care of the newlyweds, largely due to Thea's understanding of the culture and her skill with the language. Thea was filled with compassion and unrelenting zeal to help the oppressed Chinese women. She began her own ministry even though it seemed a hopeless calling. Thea would talk with Chinese peasant women in their humble, dirty homes and give them advice on cleanliness and proper diet for their children. She found them to be intelligent and curious about the Christian faith. When she spoke to the women of heaven and hell, they told her they were already in hell. One woman said that in the next incarnation she would rather come back as an animal or even an insect than as a Chinese woman.

As Taipingtien was only thirty miles north of Fancheng, the Ronnings could ride up the road along the Han river to visit: Hannah on a shaggy Mongolian pony, Nelius astride a small white donkey, and Halvor riding double with toddler Chester on Prince, the beautiful stallion that seemed destined to save Halvor's life many times. The procession was usually followed by two sedan chairs loaded with supplies and curious Chinese waving at the foreign devils. This delighted Nelius and Chester, who waved back, obviously enjoying being the center of attention.

Hannah often accompanied Thea on her rounds. Thea wrote the mission about a visit they made to Mrs. Yang, who was very ill. They entered a mud house, cold and damp with a straw ceiling. It looked like a cave, so dark they could hardly see her lying in bed. There was no window, but some light came through slits in the wall. *On one end of the bed was a bowl of food for animals. At the other end was a hole from which came an unusual smell. I asked her husband what it was. He said, "Our cow is there during the night," as though everything was as it should be. . . . "I will go to hell," said Mrs. Yang in a trembling voice, "but you, who know God, will go to heaven. If I live I will accept your teaching so that I too can go to heaven."* Thea asked the women in Minnesota to pray for her. Hannah later reported that Mrs. Yang had come to study with her and thought she would become a teacher for girls.

In the summer of 1898 the annual meeting of the Mission Society was held in Fancheng. Thea came two weeks early. She was in good health and glowing with happiness. When not preparing her report for the conference, she spent every moment with Hannah and the children. Baby Almah was almost two years old and trying to follow her brothers around. Her shimmering golden curls made the Chinese stare in awe. When Hannah and Thea could wrench themselves away from the children and mission duties, they made forays to the curio shops in veiled sedan chairs to buy all types of *dongxi* (things). It was their greatest vice. They spent hours bargaining for silks, ivory, jade, porcelain, silver, lacquer ornaments, rings, beads, and fans of all types, always careful to leave before drawing a crowd. By this time they were friendly with the shopkeepers and people in Fancheng, but there was always the possibility of vagrant ruffians from some secret antiforeign society stirring up the crowd. When time was too short to shop in the city, Hannah sent word for the curio dealers to come to the mission. It was great fun for the children to watch the wily merchants spread their wondrous wares on the floor of the reception room and to see their mother bargaining with the persuasiveness of a Syrian rug dealer over the prices.

Their favorite curio dealer was a delightful old rogue called Lao T'ang. His slight body was encased in a tattered silken robe embroidered with golden dragons, and his head was topped with a red-tasseled black mandarin hat, although he had never had any connection with mandarins except to cheat them out of their curios, which he then sold at a profit for himself. His mustache curled slyly around the edges of his mouth, joining the wispy white beard that straggled sparsely over his chest. This imposing front view was strangely balanced by a scanty white pigtail tied with a red ribbon that dangled down his back, almost reaching the white felt platforms of his curled-up shoes.

The ritual he and Hannah performed was always the same. Lao T'ang would arrive with his sturdy servant Chin, who carried two huge bundles on each end of his yo-stick. After bowing in a dignified but deferential manner, he directed Chin to undo the canvas bags, all the while cautioning him about breakage and reminding him of the great value and rarity of the objects he was handling. The junk was often treated with more grandiose respect than the genuine antiques, which to the inexperienced eye enhanced the value of the most lowly object. The children were convinced that they were looking upon priceless treasures, and they wondered why their mother was not impressed. Indeed, she often acted as if she was not interested at all in the beautiful assortment of articles arrayed before her. But Lao T'ang could always count on the children to clap their hands in pleasure at his fascinating bounty: mysterious faces peering out from carved nuts and peach pits, jade flowers, lacquer beads, ivory horses, snuff bottles painted on the inside, silver and jade bracelets, wooden carvings of all descriptions, ginger jars, porcelain vases, bronzes, rugs, and precious scrolls.

Hannah's feigned indifference was often difficult for her to maintain, especially in the presence of the enthusiastic children. But experience had taught her that bargaining in China was a fine art that had to be carried on with astute finesse if one expected to obtain anything at a reasonable price and keep face in the eyes of the Chinese. Hannah was careful not to let Lao T'ang know which article she really cherished but instead would show interest in a piece of cheap junk. Lao T'ang would then, as a special favor to an honored guest in China, ask an outrageously high price for it. Hannah, in turn, would offer a shamefully low bid, and the spirited bargaining would begin, with both opponents aware that, as this was only a warm-up process, they should be careful not to reach an agreement. Finally, with dramatic sighs and laments, Lao T'ang would bid Chin to wrap up the collection. After a few pieces had been packed up, he would look sorrowfully at the children and tell them how it grieved him to leave without satisfying their honorable mother. On cue, the children would plead with their mother to give him another chance. When she reluctantly agreed, he would happily squat down and begin to make more unreasonable offers. He was a great actor; he wheedled and whined and lied and flattered while Hannah would turn up her nose and walk away only to be persuaded by the children to return to the ring. Time meant nothing to Lao T'ang, but the game of bargaining meant everything.

One morning Hannah was fascinated by a small teak dressing case embossed with silver that Lao T'ang had opened to expose the mirror under the lid. Inside, preserved in small compartments, were all the appliances of the feminine toilet. One drawer contained the fine white powder that Chinese women fluffed on their faces after polishing their skin with a hot damp cloth; another held the carmine that tinted the whitened skin. There were separate compartments for an ivory comb, a hairbrush, toothbrush, tongue scraper, ear picker, back-scratcher, gum to keep the hair in place, jade hairpins, and a variety of gray and black pastes to enhance the eyes. In a secret chamber, disguised by a false bottom, were two gold-filigree fingernail protectors. Hannah was determined to have the box to present it to Thea as a gift. After going rather quickly through the preliminary stages of bargaining and when Lao T'ang was about to pack up for the third time, she said to him: "Lao T'ang, you are an old man and have gone to so much trouble. I would like to buy something just to please you but your prices are really too high for a poor missionary to pay."

"But for you I will make a tremendous sacrifice," replied the old man, "but for you alone."

"Well, perhaps if that cosmetic case is very cheap I would consider it."

Lao T'ang sensed that this was his chance. The words tumbled out. "That case once belonged to the empress dowager herself," he lied, "and was brought to Fancheng by the mandarin's third cousin whose daughter is a concubine of the emperor. It was smuggled out of the Imperial Palace in Peking by her favorite eunuch, Cobbler Wax Li. It is the only box of its kind in China, indeed in the whole world! But you may have it for the ridiculously low price of five silver dollars." He opened his palms to show her that he was being completely honest and smiled charmingly.

"A pity," replied Hannah, "because that is four dollars too much. Oh, well, I really don't want it anyway."

"Maybe $4.50? As a special favor."

"$1.50."

Lao T'ang assumed a posture of hurt dignity. "I would be losing money. $3.00." He sighed loudly and looked at the children mournfully.

"$2.00," snapped Hannah. "Last price."

"$2.50?" he pleaded with tears rolling down his cheeks, "but only on the condition that you tell no one what you paid, ever! It is too ridiculous!"

By now the children were on the side of the crafty merchant. "Please, Mama!" cried Almah.

"$2.25," she countered weakly.

"All right, all right," sighed Lao T'ang wringing his hands, "but please don't let me eat so much bitterness next time."

Hannah counted out the money carefully and handed it to Lao T'ang. He presented the box to her with the air of someone parting with the crown jewels. The game was over. Thea could not stop giggling.

"Oh, I just love it!" cried Hannah, losing her cool composure completely and clutching the box to her bosom. Lao T'ang wiped his tears and grinned at the children. Chester was fascinated by his straggly black and yellow teeth. Lao T'ang looked at Hannah and bowed respectfully.

10

Thea

TO MY SISTER

I look into the courtyard
Just outside,
And I am jealous
Of the smiling flowers,
Rejoicing with their sisters
In the sun.
—POETESS XI FEILAN,
    QING DYNASTY (1644–1911)

Life within the mission now took an unexpected and tragic turn, overshadow-ing concern about the growing antiforeign sentiment in the country. Halvor's mission was one of the few where women missionaries were permitted to read their own progress reports instead of sitting quietly at the conference table while their husbands or superintendents spoke for them. On the last evening of the conference, Thea, for the first time in her missionary career, gave her report in a strong, positive voice. Before adjournment, she was asked to lead devotion. This fact was recorded by Halvor because of the prophetic nature of the Bible reading she selected: Romans 5:21: "As sin reigned in death, even so might grace reign through righteousness into eternal life through Jesus Christ our Lord."

Two days after the conference, on the evening of March 22, Thea became violently ill. Carl burst into the Ronnings' room, imploring them to come im-mediately. The Ronnings and the Himles rushed to Thea's bedside and found her in an agony of cramps and convulsions. Himle diagnosed it as meningitis. She died twelve terrible hours later. Halvor wrote to Nils in detail about her death, but his brother felt it was so personal that he destroyed that part of the letter. No one in our family seems to know exactly what happened to Thea as those who knew refused to talk about it. We can only imagine how difficult it was for Halvor to write this letter to Nils in which he seemed to blame himself. When I read it many years later, two significant pages were missing.

Now Brother, you must be strong! God has taken our dear, sweet sister Thea. So swiftly . . . None of us thought that Thea was so soon to be called home . . . We have been going about stunned. It is all so incomprehensible. My son, my mother, now my sister . . . It came so suddenly we could hardly believe our eyes. And it was I who brought her out here, you know. Life can change in an instant, brother, take nothing for granted. My dear sweet innocent sister. What a nightmare! We are all in shock! She was only 33. Everyone loved her. Why? Why did He take her before her time? Still, we thank God that she fought the last good fight, ended her course, kept the faith and received the crown . . . There were several hundred people present at the funeral. The children walked ahead of the coffin singing. Our friends, Rev. P. Matson and Rev. Sen, spoke in English and Chinese. We sang a hymn and brief talks were given by others in Chinese, English and Norwegian. It made a profound impression on the Chinese to witness a Christian funeral which was quiet and dignified in contrast to burning paper money, banging gongs and the wild wailing of professional mourners.

Hannah wrote: *I shall never forget the light that radiated from our dear sister's countenance when she was nearing the gates and her suffering suddenly ceased. She is happily there now, but we miss her so. I feel lost without her. She will not come back, but we believe she sees us, that she is watching from a distant shore. Her spirit reaches us but alas, in words of human speech we can talk no more. She was true to the ideal of a missionary's life and that is to bear His Cross. We needed her so much but God took her—we do not know why?* The ink on the paper was smudged with her tears.

Grief weighed heavily on Halvor. He fell into a lengthy depression that seemed alien to his nature but was understandable considering what he had suffered emotionally. He began to write tortured letters that must have alarmed Nils. *April 28, 1898. Life here is often depressing. It is hard to let Thea go . . . I have never longed for spring more than this year. Have been looking at the trees every day. Finally, swelling buds and now, leaves, tiny, tender green leaves. Whenever I have a spare moment I work in the garden. I sit under the pomegranate tree and breathe in the seven-mile perfume from the jasmine. That is my resting place. Mother, you know was a lover of flowers. We have this in common. It is part of our heritage. I have not been well this spring. Terrible headaches and fever. Welcome be death, but for the sake of my family and the work, I hope I may live many years. My wish is that after these experiences, I may come forth purged and purified, with new life, new spirit, new strength, throw off the winter shroud and enter into a full summer with flowers and the song of birds. Sun and summer.*

There was no respite for the missionaries. Dr. Himle's wife, Gidske, who had survived smallpox and the death of her beautiful twin daughters, now died of that sudden, unknown fever that struck down so many foreigners in China. Halvor wrote: *We shall go to the mountain this summer with Himle. He feels he should stay and work but I can see it is all taking too strong a toll on him. Even the dragon flies are lazy in the August heat, but not the children, they are still full of fun and running all over . . . We will all escape the heat and heal our wounded hearts. I will have time to remember Thea and our summers in the mountains of Telemark.*

The previous fall Halvor had spent $250 to build a modest house in a high scenic valley in the Dabie Mountains overlooking Hsiangyang. It became a retreat where they could feel close to God and nature and obtain relief from the harsh realities of the decaying empire. The valley reminded Halvor of their *saeter,* the summer house in the mountain pastures of Norway where he had spent the summers with Thea and his other siblings herding cattle and goats. It had been good training for a life as a missionary in China. While Thea and sister Mori stayed in the log cabin making butter and cheese, the boys roamed with the herds, leaping from stone to stone, climbing steep cliffs, and running races with self-willed cows. It all made for good lungs, steady nerves, and tough muscles. Being alone most of the time taught Halvor to do his own thinking. He became a follower of no man.

Halvor and Hannah chose to ride horseback while Dr. Himle and Mrs. Netland and her children traveled in donkey carts followed by a team of horses pulling a wagonload of servants and the Ronning children. It was the first time Chester had seen his mother ride her Mongolian horse, a spirited sorrel with a magnificent tail. Hannah cut a dramatic figure in her brown riding skirt, red jacket, and white pith helmet. She scooped little Almah onto the pommel of her saddle and led the procession toward the river, where they ferried across and proceeded up the mountain trail. It took all day.

They all prospered in the mountain air, and Halvor showed signs of recovering his health. The missionaries were painfully aware of the growing hostility in the country, but in spite of a sense of living on borrowed time, they were determined to have a rejuvenating summer in their *saeter.* Halvor and Hannah went riding every morning, galloping over the hills, pausing only to admire the beauty of the valley, ablaze with flamboyant apricot trees. In the afternoon, while the ladies played croquet with the children, Himle and Halvor, with Chinese helpers, built an extension on the house. *August 1898. I have been well all summer and worked like a horse. Yesterday I used a sledge hammer. The hammer flew off and hit me in the face so the blood streamed. Here I am sitting with a black eye . . . But the work and fresh air have put me in the best of humor. I have ached in every limb of my*

body, but I have a good appetite and have slept well. Hannah is blooming and we are
extremely happy. Himle is also recovering. We thank God for evangelist Sen and the
other Chinese Christians who are supervising the mission so we can rest. Up here we
are in another world but must soon go back to reality.

By the time they returned from the mountain, in the fall of 1898, China was
in convulsion. Halvor was alarmed by the arrogance of the Allied Powers, who
proceeded to slice up China into spheres of influence. The Chinese bitterly resented it. The Russians brought in warships and forced the Chinese to yield
control of Port Arthur; Germany occupied the port of Ch'ingtao (today's Qing-
dao) for use as a naval base; and the British extracted a lease of Weihaiwei. Then
they scrambled for railway and cable rights. Germany won rights in the Yellow
River Districts; Russia in Manchuria; France in South China; and Britain in the
Yangtze River Valley. Halvor wrote to Nils that the staggering defeat by Japan,
however, had an interesting saving grace. It provided a lesson for the Chinese
by proving to China that a tiny country with machinery and a constitutional
government could defeat a great empire handicapped by outmoded ways and
ruled by despots. Chinese patriots and intellectuals began to look for the sources
of their country's weaknesses. The reformers pointed out the deep political and
private corruption in the Manchu court. They cited the industrial backwardness
of China and argued that if Japan could become powerful by adopting Western
ideas and methods, China could be regenerated in the same way. An activist
reform movement began in southern China that would eventually engulf the
Imperial Palace itself. Soon, in the eyes of the people, the Qing Dynasty would
lose the Mandate of Heaven. Ironically, the Japanese victory proved to be the
death knell for the Imperial dynasties that had ruled China for more than two
millennia.

The Germans had been ceded railway rights in Hubei Province and had
begun building a railroad from Hankow to Fancheng, but the peasants tore up
the tracks as fast as they were laid. Two German engineers came to Fancheng
to plead with Reverend Ronning to persuade the peasants to let them continue
to build the railway. One, a balding fat man with a red face, told Halvor that all
the peasants were stupid and could not even understand German. Halvor reluctantly went into the countryside and talked to the peasants as well as the chair
bearers, muleteers, camel men, and innkeepers along the roads, many of whom
were living on the edge of starvation. He found it impossible to explain how the
"fire cart" would benefit these people who would obviously lose their jobs. The

farmers, who tilled the land of their ancestors, complained that the "barbarians" who supervised the work were bullies who acted in crude and vulgar ways. Furthermore, they offended the spirits of the wind and water and had no respect for the burial grounds or the sacred hills that should not be disturbed lest it offend the "Great Sleeping Dragon" who influences the earth and the air above it.

Halvor returned to tell the Germans that they should not offend the people or desecrate the graves of their ancestors. He suggested that the foreign workers respect the beliefs of the Chinese and not just shunt them aside as mere superstition. He also suggested they employ Chinese engineers familiar with local customs who could map the railroad according to the geomancy principles of *fengshui. November 1, 1898. The Germans thought I was crazy, and told me so. They know nothing about Chinese sensitivities and have no room for compromise. Not one week passes without news of mobs tearing up the tracks and attacking foreigners. In spite of the chaotic conditions, our mission is thriving and our work goes on. 12 more women have been taught to read and Hannah's school has 23 girls. Carl Landahl and Sen Li-fu, along with Matson and I, are going with a coleporteur named Go, who will distribute books, on a trip east of here. Some earnest seeking souls have asked us to investigate the possibility of setting up a small mission. The trip should not take more than two days each way and there is little danger because there are so many of us.*

The journey turned out to be far more of an adventure than the missionaries had anticipated. They were soon to learn just how deep antiforeign feelings ran. Halvor rode on Prince while the others traveled in two-wheeled, springless carts pulled by mule teams. On their return trip, only ten miles from Fancheng, they stopped in the market town of Yintow for supplies. About six rough-looking men slouching beside their shaggy Mongolian ponies began yelling insults. Some wore army jackets indicating they were army deserters turned bandits and were living off the countryside. Coleporteur Go offered one a religious tract. The man threw it on the ground and stomped on it. This was an extremely hostile act in a country where the printed word held a particular sanctity. Printed characters represented the classical learning and its sacred teachings.

The rogues began to taunt the missionaries. Soon a curious crowd gathered. Halvor suggested they walk slowly back to the wagons and leave. The missionaries smiled courteously, and the people made way for them to pass. Matson and Go took the lead wagon, Sen and Landahl the next one, and Halvor followed on Prince. Suddenly a splat of mud hit Prince on the neck. The stallion reared and bolted past the wagons. Soon the air was full of mud balls. Halvor reined in Prince and shouted for the others to run for it. They whipped their frightened mules into action, but as they raced along, people in the streets unleashed their pent-up hostility and began to throw stones and mud. Three of the deserters mounted their ponies and caught up to Landahl's wagon, forcing it to stop. Sen stood up and tried to reason, but he was pulled off the wagon. The ruffians began to beat him brutally while the townspeople watched. Halvor galloped his horse into the crowd in an effort to rescue Sen, who was lying face down protecting his head with his hands. The crowd, now a mob, advanced on Halvor. He fired his revolver twice in the air and they backed away. Seizing the moment, he sprang off his horse and, holding the reins and gun in one hand, dragged his wounded friend back to the wagon, where Landahl was fighting off some attackers with the mule whip. Somehow they got the mules started and ran off.

Up ahead, Matson's stubborn mule team, frightened by the mud balls, refused to budge. Matson sat in the driver's seat with an umbrella over his head fending off the flying missiles. When Halvor's horse and Landahl's mules came streaking by, his mules seemed to think it was better not to balk any longer and started off with amazing speed. The mounted deserters followed in full pursuit, flailing sticks and shouting the now familiar but blood-chilling call of "Kill the foreign devils!" The missionaries ran for their lives. Sen Li-fu, though bruised and bleeding, threw the supplies and Bibles onto the road in the hope of slowing down their pursuers. The missionaries fled through the village gate and could not help notice the decapitated heads of three Chinese stuck on pikes. The horrible sight filled them with terror, and they whipped their already panicked animals to full speed.

The deserters did not stop at the gate as the missionaries had hoped but were now gaining on the mules. Halvor prayed aloud and circled back twice to fire warning shots, but the frenzied mob paid no attention. It was time for a miracle. Halvor noticed that the road ahead made a sharp right to follow along a narrow river. Knowing that few Chinese could swim and that most were afraid of water, he decided to try a desperate maneuver. Shouting for the others to follow, he galloped Prince straight ahead, down the inclining bank into the water. The mules, too frightened to balk, ran head-on into the river and within minutes were up to their bellies. Fortunately, the water was shallow. The missionaries jumped out of their wagons to lead the frightened animals across. By the time Landahl's wagon was in the middle of the river, Halvor was climbing up the other side. The ruffians pulled in their ponies and began to argue. When two of them started to cross, commanding the others to follow, Halvor took aim at a gingko tree and by luck shot off a thin branch. It landed on a large black dog that had followed the crowd. The dog yelped wildly and jumped into the river. The ruffians stood still. They were all familiar with the Chinese custom of kicking the dog instead of the master. They hurled their sticks at the foreigners but did not advance. The missionaries could hear the curses and sinister laughter until they were out of earshot.

Sen was cut around the head and his back bruised; Landahl could hardly move his right arm; Go was covered with bruises; Matson, thanks to the umbrella, had escaped with a few minor bruises; and Halvor had a gash on his forehead. But the men were too grateful to be alive to tend to their wounds. They knelt in prayer and thanksgiving and started home. The mules were shaking and foaming at the mouth but seemed happy to be on the way. The skinny dog followed. They drove all night. The next morning the four battered warriors staggered into the mission compound in Fancheng. Landahl's arm was broken. Dr. Himle put six stitches in Halvor's forehead. Sen was not seriously hurt. Hannah was horrified but grateful. Chester and Nelius were full of awe and admiration for this great bewhiskered man who presented them with a hungry black dog that Chester named Vesta after a Norwegian goddess.

The missionaries interpreted their survival as a sign from God that, despite the obvious danger, they should stay in China and continue their work. These pioneer missionaries were a special breed of men and women who believed absolutely in their cause. They were determined to defy all dangers to spread their urgent message: the promise of eternal life. There was no room for cowardly or doubting souls. Their mission was more sacred to them than their own lives.

Although the missionaries all lived with a nagging sense of foreboding, it was not long before the whole sinister incident had been deliberately reduced to jest. Halvor had thrown off his depression and felt strong again. About forty years later, my brother Alton asked our grandfather about the scar on his forehead and the old man told his grandchildren the story, still laughing at how ridiculous Reverend Matson had looked sitting under his mud-spattered umbrella.

In spite of these sporadic outbreaks, the Chinese Christians and the majority of the gentry in Fancheng remained friendly and supportive of the Ronnings' mission. The city was relatively peaceful, and the mission work went on. Christmas came and went. Halvor and Hannah spent a heartwarming Christmas Eve with their friends and all their children: Chinese, American, and Norwegian.

On December, 29, 1898, Halvor wrote to Nils: *A large number of Chinese friends visited us during Christmas. 160 gave us presents. We are encouraged by our progress although many Chinese warn of the anti-foreign sentiment and urge us to leave the country. We are touched by their concern. God be praised that we already have won so many friends where we knew none a few years ago. Not all of them have experienced a change of heart but we must first win their friendship before we can teach and preach. A Blessed New Year.* The New Year, however, was anything but blessed. Halvor's chase turned out to be a foreshadowing of the worst missionary slaughter in the history of China.

11

Hundred Days of Reform, 1898

We have heard of Chinese ideas being employed to convert barbarians, but have never heard of China being converted by barbarians.

— OFFICIAL IN THE MANCHU COURT WHO FEARED
THE EMPEROR'S REFORM MOVEMENT, 1898

No one escapes history, but the Chinese seem more aware of this than most other people. The Ronnings, like the Chinese, began dating events in their lives by historical episodes. The year my father was born, 1894, was the "Year of the Sino-Japanese War," and 1898 was the "Year of the Reform."

July 2, 1898. Dear Nils: We have great hopes for reform at last. The Old Buddha who has been ruling from a curtain behind the throne for 37 years has retired to the Summer Palace. The enlightened Emperor Guangxu has finally taken the reins of power and already demonstrated that he is far more concerned about the fate of China than the Empress Dowager. He has summoned progressive Chinese scholars such as K'ang Yu Wei, a Cantonese visionary who is popularly known as "K'ang the Modern Sage and Reformer" and even missionaries like Timothy Richard, to come to Peking to begin work on the Reform Decrees that could turn China into a modern state. China is now on the edge of a social revolution and I pray that reforms will make it a peaceful one. Everything has happened so fast we don't know what will happen next. Let us pray the Emperor will be able to hold power.

The Japanese victory and the infringement of the Western powers on its territories had jarred the Chinese empire from its insular illusions. The Imperial Court was forced to recognize the realities of the present and acknowledge that Western civilization was not necessarily inferior, at least in the art of war and perhaps in other ways as well. It was obvious that the lumbering Chinese war junks, dependent on the winds and tides, were, in fact, virtually defenseless against the steam-engine battleships of Japan and the Western powers. Chinese defense officials aspired to a modern navy and an army with up-to-date weapons, while scholars and court officials began to recognize the usefulness of Western science and technology as well as the need for Western learning.

The "enlightened Emperor Guangxu" to whom Halvor referred in his letter was the eleventh emperor of the Qing Dynasty. He was not the son of the preceding Emperor Tongzhi, who had died without an heir, but the son of the empress dowager's sister, Ci'an (Eastern Mistress), who had also been a concubine of the Emperor Tongzhi. The Dowager Cixi had adopted her underage nephew when her own son died so that she could retain the power of the regent. She bestowed the title "Holy Mother Empress Dowager" on herself and placed Guangxu on the Dragon Throne at the age of four. At official meetings she sat behind a gold brocade curtain hung behind the throne and told the child what to say. This continued until the boy reached his majority, at age eighteen, when he was expected to take full power.

Concubine Orchid

Empress Dowager Cixi was born in 1835, a branch of the Yehenara clan of the Manchus, and named Orchid, following the tradition of naming girls after flowers. Her parents had arranged her marriage to her cousin Ronglu (who would later play a major role in her life), but when the Emperor Daoguang died in 1850, his nineteen-year-old successor, Emperor Xianfeng, issued an edict requiring young girls eligible as concubines to come to the Forbidden City. Orchid and her sister Sakota were chosen as concubines. Sakota became empress, and Orchid became the Noble Consort Yi. In 1855, they both became pregnant. Sakota's child was a girl, and Orchid was fortunate enough to give birth to a boy, who became the only male heir to the Dragon Throne. His mother, now Consort Yi, was both brilliant and beautiful, and she soon became the most influential person in the emperor's court.

In 1858, the Chinese were forced by the British to sign the Treaty of Tientsin, which opened up additional treaty ports on the Yangtze River, formally allowed Christian missionary activity, and gave the British and other Allied treaty powers the right to establish permanent resident legations in the capital. In September 1860, during the last stages of the Second Opium War and in the midst of the Taiping Rebellion, Lord Elgin and the French Baron Gros advanced into Peking to demand a Second Treaty Settlement. The notorious Convention of Peking further humiliated the Chinese by imposing on the Qing further financial reparations and ceding additional territory around Hong Kong to the British and parts of outer Manchuria to the expanding Russian empire.

Emperor Xianfeng, warned of the advance of Lord Elgin's troops, fled to the city of Jehol (an imperial hunting park near Peking) with the court faction that had urged resistance to the British. He was accompanied by his empress and Noble Consort Yi (future empress dowager), aged twenty-seven, and her son, the three-year-old heir to the Dragon Throne. The emperor left his half brother, Prince Gong, to assume the role of de facto head of government.

When the Anglo-French troops reached the capital, General Elgin, in a shameful demonstration of Western power, ordered the soldiers to loot and burn the Yuanmingyuan (Gardens of Eternal Brightness, or Old Summer Palace), an architectural gem of pagodas, temples, and libraries that had been designed by Castiglione and built by Emperor Qianlong on Longevity Hill west of Peking. After carrying away valuable artworks, the troops razed the magnificent structures and torched the Royal Gardens, including the mulberry trees that nourished the precious silkworms. On hearing of the desecration of his sacred Old Summer Palace, Emperor Xianfeng fell into depression, turned to alcohol and drugs, and died a year later. This sordid event is one of the main reasons the empress dowager later swore vengeance on all foreigners.

On his deathbed, in 1861, the emperor summoned "Eight Regent Ministers," headed by Sushun, to be sworn in as regents to his five-year-old son, soon to be the Emperor Tongzhi. But his mother was not to be denied power. As soon as Xianfeng died, the sisters became dowager empresses and assumed new titles. Sakota became Dowager Ci'an, and Consort Yi became the Empress Dowager Cixi. The more ambitious one, Cixi soon concocted a plot with Prince Gong to wrest power from the regents, whom she charged with the "Eight Guilts," including negotiating with the "barbarians." Head Regent Sushun was sentenced to the horrible "death of a thousand cuts," but Cixi showed mercy and had him beheaded. Two others were given white silk scarves, allowing them to commit suicide. Thus the empress dowager became the first and only Qing Dynasty empress to rule from "behind the curtain."

Her son, the Emperor Tongzhi, was a healthy lad fond of sports, but as a teenager, he was led, for unproven sinister reasons, by the palace eunuchs down a path of self-destruction. It was rumored that at night he would disguise himself and sneak out of the Forbidden City with his favorite eunuch to debauch in the sordid opium dens and brothels of Peking. So great was his mother's greed for power that she encouraged rather than curtailed her son's unhealthy orgies. In 1875, one year after her addicted son reached eighteen, the age of power, he died of a mysterious illness. Word went out that he had overindulged in his pleasure quarters with the palace eunuchs. Even more sinister, shortly after his death, his pregnant consort died of an overdose of opium. This left the empress dowager with no contenders for royal power. To assure her regency, she adopted her sister's five-year-old son, who later became Emperor Guangxu, and the dowager once again ruled from behind the yellow brocade curtain hung behind the Dragon Throne.

The boy's regal name, Guangxu, meant "Glorious Succession." His reign, however, was destined to be anything but glorious. Instead, it was among the most tragic of all the Qing emperors' dominions. He was later betrayed not only by his own aunt and her reactionary establishment but also by the foreign powers who had favored and encouraged his radical reform movement.

The empress dowager, as regent, kept the young emperor under firm control. To strengthen her own family, she forced him to marry her brother's daughter, an older woman, Yehenara Jingfen, whom he detested. She became Empress Longyu, but the emperor consoled himself with Lady Tatara, his favorite consort, known as the Pearl Concubine, who later paid for the emperor's attentions with her life. When Emperor Guangxu began his formal rule, the dowager was required to retire and moved to the reconstructed Summer Palace outside Peking. She had ordered Guangxu's father to renovate the palace, with the intention of keeping him from influencing his son.

In Fancheng, Halvor and Hannah were encouraged by reports from Peking that the young emperor had progressive ideas and was advocating a reform movement. After China's defeat by Japan in 1895, Emperor Guangxu thought China could learn from constitutional monarchies like Japan and began initiating reform within the Imperial establishment. He summoned men like Kang Youwei and his disciple Liang Qichao, pioneers of the new culture movement who advocated "enlightened autocracy," which was also later espoused by Sun Yat-sen. Kang Youwei looked to Peter the Great and the Japanese Meji monarch as the political models for leadership in modernizing China. Only the emperor himself, who embodied the Imperial mystic and commanded the authority necessary to cut through the maze of ancient traditions, old customs, and established feudal family clans perpetuating Chinese parochialism and fostering national weakness, could enforce fundamental reforms and establish the foundations of a modern society. Advised by Kang and six other influential scholars including Yang Shenxiu and Song Bolu, the emperor drafted scores of reform edicts designed to change China into a constitutional monarchy.

Halvor hoped for a renaissance. The reform movement, strongly influenced by Christian concepts, was gradually arousing interest among the upper classes. A colleague, Reverend Timothy Richard, an Anglican missionary who was secretary of the Society for the Diffusion of Christian and General Knowledge, edited the *International Review,* a magazine in great demand by progressive Chinese scholars. Books on physics, thermodynamics, optics, and other sciences were translated into Chinese and discussed by scholars in contrast to the traditional philosophical controversies. New sources of energy were explored. Telegraph lines and electrical cables were installed in the main cities, and construction of railroads, under foreign lease, was begun. A shipping bureau was opened. Scores of Chinese students went to study in Europe. In all the port cities, zealous efforts were being made to enlighten the literati of the empire. The official with the most influence over the emperor was the Imperial tutor, Weng Tonghe, a brilliant Confucian scholar and a member of the Grand Council who had mentored Emperor Guangxu since he was five years old.

The Emperor's Reform Movement

In June 1898, in an attempt to save the Qing Dynasty from decline and the anti-Manchu movements manifesting in the secret societies rising up all over the country, the young emperor began the "Hundred Days of Reform." This desire for Western learning and technology alarmed the establishment. The new ideas met with bitter opposition from the dowager's powerful Grand Council, along with reactionary members of the aristocracy with their retinue of sycophantic eunuchs, who were rightly fearful that progress and education of the ordinary people would undermine their power structure. One court official declared that he would rather see the whole nation wiped out than adopt any reforms based on foreign political principles. A tangled web of party strife and petty politics was soon spun by frightened Manchu officials looking out for their own interests.

In the meantime, the empress dowager, by all accounts, was leading a life of leisure with the insiders of her Royal Court: picnicking on the Marble Boat in Kunming Lake and performing in elaborately staged Chinese opera and theatrical productions. Although keeping informed of politics in the Forbidden City, she ostensibly left the affairs of state to the emperor, who dutifully visited the Summer Palace to pay his respects and consult the Old Buddha about important decrees. At first she did not openly object to the reforms, but she watched the rapid spread of reform ideas throughout the empire with growing concern. When Prince Gong, commander of the military and naval forces, died, she seized her chance. She dismissed his appointed successor and named her kinsman and loyal supporter Ronglu as head of the military and Grand Council, thus making him the most powerful official in China with an army and navy to support him. He also had a powerful ally, General Dong Fuxiang, a Manchu prince who commanded the dreaded ten thousand Moslem Gansu Braves of the Imperial army, armed with Western rifles and modern artillery (which would later be used against the foreigners in the Siege of Peking).

On June 23, Emperor Guangxu, unaware of the forces gathering against him, issued the first of his reform decrees. He conferred on the subject with the empress dowager, who assured him she would raise no objection to his policy provided that the ancient privileges of the Manchus were not infringed upon. She also insisted that he get rid of his faithful old Chinese tutor, Weng Tonghe, whom she felt was instigating an anti-Manchu movement.

The young emperor moved swiftly to institute his reforms, and in rapid succession issued a series of Imperial edicts, which were printed on yellow paper and posted on all public buildings. Westerners considered the decrees nothing less than heroic, but the Chinese establishment, still under the influence of a highly conservative neo-Confucian traditional culture, viewed them as heretical and dangerous. Some called the emperor a Chinese traitor. The emperor, ignoring the opposition, ordered a number of radical changes in all fields, including military, industrial, financial, and educational. The edicts directed the abolition of the classical "eight-legged" essay that had to be mastered to pass the imperial examinations, which had been in force since the Song Dynasty (AD 960–1279). In the future, claimed the emperor, papers on practical subjects were to be set at the public examinations, and while the classics were to remain as a basis for the literary curriculum, candidates for the public service would be expected to display knowledge of the history of other countries and of contemporary politics. To the delight of Reverend Ronning, the emperor planned for the creation of new schools and the introduction of Western subjects into Peking University. To advance public education, even abandoned temples were to be transformed into village schools.

It soon became obvious that the young emperor was ahead of his time. One decree provided for the reorganization of the effete Manchu troops; another ordered arrangements for the publication of official newspapers, in which opinions were to be freely expressed, and all abuses fearlessly exposed all over the empire. The emperor went so far as to order Bibles that had been translated into Chinese to be sent to the Imperial Palace. Some advisors even advocated that Christianity be placed on the same level of toleration as Buddhism and Daoism. This caused great alarm in the Manchu court. For the first time in two thousand years, fundamental assumptions, structures, and ways were being challenged, and the ancient bulwarks of dynastic privilege were in danger. One official quoted Mencius himself: "We have heard of Chinese ideas being employed to convert barbarians, but have never heard of China being converted by barbarians."*

One unthinkable decree granted permission to the Manchus, who as a matter of principle had never worked a day in their lives, to leave Peking and earn their living in the provinces. The most shocking blow to the Manchus, and probably the death knell to the reform movement, was the decree abolishing a number of obsolete and useless government offices—fat jobs that had maintained thousands of idlers for generations, including high officials of the Board of Rites; they had become a useless burden to the state. This decree was loudly denounced by minor officials and their parasites as contrary to the traditions of the Manchu Dynasty. They sent an urgent plea to the Empress Dowager Cixi begging her to cancel the order and protect the privileges of the ruling class.

The last reform decree ended with a remarkable plea from the emperor himself for understanding by the people. Halvor was deeply impressed and sent it to Nils:

When I reflect how deep is the ignorance of the masses of the dwellers in the innermost parts of the Empire on the subject of my proposed reforms, my heart is filled with care and grief. Therefore do I hereby proclaim my intentions, so that the whole Empire may know and believe that their Sovereign is to be trusted and that the people may co-operate with me in working for reform and strengthening of our country. This is my earnest hope.

I command that the whole of my reform decrees be printed on yellow paper and distributed for the information of all men. The District Magistrates are henceforward privileged to submit memorials to me so I may learn the real needs of the people. Let this Decree be exhibited in the front hall of every public office in the Empire so all men may see it.

The net result of the edicts was to create an equal measure of delight among the reformers, including Halvor, and utter dismay among the more powerful Imperial hierarchy. A power struggle between the Reactionary Party and the outnumbered Reform Party was imminent.

---

*Quoted in J. O. P. Bland and E. Backhouse, *China under the Empress Dowager: Being the History of the Life and Times of Tzu Hsi* . . . (New York: Houghton Mifflin, 1914).

12

The Year of the "Boxers United in Righteousness"

There are many roads to the top of the mountain. We only know one way. No one, not even the Christians, has a patent on heaven.

—HALVOR RONNING, 1898

By 1898, Nelius was seven years old and Chester five. They were too young to understand why their parents were so involved with their mission work and the growing unrest that they had little time for their own children. By the closing months of 1898, there was serious trouble caused by the growing secret societies, the largest being the Yihequan, or Fists of United Harmony. The name Boxers literally denotes the Fists *(Quan)* of Righteous *(Yi)* and Harmony *(He)*. As "fists and feet" signify boxing and martial arts in China, the name Boxers appeared suitable for the adherents to this sect. It was first coined by correspondents of missionary journals and later accepted universally.

While their parents were attending to mission duties, working in the orphanage, and teaching in their new schools, Nelius and Chester spent most of their time with their Chinese playmates and the household servants. The boys naturally identified with the Chinese. They dressed like them, talked like them, and shared their problems. They were not looked upon as foreigners. Chester later recalled that as a child he did not think there were any differences between himself and the Chinese except for the color of his skin, hair, and eyes.

The children met with their parents during three formal meals each day. At breakfast, their mother spoke to them in English, and they answered in English. At dinner and supper, their father spoke to them in Norwegian, and they replied in Norwegian. Away from the table, however, they all spoke Chinese, which was the only language the children spoke fluently. The Ronnings were fortunate in having a cook and amah who were literate. They came from a family that had worked for generations for the Tao T'ai, the super mandarin in Hsiangyang. Cook Liu se fu was short, jolly, and fat as a dumpling, and his wife, Amah Tung se fu, was a thin, pleasant woman who oiled her hair and pulled it straight back in a tight bun. The children were entranced by her widely spaced gold teeth that sparkled in the candlelight when she laughed. Through Cook Liu and Amah Liu and their boisterous family and friends, who always filled the large mission kitchen, the children were introduced to the rich world of old Chinese folklore. At the age of ninety, my father still remembered the fables and loved to recite the childhood rhymes, riddles, proverbs, and wise old sayings that had become part of his daily life as a child.

The children received their religious education, based on the Bible, in Norwegian from their father. They believed everything he told them. It never occurred to them to wonder if Jonah could really have survived in the belly of a whale or that it would have been difficult for Noah to get a pair of all the animals in the world into his ark. The boys also believed Cook Liu when he told them that in all the world, China was the only civilized island in a sea of barbarians. "The world," said Cook Liu, "is a chariot. The square cart is the earth, and the round canopy is heaven. Because the canopy is round, it cannot cover the four corners where the barbarians with light eyes live. Heaven," he explained to the blue-eyed children who hung onto his every word, "has nine levels like a pagoda, each separated from the next by a gate guarded by fierce tigers. On the highest level is the 'celestial palace' [ziweigong] where Shangdi [God] lives. He is guarded by a wolf with piercing eyes that tosses intruders in the air and plays with them as with a ball before he casts them into a bottomless pit. The 'lowest gate' [changhemen] divides heaven and earth, and through it the west wind blows on the earth. Heaven is held up by eight pillars at the extremities of the earth. These keep the sky from falling on the earth. Between heaven and earth are the sun, moon, and stars. The sun is a fire ball shaped like a lotus blossom; he spends the night on earth. Each morning his mother, Xihe, bathes him in the Gulf of Sweetness before she lets him cross the Valley of Sunrise, where he climbs to heaven on the branches of a tree." The cook's stories seemed just as plausible as their mother's fairy tales and their father's Bible stories, but the boys intuitively knew it would not be wise to tell their father, whom they secretly called Lao Huzi ("Old Whiskers"), the stories they had heard in the kitchen.

Chester and Nelius loved their Chinese playmates like brothers. But the missionary's sons were troubled about where their friends would go when they died. Was nirvana the same as heaven? One day they approached their father. Chester just stood and glared at his papa until Halvor asked his son what was wrong. "I can't believe," said six-year-old Chester, "that my Chinese friends and their honorable ancestors will not go to heaven just because they are not Christians." The boys' mother had voiced the same concern: "How could this be when they never had the chance to know about Jesus?" Halvor put his hand on Chester's head and said something the children would never forget: "If they are good people, you don't have to worry about your friends. There are many roads to the top of the mountain. We only know one way. No one, not even the Christians, has a patent on heaven." This statement may not be startling today, but in those days of absolute, fundamentalist thinking, it was heresy. The boys were not aware of this, however, and their father's words gave them great comfort.

In spite of the antiforeign sentiment in the countryside, the Ronnings felt fairly safe in Fancheng. Chester and Nelius and their friends loved to trek up the mountain on the eastern horizon that rose up in the shape of a lion's head. There, hidden in a forest of ancient trees, stood the enchanting temple of Zhuge Liang surrounded by peony bushes and guarded by great stone monsters. The boys loved to listen to the stories about the legendary prime minister who had lived during the Three Kingdoms Period in the third century AD and won battles by wit rather than force. Zhuge Liang was the hero of Fancheng. It mattered not to these children of the walled-in cities that their hero had been dead for a thousand years. Whenever Chester returned to his hometown, he would make a nostalgic visit to the temple to sit in the chair of his hero. I have watched him do this, and even at the age of ninety his eyes shone with pride and his whole countenance took on the hero-worshiping visage of a smitten ten-year-old boy.

Seventeen centuries ago, during the Three Kingdoms Period, Fancheng was part of the kingdom of Shu. But as romantic as it may sound in military annals, that period contributed little other than entertainment, and it brought China perilously close to losing its national and cultural identity. During the Three Kingdoms Period and the Six Dynasties, which extended to AD 589, Confucianism lost its importance, but an intellectual interest in Daoism was revived. In later ages, the term neo-Daoism was applied to the new interest in the Dao, or the Way, which was a many-sided movement finding expression in the spheres of metaphysics, aesthetics, and religion. More important, a new religion, Buddhism, which was soon to become a state religion and be integrated into both Daoism and Confucianism, gained a foothold among all classes of people for the first time.

The gradual disintegration of the Han Dynasty had taken more than a hundred years. The period between its downfall and the reunification of the empire under the Jin Dynasty (AD 265–420) was known as the San Guo, or Three Kingdoms of Wei, Shu, and Wu. It was a period of division and confusion but gave rise to some of the greatest stories and poems in Chinese history. The contending generals in the continuous battles became legendary figures of romance to later generations, and their exploits, recorded in *Romance of the Three Kingdoms*, became as familiar to the Ronning boys as the Knights of the Round Table or Robin Hood are to Western children.

Beginning of the Boxer Uprising

By the close of 1898, serious trouble was afoot in northern China. The provinces had been devastated by flooding, drought, and crop failure. Large areas were threatened by famine. The prisons were packed with hungry thieves and bands of robbers. The country was ripe for rebellion. According to the on-the-spot missionary-historian Arthur H. Smith in his iconic book *China in Convulsion*, revolutionaries more than a thousand strong in the city of Woyang in northern Anhui Province had clashed with Manchu officers and troops sent against them. "Under the leadership of a former Taiping outlaw the malcontents kept up the guerrilla warfare." There were also bitter complaints against the Roman Catholics. The missionaries in many areas were already feared and hated by the superstitious and uneducated people living on the edge of survival.

Chinese secret societies had traditionally functioned as the vehicle of opposition to Manchu rule. However, antiforeign agitation in the Yangtze River Valley and south China had not yet resulted in violence because such viceroys as Liu Kunyi in Nanking and Zhang Zhidong in Hankow had sought to maintain order in their spheres. They declared the Boxer Uprising to be a rebellion and not an act of a lawful government. Halvor noted in his journal that there was a large democratic element running through the entire social structure of Chinese society. While the people were generally satisfied with the system of government that had been established two thousand years ago, they were not content with its faulty and frequently oppressive operation. The Chinese had respect for "the Practice of Virtue." For centuries, China had been honeycombed with secret societies in which vast numbers of people were connected. Secret societies can be traced back to the Ming Dynasty (1368–1644), and many more appeared after the Manchus seized the Mandate of Heaven in 1644. The societies were outlawed by the Manchus, who feared their power to stir up large political uprisings, as had occurred in the case of the Triad and the White Lotus Societies.

In the late 1890s, the Boxers were one of many secret societies supported by the millions of downtrodden peasants as their only hope to fight against a system that was driving them into miserable poverty. The peasants were rooted in the earth their ancestors had depended on for existence; their lives consisted of work, work, and more work. Periodically throughout Chinese history, the peasants in rags would rise and fight for survival with all the fervor of a people fighting for justice. Revolution in China was the only way to change governments. The Boxer Uprising began as just one more episode of this perpetual ferment arising out of the chasm between extreme wealth on one side and poverty on the other. In a deadly twist, however, when the Boxers were bribed to champion the interests of the Qing, their uprising took the form of a rebellion against foreigners under Manchu auspices. It was hardly noted that the Manchu rulers were also foreigners—brown-eyed foreigners—who had dominated China for more than two hundred years.

The empress, who had ample reason to hate the foreign powers after the Allied troops destroyed the Summer Palace, had been impressed by a special company of Boxers who claimed to be invulnerable to foreign weapons and who had been invited by the Manchu Prince Tsai Hsun to demonstrate their defensive and offensive martial arts exercises on the palace grounds. At first she vacillated between extremists and moderates on the issue of using Boxers for political purposes. But her path became clear when she found the Boxers were also against the "foreign devils." Thus encouraged, the Boxers began attacking foreigners. The empress openly blamed all the natural and man-made catastrophes in China on the Westerners. The Ronnings and other missionaries found themselves caught in the middle.

Nelius and Chester were only vaguely aware of the dangers all around them. By 1899, the Boxers were killing foreigners with the apparent sanction of the empress dowager. The popular impression was that the Boxers had orders from on high, and therefore nothing was done to stop them. The first missionaries to be killed in Hubei Province were the two Swedish missionaries Hans Wikholm and Lars Johanson, who had been murdered in 1893. Hostility had been festering in the northeastern province of Shandong since the murder of two German Catholic priests in 1897 in what was known as the Juye Incident. At that time, Kaiser Wilhelm had retaliated by landing German marines and forcing the Chinese to give them a ninety-nine-year lease on Kiaochow Bay (today's Jiaozhou), one of China's finest natural harbors. The occupation had been amazingly easy. Three German warships entered the bay and without warning began firing their guns at the Chinese fortifications. Within three hours, the disorganized Chinese troops broke and fled without firing a shot. They not only dropped their guns but removed their uniforms so the Germans would not shoot at them. Many of the soldiers, for a few strings of cash, helped the German troops carry their guns and baggage into the same fort they had just deserted.

Encouraged by the lack of resistance, the Germans went still further: they demanded railway, mining, and employment rights in Shandong Province and got them. Then, to further humiliate the Chinese, the kaiser demanded indemnity for military expenses. The action was met by a chorus of applause from many foreign powers. Few suspected these acts would foster one of the fiercest antiforeign uprisings in the history of China.

The Boxers were gaining courage day by day. The magic rites, incantations, and charms they used not only appealed to the superstitious Chinese but amused them as well. The Boxers claimed supernatural powers and invulnerability to swords and bullets. To prove this, the Boxers put on demonstrations in temples and gardens. Uttering incantations, they invited the gods from the central southern mountains and the eight caves to help them preserve China and destroy foreigners. While mumbling this abracadabra, they would go into weird contortions and violent spasms until their mouths foamed and their eyes rolled up as if in an epileptic fit. Eventually they fell into a trance from which they emerged "possessed" with protective spirits that they claimed rendered them invulnerable. This would be demonstrated by staging mock fights where the combatants appeared to deflect bullets by a wave of the hand and sword cuts and spear thrusts made no impressions on their bodies. These so-called magical happenings made a great impression on the illiterate spectators. Some believed it so completely that they tried it themselves. More than one poor soul was blown in half by a cannonball shot by a trusting friend. Others were shot and maimed. When these mishaps occurred, the Boxers explained that it was because the initiates had not uttered the right incantations or had been lax in their devotions. Throughout northeastern China, secret societies and peasants joined together; they tied red cloths around their heads and roamed the country looking for foreigners and shouting their slogans: "Save the country! Kill the foreign devils! Revive the Great Qing! Exterminate the barbarians!"

Foreign Scapegoats

The Boxers blamed all natural catastrophes on the foreigners. In early 1899, two successive harvests in Hubei and Shandong failed because of widespread drought. Plagues of locusts devoured the remaining crops. People were starving and dying of cholera. The Boxers spread rumors that the foreigners had poisoned the wells and the rivers. They warned peasants to keep their children away from the missionaries, who wanted to use them for evil experiments. They claimed the missionaries saved abandoned baby girls to mutilate their bodies for the purpose of alchemy—to use their livers to turn lead into silver—and to make medicine from their eyes and hearts.

Halvor got the first warnings of the extent of disturbances in a rather unexpected manner. He was returning home after a visit to Middleman Ting, who was recovering from his prison ordeal. Walking through town in his Chinese clothes with his false queue dangling from his mandarin cap, Halvor noticed a ruffian in a white cotton tunic and a red band around his forehead coming toward him. A long, curved knife hung from the man's wide red sash. Halvor realized the man belonged to one of the secret societies rumored to be in the area—perhaps the Dadaohui, or Big Swords, or perhaps a Boxer. The man thrust a crumpled booklet into Halvor's hands. Red Chinese characters on the cover read "Death to the Devils' Religion," but before Halvor could digest the significance, he noticed that the curious crowd behind him was turning into a hostile mob. He sensed the danger. His long legs broke into a fast run. They chased him up the street to the mission yelling "Yangguizi" (foreign devil). The gatekeeper heard the threatening noises and, unaware that his master was involved, barred the mission gate. Seeing the gate closed, Halvor made a desperate leap up the compound wall. It was at least ten feet high, but the rugged stones gave him a foothold. As he scrambled up, the ruffian grabbed his queue and yanked it off, together with his skullcap. The angry people stopped and stared in amazement at the disheveled, hatless foreigner straddling the wall with his brown wavy hair blowing in the wind. They were soon roaring with laughter at this strange spectacle. The man who had snatched the queue now stared at the object in his hand, apparently suspecting some evil foreign magic, and quickly carried the dangling queue to the gate. Halvor descended from the wall on the inside, opened the gate, took the false pigtail, and thanked the frightened man for returning his precious queue. He then stepped into the street and expressed his gratitude to the now smiling crowd for their kindness in escorting him home. He placed the cap and queue back on his head and invited them to visit him sometime when they were not in such a hurry.

Hannah, watching anxiously from the balcony, could not keep from laughing at Halvor's bravado. She thanked the Lord that he had been an athlete in Norway before he became a missionary and ran to meet him. In spite of his cool performance, he was pale and shaken. How long could their luck hold out? They both knew that as quickly as a Chinese mob could be swayed to laughter, it could turn ugly and murderous, and they had no defense. Nelius and Chester had watched their father's scramble over the wall with great delight. He was always playing funny games. It never occurred to them that this great bewhiskered man might have been running for his life. To them he was indestructible.

Hannah and Halvor left their children kicking a shuttlecock in the courtyard with their Chinese friends and went into the parlor, where their number-one boy served tea. Halvor reached into the breast pocket of his Chinese robe to pull out the pamphlet shoved at him by the Boxer. He shuddered when he remembered the man's evil smirk as he had handed him the papers. He gave the pamphlet to Hannah, who held it as if it had been conjured up from hell itself. She flipped the pages and stopped at a drawing of a hog, identified in the margin as Jesus Christ tied to a cross, with a mandarin official directing its execution by arrows. One of the Chinese terms for Christianity (Tianzhujiao) was written in characters having the same sound as Christianity but meaning "The Squeak of the Heavenly Pig." Goat-headed foreigners were being decapitated in the foreground. Hannah gasped and dropped the booklet to the floor.

Hannah's letter to her mother revealed a lack of awareness: *Dearest Mother: Don't worry about us. It's the Catholics the Chinese really blame for their troubles and the miners and railroad engineers. I can't say I blame them for resenting the Catholic missionaries when they ride so arrogantly through town in their fancy sedan chairs with a whole retinue of chair bearers, outriders, and footmen . . . But the Chinese know we aren't Catholics, so why should they harm us?* Halvor was not so optimistic. "Foreigners are foreigners," he told Hannah, "and if the Catholics are pompous or one of those railroad engineers insults a Chinese, then we all get the blame."

Halvor wrote to Nils: *Brother, it is dark out here! We have been ordered to leave. But our trip has been delayed by the untimely passing of Miss Marietta Fugleskjel, the nurse who has worked so unselfishly in the hospital for the past two years. Two years! How fast China devours those who offer themselves in good faith! Now four out of our five women missionaries have died. Hannah is the only one left. She is weary with sorrow and stress.*

Although the main turmoil was still in the neighboring provinces, it was getting dangerously close to the Ronnings in Fancheng. Halvor bribed the "King of Thieves" to keep watch at the gate with a gang of "honorable robbers" who carried swords. The King had a spear with a forked tip which he showed to wide-eyed Chester and claimed he could throw it twenty yards and spear a man in the eye. But in spite of the guards, someone managed to tack a Boxer edict written in Chinese characters attributed to the "Lord of Wealth and Happiness" onto the mission gate. It read:

> The Catholic and Protestant religions, being insolent to the gods, rendering no obedience to Buddha, are enraging Heaven and Earth. The rain clouds no longer visit us; but eight million Spirit Soldiers will descend from Heaven and sweep the Empire clean of all foreigners. Then will the gentle showers once more water our lands. Hasten then to spread this doctrine far and wide, for if you gain one adherent to the faith your own person will be absolved from all future misfortunes. If you gain five your whole family will be absolved from all evils and if you gain ten your whole village will be absolved from all calamities.
>
> THOSE WHO GAIN NO ADHERENTS TO THE CAUSE SHALL BE DECAPITATED FOR UNTIL ALL FOREIGNERS HAVE BEEN EXTERMINATED THE RAIN CAN NEVER VISIT US.
>
> Those who have drunk water from wells poisoned by foreigners should at once make use of the following Divine Prescription, the ingredients of which are to be decocted and swallowed, when the poisoned patient will recover:
>
> Dried black plums . . . half an ounce
> Selenium dulcimer . . . half an ounce
> Liquorice root . . . half an ounce.

The identical edict appeared in several northeastern provinces, indicating that the Boxers possessed a common message, but as nothing was allowed to be written about the secret societies, no one knew the extent of their internal organization. The gatekeeper delivered the edict to Reverend Ronning. Within the week, a telegram from the American consul in Hankow urged all American missionaries to evacuate. At the same time, the London Missionary Society received a telegram ordering missionaries west of Peking to seek refuge at the British legation.

Halvor to Nils: *The Boxers have been given sanction by the Empress Dowager to kill all foreigners. Britain and the U.S. governments have ordered all missionaries to leave their stations and seek refuge immediately. Conditions are worse than ever. In her desperate effort to retain the old order, the Old Buddha is trying to rid China of foreigners by the simple method of killing them all. She is in league with the Boxers and believes in the supernatural powers they claim to have. There are riots in Fancheng and rebels have set fires in Hankow to get cheap building lots. We have been here nine years and are due for home leave, but personally I would like to remain here until my death. However, I must get my family to safety . . . I will turn the mission over to our loyal colleagues, Sen Li-fu and Evangelist Huang. Dr. Himle, who has already lost his wife and children, is determined to stay on as long as he can. What can I say? He is a brave man and needed here. Brother, this cannot last long. We shall come back soon. We plan to go to America via Norway and God willing we can meet again in Telemark.*

13

The Gathering Storm

Men make their own history, but they do not make it just as they please; they do not make it under circumstances chosen by themselves, but under circumstances directly encountered, given and transmitted from the past.

— KARL MARX, *Eighteenth Brumaire of Louis Bonaparte*

The Ronnings had personally experienced the misunderstandings and wrath engendered among the Chinese by the arrogance and greed of foreign colonialists. Halvor was shocked but not surprised by the antiforeign riots led by the Boxers and encouraged by the empress dowager. The Western powers had been chipping away at Chinese sovereignty, without regard to Chinese traditions and culture, for sixty years. By the end of the nineteenth century at the height of the Scramble for Concessions, antiforeign sentiment in China was focused on two main issues: the deplorable conduct of foreign traders and the authoritarian and antiquated policy of the Manchu rulers, who, after two centuries of undisputed sovereignty, had become decadent and out of step with the modern world.

Foreigners had originally come to China for the sake of trade. In earlier centuries, the legendary Old Silk Road had brought trade with the Near East and the Roman Empire. Buddhism, carried by pilgrims from India, had been welcomed and adapted to the national temperament. The Moslem faith had taken root in the northwestern provinces, and the Jesuits had won respect in Peking. Marco Polo, with his father and uncle, who served for seventeen years with the Mongol Emperor Kublai Khan during the Yuan "Everlasting" Dynasty (AD 1279–1368), had been permitted with great reluctance to return to Italy with their fabulous tales of incredible wealth. Europeans had been welcomed to audiences with the Ming emperors if they showed proper respect and kowtowed in the established manner.

The Chinese did not begin to resent Westerners until 1832, when the colonial powers came in warships in search of trade and profit. The Chinese closed their doors, but the foreign traders battered them down. The worst suspicions of the

Chinese seemed confirmed as the Westerners demanded what the Chinese considered outrageous rights of treaty relations and commerce.

The most outrageous clash between China and the West occurred when Britain forced China to import opium, or "foreign mud." It is a shameful episode of which the British prefer not to be reminded and which the Chinese will never forget. It began around 1839, when the British, then at the height of their imperial colonial powers, seized a protected harbor, now known as Aberdeen, on the Chinese island of Victoria, the main island of Hong Kong in the Pearl River Delta. They used the bay as an anchorage for their gunboats and merchant ships to smuggle opium from the British colony of India—the center of the world's opium poppy fields—into China. They did this despite the fact that China's Emperor Daoguang had demanded action against the outlawed "happiness and longevity gum" and prohibited its import by the British East India Company. Before opium, the British trade with China had been limited to tea and silk in exchange for seal pelts, sandalwood, and tons of silver.

In the 1820s, the British East India Company, known as "the father of all smuggling," began to ship opium, grown in Bengal, into China on a large scale. They were soon joined by the British company Jardine, Matheson & Co. With the full knowledge of the English Parliament, the British traders literally forced the drug upon the Chinese.

Americans were also involved, as junior partners. U.S. vessels transported about 10 percent of the opium. Of the foreign ships that carried opium to China in 1837, sixty-one were British and fifteen American. When the opium arrived at Lintin (today's Lingding) Island off the coast of Canton (today's Guangzhou), it was unloaded and taken to China in small smuggling boats called "fast crabs" and "scrambling dragons." Fully armed and moving swiftly across the waters like running centipedes, these boats had twenty or more oars on each side and were rowed by seventy-some coolies. Evading customs patrols, they ran up small creeks, where agents waited to store the opium in floating warehouses for distribution to pushers. In 1839, Emperor Daoguang appointed the governor of Hunan and Hubei Provinces, a traditional Confucian mandarin scholar-official, Lin Zexu, as Imperial commissioner with authority to take any action necessary to halt the opium smugglers. "Unless this is stopped," Lin had written to the emperor, "there will not be a man left to make a soldier in ten years."

Lin Zexu, an impressive personage with a dignified air, a heavy mustache, and a long beard who is still honored in China today, became the leader in the struggle against the opium plague. In his own provinces, he confiscated 5,500 opium pipes and rehabilitated thousands of addicts. Then he attacked the centers of the smuggling in Canton and along the southern coasts.

Lin wrote a personal letter to Queen Victoria that was also circulated in the Canton foreign community, imploring her to halt the opium smuggling: "The wealth of China is taken to profit the barbarians . . . By what right do they in return use the poisonous drug to injure the Chinese people? . . . Let us ask, where is your conscience? . . . Why do you let it be passed on to harm other countries? Suppose there were people from another country who carried opium for sale to England and seduced your people into buying and smoking it; certainly your honorable ruler would deeply hate it and be bitterly aroused . . . Naturally you would not wish to give unto others what you would not give to yourselves."*

The letter was carried to London in January 1840. But, in a sad example of tragic missed opportunities that could have changed history, the letter was evidently never delivered to the queen. What followed resulted in an indelible stain on all the "Great Foreign Powers." The opium trade for profit intensified, resulting in the slow death of innumerable addicted Manchus and Han Chinese.

The first undeclared and iniquitous "Opium War" began with the British shelling Canton. The Chinese had no defense against the modern warships. Commissioner Lin attempted to mobilize the Chinese people. Every able-bodied man was ordered to "take a knife and kill." The emperor, in a panic, looked for a scapegoat and pounced on Commissioner Lin. He was replaced by a Manchu official, Qishan, who was determined to make peace at any cost.

The British armada took Amoy (today's Xiamen), Shanghai, and Nanking. Finally, Emperor Daoguang was forced to bend to the reality of defeat. In 1842, the Chinese and British signed the Treaty of Nanking, the first "unequal treaty" that changed the international status of China. The British now demanded and got $21 million for war expenses and reparations for financial losses of British merchants associated with the opium trade. Five coastal towns were opened as treaty ports with fixed low tariffs. The following year, in a supplementary treaty, the British were granted "most favored nation" status, by which Britain would enjoy the trading privileges that China might thereafter grant to any other nation along with the legal protection of extraterritoriality for British subjects.

The Second Opium War (1856–60) was triggered by an incident so trivial

*"Lin Tse-hsu's Moral Advice to Queen Victoria," 1839, in *China's Response to the West: A Documentary Survey*, ed. Ssu-yu Teng and John King Fairbank (Cambridge: Cambridge University Press, 1954).

that it is obvious the British were waiting for an excuse to make further demands. A Chinese patrol boat spotted an illegal smuggling ship in Canton harbor, flying the British flag. The commander boarded the ship, arrested thirteen crew members, and tore down the flag. The British consul protested, demanding release of the crew and an official apology.

An indignant British protest note was sent to the Chinese Governor Ye Mingchen, whose response reflected the Daoist mentality that many Chinese officials exhibited at that time: they were so overwhelmed with the awful present that they left the future in the hands of fate. His unique story is told by the Chinese historian Tsui Chi in his book *A Short History of Chinese Civilization*. Apparently Governor Ye was more interested in painting and poetry than politics and felt that there was no harm in pacifying the British consul, so he freed the British crew. The British consul, in his arrogance, was not satisfied with this act and demanded that the Chinese commander be severely punished for hauling down the British flag. This was too much even for Ye, who promptly sent the English crew back to prison. The British responded by opening fire on Canton. Governor Ye, outnumbered, chose to ignore the uproar and ordered his own forces to hold their fire. The British landed and marched into Canton. Riots broke out, and the French sent a fleet to assist the British.

In the meantime, Governor Ye, in accordance with the Daoist belief that everything works itself out in time, continued to paint his landscape scrolls and refused even to discuss the situation with his military advisors. In autumn of 1857, the French and British launched a full-scale invasion of Canton, and the city fell in three days. Ye was taken prisoner. He dressed himself with great dignity in his official blue brocade gown embroidered with peacock feathers and his mandarin cap set with a coral button before he was carried off to Hong Kong's prison in his golden palanquin shouldered by four uniformed bearers. During captivity he continued to paint and write poetry in the finest calligraphy. He soon charmed his English captors, who recognized a gentleman when they saw one. Unwilling to execute anyone with such remarkable skills, they sent him to Bengal with his military attaché, two servants, and his hairdresser. He died two years later in "The Hall Where the Sea Is Pacified," but his body was brought back to his native land to be buried with full honors. The Chinese did not consider him a coward for not resisting the British forces; instead, a ballad preserves his memory:

> You neither fight
> Nor make peace
> Nor prepare defense

You neither die for your duty,
Nor surrender
Nor flee to safety.
It is a minister's generosity
And a governor's liberality
Which find no example in ancient times
Nor an equal in modern history!

My grandparents were in China in 1898 when fighting between China and Britain erupted again and Britain demanded that China lease the New Territories adjacent to Hong Kong for ninety-nine years. In the meantime, Emperor Guangxu had come of age, and Empress Dowager Cixi had ostensibly retired to the Summer Palace. The emperor was too busy with his reform edicts to resist British claims. Halvor, like some other missionaries, became involved in the reform movement, and as fate would have it, ninety-nine years later I was in Hong Kong when that lease was up and the whole area was returned to China. By that time, the opium trade had been wiped out, but the drug was not made illegal until the Communists took over and in a harsh sweeping reform in 1950 executed the drug pushers and forcefully rehabilitated the addicts.

On July 1, 1997, I had been assigned as a journalist to go to Hong Kong to cover the amazing "handover" story for the *Houston Chronicle*. Britain at last returned its ill-gotten gains to China with the highest interest ever paid for the loan of a barren island. This major media event marked the final closure of the Opium Wars. Millions of viewers the world over watched television with trepidation, but the soldiers of the People's Liberation Army marched peacefully through the New Territories and into the prosperous metropolis of Hong Kong on Victoria Island. The old "Smugglers Cove" that British Foreign Secretary Lord Palmerston, in 1841, referred to as that "barren island with hardly a house upon it" had developed into an economic miracle.

I wrote: *On the morning of July 1, 1997, Hong Kong's six million people, without moving an inch, woke up in a different country. At midnight on June 30, after 156 years of British rule, the "Handover Ceremony" celebrated the unique metamorphosis of Hong Kong from a British crown colony (BCC) to Chinese special administrative region (SAR) and a new era begins—for better or for worse.*

14

The Palace Coup in Peking

September 21, 1898. I am willing to shed my blood, if thereby my country may be saved. But for every one that perishes today, a thousand will rise up to carry on the work of Reform and uphold loyalty against usurpation.

—TAN SITONG, MARTYR OF THE HUNDRED DAYS OF REFORM

In 1898, a century before the British Crown Colony of Hong Kong was returned to China, the Empress Dowager Cixi retired to the Summer Palace that had been reconstructed after its destruction by the British and French troops. The young emperor, encouraged by some progressive Chinese officials and missionaries, organized a Reform Party. Halvor Ronning had high hopes for the reforms that could put China on the road to progress and prevent the chaos that in fact followed. But fate took a cruel twist. Behind the scenes, the dowager was encouraging the Boxers to kill the foreigners. The rising antiforeign sentiment soon turned violent. Several missionaries had been killed in a series of riots, but unless the circumstances had some special horror connected with them, they were soon forgotten. The Qing Dynasty was verging on losing the Mandate of Heaven, but the empress dowager and her court blamed it all on the foreigners and continued to exist in a world of their own. Revolution against the Manchus was in the air, but the Old Buddha, with the help of the Boxers, used her "divine" power to turn it against the foreigners, especially the missionaries.

The British minister in Peking, Sir Claude MacDonald, appealed to the Chinese Foreign Ministry (Zongli Yamen), warning that if the disorder was not vigorously quelled, international complications were likely to ensue. Halvor sent word of the missionaries' killings to the American minister, Edwin H. Conger, who cabled Washington: "Situation becoming serious. The country is swarming with hungry, discontented, hopeless idlers." He requested that a warship be stationed offshore from Tientsin (today's Tianjin), the nearest port to Peking.

Halvor was incensed by the diplomats' ignorance. He wrote to Nils: *The American Minister has no idea of what is happening in China! How can a warship off the coast of China help prevent the murder of the Christians in the interior, a thousand miles away!*

In spite of the warnings, the diplomats in Peking carried on life as usual. Entertaining each other seemed to be their main mission. In contrast to the missionaries, who worked as closely as possible with the Chinese, the diplomats, with rare exceptions, believed they belonged to a superior social class and remained aloof in their international enclave. Manchu officials had assured the diplomats that everything was under control, so they had little time for unconfirmed reports from "fanatic" missionaries.

Queen Victoria's eighty-first birthday, recognized by the diplomats as a truly important event, was fast approaching, and Sir Claude and Lady MacDonald had invited the elite diplomatic corps to a grand celebration at the British legation. The guests did not have far to come. All the foreign legations in Peking, except that of Belgium, were located in a walled-in, fortified, rectangular compound (approximately two miles long and one mile wide) situated in the Tartar City near the walled-in Imperial Palace. The offices and residences of the British, Italian, French, Austria-Hungarian, Japanese, Spanish, German, Russian, Netherlands, and American legations, with their scholars' gardens, extensive servant quarters, and stables, were all located between the walls that surrounded the Imperial City and the walls around the Tartar City, where only the Manchus were allowed to reside. The Chinese lived within another walled-in area in the southern section called the Chinese City. Each legation was in a walled-in compound with access to an international enclave with foreign stores, tennis courts, hotels, including the Peking Hotel, the Hong Kong and Shanghai Bank, the Russo-Chinese Bank, the Imperial Customs, the Post Office, and the incomplete Imperial Mint. The south side of the Legation Quarter was bounded by the massive, forty-five-foot-high Tartar Wall, which ringed the whole city of Peking. Just outside the northwest wall of the Legation Quarter was the Imperial Carriage Park, an expansive area with large buildings for elephant carriages, sedan chairs, and other vehicles used by the empress and her court. On the northeast side was a wide moat marked by four stone towers that surrounded the crimson walls of the Forbidden City. Therein the golden-tiled Imperial Palaces and the royal purple-tile shrines stood in all their splendor. On the side of the eastern and western ends were major shopping streets of the city.

On May 24, 1899, when the missionaries in northern China were fighting for their lives and fleeing from the Boxers, the diplomats in Peking, from eleven nations, ignoring or oblivious to the plight of their countrymen, celebrated

Queen Victoria's birthday with traditional British pomp and ceremony. The cosmopolitan crowd arrived at the British legation in full dress regalia, uniforms and medals, white tie and tails, to toast the octogenarian queen of England with French champagne. Later they waltzed on the British tennis court, strung with scarlet lanterns, to the music of a Chinese band conducted and trained by Baron Robert Hart, the British inspector general. The next day an English journalist dispatched a rave review to the society column of the *Daily Mail* in Shanghai. "Nobody," he stated, "worries much about the Boxer stories."

The empress dowager, enraged by the reform movement and bored with her retirement in the Summer Palace, conspired with Ronglu, her lover and military commander, to stage the Palace Coup and take power from the emperor. She proved to be a shrewd strategist. The coup began with a classic royal court drama worthy of Shakespeare: intrigue, plot, and counterplot were enacted within the crimson walls of the Imperial Palace.

The lead villain of the Palace Coup was the Chief Eunuch, Li Lianying (often termed the "sham eunuch"), a handsome man with deadly charm who had managed to manipulate and bribe his way through the ranks until he became the constant companion of Her Majesty and consequently one of the richest creatures in Peking. He owned gold shops, banks, and pawn shops, and it was well known that he had obtained his enormous wealth through presents and bribes from officials hoping to obtain access to the empress dowager. They both let it be known that they loved presents. The "sham eunuch" was also known as "Cobbler's Wax Li" because, before his consented castration (which some dispute) to become a eunuch at the age of sixteen, he was a cobbler's apprentice. Li openly hated the young emperor (who once had him beaten) and feared the reformers, whom he felt, correctly, would expose his corruption and abolish the system of eunuchs. Progressive men in China and abroad realized how this barbarous medieval custom lowered the status of China in the eyes of the modern world.

History records that the Ming Dynasty, after three hundred years of greatness, had become effeminate and degenerate mainly because of the demoralizing influence of the eunuch system on the court. History seemed to be repeating itself during the downfall of the Qing Dynasty. In the late nineteenth century, the Chinese reformers and their Western supporters, including my grandfather, saw the same pattern emerging. They placed the abolition of these "fawning sycophants" with power in the Imperial Court in the front rank of the reforms necessary to bring China into line with the modern powers. Under the empress dowager, however, the abhorrent custom grew and assumed monstrous proportions. Eunuchs were the only males allowed to enter the Forbidden City, aside from mandarin officials in the Imperial Court. They were all Chinese (no Manchus were allowed to be castrated) who had been abused in their teens. Many became flagrant abusers themselves. Cobbler's Wax Li had boasted that he could make or break the highest officials at his pleasure and even defy the Son of Heaven on his throne. The story, behind the scenes, of the disintegrating Manchu Dynasty was inextricably entwined with stories of sordid sex orgies and sinister intrigues enacted by the palace eunuchs.

Cobbler's Wax Li plotted, with a number of court officials who foresaw their power eroding, a vicious scheme to destroy the young emperor. The sham eunuch began a whispering campaign, claiming that the emperor intended to murder the dowager. Rumors soon reached the ears of Ronglu, the all-important governor of Zhili Province (today encompassing Beijing, Tianjin, and parts of Hebei, western Liaoning, northern Henan, and Inner Mongolia) and commander-in-chief of the Military Guards Army. Commander Ronglu went straight to the Summer Palace to warn the dowager. Alarmed, the Old Buddha returned forthwith to the Forbidden City and conspired to destroy the emperor and his reform movement once and for all. The emperor, however, got wind of the dowager's maneuvers and decided to strike first. He called his trusted general Yuan Shikai, who professed to be a strong supporter of the Reform Party and had convinced the emperor of his complete devotion. But unbeknownst to the emperor, Yuan was actually Ronglu's "blood brother" and favored the established Reactionary Party.

The story goes that Emperor Guangxu ordered General Yuan to kill Commander Ronglu in his Yamen headquarters in Tientsin. After the decapitation, he would swiftly bring a force of ten thousand of the commander's military guards to Peking to overthrow the Reactionary Party officials. Then he was to send the empress dowager back to the Summer Palace. The emperor gave Yuan the highest symbol of Imperial authority, a small golden arrow, and bade him proceed with all speed to Tientsin. The scheme backfired. Yuan Shikai left Peking by the first train and proceeded to the Yamen. But instead of killing Ronglu, he betrayed the emperor and gave the commander the emperor's arrow to travel by special train to Peking and inform the empress. Thus Yuan Shikai brought about the effective dethronement of the emperor. (He was later suspected of betraying the emperor for his own purposes. In 1911, he became the first president of the Republic of China and, in a vain attempt to continue the Qing Dynasty, declared himself emperor.)

When Empress Dowager Cixi heard of this intrigue, she requested Manchu statesman Prince Duan (Zaiyi), commander of the Tiger and Divine Corps, to order his men to surround the Temple of Heaven and arrest the defenseless emperor as he was performing a sacred ritual in the Hall of Annual Prayer. The armed henchmen dragged the emperor to the Imperial Palace, where he was locked up in the Ocean Terrace on the Island of Immortals in the lake of the Southern Sea. His only link to his palace in the Forbidden City was by a narrow drawbridge, heavily guarded.*

After wrenching the emperor from power, the dowager ordered the prompt execution of his eight advisors on reform. Kang Youwei was sentenced to be tied to a wooden frame in the public square and suffer the lingering "death of a thousand cuts." Fortunately, the emperor was able to warn him, and he escaped to a foreign settlement in Shanghai. The city gates were closed to prevent the escape of the other reformers, but Liang Qichao managed to elude capture and fled to Japan. Other reformers fled to America, but some did not even attempt to escape. Six of the emperor's staunchest supporters were captured. The Board of Punishments condemned them to death without trial, and on September 28, 1898, they were executed.

In his book *Forty-Five Years in China,* Halvor's colleague Timothy Richard, who had scheduled an audience with the emperor for the very day of the coup, pleaded with the British minister to do his utmost to save the lives of the captured reformers. "But," he later wrote, "the minister was already prejudiced against them. His prejudice rested largely on ignorance, for I learned that he had never even heard of the chief Reformer Kang Youwei."

Cixi had intended to murder the emperor and place the son of Prince Duan on the throne, but when her plan leaked out, strong objections were raised by the foreign diplomats and missionaries as well as brave Chinese officials from the southern provinces. These included Liu Kunyi, the viceroy of Nanking and an active reformer, who pointed out that the emperor's role as the Son of Heaven was to be the symbolic intermediary of the Middle Kingdom between Heaven, Earth, and humanity. Richard's plea pointed out the fact that "His Majesty, according to the 'Mandate of Heaven,' was the only one on earth who could perform the correct rituals, pray to God on the Altar of Heaven for bountiful harvests, and achieve 'Great Harmony' of all things great and small. If the Dowager had the Emperor killed, 'all under Heaven' would fall into chaos."

*Bland and Backhouse, *China under the Empress Dowager,* 66.

Pressured to spare the life of Emperor Guangxu, Cixi pronounced him insane and imprisoned him in the Ocean Terrace, where he was guarded and tortured by the sadistic eunuchs who had betrayed him. On sacred ceremonial occasions he was escorted to perform the rituals required. The emperor's cruel confinement resulted in his prolonged illness and severe melancholy. An edict was posted declaring that, owing to ill-health, the emperor had decided to abdicate. The victorious empress dowager usurped the Dragon Throne, annulled all the recent reforms, and declared that all of China's troubles had been caused by the meddling foreign devils. Her former lover Ronglu became the most powerful official in the empire.

The missionaries were devastated by this sudden turn of events. In his letters, Halvor openly expressed sympathy for the reformers, revealing a dangerously outspoken, revolutionary attitude toward the Imperial Court: *The end came on Sept. 21. The Old Buddha arrested the Emperor and stamped out the Reform Movement. A week later the heads of 6 of the most brilliant Reformers were shorn off by the sword of the executioner giving ghastly testimony to the fact that here in China the propagation of new ideas carries grave dangers. They were all courageous men, true martyrs of a Reform Movement that could have saved the Empire and avoided revolution, but now, I fear, the storm is yet to come. They met their deaths bravely, witnessed by an immense crowd outside the city wall.*

Reverend Timothy Richard witnessed the executions and recorded the following: "As they were being led to the execution ground, Lin Xu asked for permission to say a few words but he was refused. Tan Sitong, however, boldly spoke out, ignoring permission. He said that he had heard how many reformers in other lands had died for their country's good. 'I am willing to shed my blood, if thereby my country may be saved. But,' he cried to the judges, 'for every one that perishes today, a thousand will rise up to carry on the work of Reform, and uphold loyalty against usurpation'—thus died the martyrs of Reform. The betrothed of Lin Xu, on hearing the news of execution, at once committed suicide."

On October 28, 1898, Halvor wrote: *Our hopes have been cruelly shattered! Conditions in China are standing on their head. The Emperor was a true Reformer who attempted to implement policies of modernization and Christian ethics that could have saved China. Alas, the evil dowager who ruled behind the throne for 37 years now sits at the helm. What a dark future! The Chinese ship of state is heading into a violent storm . . . I must tell you, brother, that when I read the last Decree of the Emperor written in his own boyish calligraphy on yellow paper—and knowing the terrible consequences—I fell on my knees and wept. It showed, unlike his evil aunt, how deeply and honestly he thought of his country before himself. The Dowager and her band of eunuchs now control the destiny of China.*

No intelligent observer of China could, with certainty, profess to be able to separate fact from fiction in the reports of what transpired within the impenetrable crimson walls of the Forbidden City. The emperor was a prisoner in his own palace, doomed to be a puppet of the dowager. His sole purpose was to perform ceremonial state rites in his role as the Son of Heaven.

On June 12, 1899, eight long months after the emperor had been kidnapped and imprisoned because of his courageous effort to reform the Imperial establishment and save China from war with the foreign powers, the *New York Times* published an article that had been leaked to the Shanghai correspondent for the *Daily Mail* by the emperor's loyal old tutor and confidant, Weng Tonghe. Obviously smuggled out at the risk of his life, the article was a desperate cry for help from the emperor himself.

Chinese Emperor Issues an Appeal
Proposes a Joint Protectorate by the Powers
Asks Them to Free Him

His Majesty, the Emperor Guangxu says "There Would Then Be No Difficulty in Calming the People," Empress Throws Off the Mask Entirely by Changing Personnel at the Zongli Yamen [China's foreign ministry].

London, June 12, 1899. Weng Tonghe, who was dismissed by the Empress Dowager after the Palace coup d'etat in 1898, sends with special sanction of the Emperor Guangxu and his party, including three Viceroys, a message to the peoples of the West. In part it is as follows:

"His Majesty is convinced, through trustworthy sources that the loyal support of millions of Chinese will be accorded to his proposals to put an end to the state of anarchy brought about by the action of the Empress Dowager.

"The Government of China, being virtually non-existent, the Emperor proposes that the foreign powers, whose troops dominate the Capital, shall remove His Imperial Presence from the Palace, in which His Majesty is confined as a prisoner; shall declare Empress Cixi and her present ministers to be usurpers and shall bring the Emperor to Nanking, Wuch'ang or Shanghai whichever the foreign powers deem to be the most suitable for the new capital of the Chinese Empire under the new conditions.

"It is proposed by His Majesty and his advisors that the foreign powers declare a joint protectorate and undertake the task of governing the country through His Majesty."

The message suggests that the protectorate should abolish the present government boards and appoint new ministers, abolish the existing so-called armies, take control of the customs, posts and telegraphs, and work them through Chinese officials, establish a uniform currency, readjust taxation and insure the freedom of religion. Weng Tonghe who predicts a peaceful acceptance of such a regime goes on to say: "China is ripe for the change of tide which the Reactionaries vainly seek to stem."

The emperor's proposals for peace made good sense to Halvor. When there was no response from the diplomats in Peking, he cabled mission headquarters, asking them to circulate the article, and sent an urgent telegraph to President William McKinley in Washington. There was no reply and no further publicity. Tragically, the emperor's plea was ignored. He was betrayed not only by the diplomats in Peking but by all the governments abroad. Halvor was outraged. When, years later, during my research for this book, I found the fading *New York Times* article in my grandfather's files, I, too, was appalled by the failure of responsible parties to act and support the emperor's reform movement and his urgent plea. If only the pompous representatives of the foreign powers in Peking had taken the time from their social events to listen to the enlightened emperor, the empress dowager's "War on the World" and the Siege of Peking might have been avoided, and tens of thousands of innocent Chinese and Western lives might have been saved.

In July 1899, Cixi played her trump card. In an obvious attempt to draw attention from the plight of the pitiful emperor, she sent fanciful invitations embossed with gold characters on red paper to all the wives of the foreign ministers, inviting them to a tea party in the Summer Palace. This was unheard of. The diplomats' wives were elated! The empress made a dramatic entrance with the silent, stony-faced emperor in tow. Swathed in a royal robe embroidered in gold threads with the five-toed Imperial Dragon, and crowned with a shimmering Manchu headdress inlaid with azure kingfisher feathers, red coral, and pearls, she oozed charm as she welcomed the guests personally with every token of cordiality and esteem, assuring each one that "we are all one family." There was no further conversation as none of the ladies spoke Mandarin. After tea and delicacies, they were given presents and dismissed. A few months later, the diplomats' wives, exhilarated by the touch of royalty, insisted on a return courtesy visit. They were received under even more elaborate conditions. After a delightful afternoon, they returned to the Legation Quarter full of admiration for the empress and hope for a peaceful China.

None could imagine that five months later, her Gracious Majesty would attempt to kill them all. In January 1900, she issued a direct royal edict: "Exterminate the Foreign Devils!"

15

Escaping the Boxers

Dear Halvor: Make evacuation plans to be used as soon as possible, if conditions worsen. It does not look good. God bless and keep you all.

—DR. GRIFFITH JOHN

Halvor implored Hannah to leave with the children, but the stubborn look on her face told him differently. "My place is with you," she replied simply. "If you stay, we all stay. We will live or die together. It is in God's hands. There is nothing more to say."

Halvor heard nothing more about the Boxers until June, when a dispatch published in the *North China Daily News* of Shanghai, the principal foreign-language newspaper in China, arrived several weeks late by post boat from Hankow: "The secret societies are now organized. The 'Boxers' say they will unite to uphold the cause of righteousness, by force if necessary."

The violence spread like a forest fire. Throughout northeastern China, secret societies and peasants joined together, creating a widespread state of anarchy. The Boxers were openly murdering Chinese Christian converts, the so-called "secondary foreign devils."

On September 22, an urgent telegram arrived from mission headquarters in Minnesota: "Leave China immediately stop, repeat immediately." A week later, Carl Landahl and his new wife, Alice, arrived in Fancheng by boat, having fled their mission in Taipingtien with nothing but the clothes on their backs.

Halvor wired Shanghai to secure passage on a freighter leaving Shanghai in December 1899. The problem was how to get to Shanghai. He could not find a *laopan*, junk captain, willing to take them downriver to Hankow. The French Catholics and Swedish Lutherans had left a week earlier. *Pray for us, brother, the viceroy of Hubei is a man of intelligence who sees the folly of the royal edict. He is not yet willing to carry it out. We have many faithful Chinese friends who have offered their help if needed.*

Another warning was tacked on their gate: "The foreign devils disturb the Middle Kingdom urging the people to join their religion, to turn their backs on

Heaven, to venerate not the gods, and forget the ancestors. Foreign men violate human obligations, women commit adultery. Foreign devils are not produced by mankind. If you doubt this, look at them carefully. The eyes of all foreign devils are blueish."

The residents of Fancheng remained behind barred gates. Many hid Chinese Christians in their homes. The mandarin sent word urging the missionaries to leave immediately but offered no protection. Each night the Boxers got bolder. They banged on the locked gates and sang out their threats in unison: "No rain falls because the Christian religion stops the heavens. The gods are angry, the genii are vexed; both have come down from the mountains to deliver the doctrine. This is not hearsay. Burn the written prayers, light the incense sticks, exterminate the foreign devils. Push aside the railway tracks, pull out the telegraph poles; immediately after this, destroy the steamers. May the whole elegant empire of the great Qing Dynasty be ever prosperous!" Bloodcurdling screams of "death to the foreigners" pierced the night air.

The mandarin had no authority to control the Boxers, and a general uprising was feared. Chinese Christians from the countryside came to the mission with dreadful rumors. Foreign missionaries in Shanxi and Henan Provinces fled for their lives. The railroad from Peking to Hankow had been torn up. Christian refugees headed toward Fancheng, hoping to go downriver to Hankow. One man, Lao Li, sought refuge at the mission after having been almost beaten to death. Li said that in his village, thirty miles upriver, more than a hundred Chinese Catholics had been murdered and their homes burned. He said that the Boxers had offered to spare those who stamped on a picture of Jesus and renounced Christianity, but none would do so. At one home they killed the whole family except for two small boys. Lao Li tried to stop the killing, but they beat him unconscious. "When I opened my eyes I saw their headless bodies. The house was burning. I fled to the river bank and collapsed, thinking it was the end for me." The postman found Lao Li and brought him to the mission.

Early the next morning Halvor, in Chinese clothes, went with Evangelist Sen to the cable office in Hsiangyang to send urgent telegrams to the American minister in Peking, Edwin H. Conger, and the American consul general in Hankow. He reported the massacre of the Catholics and warned that all foreigners and Chinese Christians in the interior of China were in grave danger. He requested that American gunboats be sent immediately to evacuate the Christians, signing the message "Immanuel" (God be with us). On the way back, a group of men followed Halvor and Sen to the mission gate, and when the old gatekeeper, Da Sun, opened the gate, the men let loose with a hail of stones. Sen was struck on his back. As Halvor helped him through the gate, a ruffian grabbed the gatekeeper and dragged him into the street, where the whole mob began beating him. Carl Landahl and Halvor ran out, yelling and swinging sticks, until the mob backed away. The gatekeeper remained unconscious for an hour before Dr. Himle could revive him.

That night the missionaries, with loaded rifles at hand, planned their escape. The Boxers were inspecting all rivercraft suspected of carrying foreigners. Halvor considered putting the women and children in water barrels to be pulled in carts by the men disguised as Chinese coolies. When the barrels proved too small, they decided to dress as soldiers and ride out of the city on horseback, but they were unable to find uniforms. They even thought about dressing as a band of beggars, but the risk was too great: their blue eyes would betray them. Escape seemed hopeless. The city was in ferment. Robbers and rioters, sometimes in the garb of Boxers or members of other secret societies, were fighting in the streets. At night the "King of Thieves" and his band of "honorable robbers" guarded the mission gate, but he would not agree to escort the missionaries out of the city. Why should he lose his rice bowl?

The next morning a runner arrived bearing an urgent message from the postman: "Make haste. You must fly tonight! The Iron Fists have sworn to kill you tomorrow. They have been encouraged by reports that the Empress is sending troops against the foreigners in Peking. There is a junk beside the post dock; look for the sign of the Red Spear Society. Bring money." Sen promised to carry on the work of the mission school and orphanage as best he could. Dr. Himle, who had elected to remain in Fancheng, volunteered to escort the Ronnings to Hankow and then return to work in the mission.

That night Carl and Alice Landahl, the Ronnings, and Himle donned black caps and peasant garb and headed for the waterfront. The King of Thieves, looking every inch the part, escorted them through the South Gate. The moon was too bright for comfort, but they had no trouble reaching the Red Spear Society junk with a red-handled spear painted on the prow. Halvor handed the King some cash. The King hesitated a moment and shook his head. "But you can't refuse," said Halvor. "You are the King of Thieves."

The King, with a wide grin, accepted his fee. "May the winds be favorable, honorable Teacher."

A man in black pajamas standing on deck of the junk motioned for them to hide below. The captain demanded three hundred taels, or about one hundred dollars, an outrageous sum, but Halvor could not risk an argument, so he agreed to pay half now and half when they reached Hankow. They crowded into a small, hot cabin. Before the captain could pull up the gangplank and cast off, a gang of Boxers came running toward the junk shouting, "Kill the long hairy ones."

The captain tried to stop them, but they shouted: "Kill him too! He is a secondary hairy one. Kill them all!" The captain ordered a coolie to run to the mandarin for help. There was no stopping the Boxers now. About ten of them swarmed onto the boat. Halvor commanded Hannah to hide the children. Himle took them below. Halvor grabbed an oar from the deck and began to swing wildly. Carl found a rope. Both men fought as never before, calling loudly for the Lord's cooperation as they struck out savagely at anyone within their reach.

Below the deck, Hannah and Alice were terrified. Unable to find a place to hide, Hannah squatted on the floor trying to hide Almah under her skirt. "Oh, God, save us now!" Himle grabbed a sword from the wall and joined the battle on deck. Hannah could stand it no longer. She took a wooden stool as a weapon and ran out. "Guard the kids!" she called to Alice. Terrified by the brawl on deck, she jumped on the cabin roof. Halvor and Carl were standing back to back against the mainmast holding their own against the Boxers, with Halvor swinging his oar and lashing out with his foot, Carl whipping his rope like a western cowboy, and the good Dr. Himle thrusting his sword like a scalpel. A Boxer looked up and saw Hannah atop the cabin. "Ai ya! More foreign devils!"

She smashed him on the head with the stool. He rolled back on the deck. Then, to her horror, she saw the captain and the sailors advancing toward Halvor with their spears ready. "Look out, Halvor!" she yelled. She felt a hand on her ankle, pulling at her; she swung the stool blindly and heard a thud. A startled face looked up at her. "Shoo!" she said, and stamped her foot. "Out, Out!" The victim ran off screaming. When Hannah looked for Halvor, she saw the captain and crew fighting with the missionaries against the Boxers.

"Oh, thank G—," but her prayer was interrupted by a fresh volley of stones being hurled from shore. Halvor was hit full in the chest and fell to the deck on his back, feet up. Two Boxers leapt on him. By this time, Chester and Nelius were on deck, eager to join the fighting.

Years later Chester gleefully recounted the events: "One fellow landed, stomach down, on the soles of Papa's two feet and found himself suspended in air. Papa launched a quick kick and catapulted the surprised Boxer up and over the railing into the river on the deep side. You know, very few Chinese can swim. He let out such a scream of terror that the others froze in their tracks. Papa jumped up and with a savage yell dived off the rail into the water after the Boxer. We thought he was going to drown him."

Now the battle was forgotten. Boxers, rabble, sailors, and missionaries almost tipped the junk by running to the side of the deck to look. There was no visible trace of either the missionary or the Boxer—only a flurry of ominous bubbles. Carl was about to dive in after Halvor when two heads appeared. Halvor, swimming on his back, had his left arm clenched around the Boxer's neck. He towed him ashore. The Boxer looked dead. Everyone, including Chester and Nelius, ran down the gangplank. Dr. Himle laid the Boxer face up and applied artificial respiration. There was total silence. Minutes seemed like hours. The Boxers crowded closer, encircling the missionaries. "They are surely killing him. They really are devils. This proves it." "What are we waiting for? We have them now! Let's kill them!"

Although some joined in heaping scurrilous abuse on the missionaries, no one lifted a hand against them. Instead they waited, watching the doctor suspiciously. The suspense seemed endless. The missionaries knew that if Himle failed to resuscitate the man, they would all be killed. Perspiration rolled down the doctor's face as his hands attempted to press and pull. The mood of the crowd was dangerous. "Keep calm," whispered Halvor as he put his arms around Hannah and the children. The mob was losing patience. With evil looks, sinister innuendoes, and threatening gestures, the Boxers left no doubt as to what they were intending to do. They began to discuss how they should put the missionaries to death. "Build a fire," cried one, "roast them!" "No, no," shouted another, "they should be beheaded like common criminals."

"Who are they talking about, Papa?" asked Chester in alarm.

"Be calm my son. God is with us."

Suddenly the Boxer moaned. "He lives!" cried Himle. This was the second time he had brought a Chinese patient back to life. Tears and sweat rolled down his face. The missionaries gave thanks to Jesus Christ, but the Boxers quickly took all the credit.

"He lives! Now you see," cried the head Boxer. "We are invulnerable! We can live forever! This proves it."

The junk captain touched the man and found he was indeed alive. The Boxer sat up and coughed. The captain must have thought he had seen a miracle but wasn't quite clear who had accomplished it. The winds were favorable. He cast off quickly and headed the junk downriver toward Hankow.

The missionaries remained on constant guard. At night the captain tried to locate a deserted cove to anchor, but it was impossible to find a deserted place in China, and no one could be trusted. When food supplies dwindled, the Ronnings shared the remains of their tea, two hams, and a box of oranges with the crew, who in turn shared their preserved fish, fermented bean curd, and kumquats. Occasionally Halvor would catch a fish, but as they were obliged to stay in the middle of the river where the current was strong, the fish were few. Halvor shot two geese. The crew members grew fond of the children, who spoke like natives, without their parents' foreign accents, and the captain took delight in teaching the boys riddles and nursery rhymes.

About seven days from Fancheng, the captain spotted a gunboat approaching from behind and ordered the missionaries to hide. It pulled alongside. "Aye, there!" someone called in broken Chinese. "Have you seen any foreigners on the river?"

Halvor recognized the voice. Sure enough! There was Sanford, the grizzly old English sailor he had met on the Yangtze River steamer. His curly red beard was now salted with white, but his nose was as bulbous and purple as ever. What a sweet sight. Halvor hurried on deck and waved: "Hey, Sanford! You old scoundrel. We're here! Thank the Lord you have come. We're starving!" Sanford flashed a gap-toothed grin. "Aye, Preach, we've been looking for ya. Where the 'ell 'ave you been?"

Halvor thanked the captain and crew for saving their lives and paid generously for passage. "We'll pray for you."

Captain Sanford dropped a thin rope Jacob's ladder onto the deck of the junk. The missionaries and children climbed up carefully, one by one.

"And we will pray for you, honorable Teacher," yelled the captain.

Halvor laughed as he climbed the ladder carrying little Almah.

On board, Halvor and Sanford embraced like old buddies. The gunboat was heading for Hankow loaded with refugee missionaries from the interior. They looked as weary as the Ronnings. Hannah noted that the British gunboat was the dirtiest little steamer that ever the eye of man beheld, but to the refugees, it was beautiful. Although some of the passengers were wounded and still wearing their bloody clothing and others lacked shoes and shirts, they could not have been a more grateful crowd. They were the fortunate ones. Hundreds of others had been massacred by the Boxers, but that story would not be known for months. In the ship's saloon, the flies were thicker than black molasses. The missionaries deferred to the miserable insects and ate their scanty meals on deck. There were no sleeping accommodations, so they were obliged to sleep on deck—men on one side, women and children on the other. Hannah could not help laughing at the curious spectacle they must have presented lying like rows of sardines wrapped in rugs and huddled together for warmth. Although it was hot when the sun shone, the chilly wind whistled around them at night, and they shivered in spite of the rugs. Nelius and Chester looked at the gentle, smiling face of their mother and thought everything was fine. It had all been a great adventure. The gentlemen gave up their blankets to the ladies. Halvor crept over more than once each night to see if Hannah and the children were all right. Carl Landahl kept a constant watch on Alice, and she seemed to blossom under his attention. During the day they huddled together in small groups exchanging escape stories.

The Ronnings did not realize the extent of the turmoil they had left behind until they heard the heartrending tales of the other missionaries. The Reverend Walter Seaman, an English Presbyterian, had escaped with his wife and two children from Shandong, where hundreds of Christians had been murdered in the past few months. They had been given no protection even though they had made their plight known to Mr. Conger, the American minister in Peking, who did not believe his own countrymen because the Manchu officials had assured him that all was peaceful. Captain Sanford had managed to rescue about seventy-five missionaries. His offer of rum was eagerly accepted, even by the teetotalers. Three days later, they steamed into Hankow just as the sun was rising in all its glory over the Yangtze. To Hannah, this feast of color was God's reward. She would never forget the glorious glow that pervaded the whole scene and stirred her very soul.

While waiting in Hankow for a steamer to take them down the Yangtze to Shanghai, the Ronnings met two American Presbyterian missionaries, the Reverend Edmond Simcox and his wife, Ellen May, with their three children, all born in China. Chester and Nelius were happy to find kids their own age. The Simcox family was on the way back to Paotingfu (today's Baoding), a mission station about 120 miles southwest of Peking in Zhili Province. Mrs. Simcox, a warm, vivacious woman in her mid-twenties with expressive brown eyes and dark auburn curls, was dedicated to missionary work. Ellen May and her husband had met at Grove City College in Pennsylvania. In her junior year she was drawn to foreign missionary work. Halvor strongly advised Edmond Simcox to leave China because of the antiforeign uprisings, but the determined missionary claimed that in Paotingfu everything was peaceful; he was confident the Lord would protect him and his family. When they parted, Ellen May Simcox wrote a short verse in Hannah's autograph book:

> Life is a leaf of paper white
> On which each one of us may write
> His word or two, and then comes night.

Hannah did not realize, until after she had heard of the horrible massacre of missionaries at Paotingfu, how prophetic the message was.*

Coming from a walled city in the interior where the only foreigners were missionaries, Nelius and Chester had never seen a foreign-occupied city like Hankow, but it was not long before they witnessed an example of foreign control. One afternoon Halvor took the boys walking down a paved, tree-lined street in the German Concession. He had donned his preacher's coat for the occasion. As they passed the manicured front lawn of a large house flying a German flag, the boys stopped to stare at a Chinese man chained by his feet to a huge block of cement. Around his neck was a large square frame made of heavy wooden planks. The prisoner could hardly reach his mouth through a small hole in the frame. Their father tried to hurry by the sordid scene, but the boys were riveted by the sight. The victim pleaded with his eyes. Chester began to cry: "Papa, how can Christians behave like heathens?" Having known only missionaries, Chester assumed that all foreigners were good Christians.

His father tried to explain that in China foreigners were above the law: "You are too young to understand. This is not China, but a foreign concession in China. The man has perhaps done something wrong and is being punished all out of proportion to his crime. You see, all foreigners in China have extraterritoriality. But that is too big a word for you." Suddenly Halvor turned back. "This is too much! Wait here!"

Chester and Nelius watched in amazement as their father strode to the gate, defied the armed guards, and forced his way into the manicured yard. He loosened his white collar and pounded the brass door knocker. After some wrangling with the Chinese servant, the German owner came puffing to the door and to his astonishment recognized Halvor as the missionary in Fancheng whom he had asked to persuade the Chinese to let the Germans build a railway from Hankow to Fancheng. Chester had never seen his father so angry. "Why are you torturing this man?" demanded Halvor.

The red-faced German said the man was the amah's husband and had stolen food from the kitchen. "Papa," recalled Chester many years later in his *Memoir of China in Revolution*, "took some money out of his pocket and offered to pay the German for the food if he would release the man. Papa pointed to the wretched

*For an account of the events in Paotingfu, see Isaac C. Ketler, *The Tragedy of Paotingfu: An Authentic Story of the Lives, Services and Sacrifices of the Presbyterian, Congregational and China Inland Missionaries Who Suffered Martyrdom* . . . (New York: Fleming H. Revell, 1902).

man and shouted in an angry voice: "*Dummkopf!* Don't you understand? This is the very reason the Chinese refused to let you build the railroad!" The embarrassed German released the man, who ran for his life. At the age of five it was not easy to understand "extraterritoriality," but Chester did begin to understand why the Chinese were antiforeign.

A week later they steamed into Shanghai. Hannah mailed a letter to let her family know they were safe. *December 1899. Dear Mama: Thank the Lord! We have finally arrived in Shanghai, all safe and sound. In the morning we shall continue our journey to Telemark, where we will spend the rest of the summer before returning to Iowa. I can hardly believe it. Carl and Alice Landahl will sail to San Francisco. Oh when will men learn that violence is never an answer to our problems? Love is the only answer. That is all I really know. Your beloved daughter and sister Hannah.*

The Reverend and Mrs. Halvor N. Ronning, 1891.
Ronning Family Archive

Teacher Sen with young missionaries Halvor Ronning (clean-shaven), Daniel Nelson, and Johannes Brantzaeg, 1892. This photo was taken just before the missionaries' first journey up the Han River to Fancheng. *Ronning Family Archive*

Hankow waterfront on the Han River.
Ronning Family Archive

Halvor's sister Thea, Hannah, baby Nelius, and Halvor, 1893. Nelius was born in Hankow.
Ronning Family Archive

A view of the compound of the Lutheran mission in Fancheng, with Halvor's church at center (enclosed in white wall).
Ronning Family Archive

The living room of the Ronnings' house in Fancheng. Note the photo of Halvor on skis, propped on the settee.
Ronning Family Archive

The streets of Fancheng, 1894.
Ronning Family Archive

A formal photo of the eldest son of the Hsiangyang civil mandarin and his new wife, 1894.
Ronning Family Archive

The Ronnings' cook and amah with their children,
playmates of Nelius and Chester.
Ronning Family Archive

Young Nelius and Chester with their amahs (*left front*), with servants and friends at Halvor's mission. Hannah is at the far right.
Ronning Family Archive

Halvor's professor of Chinese philosophy in Fancheng, 1894.
Ronning Family Archive

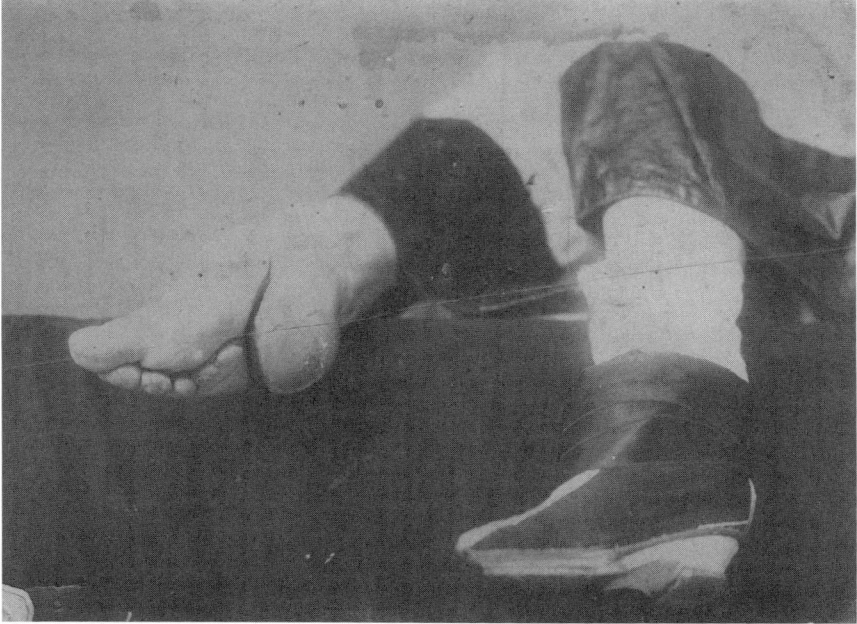

Unbound foot of a young Chinese girl showing disfigurement, 1894. Only girls with unbound feet were allowed to enter Hannah's school.
Ronning Family Archive

The Ronnings' gardener takes four-year-old Chester (*left*), Hannah, and Nelius riding in an old-style Chinese wheelbarrow, 1898. Many Chinese families traveled this way on short trips.
Ronning Family Archive, photograph by Halvor Ronning

Halvor (holding daughter Almah) and Dr. Thorstein Himle (holding son Sven), with Chester, Edwin Himle, and Nelius seated at their feet. Fancheng, 1898.
Ronning Family Archive

Reverend Li, a Christian convert who later became pastor at Fancheng, and Mr. Hsu, the doctor.
Ronning Family Archive

Halvor (*far left*) with students and teachers outside Fancheng city gate, 1898.
Ronning Family Archive

Belltower and wall surrounding the Lutheran mission compound in Fancheng. This is the wall Halvor scaled, losing his Chinese pigtail, as he retreated from a hostile mob in 1899.
Ronning Family Archive, photograph by Halvor Ronning

Hannah and Halvor with Chester, Almah, and Nelius in Hankow, 1899.
Ronning Family Archive

Members of the Red Spears secret society during the Boxer Uprising.
Ronning Family Archive

The Ronnings as they returned to China after the Boxer Uprising, 1901. Another boy, Talbert (*seated, center*), has joined the family.
Ronning Family Archive

Chester and Nelius in Chinese clothes, Fancheng.
Ronning Family Archive, photograph by Halvor Ronning

The Ronnings on the balcony of their home in Fancheng, 1903. Nelius is on the left with a Chinese friend; Halvor is at center with Almah and Talbert; Hannah stands with the twins Hazel and Harold; and Chester is playing the flute on the right.
Ronning Family Archive

Halvor's high school in Fancheng, 1905. Halvor is on the far right.
Ronning Family Archive

Hsu Ta-yin, one of Halvor's former students, gave him this portrait as a gift.
Ronning Family Archive

Hannah's Bible class, 1906. Note the bound feet of the Chinese women. Hannah is seated on the far right.
Ronning Family Archive

Teacher Huang, Halvor's friend and a fellow pastor, holding a candle in memory of Hannah after her death.
Ronning Family Archive

Halvor Ronning stands alongside the tombstones of his sister Thea (d. March 23, 1898) and wife Hannah (d. February 9, 1907). The tombs still stand to this day in the courtyard of the school Halvor and Hannah founded in 1894. *Ronning Family Archive*

Nelius, thirteen, and Chester, twelve, with father Halvor in 1907, after mother Hannah's death. The boys were preparing to leave Fancheng for school in Iowa.

Ronning Family Archive

Reverend Ronning's congregation gathered to bid farewell to Nelius and Chester (in front with hats), 1907.
Ronning Family Archive

PART II

HOME
LEAVE
and
RETURN

"Foreign Devils" in the Homeland

WELCOME HOME

How swift was your departure,
How slow your coming home!
Let's drink deeply of the good warm wine,
And drown the years between.
—SU CHANYI,
SUI DYNASTY (AD 581–618)

In Shanghai, the Ronnings boarded the *Villanger,* a 20,000-ton Norwegian freighter, to sail along the east coast of the Pacific to the Indian Ocean, with stops in Ceylon and Alexandria, Egypt. They then proceeded through the Suez Canal on to Germany, from where they went by train to Naples. There Hannah bought Chester a smooth little mouse carved out of red marble from Mt. Vesuvius. He kept it in his pocket so he could feel the cool marble as they continued by train to Florence and Rome. Hannah thrived in this exhilarating atmosphere where she could forget about the suffering Chinese.

The last part of the journey from Liverpool across the North Sea to Norway was by far the worst. Years later, Chester remembered how terrified he was when the boat pitched and screeched its way over the gigantic waves. His father, however, seemed to love it. Halvor stood on the bow, wet hair flying, coat collar upturned, braced stiff against the wind, searching the dawn for the first glimpse of his beloved homeland. Finally some high cliffs and a long shoreline appeared in the distance. It was Norway! Halvor ran below to get Hannah and the children. "Hurry, hurry!" he called, as if Norway were about to disappear any minute. "It's Norway! I can see Norway!"

Halvor ignored Hannah's protests. He scooped Almah up in one arm, dragged Chester by the other hand, and headed for the bow. "Let this old steamer roll to its heart's content," he called to them. "Let the wind blow and burst its cheeks, let the spray leap as high as it wants! What do we care? This is Norway!"

The boys were caught up in their father's wild enthusiasm. All memories of China were forgotten. They stood wet and wind-lashed, watching spellbound as the land of their ancestors, furrowed and weather-beaten, emerged out of the North Sea.

The next morning they hit calmer waters as they steamed up the Oslo fjord toward Norway's capital. By afternoon they were walking up Carl Johan Street to buy some Norwegian outfits. Nelius and Chester put on Western clothes for the first time in their lives. They burst out laughing when their father showed them what suspenders were for. Then, in their strange garb, they strode self-consciously among all the tall, fair-haired people who resembled their parents—the ladies in long skirts and strange bonnets, and the men in hats like their father.

"Papa, why do the men bob their hats?" asked Chester. Halvor told them to speak Norwegian, but their mother answered in English.

"That's the way gentlemen greet ladies in Norway," she explained.

"Ay ya!" shouted Nelius, "what funny people these barbarians are." The boys put their hands over their mouths and doubled up with laughter until their father reminded them that they were the ones acting like barbarians. He explained that these people were Norwegians, the natives of Norway, and that the Chinese were the foreigners here. But, for the first time in their lives, the boys felt like foreigners, even if they did not look it.

The Ronnings took a small steamer to Aarnes in Telemark, where three horse-drawn wagons were waiting to carry them and their trunks filled with gifts the seven miles to Halvor's family farm in the Bo Valley. This is where Halvor's Teler forefathers had lived for generations. The oldest church record of the family goes back some seven hundred years to one named Steinod Folkstad. Halvor's namesake was a celebrated bishop named Halvor Folkstad, whose descendants were rich and powerful members of the rural aristocracy. The Ronnings made only hushed references to their un-Christian Viking ancestors but claimed that Eric the Red and Leif Ericson were among them. The Vikings in Telemark had been the last to forsake their Norse gods and accept Christianity. According to my father, because these things were told but not written down, one stubborn ancestor killed three priests who had dared to come to the valley to convert the heathen Vikings. But later, according to family lore, the old Teler repented and attempted to improve his manners: when he was drunk, he prayed to Thor, god of thunder, to let him stay drunk because if he sobered up he was afraid he would kill another priest. And now, ironically, the descendant of the converted heathen Viking was returning from his mission to convert the heathens in China, where he was treated no better than his ancestors had treated the early Christians in Telemark.

Some of the fiercest Vikings and rebels were Telers, but the area also produced great musicians, writers, poets, and painters. Telemark has been a land of romance from time immemorial. Halvor constantly reminded his children and grandchildren that Telemark had produced more fairy tales, legends, ballads, music, and songs than all the other parts of Norway combined. Nowhere, he claimed, had the old culture been better preserved than in Telemark.

The Telers finally embraced Christianity with the same zeal that they had fought it. The second of our forefathers to appear in the church record is one Halvor Ryan, who was born in 1580 and owned several farms in different parishes. Family lore claims that one of his five daughters brought him fame by marrying the king of the Bo Valley, where the family lives to this day. That was when every valley in Norway was a small kingdom. Halvor Ronning was the first Teler of his ancient clan to leave Norway, become an American, and go to China. His return, after sixteen years, caused a sensation in the valley.

Halvor recognized every glen, mountain peak, and hill where he used to ski with his five brothers and sisters; he was one of the early skiers who developed the "Telemark turn," which he later brought to Minnesota. Their carriages rolled past a picturesque waterfall and the old swimming hole that Halvor and his brothers had enjoyed so long ago. He pointed everything out to Hannah and the children and told them enthusiastically about the invisible realms that nourished the imaginations of Telemark's children.

Chester and Nelius were amazed at the change in their father. They wondered why he acted more like a Norwegian than a Chinese. When they spoke to their father in Chinese, he pretended he didn't understand and began to tell them stories in Norwegian. "As children we never ventured outside the wall of mountains surrounding our parish," he told them. "We knew nothing of the world beyond the mountains. We had a world of our own—a world of make-believe, but it was all very real to us." Nelius and Chester, holding hands with their little sister Almah, listened intently. "You see, in these mountains live the underground folk, *de underjordiske*. They are all around here. Keep your eyes open! The woods are full of trolls and little fairies called *fossegrim*. They even live in the waterfalls and sometimes play the violin. I never saw one myself, but your Uncle Nils told me he saw one. But I have heard their beautiful music in the distance. As children, we thought we had *nisser*, tiny men, living in our barn. They bring luck to the farmers, you know. Nils always used to put a bowl of cream-porridge out for them by the barn door on Christmas Eve. One of our neighbors forgot to do this one Christmas, and the next night when he put his horse in the barn, a *nisser* in knee pants and a three-cornered hat blocked his way. When the farmer tried to kick him aside, he found himself on his head in a pile of snow. He told Nils this himself, so it must be true." Halvor threw his head back and roared with laughter.

The children were delighted to learn that Telemark, like China, was full of invisible spirits. They had never heard their father talk like this before. "You sound just like Cook Liu," said Chester. He wondered why his father thought Norwegian spirits were funny and Chinese spirits were evil.

They pulled up by the old cemetery between two wooden churches standing on a hilltop overlooking the village. Halvor took the family to pay respects to his mother's last resting place in front of the old church. The family knelt at the grave. When they came over the last hill, Halvor could see his old home in the distance. He was coming home after sixteen years abroad. It was the first time Chester had seen his father cry. "My heart," wrote Halvor later, "was filled with the sweet, solemn joy which is akin to pleasant pain."

The little wooden house with lace curtains, where uncounted generations of Ronnings had lived, was surrounded by flower-decked meadows and green fields, with a fruit orchard on one side and snowcapped mountains on the other. In one corner stood the old apple tree that Halvor's father had once wanted to cut down, but Nils had stood in front and begged tearfully for its life. It sparkled with fine apples now. There were people in the garden looking up the road expectantly. Halvor grabbed the reins and urged the horses into a gallop. The wagons bounced down the slope accompanied by great Viking whoops of joy from the returning missionary. Relatives and friends crowded around them. Chester was almost crushed by a hug from Uncle Svein, Halvor's older brother, who wore the same brush mustache as Halvor. Chester's two new aunties, Mari and Hildeborg, smelled good and reminded him of his Auntie Thea. The Ronning clan all lived with their own families in wooden chalet houses with lace curtains on farms spread neatly around the Bo Valley.

Old Ronning stood silently in the doorway until the excitement died down. Nils had arrived from America two days earlier. He later wrote about Halvor's homecoming: *Father and son embraced each other in silence. Everyone sensed that Mother and Thea were not there. No words could express their feelings, so no words were spoken.*

Halvor's father, Sven, my great-grandfather, had been the superintendent of road building in Telemark. He had a splendid voice and knew many ballads, which put him in great demand as an entertainer at social gatherings. According to family lore, he became famous in Telemark for a very strange reason. In Skaane, Sweden, in 1848, he was a soldier in training, preparing to join the

Danes in fighting Germany. The Norwegian-Swedish king, Oscar the First, came to the Teler camp and learned that Ronning was an expert dancer. To test him, the king placed a hat on a high pole. When Sven made a *hallingkast*, or a high kick, and sent the hat spinning to the ground, the king laughed aloud. The story made headlines in Norway. When Halvor tried to demonstrate to his boys how his father had kicked the hat, he landed on his back on the ground, causing their grandfather to roar with laughter. The old athlete's famous legs had been injured in a landslide. Now he hobbled on a gnarled applewood cane. His still strong but lined features were framed with white hair and a full triangular beard.

Halvor's old friends had come to greet him. He saw how time had chiseled furrows of sorrow and care into their faces. Those who were old when he left were now tottering toward the grave, the middle-aged had become old, and the children were now young men and women. The mountains had endured, but the people had changed.

Inside the house, however, Halvor found everything the same: the wide fireplace with the red bellows and iron kettles where his mother had done the cooking, the hand-carved Mother Hubbard holding blue-and-white china. The old rocking chair, the dining table, the wooden chairs, the bedposts, and the spinning wheel had all been painted with intricate, intertwining *roser* flowers by his grandfather, my great-great-grandfather, a skilled *rosenmaler* whose paintings can still be found in a museum in Oslo. He mixed his own paints and made his brushes of feathers and hair. Only on the table did Halvor see something different: a pile of well-read letters from China.

Over the next month, old friends and other people came from all over Telemark to meet the missionary and his family. They listened to stories of China and admired the strange curios Hannah had bargained for and packed in camphor trunks to bring to Halvor's family. The Norwegians could hardly believe that the heathen Chinese could produce so many beautiful things. The Ronning brothers explored the old haunts and rode horses to the *saeter* in the mountains to camp out. Nils took the boys on a hike up the mountain to see the charred remains of an old hut that had once stood proudly in a grove of silvery birch trees. It had been the home of Nils's favorite storyteller, Eilef Braaten. He had called his cabin Valhalla, the home of the gods, but the only similarity between his tumbledown dwelling and heaven was that both were far removed from the people below. According to Nils, Eilef Braaten was one of those storytellers in Telemark who had planted the seeds that made Norway a land of literature.

Nils wrote: *It was interesting to get acquainted with Nelius, six and a half; Chester, four and a half; Almah, two and a half. They spoke a delightful mixture of Chinese,*

English and Norwegian. The boys asked me to tell them a story. Boys are funny. Nils told them that Eilef was the king of storytellers. His greatest joy as a child was when he saw the troll-like figure of Eilef limping down the mountain leaning heavily on the axe he used as a cane and carrying a bundle of mysterious rags on his back. Halvor and Nils would scramble up the path to meet him. "Have these rascals been good since I was here?" he would ask their mother, and the children would scream with delight because they knew that after he had eaten a bowl of their mother's finest porridge, they would all gather around the fire and listen to Eilef's fairy tales.

Nils never forgot the spell the little old man cast upon the whole household: *We sit there with large shiny eyes and swallow every word. Soon we are far away in distant places, moving among kings and queens or visiting the "Palace East of the Sun and West of the Moon." Father, who is reading the newspaper, looks hard at the page but sees nothing; Mother stops in the middle of the floor. There is perfect silence in the room except for the crackling of the fire and Eilef's low, pleasant voice. Eilef was conscious of the power he could wield, and he found great pleasure in stopping when he came to the most dramatic places. At this point he would be seized by a sudden fit of coughing or reach out for a piece of wood to throw on the fire. If he had stood up and walked out, I believe the whole family would have followed him to his cabin on the mountain.* One spring, coming down the mountain to visit the Ronnings, Eilef fell through the ice on the river and drowned. The Ronning children never forgot the sweetness and light he had shed on their childhood.

The summer passed all too swiftly. The last evening, neighbors came uninvited bearing cakes and rich pastries. Halvor was moved to speak some words of farewell: "To come from the dust and sorrow of Chinese cities filled with strangers to the peaceful parish of Bo with its inhabitants of the same blood, speech, and faith was like slipping from the turmoil of life into a delightful dream. But, alas it cannot last. We must return again to our work in China."

Before returning to China, they planned to visit Hannah's home in Iowa. Nils left Telemark with his brother and family to travel first to Oslo, and then across the North Sea to England. Their dream turned into a nightmare when, while passing through a gate in Oslo, Halvor scratched his arm on a rusty nail. As they crossed the North Sea, his arm began to swell and turn color. By the time they reached Liverpool, Halvor feared the worst. The doctor uttered ominous words: "blood poisoning!" On his orders, they canceled their plans to sail to America and moved into a hotel.

For two long weeks, Hannah and Nils took turns caring for Halvor. Hannah was expecting another baby, so Nils bore the brunt of the work. He slept in his clothes with an alarm clock beside him so that he could change his brother's poultices every two hours. The pain was excruciating. The best doctors in the city, called in for consultation, concluded that the only hope of saving his life was to amputate the arm. Halvor refused, demanding that they lance the arm instead. After stern warnings, they finally consented and thrust the knife into his arm in eight different places. There was no anesthetic, and the pain was so terrible that Halvor finally pleaded with them to stop cutting him up and amputate. Then Hannah stepped in and insisted they finish the lancing. She knelt in prayer. Halvor could never really explain what happened next, but his pain suddenly disappeared. He was still conscious and could see the ugly black pus draining out, but the arm seemed to belong to someone else. He felt detached from his body and, to the astonishment of his doctors, he relaxed completely. In a strange "out-of-body experience," he left his body in the bed while he floated joyfully around the universe. He later remembered every detail and even told his grandchildren how great it felt to fly among the planets. When he returned to full consciousness, the operation was over. The pain was still there but bearable.

The doctors agreed that Halvor would recover but insisted that he stay in bed for several weeks. The next ship, a luxury liner leaving from Liverpool, was due to sail for America in three days. Halvor said nothing, but as soon as the Liverpool doctors left, he sent for the ship's doctor, got up and dressed, and asked Hannah to put his arm in a sling. The children watched in amazement as their father opened the door for the doctor, invited him in, and walked back and forth, head high, laughing and talking about how quickly he had recovered. The doctor at first shook his head, but when Halvor insisted and kept up his bravado, he relented and gave Halvor and his family permission to sail with the ship. When the doctor left, the show was over, and Halvor staggered back to his bed and passed out.

Two days later on the crowded dock, it seemed like everyone had to bump into Halvor's sore arm. They were hoping for comfortable cabins, but because of their last-minute booking, they were forced to travel steerage. Chester and Nelius could not have cared less; they were bound for America, the "land of the free and the home of the brave," where, at last, they wouldn't feel like foreigners.

17

Hannah Returns Home

THE YEARS BETWEEN

So,
After all these long years,
You have come back!
But who can see on my sad heart
The scars graved deep
The unhealed wounds
Of the bitter years between?
—POETESS JIANG YUN,
   TANG DYNASTY (AD 618–907)

After nine years in the Middle Kingdom, Hannah was coming home again. Nils bade his loved ones farewell in New York and returned to Minneapolis, where he edited a newspaper called the *Friend*. The Ronnings boarded a train to Radcliff, Iowa. Three horse-drawn wagons waited to carry them the last lap to the Rorem family farm. Driving along a dirt road through waving wheat fields and tall, rustling corn, they soon came to the land where Hannah had spent her childhood. She knew every tree and every field. She could hardly hold back the tears as they drove across the green pastures where, as a young girl, she had ridden her horse like the wind, rounding up the cattle with her brothers. Could that be the same herd of fat jersey cows and two handsome bulls with long wide horns all grazing quietly? At the sight, the boys shouted with joy and the cattle raised their heads to stare curiously.

The old road was wider now and smoother. Hannah recognized the neighbor's house where her friend Belle Lexvold lived. Later, in 1957, Belle wrote about her first meeting with the Rorems:

> The Rorem family lived northwest of our place and they had four boys and three girls, and they each had an Indian pony, and herded hun-

dreds of cattle, and of course we all thought they were Indians, and we were afraid of them. One day the girls' ponies and some of their herd got stuck in big ponds close to our home, and they came and asked for help and we learned they were white people and also Norwegians. Boy, were we happy! It was a joyous feeling, and after that day Ed and I sat on their ponies with them every day whenever our folks would let us. The seven Rorem children were Austin, Ole, Tom, Edward, Julia, Hannah and Rebecca. Rebecca is my age and we still write letters. She lives in Robbinsdale, Minnesota, and is a mother of nine children. Our first school for three years was in the Rorem kitchen. When those terrible blizzards came, all the children had to stay overnight at our school house and Hannah and Tom would bring some of their little sheep, pigs, and chickens around the stove for fear they would freeze to death. We children had no fear. [Belle's husband, H. H. Lexvold, worked in the Ballard Bank in Radcliff. She lived to be 101.]

There was the scorched oak tree that had miraculously sprouted new branches after it had been struck by lightning. The old burned branches jagged out sharply. Then Hannah could see, at last, the big white house with green shutters where she had lived until, as sister Rebecca used to tell it, "she met her knight in shining armor and was swept away to the mysterious Celestial Kingdom." There they were: her mother, brothers, and sisters surrounded by dozens of children Hannah had never met. No one moved when she stepped out of the carriage; even the children stared in silence at the legendary aunt who had ventured around the world on a mysterious mission and had now returned with her husband and China-born children with their smelly camphor trunks and curious bamboo cases. Her family was all there: beautiful Julia, a little matronly now, and Rebecca, no longer a chunky girl of seventeen but a svelte woman with a handsome husband and a babe in her arms. Could that be gray at Austin's temples? He looked so wise—these young men must be his sons. There was her dashing brother Ole, holding his son Rufus; he now looked like Papa. And there was Tom, robust, ruddy-cheeked, shirt sleeves rolled up, tousled hair, smiling broadly with his arm slung carelessly around Edward, her youngest brother, who sported a mustache and wore an expensive stiff-collared suit that made him look older than Tom. Standing in the background was a white-haired figure, grown so old and bent—could it be her mother? Hannah walked slowly forward to put her arms around her mother, but the old lady held her at arm's length, squinting to see her daughter clear and straight. It was a long, silent, penetrating gaze.

Hannah was different. Her face was hauntingly gaunt; the high cheekbones, once hidden by teenage flesh, were now defined, giving her a sophisticated, almost mysterious aura. The Iowa cowgirl was gone forever. Hannah had taken on a new stateliness. Her hair was brushed high and rolled softly around her high forehead. Above the lace collar, her neck was long and graceful, and her skin, though smooth and creamy as a child's, was shaded slightly under her eyes. The hardships, sufferings, and violent deaths she had experienced in China had made something of her that Iowa never could. Mother Anna could see the pain in her daughter's eyes. They still blazed bright and blue as the Iowa sky, but they were deeper, sadder. But it did not matter to the old lady how Hannah had changed. This was still the baby she had cuddled and diapered, still the little girl she had laughed with, whose tears she had dried, whose hurts she had kissed and rocked away in the creaky old chair. Only now the wounds her daughter harbored could never be shared or understood. Where was the care-free, wild, laughing girl who rode bareback like an Indian brave? With a stab of pain, the mother realized that her daughter's hurt was now beyond her power to heal. She pulled her long-lost child to her breast, sudden tears streaming down her face. Mother Anna looked over Hannah's shoulder at Halvor, his arm still in a sling from the blood poisoning. He had changed, too. It was not only the robust ram's-horn mustache that had matured him. The young preacher who had come to Radcliff to raise money for China and stolen her daughter's heart had gained an appearance of authority and strength. He had acquired the dignity of a man of the cloth.

Then everyone was laughing and crying, hugging and kissing, whooping and hollering, and cooing over the children. Almah loved the emotional fuss and responded warmly like her mother, but Chester and Nelius hung back red-faced, kicking the dirt in their Norwegian boots, hopelessly embarrassed, peering from the corners of their eyes at this uncouth, un-Chinese behavior. Even the Norwegians in Telemark had shown more reserve. Hannah was delirious with joy. None of the others would ever know how she had longed for this moment. They would never know what it was like to be home, home again.

Three weeks after their arrival, Halvor wrote to Nils: *This is my first writing. The hand is still stiff but the sores are healed. A great reception was given us here, and we met many old friends and supporters. Hannah just looked over my shoulder and said, "Is it possible you are writing again?"*

Halvor was soon playing horseshoes and arm wrestling with Hannah's brothers, but he felt compelled to travel continually on fund-raising missions to visit other congregations of Norwegian Lutheran churches, Hauge Synod, and the United Lutheran Seminary. Generous offerings were received for his China mission. Hannah was glad to stay home doing family chores, waiting for her fourth baby to arrive. Without Chinese servants, the tasks of everyday life had a new excitement, and she was continually grateful for all the things she had once taken for granted. What a pleasure to make fresh bread with clean, vermin-free flour, to drink the clear water fresh from the well without boiling it for twenty minutes to kill deadly parasites, to churn real butter, drink cow's milk, and eat ice cream—most of all she loved the ice cream. She served it to the many visitors who came eager to hear about her experiences in China. But Hannah was trying to forget China and savor the memories of Iowa. Never had she seen such a glorious autumn. From the window of her own old room she watched the leaves on the aging maple flame yellow and red.

Hannah visited each one of her sisters and brothers in their homes and shared in the cooking, housecleaning, and washing while she talked with them, tenderly drawing them out, listening carefully to every detail of their lives, but somehow unable to tell them about her own life in China. It was too different. She began to realize she was not like them anymore. It was only in the evenings when they sang the old songs in harmony around the piano that she felt like a part of them again.

Before Hannah was born, her parents (my great-grandparents), Anna and Torgrim Rorem, with their five sons, had left their large farm, called Rorheim, on the island of Ombo, in the Stavanger fjord on the west coast of Norway, to sail for America. Torgrim's restless Viking blood had been stirred by glowing tales of a rich land with universities, libraries full of books, and freedom to expand beyond the limiting shores of Ombo. It was not an easy decision for the Rorems to leave Norway, the beloved land that had nourished their forefathers for centuries. At Rorheim there were three burial mounds from the Viking period, but the earliest ancestor recorded on the Rorem side was a Judge Halldar of Kroll, who died in 1256. Torgrim and his twin sister, Eli, were born in 1824. His mother called him a "bookworm" because he preferred reading to farming. He married Anna Tendeness, a Quaker from Erfjorod, and they had five sons. Torgrim was determined to give his sons the opportunity to attend good universities and seek their fortune in a land of opportunities not available on their beautiful but confined island home. He could not afford passage for his family on an ocean liner so, with the help of some neighbors, he rescued a condemned, ten-ton freighter from the shipyard and in a year, with shipbuilding techniques first used in the Viking ships, made it seaworthy. They set sail in 1867.

As a child, I listened to my great-uncle Tom, Hannah's older brother, tell stories about the adventures of his family while crossing the Atlantic Ocean. I met him long after he settled in Bardo, Alberta, and raised his family on a large farm with ten horses and lots of cattle. He was a big burly man with a raucous laugh and a weakness for beer. He was sometimes referred to as the black sheep of the family, and there were whispers that he had moved to Canada to get away from his pious family in Radcliff so he could drink beer in peace. He lived to be ninety-seven. We know this because when my father became the Canadian ambassador to Norway in 1956, he invited Uncle Tom to visit him there. Tom had left Norway at the age of six and was eager to return but couldn't get a passport because he didn't have a birth certificate. So Dad went to the old church in Tom's birthplace on the Island of Ombo and found proof of his birth. When Tom found out he was ninety-seven years old, he sent word to Dad that he was too old to travel. He died a few months later.

Uncle Tom liked to tell the story of when he went missing on the journey to America. He was six. When no one was looking, he would climb up the ship's mast into the crow's nest. But one night a sudden storm blew up and he was afraid to come down, so he went to sleep there. His parents were terrified that he had been swept overboard until his father discovered him sound asleep in the crow's nest. Uncle Tom had turned all the danger, illness, and suffering the family must have endured during their nine weeks crossing the Atlantic, crammed into the hold of a decrepit freighter, into a romantic adventure. Like most Norwegians who had endured the long northern winters and rejoiced in the short, beautiful summers with the midnight sun turning darkness into a white fantasy, they were not sufferers but were dreamers by inclination and optimists by nature.

The Rorems often talked about the good old days in Norway and the fun journey to America, but Hannah was aware that her mother, like most women, often bore the brunt of the suffering. She noticed how her mother sometimes sat silent, a pained little smile on her face and a resigned look in her eyes as she listened to her husband tell his friends about the trip. The others may have suffered a bit, Torgrim would sometimes admit, but not the Rorems, as they were from tough Viking stock. What an adventure it had been for the boys!

Then they would talk about the idyllic farm they left behind, with a beautiful view of the mountains and sea and delicious wild plums growing everywhere. It had always sounded like a paradise to Hannah. "Well, if it was so great, why did you leave?" she asked her father. "Well, we could not live on wild fruit and scenery alone," he mumbled.

After six weeks at sea, the Rorems cried tears of joy when the shores of New-foundland rose gradually out of the vast Atlantic. But the toughest part was yet to come. Their joy turned to sorrow when Canadian authorities refused to let them land because of the illness on board. Almost a third of the twenty-five pas-sengers had died of influenza. They were forced to spend another three weeks at sea, sailing from Newfoundland to Quebec, sharing the last box of wild plums they had brought from their farm. Torgrim liked to tell his children that their lives had been saved by the Norwegian plums. When they finally stepped ashore in Quebec, Torgrim fell on his knees, kissed the earth, and thanked the Lord. Almost every other family had lost at least one. It is hard to imagine how my great-grandmother Anna, with five children and expecting another, could have survived the journey.

From Quebec, the Rorems sailed up the St. Lawrence River and through the Great Lakes to Chicago, where they boarded a train to Fox River in La Salle County, Illinois. They spent their last penny buying a house surrounded by ha-zelnut trees. They were very poor. After fixing up their new home, the older boys picked baskets of nuts that they sold for fifty cents per milk pail. What little money they had left after buying food went to buy raw wool so that Anna could make her boys shirts and coats to wear to school. They all helped to wash, card, spin, and weave the wool the way Anna had learned from her mother in Norway. Torgrim carved wooden shoes for his sons, and Anna made their pants from gunny sacks. While the girls helped their mother with the housework, Tom and the older boys helped their father clear the land of trees and cockleburs so that they could plant corn and grain. When fall came, the boys pulled on their homemade clothes and wooden shoes and walked two miles through timberland and prairie to school. They were robust, fair-haired, and tall. Working on the land, they resembled their Viking ancestors, but dressed for school in coarse, ill-fitting clothes and speaking no English, they felt and looked like awkward clods. They soon became a prime target for the children of English-speaking settlers. The worst bullies were Elias Nelson's boys, led by the oldest one, Emall, who was not only big for his age but also a show-off. Tom often recalled how he and his brothers had to endure the taunts of the Nelson boys, who lived on the prairie beside the rough timberland where the Rorems lived. Tom was the youngest boy at school and because of his hot temper got teased unmercifully.

One day when the Rorem brothers were near the schoolhouse, Emall Nelson gave Tom a big push and said, "I'm going to cut a slice out of your cheek." Tom's temper flared. Emall was twice as big, but Tom challenged him to turn and fight. Emall slipped and fell, and before he could get up, Tom jumped on him and hit him over the head with the new wooden shoe his father had carved for him. The shoe split in half, and Emall ran crying to the schoolteacher. "The teacher blamed me, of course," said Uncle Tom, looking extremely put upon. "I thought she was a witch anyway because she always took the Nelson kids' part. The teacher tied my shoe together with some twine and, after a scolding, sent me walking the two miles back home with orders to tell Father what a bad boy I was. I was not sorry for Emall, but I was really sorry I had broken the shoe Papa had worked so hard to make. I arrived home tired, and afraid that Papa would punish me, but somehow Papa seemed to understand. He looked at me hard with those fierce eyes and touched my shoulder. Then without a word he went to his workbench. When I woke up the next morning, there was a new shoe beside my bed." Tom's eyes glistened with pride. "The next morning I walked back to school in my new shoe."

In two years, the Rorems had made about two hundred dollars selling nuts, and Torgrim purchased a half section of land on the prairie near the Nelsons. He bought a horse, and the boys took in the neighbor's cattle to herd at one dollar per head. In a month they could afford another horse, and the Rorem boys were in business. The first year they took in two hundred cattle and the second, four hundred. In four years, they saved more than $1,500. In 1868, Julia, Hannah's oldest sister and the first girl in the family, was born. Hannah was born in 1871, when her mother was forty-three. When she was a year old, the family moved to a new farm, four miles southwest of Radcliff in Hamilton County, Iowa, and invested all their hard-earned money in land and horses. The boys continued to herd cattle for the farmers in the area, which proved to be a very lucrative enterprise.

Shortly after their arrival in Iowa in 1874, their eighth and last child, a girl named Rebecca, was born. The Rorem family was complete at last. Torgrim and the boys built a two-story wooden frame house of which they were justly proud. There was no school, so Anna established her own school in the kitchen and hired a stern-looking teacher named Mrs. Sharpe, who lived with them. All eight children attended classes and were equally terrified by the little lady who seemed to have eyes in the back of her head. After a few years, they built a schoolhouse and called it the Rorem School.

The winters were cold and difficult. One winter Tom and his brother Austin got caught in a sudden Iowa blizzard and were lost for three days. Their father found them half-starved and freezing in the snow cave they had dug for shelter. It took them all a week to recover, but after that the adventure made for a great story.

It was not until Hannah was married and had children of her own that she began to comprehend the secret, unspoken sorrows behind the bravado of a Norseman. By that time it was, by necessity, so much a part of her own life that she could face the truth of it without resentment, even coming to treasure it. After all, we are what we think we are, she would say in her letters; why should we dwell on our suffering or shatter our dreams with reality? She knew that the real story of the hardships of the family's early days in Iowa would never be told, but as a child she believed every word her brothers said and was filled with a sharp envy because she had been born too late to be part of it all. "You had all the fun before I was born," she would say. "Just wait until I grow up and then I'll sail all over the world—I'll go everywhere—you'll see."

Hannah was especially fond of brother Tom, although she was sometimes concerned about his quick temper. By sixteen, he was the tallest of the five boys, who were all over six feet. Although he wrestled fiercely with his brothers, he was always kind and gentle with Hannah. When she was ten, he let her ride with him out on the range to help herd the cattle. The greatest danger, even on horseback, was the rattlesnakes, which could terrify the cattle and cause a stampede. The Rorem kids carried whips to frighten the rattlers. It took an alert and confident rider to control a horse. Tom was a crackerjack with his whip; Hannah had seen him snap the head right off a rattler with one crack. Then he would throw his big towhead back and, like his Viking ancestors, let out an evil, roaring belly laugh. Tom made beads from the rattles. Julia would never touch them, but Hannah and Rebecca wore them around their necks and listened to the rattles when they raced across the fields.

Hannah and Tom were the restless ones in the family. It seemed when they were together they could make fun out of almost anything. They loved to feel the wind in their faces as they galloped across the range at sundown standing up in the saddle. Hannah's long hair flew behind her like a flaming mane. She had her first brush with death when she was ten years old. Riding with Tom one hot dusty day, she felt an uncontrollable urge to swim in the cool waters of the pond waiting seductively in the nearby woods. Sighting her brother on the other side of the range, she quickly slipped into the woods, threw off her clothes, and jumped into the glorious water. Then she dressed and stretched out in the soft grass to let her hair dry. It was almost sundown when Tom noticed she was missing. He found her horse tied to a tree near the pond and suspected the rest. Dismounting, he crept toward the pond, hoping to catch her in the water, but she was lying on the bank facedown with her head resting on her right arm. Then, to his horror, he saw a huge rattlesnake curled near the tip of her right hand. His whip was back in the saddle, so he quickly found a stick. Slowly and quietly he stalked up to Hannah and then suddenly grabbed her by a foot and pulled her away. She woke up screaming and saw Tom beating the snake with the stick. Tom picked up the battered reptile and took it home to show the family. It was more than six feet long. Tom felt very proud of himself. Hannah looked at him with loving eyes and felt that she must have been spared because God had some important work for her to do.

The future, however, seemed light years away. By the time Hannah was in her teens, the Rorems had more than three hundred milk cows and seven hundred steers that had to be collected from the various farms every morning, driven to the grazing land, and returned at night. In the summer, the Rorem kids were in the saddle from dawn until dusk. The only social function for the girls was after church on Sundays, when the congregation would gather for coffee and cakes, but since even on Sunday the cattle had to be fed and the cows milked, Hannah and Rebecca took turns going to church; Julia, as the oldest girl, had priority. From the hot, dusty pastures, the sisters could hear the church bells ringing in the distance. How they longed to get out of their dirty britches and put on the Sunday dresses that Julia had made for them. What had once been Hannah's fun-filled adventures rounding up the cattle with her brothers had become a tedious chore, and she felt a deep yearning to escape—to sail the seven seas like her ancestors and experience the world beyond the wide, open range where she spent her days.

During her high school years, Hannah grew into a tall, beautiful woman with a zest for life. How she loved to dance! She could hardly wait for Saturday night, when she would dress up and go to the local squaredances with her brothers and sisters. Although their parents did not approve of dancing, nothing could dim their enthusiasm. When Torgrim refused to let Tom have the buggy and horses to drive to the dance hall, they walked the five miles there and back. After that, their mother gave in and let them have the carriage. When Hannah graduated from high school, her parents sent her twenty-five miles away to a Teacher's Normal School in Dexter. Oh, it seemed so far away! She had any number of attentive admirers who escorted her to the social functions there, but she longed for her family. When she received her teacher's certificate, she returned to Radcliff to teach at the Rorem School. But she could not find peace within herself. Her spirit was restless. Sometimes she would jump on her horse and gallop around the range. When her parents cautioned her about her recklessness, she just laughed. She still had the feeling that she was born to fulfill a special destiny. But what was her destiny? What was the meaning of her life? It was still only a vague, restless feeling deep inside her that drove her into impulsive acts in a wild search for expression.

Hannah's second brush with death also involved Tom. One hot, humid night in August, a fierce electric storm suddenly broke with tremendous force. Clouds spat out torrents of rain, thunder cracked, and lightning blazed until the heavens reeled. Hannah loved it. It gave her an odd sense of exhilaration, and energy seemed to shoot through her. She imagined the Norse gods at war, with Thor and Loki roaring across the sky in golden chariots drawn by flying white horses, lances clashing, sparking jagged streaks across the raging sky, illuminating the earth around her. Hannah felt strangely drawn to this mythical world. In her enthusiasm, she ran outside to see the full glory of the storm, to be a part of it. Her mother was horrified when she looked out the window to see Hannah dancing under the maple tree, arms outstretched, spinning around and laughing.

Tom saw her out the window and ran out calling, "Hannah! Are you crazy?" His cry was drowned out by a tremendous flash of light that exploded with a roar of thunder. Hannah was thrown to the ground, blinded momentarily by the light as a great ball of fire rolled up the red oak. Then the inferno was crashing toward her. Screaming, she sheltered her face with her arms—a hopeless gesture against certain destruction. Then she was rolling over and over as if being whirled by a strong wind. Why was she not afraid? When the crash came, she was covered by soft, wet leaves. They felt warm and protecting. She wanted to lie under them forever. Tom, grim and shaking, pulled her out. Her father, who had been ill, jumped out of bed and ran out to help Tom. When she stood up unhurt, Papa put his arms around her and cried, sobbing aloud. She was confused. She had never heard her father cry. Then she realized what had happened. She was alive! She had been struck by lightning and was saved. It was a kind of miracle. She was in a daze. Why? She wondered. Why? Tom and Papa carried her into the house.

"I'm sorry, Papa," she kept saying. "Oh, I'm so sorry! Forgive me, Papa, I don't know why I ran out. It was just such a glorious sight."

That night Hannah prayed as she had never prayed before. "Dear Jesus, have mercy upon me, a sinner, come into my heart and help me find my way." She didn't know that her father had entered the room until she saw him standing beside the bed, looking down at her with his dark, understanding eyes. She broke into tears. "Oh, Papa, I don't understand myself." He put his hand on her head and said softly, "It's all right, Hannah . . . It's all right now." A flow of comforting warmth spread through her body. "Thank you, Papa," she whispered.

A week later, her father, Torgrim Rorem, was dead. No one in the family was able to comprehend the words of the doctor. "Mr. Rorem is dying," he said sadly. "The flu has developed into influenza . . . There is no way to save him." The family gathered around the bed. Torgrim took his wife's hand and said hoarsely, "Do not worry, Anna, I have prayed to God that all my children will come to Jesus and be saved and He told me that my prayers would be answered . . . so you see it's all right . . ." His voice trailed off, and with one last gasp, he died.

That night Hannah gave herself to God. She had no idea what God would do with her or even if He would accept her, but she was ready. "Show me the way!" She slept peacefully for the first time in months. The maple tree lay seared and broken in the garden. Sticky, orange sap oozed slowly out of the burned trunk. Two months later, the handsome missionary came to town on his way to China, and Hannah Rorem's prayer was answered. Her life was changed forever.

Sixteen years later, in her old bedroom on a clear Sunday morning in autumn, Hannah gave birth to her third son. How good it was to be surrounded at a time like this by loving sisters and a ministering mother. She looked at this wondrous creation she had brought forth and gave thanks for another miracle. Blue eyes, light hair, dimple in his chin. She laughed at the resemblance to his brothers. "He's a Ronning all right!" She hugged him to her breast and felt the deep well of motherly love renew itself. Halvor picked up his new son more roughly than Hannah approved of. The church bells rang in the distance as Halvor held him high. "We shall call him Talbert," he shouted for all to hear, "and he will be a fighter for righteousness!" The next day Halvor gave firm orders for the older boys to help their mother and then rode off to preach a sermon in North Dakota. Years later, Chester admitted that he was angry with his father for not staying longer. It was the same thing in China: his father was always away. He felt sorry for his mother, but she never complained.

With their father gone, Chester and Nelius assumed more responsibility. Uncle Tom taught them how to leap on their horses and round up cattle like western cowboys. When the leaves turned crisp and the snow began to fall, the Ronning kids were beside themselves with joy. They had never seen snow. They watched in awe as layer after layer of fairy-like flakes fluttered from the sky and piled high on the house, the barn, the garden, the trees and fields, turning their world into a sparkling wonderland. Hannah watched her children, indistinguishable from their cousins, gleefully set forth with their sleighs in search of a hill. They cleared the pond, and Hannah impressed her children by giving a figure-skating exhibition they couldn't begin to match. The days rushed by. Christmas Eve came. All the cousins, brothers and sisters, mothers and fathers gathered together under the roof of the great white house Torgrim Rorem had built: music and laughter, endless platters of Norwegian pastries, *belenacrunsa, lutefisk,* and *lefsa,* homemade presents. Almah got a doll that cried "Mama." The children had never received so many gifts.

But Hannah could not enter fully into the Christmas festivities in her home. She had changed too much. A hidden part of her was in another place, another land far away from this secure, sheltered world of her kinfolk. The sense of difference could not be thrown off. Memories of China haunted her: other faces, other times in a miserable, crowded, cruel world; suffering people fighting for existence; dark, short lives reaching for the light. As she watched her own young ones play, the faces of other children, as dear as her own, swam before her eyes: Peter, the rescued prisoner; Lydia, their first foundling. Hannah and Halvor knew they must soon return to China—where they belonged. It was their destiny. Rebecca was adamantly against her sister returning to China. She tried to persuade Hannah to let Halvor go alone, if he must. But Hannah had sworn a total commitment to her husband and his mission. She knew she must cut herself off from her American family and accept the misery and pain in the other world where she felt she could make a difference. China needed her; America did not. She later wrote: *December 25, 1899. It was on Christmas Eve, I came to know that rooted by birth as I am to America I can never stay home again, for I am bound to China by invisible cords tied to my very soul. Only Halvor can understand this.*

In January 1900, as the Ronning family was preparing their return to China, Halvor received news from mission headquarters ordering them to postpone the trip. The Boxer Uprising had erupted into a deadly conflagration of enormous proportions. Two Roman Catholic missions and two American Protestant missions had been savagely attacked. An Italian priest reported that the homes of between five hundred and six hundred of his Chinese Catholic converts had been looted, ten persons killed, and five thousand made refugees. The news got worse. Thousands of Chinese Christians had been butchered by Boxers and entire villages burned to the ground. Hundreds of British and American missionaries had been forced to flee for their lives. There was no news of the Reverend Frank Simcox's family, who had chosen to stay in Paotingfu with their three China-born children. Halvor feared the worst. Empress Dowager Cixi and the antiforeign governor of Shandong Province, Yu Xian, were encouraging the Boxers.

One of the first to be murdered by the Boxers was an English Protestant missionary, Reverend S. M. Brooks, a friend and colleague of Halvor's who had worked with him in Hankow. Brooks was killed on December 31, 1899, in Shandong Province, where the infamous Governor Yu Xian had openly declared his hatred for foreigners. The missionary had been riding a donkey near the village of Changchiatien when he was brutally attacked by a gang of Boxers. A Chinese boy driving a cart behind Brooks managed to escape. The frightened boy reported that some Boxers had pulled Brooks from his donkey, stripped him, put a hole through his nose, and led him through the village like an animal for hours while he was taunted by villagers. At one point he managed to escape and ran for his life, but the Boxers pursued him on horseback. When he was caught, they cut his head off with swords and threw his mutilated body into a ravine by the roadside. It was later recovered by Reverend Mathews and laid to rest in a decent grave with the red cross of martyrdom on his chest.

The missionaries were somewhat encouraged by the news that the "Iron Fists" who killed Reverend Brooks had been caught and tried three months after the murder. The trial was attended by the British consul, C. W. Campbell. Two men were executed and one sentenced to life imprisonment, which in China was worse than death. Another was imprisoned for ten years, and two more were exiled. The head men of the village were fined five hundred taels (about twenty-five dollars). A memorial tablet marked the spot where the murder took place.

The British minister, Sir Claude MacDonald, had written an indignant letter to the Zongli Yamen, China's foreign ministry, warning that if the disorder was not vigorously quelled, international complications were likely to ensue. There was no reply. Instead, in what seemed like a reward, Governor Yu Xian, who had cut his political teeth by suppressing bandits and was openly antiforeign, was transferred to a province near Peking and was hailed as a hero by the empress dowager in Peking, which foreshadowed violence in the capital.

The Ronnings delayed their return.

18

The Siege of Peking

There are things which could never be imagined, but there is nothing which may not happen.

— CHINESE APHORISM

It is safe to say that where one real Boxer has been killed since the capture of Peking, 50 harmless coolies or laborers on the farm, including not a few women and children, have been slain.

— GENERAL ADNA R. CHAFEE, AMERICAN COMMANDER OF
THE CHINA RELIEF EXPEDITION, SEPTEMBER 1900

On June 21, 1900, China declared a "War on the World." Empress Dowager Cixi ordered an attack on the international legations in Peking. Two thousand foreign diplomats, representing eleven nations, along with 2,800 Chinese Christians and missionaries, were trapped in the walled-in Legation Quarter, surrounded and vastly outnumbered by 72,000 armed Imperial troops, Manchu Bannermen, Moslem Gansu Braves, and Boxers with orders from the empress to "Exterminate the Foreign Devils."

The strangely worded declaration was published in leading newspapers abroad and in the *Peking Gazette:*

IN THE NAME OF THE EMPEROR

. . . With tears have we announced in our ancestral shrines the outbreak of war. Better is it to do our utmost and enter on the struggle than to seek self-preservation involving eternal disgrace. All our officials, high and low, are of one mind. They have assembled, without official summons, several hundred thousands of patriotic soldiers (Boxers and Imperial troops) . . . Even children carry spears in the defense of their country. Exterminate the Foreign Devils!

That same morning, an editorial pointing out the difference between the Chinese people and the Manchu government of China was published in the *North China Daily News:*

> The Manchu Empress Dowager is reaping the whirlwind with a vengeance . . . Instead of having one or two Powers to pacify, China is at war with all the Great Powers at once, and she is at war by the choice of the Empress Dowager and her gang . . . It is to be hoped that it will be possible to get the Emperor Guangxu out of house arrest and place him on the throne. Meantime it should be made perfectly clear that it is the Empress Dowager who has undertaken the present war, and that we [the British] are not fighting China, but the usurping [Manchu] Government of Peking.

The War on the World was the culmination of the antiforeign movement that had been raging for decades in the countryside. But now it took on an international character. The Chinese diplomatic ministers to Great Britain [Luo Fenglu] and to France and the United States [Wu Dingfang] announced that at a meeting of the officials of the Grand Council in Peking, the Manchus were unanimous in favor of defying the world while the Chinese offered strenuous objections. They claimed that responsibility for the Siege of Peking, which was a violation of the laws of nations, lay on the Manchu clique. But there was enough guilt to go around.

The sensational details riveted the attention of the world. The Siege of Peking became one of the most extraordinary tales in the annals of war, comparable to the Black Hole of Calcutta in 1756, when Europeans were imprisoned by the ruler of Bengal after he defeated the garrison of the British East India Company and captured the city. The *New York Sun* called the Siege of Peking "the most exciting episode ever known to civilization."

In early May 1900, three villages near Paotingfu were destroyed by Boxers, and scores of Chinese Catholic Christians were slaughtered. On May 10, an article appeared in the *North China Daily News* written by its "native correspondent," who, at the risk of his life, published a warning to the foreigners of the coming attack: "I write in all seriousness to inform you that there is a great secret scheme to crush all foreigners in China. The Chief leaders of the movement are the Empress Dowager, and Li Bingheng. The forces to be used are all Manchu . . . 72,000 men are to form the nucleus of the Army of Avengers, whilst the Boxers are to be counted upon as auxiliaries to the great fight that is more imminent than foreigners in Peking or elsewhere dream." These predictions were ignored by everyone concerned—until they came true. Shortly after the article was published, the reporter disappeared.

May 28: Nine Belgian railway engineers are killed at the railway station at Fengtai. The Peking–Tientsin railway is burned.

May 30: The diplomats request that foreign soldiers come to Peking to defend them. The next day, 425 armed marines of all nationalities come by train from Tientsin to guard their respective legations.

June 1: Two British missionaries are killed just south of Peking.

June 4: The day after the last troops arrive, railway connection from Peking to Tientsin is severed by Boxers. Peking is isolated.

June 8: Chinese troops, under the command of the infamous Manchu General Dong Fuxiang, along with hundreds of Boxers, enter Peking. An orgy of arson, looting, and murder of "secondary foreign devils" takes place.

June 9: The splendid grandstand at the local race course, a symbol of the foreigners' artificial world of privilege, three miles from Peking, is burned to the ground by Boxers. A native Christian is captured and roasted alive in the fire. The previously sanguine diplomats become seriously alarmed.

June 10: The British summer legation in the Western Hills outside Peking is destroyed. Prince Duan, a leading Boxer supporter, is appointed to the Zongli Yamen. An international body of about two thousand troops under British Admiral Edward Seymour leaves Tientsin by train for Peking. It is later attacked by Boxers and forced to return.

June 11: The foreigners are no longer planning dinner parties. In the official drill grounds just opposite the British legation, the Boxers are openly practicing the magic rituals believed to make them invulnerable to Western bullets. It is this supernatural element in the Boxer claims that gives the sect its powerful hold upon the imagination of the uneducated Chinese. At the end of the ritual, the Boxers act like madmen, daring everything, fearing nothing, all the while shouting their slogan: "Support the Great Qing! Exterminate the Foreigners!" (*Fu Qing, mianyang*). On the same day, the secretary of the Japanese legation, Sugiyama Akira, who had left for the train station to meet the troops, is dragged from his cart by Manchu soldiers at the South Gate of Peking and hacked to pieces. His heart is cut out and sent to General Dong Fuxiang.

June 13: The German minister, Baron Klemens von Ketteler, and German soldiers capture a Boxer boy and execute him. In retaliation, thousands of Boxers, led by the brutal Manchu Prince Duan, armed with old rifles, bamboo spears, and all manner of makeshift weapons, screaming for revenge, climb over the Peking city wall. They attack members of the twelve Christian missionary organizations and some five hundred citizens of Western countries and Japan residing in the city. Hundreds of Chinese Christians and their servants are slain. A witness, Dr. G. E. Morrison, correspondent of the London *Times*, wrote: "Women and children hacked to pieces, men trussed like fowls with noses and ears cut off and eyes gouged out." The Eastern Cathedral and the Southern Cathedral (both more than three hundred years old) are torched and hundreds of converts burned alive.

June 17: The Western powers retaliate. The forts at Dagu, commanding the approach from the sea, are stormed and captured by the Allied fleets. The empress dowager expresses shock and outrage at this action.

June 19: The Tientsin concessions are attacked by Imperial troops. The Zongli Yamen in Peking, under orders from the empress, sends an ultimatum demanding that all foreigners leave China within twenty-four hours. The legations agree to leave, and all diplomats in Peking are so notified.

June 20: The fatal day. At 8:00 a.m., German minister von Ketteler and his interpreter, Mr. Cordes, in an attempt to make arrangements for the evacuation, set forth in two official sedan chairs to negotiate with Chinese authorities at the Zongli Yamen. As they near the Yamen, Cordes, who was riding behind, sees an armed and mounted Manchu officer, identified by a white button and a feather in his cap, ride up to the sedan chair, take deliberate aim at the baron, and shoot, killing him instantly. Cordes, though wounded in both legs, manages to crawl to a diplomatic mission compound with the news. In the British embassy, 470 foreign civilians take refuge.

At 4:00 p.m., the Legation Quarter is attacked by a joint force of Imperial soldiers and Boxers. A kindly English professor returning from lessons is captured in the street and tortured for three days before his head is spiked and displayed above the legation wall as an example of what lay in store for the foreigners.

June 21: The Imperial Court issues a "Declaration of War" as Boxers are officially enlisted into the militia under the command of Prince Duan.

The Epic Siege Begins

The occupants in the foreign legations who had once entertained one another so lavishly now set out to defend themselves against overwhelming odds. They were joined by other foreigners and Chinese Christians who had come for refuge and fought with incredible ingenuity. The British minister, Sir Claude MacDonald, an impressive figure sporting a waxed handlebar mustache with twirled tips, had once been a soldier in the Fourteenth Highlanders. He became their commander-in-chief, organizing the 425 legation guards and all other able-bodied men while imposing discipline on the women and children. Orders were issued on diplomatic calling cards. The men erected barriers while the ladies sewed sandbags out of their silk pajamas, monogrammed pillowcases, and multicolored brocade draperies. They were stacked in front of the exposed outer perimeter, making the barricades look like a backdrop for a New Year's ball.

The empress dowager, who had obviously expected a quick victory, was surprised. She ordered her Manchu troops to smoke the foreigners out by tossing lighted firebrands into the Forest of Ten Thousand Pencils of the Hanlin Academy, the oldest library in the world. MacDonald appointed the American Methodist missionary Frank Gamewell as chief of the Fortifications Committee. The diplomats and missionaries managed to quell the fire with bucket brigades using Ming vases, antique bronze vessels, and incense burners to bring water from the eight wells in the Legation Quarter. The "Fighting Parsons" prayed fervently and providentially. They were not surprised when the fierce wind that had been spreading the fires subsided.

Every night the enemies beyond the walls bombarded the legations with a hail of artillery fire. Between blasts, the Boxers threw firecrackers, keeping the sleep-deprived foreigners on constant alert. On one night alone, an estimated two hundred thousand rounds were fired into the legation. There was no safe place, and the casualties mounted steadily. American Minister Conger claimed that some nights the furious firing exceeded anything he had experienced in the American Civil War. The legation guards saw their number diminish daily.

The summer heat often reached 110 degrees Fahrenheit in the shade. Corpses lay unburied around the defense perimeter, and the stench was suffocating. Flies proliferated in the putrid air. Food was scarce. Dogs that came to feed on the dead on the Chinese side of the wall were caught on hooks and hoisted into the Legation Quarter for food. Scavenging crows were shot and cooked. Racing ponies had to be slaughtered for food. Only one cow was kept for milk. Six European babies died in the first weeks. Yet the defenders carried on. A newborn infant was christened "Siege."

In spite of the terrible conditions, the English remained steadfast. Some forty people—missionaries, Belgian railway workers, Royal Marines, customs officials, lady's maids, valets, and an entire Chinese girls' school—ate every meal in Lady

MacDonald's dining room. The staple diet was pony meat and rice, but it was washed down by vintage French champagne, of which there was no shortage. Tobacco was also plentiful, and even the ladies smoked cigarettes, saying it muted the malodorous air.

As the legation was being stormed, the Northern Cathedral, where the French bishop of Peking, Favier, and twenty-two nuns had given refuge to three thousand Chinese Catholics and eight hundred children, also came under attack. The sole defenders of the cathedral were forty-three heroic sailors led by a young Englishman, Paul Henry Breton.

Missionary Martyrs

The atrocities were not confined to Peking. Missionaries and Chinese Christians in the northeast countryside were hunted down and slaughtered. It was later learned that the Boxers had killed 250 missionaries (including more than fifty children) and more than thirty thousand Chinese Christians (mostly Catholic).

The first large massacre took place on June 30, 1900, at Paotingfu, 120 miles southwest of Peking, where some thirty-two foreign residents in the Protestant missionary community were killed, including the Reverend Edmond Simcox and his wife, Ellen May, and their three children—a daughter, Margaret, and two sons, Paul and Francis, who had been playmates of Chester and Nelius. The missionaries in Paotingfu were living in three compounds. Seventeen had escaped before the road was destroyed on June 8, but the others were unable to get transportation. About twenty Boxers, joined by a hostile mob, piled stubble against the outer gate of the Presbyterian compound and set it afire. The hospital, the church, and three missionaries' homes were looted and burned to the ground. Two Chinese gatekeepers and some loyal servants were killed and thrown into the well.

Dr. G. Y. Taylor and Dr. C. V. R. and Mrs. Hodge of the American Presbyterian Mission had taken refuge in the Simcox home. Dr. Taylor addressed the crowd from an upper window in a vain effort to curb the madness. In a last desperate stand, the missionaries attempted to hold the Boxers at bay with one rifle, two revolvers, and a shotgun. The leading Boxer, Zhu Duzi, was killed and ten others wounded. In a fierce frenzy, the mob, shouting, "Kill! kill! burn! burn!" set the house on fire. All the missionaries within perished in the flames.*

On the outskirts of Paotingfu, a group of missionaries from the American

*Ketler, *The Tragedy of Paotingfu*, 34.

Board—Reverend H. T. Pitkin, a brilliant Yale graduate from Philadelphia; Miss Mary Morrill, and Miss Annie Gould, both in their early twenties; along with Mr. Cooper and Mr. and Mrs. Benjamin Bagnall, with the American Methodist Mission, and their little girl Gladys—took refuge in a house in the Pitkin compound. Captain Grote Hutcheson of the Sixth U.S. Cavalry, who arrived too late with a rescue party, related what happened in an official report:

> Mr. Pitkin was armed with a revolver with which he defended himself and his charges until the ammunition was exhausted, whereupon the crowd poured into the house and seized the occupants, dragging them out. In the melee Mr. Pitkin was shot and then beheaded, his body being buried with six or seven Chinese in one pit just outside the compound wall. The head was carried away and into the city, and it is generally reported, taken into the Yamen as evidence of the good work of the Boxers, and was seen no more.
>
> Miss Gould and Miss Morrill were taken out of the Compound and into the city. Miss Gould appears to have been so greatly frightened by the rough and brutal conduct of the Chinese that she had fainted from shock and fear, and remained in a more or less comatose condition for some time and was unable to walk. She was accordingly bound hand and foot and slung on a pole or lance, as pigs are carried in China, and taken to the city. Miss Morrill being a fearless woman of considerable moral strength, was able to walk, and did so. In this manner, Miss Gould being carried and Miss Morrill walking, but being led by the hair, they were taken to the Jisheng An Temple in the South East corner of the city, near the wall, one of the headquarters of the Boxers, where they remained all day. En route the streets were thronged with people, many of whom clutched and tore the clothing of the two women, which soon was much tattered, but no deliberate effort to parade them in a nude state was made. Neither does it appear that they were violated,—such in fact is highly improbable, but they were roughly handled and knocked about.

The Bagnalls and Coopers were later brought in and the missionaries taken out of the city. Miss Gould had recovered her strength and was able to walk. The report continued:

> The following method was adopted: The hands were bound and held in front of the body, the wrists about the height of the neck; a rope was

then tied about the wrists, passing to the rear around the neck, thence to the wrists of the next person behind, and thence about the neck and so on. The child was not bound, but ran alongside clinging to her mother's dress. The end of the rope in front was seized by two men and the doomed party, thus led in single file all bound together like common criminals, viewed by an immense throng were led through the South gate to the place of execution at the Southeast corner of the wall. Here all were executed by being beheaded, except the child who was speared by a Boxer. The bodies and heads were insecurely buried in one pit about forty yards from the South wall. Both Compound and graves were personally visited by me.

I certify this to be a true account, as gathered from various sources, and substantially correct.*

Nine days later, the killing of the largest number of victims in one day took place at T'aiyuan in Shanxi Province. The victims included China inland missionaries Dr. and Mrs. Millar Wilson and their baby, Alexander. The man responsible was the notorious Yu Xian, the former governor of Shandong who had been involved in the murder, in 1899, of Reverend Brooks and at least two other missionaries. With the encouragement of the dowager, Yu openly continued his persecutions of the Christians. In July 7, 1900, he rounded up forty-four Protestant and Catholic missionaries, including women and children, and brought them to his official residence in T'aiyuan. Two days later, they were surrounded by armed soldiers and lined up in a public square outside the Yamen entrance. All of them, including the children, Protestant women, and seven Sisters of Mercy were forced to strip to the waist and ordered to wait for His Excellency. After several hours of cruel exposure to the scorching sun and taunting crowds, Governor Yu arrived wearing his official robes and inspected the rows of innocent victims. He prodded one missionary with his sword and asked him where he was from. The answer was "*Daying guo*" (Great Heroic Nation), the official title for England. At this, Yu Xian, with a sweep of his sword, ordered the slaughter of all the missionaries. When Chinese witnesses protested, they were beheaded. The provincial borders had been closed, so no news of his deeds would leak out. One witness, however, Mr. Fei Jihao, a schoolteacher employed by the American Board, managed to escape and two months later brought the first eyewitness report of the massacre to his mission in Tientsin.

*Arthur Henderson Smith, *China in Convulsion*, 2 vols. (New York: Fleming H. Revell, 1901), 253–56.

According to this report, the first to be led forth was Mr. Farthing, an English Baptist. His wife clung to him, but he gently put her aside and knelt down before the soldiers with a prayer on his lips. His head was struck off with one blow of the executioner's sword. Next came four more missionary men, including Dr. A. E. Lovitt and Dr. Wilson. They were all beheaded. Then the governor grew impatient and ordered his bodyguard to kill the other men. Some required several blows.

When the men were dead or dying, the ladies were taken. Mrs. Farthing carried a baby and her two children, Ruth and Guy, held tightly to her other hand. The soldiers tore the children away and beheaded them all. Some of the ladies suffered several cuts before death. Mrs. Lovitt was wearing spectacles and held the hand of her little boy. She spoke to the people: "We all came to China to bring you the good news of the salvation by Jesus Christ; we have done you no harm, only good, why do you treat us so?" A soldier took off her spectacles before beheading her, which required two blows.

After the Protestants were killed, the Roman Catholics were led forward. The bishop, an old man with a long white beard, asked the governor why he was doing this wicked deed. The governor gave no answer but drew his sword and cut the bishop across the face. Blood poured down his white beard, and he was beheaded. Another bishop, two priests, the seven nuns, and one lay brother were then quickly executed. All the witnesses were amazed at the quiet courage of the martyrs in their terrible hour of death. None cried out except for three children.

Some of the heads were placed in cages on the city wall. Six other missionaries of the American Board in T'aiku were also executed that day on the orders of Yu Xian, and their heads were sent to the sadistic governor in a box. Later he boasted that he had killed fifty-one foreigners in one day and claimed a reward from his partner in crime, the empress dowager in Peking.

Around the same time in another part of Shanxi, two of Hannah Ronning's good friends, Miss Emily Whitchurch and Miss Edith Searall, were murdered in their China Inland Mission home. In late June, a group of Boxers broke into their house, picked up the ornaments in the room, and flung them violently at the helpless women, who were slowly battered to death while they remained kneeling in prayer. Their bodies were stripped, exposed, and defiled in the most gruesome way. The magistrate supplied two cheap coffins used for pauper criminals, and their battered bodies were laid to rest in the chapel.

Before the governor of Shanxi and the Boxers ended their orgy of killing, in that province alone they had butchered 102 Protestant missionaries and 41 children, as well as thousands of Chinese Catholic Christians.

Meanwhile, in Ronning's mission in Fancheng, Dr. Himle and his son were looking for a way to escape to Hankow. They were smuggled out of the city in a mule cart, and Himle bribed a fisherman to take them downriver in his sampan. He hid his son under a mat on the bow and sat on top of it. Before they could set sail, however, some Boxers spied Himle. They robbed him of everything he had, even his coat and shirt. In his inside waistcoat pocket they felt a little Bible and must have thought it was silver because they all grabbed for it furiously. "I could not help laughing," he later told Halvor, "so eager were they now to grab the word of God that I had been trying to give them for years. When they finally tore my coat apart and found it they looked at my smiling face in disgust. They took my shoes and left me completely naked. When they left I wrapped the mat around me and that night we made our way back to the Fancheng mission."

In Peking on July 18, an extraordinary thing happened. In the middle of the siege, the empress dowager ordered a cease-fire. Then she personally sent fifteen cartloads of melons, vegetables, and fine white flour to her enemies with her compliments. The same Chinese soldiers who the day before had been bent on murdering the foreigners now came to the barricades to talk. One received treatment for a slashed ear. Eleven days later, the shelling was renewed and the last effort to raze the legation began.

The Siege of Peking lasted fifty-five days. The battle came to a dramatic finish when the joint relief force of fourteen thousand men from the eight Allied Powers—America, Britain, France, Russia, Japan, Italy, Austria, and Germany—marched triumphantly into Peking while each country played its national anthem. What the cheering diplomats did not know at the time was that the Allied troops had cut a trail of devastation in a rampage of vengeance on the march from Tientsin to Peking. Even though the admirals commanding the relief force had declared they would use force only against the Boxers, the Allied forces ruthlessly and indiscriminately scorched villages and slaughtered peasants. The city of T'ungchou east of Peking, where two British diplomats had been captured forty years earlier, was looted and burned. Inhabitants were raped and slaughtered. The wells were choked with the bodies of women who chose suicide rather than fall into the hands of the foreign devils.

In 1900, the commander of the American forces wrote from Peking: "It is safe to say that where one real Boxer has been killed since the capture of Peking, 50 harmless coolies or laborers on the farm, including not a few women and children, have been slain." During the siege, 66 foreigners in the Legation Quarter had been killed and 150 wounded. The Chinese Christians who had died in the fighting were not counted in the official death toll. Astonishingly, none of the leading members of the diplomatic corps had been killed. They were united in declaring the miraculous nature of their survival.

In Peking's Northern Cathedral, 166 babies had starved to death, but thousands of other people were saved, thanks largely to the British sailor Breton, who after an inspired resistance was shot in the throat just two weeks before the cease-fire. The cathedral was liberated by Japanese troops, the only non-Christians in the relief force. Meanwhile, in the Imperial Palace, the defeated empress dowager and her Imperial Court were planning their escape.

The Empress Dowager Flees to Sian

On August 15, 1900, at the Hour of the Tiger (3:00 a.m.), the empress dowager hid her most precious jewels under the floor of a secret room in the Forbidden City, removed her enamel nail protectors, cut her six-inch fingernails, dressed in the common blue garments of a peasant woman, and pulled her hair back in Chinese fashion. Three wooden donkey carts were driven into the palace. At 3:30, the Manchu concubines and Chinese eunuchs with the emperor, who was still under house arrest, were summoned. The emperor begged to stay, saying that he was the only one who could negotiate with the Allies. The Pearl Concubine, the emperor's favorite, dared to plead with the dowager to let him stay behind, emphasizing his official capacity. In a jealous rage, the empress commanded two eunuchs, Li and Sung, to wrap the Pearl Concubine in a rug and throw her down the well that still exists just outside the Ning Shou Palace. Then the emperor, trembling in grief and wrath, was forced into a cart behind a screen so he would not be recognized. He was guarded by two soldiers riding on the shafts. The dowager got into another cart with Pu Jun, Prince Duan's son, whom she had designated as her heir apparent. The Manchu court, now reduced to a frightened retinue of grand councillors, eunuchs, and other sycophants, were followed through the North Gate (the Gate of Military Prowess) of the Imperial Palace by three grand councillors on horseback. They reached the Summer Palace, north of the city, at about 8:00 a.m. Her Majesty gave orders to pack all valuables into carriages. General Ma Yugun, with a force of one thousand men and several hundred Bannermen, escorted the entourage to Kalgan (today's Zhangjiakou) in Hebei Province.*

The royal refugees spent the first night in a mosque thirty miles north of

*Bland and Backhouse, *China under the Empress Dowager*, 210.

Peking, where a Mohammedan trading firm supplied food and mule litters (palanquins borne by poles on the backs of mules, one in front and one behind). Peking was abandoned to the mercy of the Allied Powers. As the cortege caravan advanced toward the ancient capital of Sian (today's Xi'an), it was joined by fleeing officials and chamberlains of the court. To obtain supplies, the escorting troops plundered every town and village on their line of march.

On September 10, the court arrived at T'aiyuan in Shanxi Province and took up residence in the governor's Yamen, the same bloodstained building where, six weeks earlier, Governor Yu Xian had massacred the missionaries. The governor met the court as they approached the city gate and kowtowed to the dowager's palanquin. She bade him come forward and said: "At your farewell audience, you assured me the Boxers were invulnerable. Alas! You were wrong, and now Peking has fallen! But you did splendidly in carrying out my orders by ridding Shanxi Province of the whole brood of foreign devils. Nevertheless, because the foreign devils are calling for vengeance, I may have to dismiss you from office. But, don't worry, it is only to throw dust in the eyes of the barbarians."

Yu Xian kowtowed, banged his head on the ground nine times, and boasted: "Your Majesty's slave caught them as in a net, and allowed neither chicken nor dog to escape. As to the Boxers, they have been defeated because they killed and plundered innocent people who were not Christians."*

Empress Dowager Cixi then eagerly visited the courtyard where forty-five missionaries had been beheaded and a number of native Christians who had tried to save them were also killed. According to a report in the *Shanghai Daily Mail,* the dowager cross-examined Yu Xian to extract every sordid detail of the massacre. He claimed that not only had he participated personally but he had given orders to kill all foreigners throughout his province. Before the royal court left T'aiyuan, the two psychopaths met for the last time. The Old Buddha, in true form, handed her loyal subject a white silk scarf and told him that the price of coffins was rising—a euphemistic hint to commit suicide before a worse fate overtook him. It was clear that Cixi needed a scapegoat. She ordered the executions of the Boxer leaders and offered numerous others the white silk scarf. One notorious Boxer, Duke Kung, refused and followed the court to Sian with his family. No one dared help him. To avoid starvation, he became the servant of a warlord, and his beautiful young wife was sold into slavery.

Ronglu, the military commander and the dowager's former lover, who was

*Peter Fleming, *The Siege at Peking* (New York: Harper, 1959), 167.

hated by the reformers and reactionaries alike, joined the court at T'aiyuan along with many other officials. Intrigue, jealousy, and quarreling over status became rife. In the old capital formerly known as Ch'ang'an, the walls of two Yamens were painted crimson in preparation for the empress. A throne in the Reception Hall was upholstered in yellow silk. The Old Buddha soon officiated over the exiled royal court as if she were still in Peking. For entertainment after twenty-course banquets, Her Majesty permitted the presentation of her favorite plays. A short excerpt from a confidential letter written by an official who had carried news from Peking sheds some light on the court life in exile:

> The Empress Dowager controls everything in and around the Court: those who exercise most influence are Ronglu and Lu Juanlin. She looks very young and one would not put her age at more than forty, whereas she is really sixty-four. The Emperor appears to be generally depressed. The Heir Apparent is fifteen years of age; fat, coarse featured, and of rude manners. He favors military habits of dress and to see him when he goes to the play wearing a felt cap with gold braid, a leather jerkin and a red military overcoat, one would take him for a prize fighter. He knows all the young actors and rowdies and associates generally with the lowest classes. He is much in company with the chief eunuch Li Lianying who leads him into the wildest dissipation . . . His last offense was to commence an intrigue with one of the ladies-in-waiting of Her Majesty. The Dowager immediately sent out a decree to cancel his title to the Throne. Without any official duties he is condemned to a life of poverty.

While the empress dowager was enjoying her theatricals in Sian, the foreign powers in Peking found themselves in a unique position. The defeat of the Imperial troops left the foreign generals with no one to fight, and the flight of the Imperial Court left the diplomats no one with whom to make peace. The generals organized another triumphal march through the Imperial City, but no one came to witness it. In the chaos of the past weeks, thousands of Peking residents had been murdered or committed suicide, and tens of thousands had fled the city. The population of Peking had been reduced to a quarter of its former size. When the fighting stopped, boredom became the enemy. The Imperial palaces and shops were filled with unguarded treasure. Greed took over, and the Allies began quarrelling among themselves over the loot. They divided the Celestial City into zones garrisoned by troops from the various countries. The British occupied the

Temple of Heaven, and the Americans quartered their troops in the Temple of Agriculture, desecrating both those hallowed shrines. All indulged in a frenzy of vengeance and plunder except for the comparatively well-disciplined Japanese troops. Soldiers rampaged through the streets, breaking into shops and homes, stealing silks, furs, antiques, and jewels and forcing the residents to reveal where they had buried their valuables.

The foreign ministers concentrated on the Imperial palaces. Even the highest-ranking diplomats and their wives participated in the sordid scramble for royal treasure. For the first time in history, foreign troops penetrated the sacred Forbidden City, burning and stealing treasures from the private apartments of the dynastic emperors. Common soldiers sprawled haughtily on the brocade-curtained bed of the empress dowager and scribbled graffiti on the scarlet walls; all her elaborate theater costumes went up in flames. Considerable fortunes were stolen and shipped abroad. Officers and diplomats left the capital with shiploads of crates loaded with treasures. The plundering went on for months, with each nationality charging the others with deplorable greed. On September 24, 1900, the British journalist Dr. George E. Morrison of the *Times* of London reported: "The systematic denudation of the summer palace by the Russians has been completed. Every article of value is packed and labeled." He did not mention that the British aristocrats were no exception. Peter Fleming, in his book *The Siege at Peking*, quotes a letter from a British officer: "Lady MacDonald was out with a small force . . . and devoted herself most earnestly to looting."

When the dowager read about the desecration of the Summer Palace, she was filled with wrath. She decided to return to the Forbidden City.

19

The Ronnings Return to China, 1901

Something told us that the return of the Court to Peking was a turning point in history, and in our breathless interest we forgot our resentment against the woman who was responsible for so much evil.

That little bow, and the graceful gesture of the closed hands, took us by surprise. From all along the wall there came, in answer, a spontaneous burst of applause. The Empress Dowager appeared pleased.

—ITALIAN DIPLOMAT AFTER THE SIEGE OF PEKING

In 1901, shortly before the dowager Cixi returned with her royal court to Peking from her exile in Sian, the Ronnings returned to China to continue their work in the mission. While the family was traveling by train from Iowa to board a ship in Vancouver, an extraordinary coincidence occurred. At the station in Calgary, Halvor recognized John Anderson, a fellow classmate from the Red Wing Lutheran Seminary, who was talking with some other men about homesteads they had just purchased southeast of Edmonton. Anderson encouraged Halvor to invest in a half section, 320 acres, of Canadian Pacific Railroad land in Bardo, Alberta, since someday he would surely need to settle in a home of his own. The land was available at three dollars an acre, with twenty years to pay and at a very low interest rate. Halvor said he was interested but could not buy land in Canada because he was an American. At this point Anderson introduced Halvor to "the Honorable Frank Oliver," an impressive elderly gentleman wearing a stovepipe hat. Oliver patted Halvor on the back and generously declared, "Reverend Ronning, if you vote for me in the next election, I will make you a Canadian."

They sailed back on the Canadian Pacific *Empress of China*, which was even more luxurious than the SS *Oceanic* that Halvor, Hannah, and Thea had taken ten years earlier. Hannah missed the romantic sails. All the way to China they discussed the possibility of buying land in Canada. Nelius and Chester grew more enthusiastic every day, dreaming about a ranch where they could ride the range like their uncles in Iowa. In Yokohama, Halvor made a decision that would change their lives and the lives of their descendants. He sent a cable to Anderson to buy land in Canada. (Seven years later, Halvor would take advantage of Frank Oliver's promise: he voted for Oliver, and the Ronnings became Canadians.)

When they reached Shanghai, Halvor learned from the *Shanghai Daily Mail* that the Allied Powers in Peking had agreed to a peace agreement among themselves called the Boxer Protocol. There had been no Chinese government officials with whom to negotiate. The dowager had left an aged official, Li Hong-zhang, to salvage China's damaged foreign relations, but after prolonged negotiations and much wrangling among the powers, he died of a heart attack before the settlement was signed. Its terms were drastic.

Indemnities

Ronning found the Chinese smarting from the indemnities demanded by the Boxer Protocol signed on September 7, 1901. He was relieved that the Americans had at least exercised a moderating influence but was troubled to read that "Punishment and Indemnity" topped the list of the fourteen points agreed on. China had agreed to punish all those involved except the main culprit, the empress dowager herself, who had betrayed the Boxers by claiming to be their victim. Her first victim was her co-conspirator in murder, Shandong's Governor Yu Xian, who, after denouncing the empress, was allowed to strangle himself with the white scarf.

The dowager's irrational actions resulted in four decades of humiliation for China. The country was forced to pay an indemnity of 450 million so-called *haiguan* taels—about $333 million—at 4 percent interest, in thirty-nine annual installments ending in 1940, to be distributed among twelve of the powers, with Russia receiving the largest share, about 30 percent. The others were to get amounts progressively smaller in this order: Germany, France, Great Britain, the United States, Italy, Belgium, Austria-Hungary, the Netherlands, Spain, Portugal, and Sweden. Halvor was glad to note that the Norwegians were not involved. The Allied Powers immediately engaged in indiscriminate punitive expeditions against the Boxers that revealed a shocking lack of concern for innocent Chinese lives. It was commonly accepted that for the death of one real Boxer, many innocents were slain as the "accidents of war." This was borne out in a letter written by a British officer in October: "We fired about 2000 rounds, mostly at inoffensive people. I believe I killed 15 of them." The foreign victims of the Boxer Uprising were all counted and their names recorded on various monuments. The thousands of innocent Chinese victims remained unnamed and uncounted.

Adding to China's humiliation and Halvor's dismay, many foreigners took on the arrogant attitude of conquerors. As Grandfather often said, "It was not a reputable page in the history of either East or West."

From Shanghai, the Ronnings steamed up the Yangtze River to Hankow and sailed by junk up the Han River to Fancheng. They were welcomed by both Chinese officials and gentry with the firing of cannon, the sputtering of firecrackers, and a military escort. Dr. Himle, Sen Li-fu, and Evangelist Huang, who had carried on the mission work, were at the waterfront. Middleman Ting, recovered from the horror of his imprisonment, was there with a multitude of students eager to resume their studies. Halvor proudly held up his American-born son, Talbert. Nelius and Chester felt they were home at last.

Halvor to Nils: *Fancheng, December 1901. The Children were happy to meet their Chinese playmates. Chester and Nelius were presented with a rabbit by their school chum, Shi Gun-ching, and the boys had lots of fun. Great sorrow when the rabbit died. The dear friend was given an honorable burial. Their sorrow turned to joy when Gun-ching gave them a pup, that Chester named Vesta. It is great to be back . . . Things look very promising. The defeat of the Manchu Empress in Peking has given the Chinese here great joy. I brought back some Iowa potatoes and some tomatoes which I believe will grow very well in this climate . . .*

There are nine missionaries here now, including Hannah and me. Dr. Himle is back with his new wife, the former Alma Carlson, and two other medical missionaries. Dr. and Mrs. I. M. J. Hotvedt are a tremendous help to Himle in the hospital. Rev. and Mrs. O. R. Wold have also returned and a new missionary, Miss Ida Groseth, has arrived. We are all working as hard as we can to expand the mission and bring the gospel to the Chinese. The new Mandarin has taken an interest in our work so we are hoping to gain the support of the gentry.

In the fall of 1901, Empress Dowager Cixi prepared to bring her enlarged Imperial Court back from their exile in Sian. They set off in a mile-long caravan of two thousand carts flying ten thousand flags on a seven-hundred-mile journey back to Peking. The Imperial party traveled in yellow palanquins carried by mules in the center of the procession with cavalry and mounted officials on the flanks. The last lap was completed by rail. Four freight trains, provided by the Belgian railway authorities, conveyed all the princes, grand councillors, concubines, eunuchs, servants, chariots, horses, and mules of the royal retinue back to the capital. The Belgian official who had appointed the "fire carts" with yellow silk upholstery, two thrones, and several opium dens was decorated with the Order of the Double Dragon. Ironically, the same foreigners whom the empress had tried to exterminate now gathered on the city wall to watch the monarch's ceremonial procession from the train station into the devastated city.

An Italian diplomat who witnessed the extraordinary event described it thus:

> There was a strong wind and much dust but all of Peking had collected on top of the [city] wall. First to arrive were the Manchu Bannermen on their fiery little horses. Next came a group of Chinese officials in ceremonial robes, and finally the Imperial palanquins, which advanced at an almost incredible speed between two ranks of kneeling soldiers.
>
> As she got out of her chair, the Empress Dowager looked up at the smoke-blackened wall and saw us: a row of foreigners, watching her arrival from the ramparts. The eunuchs seemed to be trying to get her to move on, as it was not seemly that she should remain there in full view of everybody. But the Empress was not to be hurried, and continued to stand between two of her ladies-of-waiting who held her up under the arms on either side, not because she needed any support but because such is the custom in China.
>
> At last she condescended to move, but before entering the temple where the priests were all ready to begin the ceremony, she stopped once more and, looking up at us, lifted her closed hands under her chin and made a series of little bows.
>
> The effect of this gesture was astonishing. We had all gone up on the wall in the hopes of catching a glimpse of the terrible Empress, whom the West considered almost an enemy of the human race. But we had been impressed by the magnificence of the swiftly moving pageant and by the beauty of the picturesque group, by the palanquins of yellow satin flashing with gold. Something told us that the return of the Court to Peking was a turning point in history, and in our breathless interest we forgot our resentment against the woman who was responsible for so much evil.
>
> That little bow, and the graceful gesture of the closed hands, took us by surprise. From all along the wall there came, in answer, a spontaneous burst of applause. The Empress Dowager appeared pleased. She remained there a few moments longer, looking up and smiling.*

Then, in a strange twist of fate, the empress dowager, after authorizing one of the greatest crimes in history, entered the Confucian temple and was ceremoni-

*Bland and Backhouse, *China under the Empress Dowager*, 210.

ally restored, by permission of the Allied Powers, to the Dragon Throne she had so cruelly usurped from the real emperor, who was once again confined to the island prison of the Ocean Terrace. The Old Buddha spent the rest of her life trying to drive him insane.

The empress now blamed the Siege of Peking on the Boxers she had commanded to attack the foreigners. To prove this, she publicly executed any Boxer that could be found and then hypocritically took credit for the reforms the emperor had advocated and for which she had beheaded six scholars after the tragic Palace Coup. The true emperor, Guangxu, remained in prison, and the fallen heir to the Dragon Throne, Pu Jun, became a drunkard and a disreputable character, notorious in the bars of Peking as a swashbuckler with a romantic past—one who, but for adverse fate, could have been emperor of China.

The dowager returned to find her looted palace partially destroyed, but she was delighted that her most precious jewels, the ones she had hidden under the floor of the Red Room, had not been discovered.

The Civil Mandarin

Two months after their return, the Reverend and Mrs. Halvor Ronning received, with great flourish, an invitation to dine with the Hsiangyang civil mandarin at his residence. Fifty years later, my aunt Almah recalled how wonderful her mother had looked that evening dressed in a Western-style blue brocade dress she had designed and had sewn by their Chinese tailor. She wore it with a blue velvet cape she had purchased in Naples. Her father looked splendid in a black silk Chinese robe with a scarlet brocade vest. He tipped his new fedora at Almah as they walked out the mission gate to board a launch to ferry them across the Han River.

On the Hsiangyang side of the river, eight uniformed bearers carrying two curtained palanquins sent by the mandarin awaited to take them to the Yamen. They were set down between the two high poles that marked every official residence in China. Near the top of each pole was a V-shaped construction intended to catch any evil spirits that might chance to drop from the netherworld. A three-gun salute announced their arrival. The wrought-iron gates, guarded by massive stone lions, swung open, and the Ronnings were welcomed by two of the mandarin's male secretaries, who led them past a detachment of armed guards through the outer and inner courtyards, past a pool filled with golden carp and surrounded by Tai-ho rocks. The mandarin was waiting at the open door of his reception hall. He walked toward them in short, quick steps, the upturned toes of his black satin boots pointing outward. Pushing the gold-rimmed spectacles, obtained for him by Reverend Dr. Himle, back to the bridge of his flat nose, he peered up at the tall foreigners. His white-lacquered queue matched the sparse white mustache straggling around his lips to join his straggly beard. He was wrapped in his official purple robe with a mandarin square on the chest, embroidered with a golden peacock that marked him as an official of the third rank. His sleeves were considerably longer than his arms to conceal his hands, which was considered the proper etiquette. A red coral brooch pinned on a crimson tassel on the front of his velvet-brimmed hat was another symbol of status, along with a mandarin rope of 108 jade beads as big as marbles hanging from his short neck to his protruding stomach. Placing his fists together under his chin, he bowed slightly and welcomed them in English.

The civil mandarin had been appointed shortly after the Ronnings' flight from Fancheng. During the Boxer Uprising, he had helped Dr. Himle escape and saved the lives, directly and indirectly, of many Chinese Christians. Like all civil mandarins, he had attained his position not through heredity but by taking the highly competitive Imperial examinations. According to the ancient tradition, he had written the exams in one of the windowless, four-foot-square tiled sheds that stood within a walled enclosure on the Imperial Palace grounds in Peking. To Western sensibilities, the competition verged on burlesque. Each candidate was required to be shut up for three days and two nights in the fierce heat of August in a box-like cell with only a peephole for the guard to observe them. The scholar was not allowed to lie down and was permitted to relieve himself only under escort. Other than a little food and a red candle for light, he had only his paper, calligraphy brush, a stick of ink, and a board for a seat. The scholars were obliged to write the Chinese classics from memory, compose formulaic "eight-legged" prose, and write essays about ancient Confucian philosophy as proof of their fitness to govern in the modern world. If a drop of ink accidentally fell on their paper, all hope of success was blotted out. It was not uncommon for a student who failed the examinations to commit suicide or turn to opium. Fear of failure and the thought of disgracing their clan drove some men mad. Barely an examination passed without a student being found dead in his cell. When this happened, a hole was cut in the wall of the shed to allow the removal of the body, for the doors, once sealed by the Imperial commissioners, could not be opened for any reason. Only those who passed all three of the examinations were eligible to become state officials, a group divided into nine ranks. Each of the nine ranks of civil officials was designated by a different bird; from the highest (first) to lowest (ninth), the birds were: the crane, golden pheasant, peacock, wild goose, silver pheasant, egret, mandarin duck, quail, and paradise flycatcher.

The mandarin of Hsiangyang was one of three local scholars of the more than four thousand entrants from Hsiangfan County who had passed the highest Imperial exam in the preceding three years. After years of study in Peking that aged him before his time, he was welcomed back home in 1900 as a great hero.

In the house of the mandarin, the missionaries were escorted into the elaborate reception hall and introduced to Morning Glory, the mandarin's second wife, and also his eldest son by his first wife and three officials. It was the first time Hannah had met the wife of a high-ranking official. Her keen eyes did not miss a detail of the woman's clothing. In a letter to her sister Rebecca, Hannah noted: *It seems to me that the main object in the dress of a Chinese woman of rank must be the combination of a diversity of color and a variety of embroidery. There was no attempt to match anything. She looked very fragile. Her melancholy face was powdered white with daubs of rouge like a porcelain doll, and her eyes outlined in black kohl. Her hair was lacquered tightly back in an elaborate chignon held by silver filigree hairpins hung with tiny bells and inlaid with blue kingfisher feathers. They were exquisite but my heart went out to her. She looked at least thirty years younger than her husband and seemed almost lost in layers of clothing. She wore three jackets of different lengths, a pleated skirt over trousers and a girdle, all embroidered in different colors. Her ankles were wrapped in black ribbons and her tiny spangled shoes were bound to her poor crippled feet with gold tinsel. She barely reached my shoulder.*

The mandarin was a man of many facets. He had invited Halvor to discuss the aftermath of the Boxer Uprising and to assure Halvor that as chief magistrate, he was not averse to the teaching of Western ideas in the mission school. He showed Halvor an edict issued from the Central Government last year in Peking ordering the immediate massacre of all foreigners. Halvor was stunned by the first sentence: *Feng yangren bi sha, yangren di hui bi sha* (Whenever you meet foreigners you must kill them, and if they attempt to escape they must still immediately be killed). The magistrate told Halvor that, at the risk of their lives, he and several other Chinese governors had altered the character for "kill" (*sha*) into another character meaning "protect" (*bao*).

Halvor to Nils: *The Civil Mandarin is a progressive man. I sincerely thanked him for saving the lives of the native Christians and helping Himle escape. He told me that the danger was by no means over. There are still many Chinese who blame the foreigners for the troubles in China. There is also lots of bad feeling because of the looting of the Imperial Palaces and the indemnities imposed by the Allied Powers. The*

Mandarin said he could not be responsible for our safety but then we never expected him to be. He also complained that certain Christian converts refused to pay taxes in the belief that the missionaries will protect them.

After dinner he showed me his very impressive library with books in both English and Chinese. He was anxious for me to understand why the Chinese, high and low, regard the missionaries with fear and suspicion. He thinks that missionaries are by the nature of their calling a revolutionary challenge to Chinese culture and tradition even though some of us seem to appreciate many aspects of Chinese culture and seek, through Christian conversion and morals, to enrich and fulfill their culture rather than destroy it. But he said that even though some missionaries concentrate on the establishment of a new order rather than attacking the old order it amounts to the same thing in the end. I think he is right and that is why the Manchus fear us.

The Mandarin assured me that among the Chinese intellectuals there is a growing recognition of the need for fundamental change and that it was obvious that the fragile balance of social, political and cosmic forces in China could easily be upset by the teaching of missionaries who plant new ideas and attitudes in the mind of the common man. He gave me his full support to educate the youth of our district and to introduce them to Western political theories as well as science and technology.

Mountain Retreat

The mission was expanding in all fields when the summer heat and humidity brought the dreaded illnesses on again. Typhoid fever, malaria, and cholera infested Fancheng. Evangelist Huang caught typhoid. He collapsed in a school-room and died three days later. Halvor was compelled to close the schools and place the mission under quarantine. Halvor to Nils: *We shall miss Evangelist Huang terribly. He was the man that from a human point of view we could not afford to lose. He was the first adult baptized here and did fine work in the absence of the missionaries during the Boxer Rebellion.*

Hannah was expecting another baby. The Ronnings and Himle took their families to their cool mountain retreat in Hai Shan, but there seemed to be no escape. On July 29, 1902, Hannah wrote her mother: *One step between us and death. Last night was exceedingly warm and sultry yet Papa and the children managed to sleep but I could not find rest till about three o'clock when my good husband woke up and fanned me with a large palm leaf until I fell into a calm sweet sleep . . . About six, the Chinese workers arrived to continue work on our cellar. Himle joined them and noticed they had forgotten to place supporting pillars under the roof on*

which they had already piled all the tiles (we do not have shingles here, remember).
Halvor, shouting "the roof will fall," hurried into the cellar with some men to put
up the pillars. They were too late. I was horrified to see the roof crash—the whole
roof was down in a second—burying Halvor and the workers alive. Himle escaped
because he was on top. I ran to the scene with the others to help. We dug frantically
with anything we could find, praying all the while. You can imagine my relief when my
dear husband miraculously emerged, covered with dirt but with a thankful smile on
his face. He had been saved by the same beam he was putting up at the time. Others
were not so fortunate. Two were killed and Dr. Himle is treating six others for injuries.
It was no wonder that the twins, Hazel and Harold, were born three weeks early.

Halvor: *September 13, 1902. This afternoon twins were born, a boy and a girl.*
Mother and twins doing fine. The other children are wild with joy, especially Almah,
who finally has a sister. We named them Harold Gerhard and Hazel Marion. The
twins grew strong on the milk of a Chinese wet nurse, but Hannah became
weaker. They carried her down the mountain on a litter to the mission hospital,
where Dr. Himle treated her for puerperal fever, an often fatal infection appearing after childbirth.

October 13. Hannah has been very sick. I took the four children to her bedside
and we knelt in prayer. It seemed to me that the Lord must hear the small children.
Hannah improved amazingly fast and was soon strong enough to resume her
mission work. Halvor and the children were convinced that their prayers had
been answered.

Before the Boxer Uprising, it had been mainly the common people who
took an interest in the church and schools. Now the prominent people of all
ranks began to send their children to school and attend church meetings. By
the end of 1903, there were 240 children in school, and the mission field had
been extended to include, according to Halvor's estimate, "in all more than three
million souls." At the beginning of 1904, another missionary, Miss Anna Lee,
arrived, and in 1905, Reverend and Mrs. G. M. Trygstad came to help. A new
high school was established, and the Mission Board elected Halvor as principal.
Halvor would have been pleased to know that a hundred years later, it would be
the largest high school in Hubei Province, with four thousand students and a
museum named in his honor.

20

Roots of Revolution, 1904–1905

In their translation of the American Declaration of Independence, our Chinese students had substituted the "Empress Dowager" for "King George the Third."
— CHESTER RONNING, *A Memoir of China in Revolution*

By 1905, the high school was filled with a new type of student. During the young emperor's Hundred Days of Reform back in 1898, thousands of students from wealthy families had gone abroad—especially to Japan—to be educated. They returned to view afresh the tyranny of their own government and the backwardness of China. Nelius and Chester soon discovered that the seeds of revolution were being sown in their own father's school. They were only eleven and twelve years old but were already as tall as most of the eighteen-year-old Chinese students. Chester resembled his father, with the same mass of wavy brown hair, the deep cleft in his chin, and the penetrating blue eyes questing for action. Nelius, with fairer hair, was more like his mother, with the same glow in his light-blue eyes that seems to come from unquestioning faith and inner strength. They wore the same school uniforms as the high school students and were never treated as foreigners by their Chinese friends.

Chester and Nelius had learned English during their stay in America and were soon in constant demand by the senior boys of their father's school, who were eager to practice English. Many of the high school students had come on recommendation of the new mandarin after failing to qualify for the demanding official exams. Some had studied English by correspondence courses and needed practice in the spoken language.

One day Nelius and Chester were invited to the room of the most senior student, Tung Tse-pei, a strikingly handsome eighteen-year-old with intense eyes, a vivid imagination, and an adventurous spirit. Like the other students, he wore the Manchu-enforced hairstyle—a shaven hairline and a long queue—that had been forced upon the Chinese in the 1640s as evidence of Chinese subservience to the Manchu rulers. Brilliant and hardworking, Tse-pei was most dissatisfied with the state of affairs in his country. He had come from a village where he had memorized Chinese classics, passed the local-level government examinations at seventeen, and was preparing for the second-level examinations when his father became ill. No longer able to afford a tutor, he sent his son to the mission school. Tse-pei was not displeased. He had grown restless with the old ideas and constant repetition of the classics and longed for new concepts and independent thinking.

Chester and Nelius were flattered by the attentions of the senior boys. Tse-pei invited them to sit down while he stood with six fellow students dressed in the smart new school uniforms Hannah had designed. He produced a hidden paper from under a floorboard, and the students began to read together from the document in singsong unison. When they were finished they stood smiling, waiting for the reaction of the American boys. But Nelius and Chester had not understood a word. It had sounded like a chant of Chinese nonsense syllables. Not wanting to disappoint their new friends, Nelius stole a look at the document they had been reciting and was surprised to discover it was the American Declaration of Independence.

With typical Chinese courtesy, the American boys congratulated the students on their splendid English and after urging, agreed to give them a few insignificant constructive criticisms in pronunciation. Nelius asked them to read it one at a time so he could hear it better. The students were delighted, and they all read the document repeatedly, each time improving their enunciation. The Chinese boys had, in fact, substituted the name "Empress Dowager" for "King George the Third" and had listed her corresponding crimes. Although the students joked when they listed the faults of the old empress, inwardly they were deadly serious. The older generation would never have dared defy the ruler who reigned by the Mandate of Heaven, but the students, reflecting their new knowledge and Western lack of respect, scoffed at their supreme ruler. The following week, Tse-pei received another document from Hankow. It was Lincoln's Gettysburg Address. Nelius and Chester were called to help them read it, and Tse-pei told the American boys that a man called Sun Yat-sen had promised to bring "government of the people, by the people and for the people" to China. They had translated the line as "people-owning, people-ruling and people-enjoying."

The young Americans were thrilled to be a part of this Chinese conspiracy. They had never thought of the Declaration of Independence or the Gettysburg Address as revolutionary documents, but they felt proud that their Chinese friends were using them as inspiration for claiming their country back from the Manchu overlords. The missionary's sons were soon spending every evening teaching English to the Chinese boys. They were only vaguely aware that they were also teaching revolution. The Chinese students expressed deep resentment not only against the Manchu court but against the old patriarchal family tyranny. Tung Tse-pei, for example, like most of the other students, had been engaged since birth to a girl he had never seen and would not see before their arranged wedding. The resentment increased when they learned from Nelius that in Western societies young people are free to choose their own life partners. Tse-pei was in love with an educated young woman with unbound feet from Hannah's girls' school, and as the time approached to marry the girl of his parents' choice, he became moody, unhappy, and rebellious. The students yearned to change the old traditions that deprived them of their freedom—by revolution if necessary.

One evening at dusk, Tse-pei invited Nelius and Chester to his room, where the other six were already assembled. They all sat in a circle on the floor, and Tse-pei confided that he had organized, through instruction by correspondence, a local cell of Dr. Sun Yat-sen's famous United League (Tongmenghui). From a secret box hidden under a floorboard, he carefully extricated some forbidden articles copied from the revolutionary Shanghai newspaper *Subao* concerning reform and modernization. The articles pointed out the importance of protecting Emperor Guangxu from the empress dowager, urged establishment of a Chinese constitution, and even went so far as to recommend the killing of Manchus. The most dangerous document, however, was part of a manifesto entitled *The Revolutionary Army* written by Zou Rong, a courageous young revolutionary from Shanghai. In his book-length manifesto, secretly copied and distributed by Sun Yat-sen's followers, Zou Rong pleaded with his countrymen to "seize back their land and dare to be free." He invoked the spirits of Washington and Rousseau and recalled the achievements of the British, French, and American revolutions. He mocked the Chinese for accepting Manchu domination like servile cattle and described as "butchers" the Chinese officials who served the Manchus. He advocated forcing out the Manchus and executing the emperor, and called for equal rights between men and women, freedom of speech, freedom of the press, and a constitution based on the American model.

As recalled in *Memoir of China in Revolution,* written by Chester as an adult, Tung Tse-pei stood up and turned on the lantern. He began to read from Zou Rong's writing with such an impassioned voice that it brought tears to the eyes of the missionary's sons.

How sublime is revolution! How majestic!
For this I march the length of the Great Wall, scale the K'unlun Mountains, travel the whole of the Yangtze, and follow the Yellow River to its

source; for this I plant the banner of independence and ring the bell of freedom. My voice reechoes from heaven to earth, I tear my lungs to shreds in crying out to my fellow countrymen: Listen! Our China must have revolution today! If we are to throw off the Manchu yoke, we must have revolution today. We must have revolution if China is to be independent. We must have revolution if China is to take her place as a powerful nation on the globe, if China is to survive long in the new world of the twentieth century, if China is to be a great country in the world and play the leading role.

Revolution is a universal rule of evolution. Revolution is a universal principle of the world. Revolution is the essence of the struggle for survival or destruction in a time of transition. Revolution submits to heaven and responds to men's needs. Revolution rejects what is corrupt and keeps the good. Revolution is the advance from barbarism to civilization. Revolution turns slaves into masters.

When the Manchus assumed the Mandate of Heaven from the Ming in 1644, the main opposition to the Manchu conquerors concerned not politics or territory but hairstyles. The Manchus ordered the Chinese men to shave their foreheads and wear one long queue down their backs as a sign of subjugation to their new rulers. This violated the Chinese sense of honor and decorum. The traditional Chinese hairdo for men was a topknot, like the first emperor's terracotta soldiers had worn. The Mongol Emperor Kublai Khan humiliated the Chinese by ordering the men to let their hair down and wear it in two braids. When Chinese rule was restored with the Ming, the first thing they did was to coil their hair on top of their heads. When the Manchus defeated the Ming, they ordered the Chinese, on pain of death, to wear their hair in pigtails. The Chinese rioted. Some areas, like the town of Chiating in the southeast, refused outright and offered armed resistance. The men in Chiating held out for eight days against the Manchu Bannermen. When the town was finally subjugated, a three-day massacre took place as a warning to anyone with similar ideas. Records show that ninety-seven thousand townspeople and seventy-five thousand in the surrounding areas died in the battle over the pigtail.

All the boys knew that even talking about cutting their hair was dangerous. Manchu soldiers and their spies were on constant lookout for short-haired rebels. Any Chinese caught without a queue was beaten to death or decapitated. What the boys didn't anticipate at the time was that, within the year, their hero journalist Zou Rong and the entire *Subao* newspaper staff would be jailed for treason. In the spring of 1905, the young revolutionary whose rhetoric had inspired students all across China died mysteriously in jail. There was widespread talk that he had been tortured to death. He was nineteen years old.

When Tung Tse-pei was finished reading Zou Rong's inspiring words to his fellow students, they stood up and cheered; then Tse-pei, in a gesture Chester would never forget, suddenly bent forward and whipped his long queue over his head from behind. "Look at this disgrace to all patriotic Chinese!" he shouted. "You call it a pig's tail, and that's exactly what it is. For over 200 years we have been forced to wear these miserable things because we have become pigs to show our inferiority to the Manchus." He looked up and, using his fingers like a pair of shears, added: "We are going to cut them off like this." Tung Tse-pei's eyes shone with a fierceness Chester had never seen before. "When Dr. Sun cut off his queue he did more than disguise his appearance, he changed from inside out and resolved nevermore to be subject to the Manchus. There are students like us in all the schools in China," he said. "We shall overthrow the Manchu Dynasty!"

Chester and Nelius were sworn to secrecy. Tung Tse-pei told them that their father ("Old Whiskers") would not like to hear that his students were plotting revolution, but Chester thought he would be pleased to hear that his students wanted China to become a republic like the United States of America.

Tung Tse-pei and his fellow student conspirators were in fact seeking to renew a revolutionary movement called the Taiping Rebellion that had begun forty years earlier. Chinese historians describe it as the first peasant uprising against Manchu domination. It raged across the rich, productive heartland of the lower Yangtze provinces, affecting sixteen out of the eighteen provinces. It destroyed six hundred cities and killed an estimated 20 million people. It also constitutes a strange chapter in Christian missionary experience in China. The rebel leader was Hong Xiuquan, a mystic who became interested in Christianity after reading missionary tracts.

Hong was a frustrated Confucian scholar who had failed the civil service exams four times. He collapsed during his last effort, and a hole was cut in the wall of the shed to allow the removal of the unconscious student. Hong was delirious for forty days and saw visions of God. When he recovered, he was a different man, changed in both appearance and personality. Some believe he had suffered brain damage. He went into the countryside proclaiming himself the younger brother of Jesus and declared that a great calamity would befall mankind unless the people repudiated their idols, overthrew the Manchus, and worshiped the Christian God. Thousands of impoverished peasants, restive under the Manchus, rallied to him. The Taipings managed to conquer half of the Manchu empire, and Hong set up a government in Nanking, the "Heavenly Kingdom of Great Peace," and organized a church in the Purple Mountains of Guiping, Guangxi Province, called "God's Mission." He declared himself king and governed for fifteen years.

The end came with the help of a foreign intervention. In 1860, when the Taipings were attempting to conquer Shanghai, a Chinese financier Yang Feng, known as Taki, hired a young American soldier of fortune, Frederick T. Ward, to assemble a force to drive the Taiping rebels out of the city. Ward's forces of European officers, Chinese soldiers, and Filipinos, which the Manchu emperor named the "Ever Victorious Army," twice drove the Taipings back. When Ward was killed in battle, an English soldier known as "Chinese Gordon" replaced him and expanded the army. The Taipings were wiped out, and Manchu troops slaughtered millions of Chinese who were suspected of supporting the Taipings. Many fled from Canton to Southeast Asia and became overseas Chinese known as *huaqiao*. Cities that had welcomed the Taipings were razed.

When Nanking was retaken by the Manchus, Hong, the "Heavenly King," poisoned himself. The Manchus killed more than one hundred thousand residents of Nanking. The remnants of China's revolutionaries went underground to join the Heaven and Earth Society, which kept alive the idea of a nationalistic revolution that finally resulted in the overthrow of the Manchus in 1911. Dr. Sun Yat-sen, whom both the Nationalist and Communist parties later claimed as "Father of the Revolution," said that as a boy he had been inspired by the Taipings. In Europe, Karl Marx gained a new perspective on peasant revolution.

More than a century later, my father and I visited the site of one of those unfortunate cities not far from the present city of Shashi in Hubei Province on the Yangtze River. The walls had never been rebuilt, and every building in the city still lay in a heap of shapeless rubble. A dark cloud of horror hovered over the remains. As we looked at the devastation, it was not hard to imagine the inhumane butchery and wanton destruction of that terrible day. The ruined city was still haunted by the ghosts of the Taiping Rebellion, the first and largest of the anti-Manchu revolutions.

21

Sun Yat-sen

Three Principles of the People: To establish Ultimate Peace, Freedom, and Equality.
— SUN YAT-SEN, *Manifesto*, 1905

The gospel of revolt seems to be spreading more rapidly throughout the country than the gospel of Christ.
— HALVOR RONNING, 1905

March 25, 1905. Dear brother Nils: All my interests are now in the mission work with its joys and sorrows. Doors are opening all over and strange things are happening. The old Empress has abolished the Imperial Examination System and the students of higher learning are pouring into our school. We have obtained more property and have over a thousand students. It has always been my hope to train enough Chinese evangelists and teachers so eventually they will have their own independent churches and schools. We already have 30 Chinese teachers to help us, six of them are women. But, in spite of our hard work or perhaps because of it, the gospel of revolt seems to be spreading more rapidly throughout the country than the gospel of Christ. The suffering of the people of China is unbearable. They are tired of Emperors with total power but no compassion. The handwriting is on the wall. The Middle Kingdom has survived countless revolutions but none have brought basic change. This time we are hoping for true reforms. Sun Yat-sen is a Christian so let us pray that change may come without violence.

Sun Yat-sen appeared at a time when the Chinese nation was suffering grievously. Japan and the Western powers were tearing the country apart, and the Manchu rulers had lost the respect of their subjects. Sun introduced a new political philosophy to China that would eventually destroy the two-thousand-year-old dynastic cycle. Like most revolutionary leaders in China, Sun had received his education in mission schools. He was born in 1866, in Cuiheng village in Guangdong Province. As a child, Sun was intrigued by an uncle who had been a Taiping veteran, and the seeds of hatred against the Manchu conquerors were deeply ingrained. At the age of twelve and partially educated in the Chinese classics, he was sent to Hawaii. He attended the Church of England's Bishop's School in Honolulu, where he adopted Christianity and began to look at antiquated Chinese traditions in a new light. When he returned to Canton, he studied medicine at the American Presbyterian Hospital under the missionary John G. Kerr. Sun continued his medical studies with Dr. James Cantlie, a Scottish physician in the Medical College in Hong Kong, called Yale-in-China, where he formed a revolutionary group with three close friends who became known as Si Da Kou (the Four Bandits), In 1892, Sun graduated with honors in medicine and surgery and returned to Canton, where he opened a pharmacy and brazenly sold his political opinions along with his prescriptions. In 1894, the year Chester was born and China was at war with Japan over Korea, Sun escaped to Hawaii to found China's first political party, the Xing Zhonghui (Revive China Society). The purpose was to kick out the Manchus, unite all progressive Chinese in China and abroad, use Western scientific and industrial skills to make China strong and prosperous, and direct the intellectuals toward a reasonable political theory. Sun's whole revolutionary movement was strongly supported by the Overseas Chinese, many of whom had escaped during the fall of the Taipings. In 1895, Sun led his first revolutionary plot to seize Government Headquarters in Canton. The scheme was a terrible fiasco. His shipment of six hundred pistols bought in Hong Kong was intercepted by Chinese authorities. Several of Sun's comrades were executed, and seventy more were arrested. Sun escaped again, this time with a price of 10,000 taels on his head. While hiding out in Japan, he cut off his queue and grew a mustache so he could pass for a Japanese. When the students in Halvor's school heard this, they became determined to cut off their pigtails.

The next year Dr. Sun went to London, where a bizarre incident brought him to the world's attention. Sun was kidnapped in London by Peking's agents and imprisoned in the Chinese embassy. Before the Chinese ambassador could transport the prisoner to China for execution, the plot was foiled by an embassy porter, who brought the news to Sun's former professor, Dr. Cantlie, who had since been knighted by Queen Victoria. The doctor went to Scotland Yard for help but was ignored. He appealed for a writ of habeas corpus, but a judge at the Old Bailey threw it out. Then, in a stroke of genius, Cantlie leaked the story to the press. On October 22, 1896, the London *Globe and Mail* headlined the sensational news. The next morning, Prime Minister Salisbury demanded Sun Yat-sen's release. After twelve days of confinement, the unknown Chinese revolutionary walked out of the embassy a free man and became famous the world over. The international press was there to photograph him and record his story, which appealed to the democratic nations. The little room at 49 Portland Place where Sun was secretly detained is still preserved as a historic landmark.

Dr. Sun spent the next eight months in London, where he is said to have spent fifty-seven days in the British Museum reading books ranging from philosophy, political science, economics, engineering, and agriculture. He was influenced by the socialist tax-equalization and land-distribution theories of Henry George and swapped ideas with many Russian exiles studying revolutionary ideas in the library, including Karl Marx. It was during these years that he molded his "Three Principles of the People": Nationalism, Democracy, and People's Livelihood.* Dr. Sun went back to Japan, where he organized secret revolutionary societies among the eager students. As a political reformer, Sun Yat-sen exuded the same indefatigable energy that Reverend Ronning displayed as a religious reformer. Both men were visionaries with the same goals: the reform and modernization of China. They differed, however, about how to reach that goal. Halvor, the idealist, was convinced that education of the masses could result in social reform and modernization without revolution. Sun Yat-sen, the realist, felt the only way to achieve democratic reform was through an anti-Manchu revolution. Education of the masses, he believed, would come after the revolution, not before. Chester agreed with Sun Yat-sen, and a philosophical difference began to develop between father and son.

For the next years, Sun traveled constantly to places like Hong Kong, Macao, and Annam, where he founded societies, printed pamphlets, and trained agents to spread the word in China. Although there was a high price on his head, he traveled freely. In 1904, he was received by President Theodore Roosevelt and honored by Chinese merchants in Philadelphia. He was an eloquent speaker who could hold an audience spellbound for hours. His greatest talk delineated his version of a Lincoln-type government for China "of the people, by the people and for the people" on which he based his Three Principles.

Basically, the principle of Nationalism was to free China from Manchu domination and foreign pressures and make it an independent nation, equal among the nations of the world. But the first task was to unite the five subraces, Han, Mongol, Manchu, Tibetan, and Uyghurs, that make up the Chinese people and to win political, economic, and social equality. Dr. Sun envisioned the building

*Mike Peng, "A Study of Chinese History" (unpublished typescript).

of a new China in three stages: armed revolutionary activity, political tutelage, and, finally, constitutional government. The first stage meant military operations: the revolutionary army would unify the country by force, and at the same time reformers would explain the aim of their leader by extolling the "Three Principles of the People." In the second stage, educators and propagandists would be sent into all the occupied areas to educate the people in self-government, and a provincial governor would be elected by popular vote. Eventually a People's Congress would be set up and a national constitution created. In the third stage, a constitutional government—"by, of, and for the people"—would be ushered in.* The designer of this scheme could not foresee that for the next half century, until 1949, China would be stuck in the first stage: military operations. The third stage is still in process.

Ever since his acceptance into Tung Tse-pei's secret society in his father's school, Chester had been uneasy about the false queue his Papa often wore. One evening when Halvor was going to a meeting, he asked Chester to fetch his skullcap with the attached queue. Chester handed it to him and said cautiously, "I have heard, Papa, that the Chinese call the foreigner without a pigtail a 'true devil' but the foreigner who wears one, like you do, is called a 'false devil.' Is it not better to be true than false?"

Reverend Ronning was about to place the absurd apparatus on his head but hesitated and studied the reflection of his son in the mirror. Chester stood stiffly with his eyes cast discreetly downward in the manner of a modest filial son whose greatest fear was to cause his worthy father to lose face. Then his father burst out laughing. "You are right, my son," he said. "Get the scissors and we shall cut off this degrading symbol of Manchu domination!" Chester ran for the scissors. He wondered if "Old Whiskers" knew more about what was going on in his school than the students thought he did.

In 1905, Sun Yat-sen's United League proclaimed the expulsion of the Manchu monarchs as its first objective. But by fall, for the people in Hubei, all thoughts of reform were obliterated by a more urgent problem—hunger.

*Ibid.

22

Famine

See the rain does not come
The sky is as brass
Foreign blood must be spilt
Before the drought shall pass.
—CHANT OF THE RAINMAKERS, 1905

When Hannah became pregnant again, she was filled with both joy and fear. She struggled to conceal the latter from her husband but wrote of her trepidations to her sister Rebecca, who had recently given birth to the fourth of her nine children: *Pray for me about the middle of February—it is too much to ask to have the easy time you had but I should be thankful with less struggle than last time. You urge me to come home with the children. Oh would I for the children's sake but it is an impossibility unless I part with my husband. We have so much more work to do here. I am not strong but God will have to take care of me. If I shall live, He will have to supply strength and protection for the children. I am in God's hands. Don't worry, dear sister.*

Halvor to Nils: *February 1905. A healthy baby girl, Lilly Victory, was born! Nelius is twelve, he plays the flute already very well. Chester, only ten, is perhaps going to be a writer like his uncle. He writes long stories about China in revolution. Sometimes I wonder where he gets his ideas. Almah, eight years old, is an artist. She paints better than either her father or mother and that is saying a good deal, isn't it? Talbert is round and fat but a good chap. The twins, two and a half years old, run around like little terrors and are healthy and happy. But brother, I fear for Hannah and the children. It is hot and dry here. If we don't have rain soon we might have a drought and terrible famine. Thank God the potatoes I brought are flourishing here.*

Had it not been for the lack of nutrition, Hannah might have recovered. When the famine struck, it was so devastating that even those who survived its ghastly tentacles were scarred for life. The missionaries learned that nothing on earth is as horrible as hunger.

In the fall of 1905, drought in the Yellow River Valley spread north. The food shortage was not yet critical in Fancheng, but refugees from the countryside filled the streets of the twin cities and told terrifying tales of famine. Food was hoarded, leaving little for the hungry to buy. Fancheng was soon overflowing with the wretched creatures, and still they came, staggering skeletons, haggard, grim, exhausted, dying, carrying shelters of rolled straw matting on their backs. Each day hungry eyes searched the sky for the rain clouds that would save the harvest, but the sun blazed relentlessly until the green rice shriveled and fell to the parched earth. Small rivers became muddy streams, and the ponds dried into cracked mud cakes glinting with dead fish. The Han River was lower than Halvor had ever seen it, but thank God it continued to flow. It was the life force that kept the hungry alive. They ate the fish and mixed the water with flour made from ground leaves. When all the sweet potatoes were gone, they ate the vines and roots; when the corn and sorghum were finished, they ate the cobs and stalks; then they ate sawdust, thistles, and tree bark and added dirt to the leaf flour.

Rainmakers marched in from the countryside—men and boys stripped to the waist, wearing dried-leaf garlands around their heads. They paraded through the streets carrying cudgels to beat the gongs and anyone who got in the way. If a man crossed the path of the rain procession, he was beaten severely; if a woman stepped in the way, she was beaten to death. When the rainmakers discovered the foreign mission, they stopped their daily march, pounded on the gate of the mission, and chanted:

> See the rain does not come
> The sky is as brass
> Foreign blood must be spilt
> Before the drought shall pass.

Hannah and Halvor were sickened to think that after all the progress they had made, they would still be blamed for natural catastrophes. They were moved to almost unbearable fear and despair. The potatoes and tomatoes that Halvor brought from America thrived, but the missionaries had barely enough to feed the mission workers and students. They began storing rice and river water in barrels. At the beginning of the drought, Halvor and Himle had gone into the streets to distribute relief, but they were mobbed and forced to run for their lives. It was not long before the refugees gathered in front of the mission. They huddled in dreadful, trembling hordes against the walls, banging on the gates with wooden bowls, begging for food. The missionaries knew they were endangering their own lives but felt they had no choice. They cooked some of their precious fruit and vegetables with rice and potatoes in large cauldrons and distributed what they could to the starving people. Hannah made sure that all the mission children had adequate food, but her own food turned to ashes in her mouth. Halvor appealed to the civil mandarin, who sent some rice, but there was never enough to ease the hunger.

One old man collapsed at the mission gate. Halvor and Himle carried him into the already-overflowing hospital. After he had sipped some warm broth, incoherent words began to tumble out of him. Halvor later wrote: *His name is Lin. His eyes were wild and haunted and his body so emaciated he could hardly walk. He was a farmer and the only survivor of a family of fourteen that had started from a town 100 miles north. He talked in a whisper because he had not the strength to speak louder: "They fell by the roadside until there were only five of us left, I could not bear to see my children suffer anymore, out of mercy I smothered three of them in the snow. Some others saw me and they dug them out and carried them away. My wife screamed because she knew they would eat them. I tried to drag them back but it was hopeless. When they were gone my wife made a hole in the ice and drowned the baby. Then she went in the water herself, begging me to cover the hole so no one would find them." When he finished his terrible story Hannah was in tears. I comforted Old Lin as best I could. He looked at me with half-crazed eyes, and said, "What kind of people are you then that will weep for strangers?" I told him that we were children of God just like he was. He has since grown stronger and helps us in the vegetable garden. Food is the most urgent problem in China. Famines and floods have been the scourge of China for centuries. Cities crumble but somehow the people go on. Untold millions have died of starvation and no government has taken steps to prevent it. There must be a way even if it means revolution!*

Days passed into weeks and months, and still no rain fell from the unmerciful heavens. Geomancers used every type of cosmic persuasion known to them, but to no avail. The people stood about, listless and starving, their faces turned upward. But the sky remained empty, and every day the cruel sun made its unhampered march across the blue. At night the moon shone clear and the stars hung like burning sparks in the heavens, but to Hannah there was no beauty in the sky anymore. She began to question her faith. *Dear Mother: How can we fathom His ways? Why does God hide himself from us? How can He let His people suffer so? My mind is too small to see the eternal pattern of things. I am in despair but I feel we must know in our hearts, not in our minds, that God loves us. The meaning of it all does not reveal itself to me but I must not lose touch with God because He does not do things my way . . . We are still trying to keep the schools going but have lost heart. Nelius and Chester and their Chinese friends are helping us distribute what food we can muster up. Almah protects the little ones from seeing the terrible sights outside the gate but she is not strong. Halvor is skin and bone but is working harder than ever. I don't know where he gets his strength. We cannot take the horses out because we are afraid they will be killed and eaten by the hungry hordes. Chester keeps his dog Vesta close to him for the same reason. Pray for us. Maybe God will hear your prayers. He doesn't hear mine.*

It was almost Christmas when relief finally came in the form of a small British gunboat. The river was too low for regular gunboats. Halvor ran to the dock waving an American flag. The captain was a bear of a man who looked familiar. Could it be Captain Sanford, who had rescued them during the Boxer Uprising? Sure enough, it was the same old English sailor who had rampaged up and down the China coast for almost two decades before he retired to gunboats. His face was even more sun-damaged and his nose as rosy as his curly beard. He still reeked of rum, but to Halvor he was a patron saint. The two old friends embraced.

Sanford informed him that cartloads of food headed for the city had been stolen and the mules killed for food. The weaker refugees had fallen prey to wolves. Bleached skeletons lined the roads. The villages were silent except for the moans of those who waited in stupefied misery for death. Hundreds had been reduced to cannibalism, and butcher shops trafficked openly in human flesh.

The sailors from the gunboat began hauling sacks of rice and soybeans down the gangplank and stacking them on the dock to be loaded into carts and taken to the mission and distribution centers. Suddenly a tidal wave of refugees surged forward, grabbing for the sacks, tearing them open, filling their pockets, trampling over one another, fighting and growling. Hannah, watching with horror from the balcony, feared that Halvor would be trampled by the half-crazed mob fighting like wild beasts over the kill. She was shocked by what hunger could do: friend pitted against friend, husband against wife, mother against child.

Halvor and Sanford called in vain for reason. One ruffian jumped on a cart and encouraged the mob to grab the food and kill the foreigners. Once again came the dreaded call, "*sha yangguizi!*" (kill the foreign devils!). Captain Sanford fired his pistol in the air, causing only a moment of hesitation. Then he fired at the man on the cart. The bullet ripped open a sack of rice on his shoulder. The kernels flooded over him and the man screamed. Halvor seized the moment.

"Put down your sacks!" he shouted. "God has sent this food to be shared by all of us. You will all get your share!" The hungry people continued to riot. Small children were trampled.

Sanford was about to order his armed men to fire when the cavalry of the civil mandarin came galloping to the waterfront. The people backed off. The mandarin took half the supplies to set up a distribution center across the river in Hsiangyang. The Swedish mission joined with the American mission to distribute food in Fancheng.

Captain Sanford returned the following week with more supplies, but it was never enough. Hannah was tortured by the sight of starving innocents—bones cracking through parched skin, vacant eyes, bellies swollen with foul wind. There were no animals left in the city except the Ronnings' horses and Chester's dog. Even the rats had been devoured. Specters wandered over the distant hills in search of roots and bark from the few remaining trees.

Early on the morning of March 25, 1906, when the Ronnings were in the middle of their prayers, there was an ominous hush in the air. A wind began to blow from the south, bringing gray clouds with a hint of humidity. Then it happened. Wondrous curtains of shining pearls came trickling down the windows, and soon the heavens resounded with the sound of falling water. Doors flew open and people filled the streets. All decorum was forgotten as everyone splashed in the puddles with the children. Glorious, glorious rain! God had shown his face at last. Why had He taken so long? Why? Why?

The spring rains continued. Gradually, miraculously, the countryside rejuvenated, the parched earth softened, and a shimmer of green appeared on the hillsides facing the sun. The rice paddies filled with rainwater and turned the gray ashes into emerald green. The lotus buds unfolded their pink blossoms on the ponds. The birds, chirping and flashing their brilliant wings, returned to build new nests. Eternal China began to rise again.

Soon the markets were filled with food, but no one would ever be the same. Halvor and Old Lin planted a garden of flowers and vegetables. When the first sprouts popped up, Lin watered and guarded them as if his life depended upon it. He stayed at the mission as a gardener, but his eyes never lost their look of horror. The missionaries thanked the Lord, but their hearts still ached for the thousands who had perished. The scars ran too deep to heal, but perhaps their painfully acquired wisdom had somehow added another dimension to their lives.

Halvor to Nils: *Thanks be to God that we survived the famine. The Shanghai and Peking newspapers hardly considered it worth writing about. It was the most trying time of our lives, but we had it easy compared to thousands of Chinese peasants who starved to death. I am worried about Hannah. She is weak from exhaustion. The present bad conditions here are chiefly because of the political disorganization of the country and this cannot be dealt with effectively except by a stable and just government. We live in fear of another famine. There is no such thing as fair distribution of food. We are now teaching agriculture in our school and urging the Mandarin to begin reforestation . . . The hope for China lies not in foreign aid but in the Chinese themselves. They must bring about the reforms themselves. When that day dawns, there will be a new and happy China. Spiritual awakening must go hand in hand with material progress.*

23

Missionary Conference in Peking

THE SCHOLAR

The evening wind
Has rolled back
The curtain
Of the clouds.
The moon shines clear,
And the sky is bright
With the gleam
Of distant stars.

Though you
Are far away
From home and me,
I see you
As you always were
At this hour of the night,
In your study,
Poring over
Your loved books.
—CHEN SHENGZHI,
QING DYNASTY (1644–1911)

In the summer of 1906, Reverend Ronning was invited to attend a convention of the Mission Society in Peking concerning plans for expanding the missions. Halvor was eager to participate but felt uneasy about leaving Hannah. She, however, urged him to go. He was accompanied by Sen Li-fu and his brother-in-law Carl Landahl, who, a year after Thea's death, had married Alice Holmberg, a secondary missionary called a Bible Woman, who worked with him in the Sinyeh mission in Henan. Alice agreed to stay in Fancheng with Hannah while Halvor and Carl went to Peking.

The journey took about two weeks. The three men sailed down the Han River to Wuhan and down the Yangtze to Nanking, where they boarded the recently constructed Jingpu Railway to Peking. The sleeper cars were a welcome relief, even though the bunks were too small for the tall Norwegians. The sun was nearing the horizon when they arrived at the Peking station and hailed a mule cart to ride through Qianmen Guardhouse to the main gate of the city wall, Qianmen Gate. In the broad avenue leading to the Legation Quarter they ran into an incredible confusion of vehicles, beasts, and people: sedan chairs whose color and style varied with the rank of the owner; caravans of furry, two-humped Bactrian camels trekking back and forth from the Silk Road carrying saddlebags bulging with brocades and spices. Mongolian horsemen galloped their fine ponies through the streets sending the Chinese coolies, shouldering baskets of squawking chickens on the ends of yo-sticks, scrambling for cover. Naked urchins scavenging for food looked enviously at the children of the upper classes clasping the hands of their amahs as they walked proudly down the streets wearing red pajamas with conveniently split pants. The small boys wore beribboned tufts of hair growing from the middle of their shaven heads to fool the malevolent spirits into thinking they were only girls and not worth bothering with. The boulevard was paved with crooked flagstone, making it even more difficult for the mules to pull the missionaries' cart through the crowds. Lanterns hung from the shop fronts, sometimes three deep, where merchants, smoking opium pipes, displayed their wares in the open, haggling loudly with customers. Soup vendors, fortune-tellers, barbers, letter writers, and storytellers all carried on their trades outdoors as there is no privacy in China. Manchu women, whom Halvor had seldom seen in the interior of China, did not have bound feet like Chinese women, but strode among the men with long steps, bright flowers in their hair, their faces white with rice flour, and their high cheekbones daubed with red.

Once the missionaries arrived at the gate of the Legation Quarter, where the Siege of Peking had been fought six years earlier, they paid the muleteer and walked along the banks of the Jade Canal that reportedly had run with blood during the siege. There was barely a building that had not been flattened or partially destroyed in the fighting. Gray stone walls topped with spiked glass surrounded each compound. They checked into the Grand Hotel des Wagon-Lits. The grandiose lobby, studded with gold and red pillars, was already filled with missionaries. Halvor and Landahl changed into their formal black Prince Albert coats and high white-starched collars to attend the convention, which was held in a bullet-ridden compound on the Street of Intercourse with the People. The attitudes of the new missionaries meeting to discuss the problems facing their rapidly expanding missions came as a shock to Reverend Ronning and the other veteran missionaries from the interior. A sharp difference of opinion existed about which, if any, Chinese manners and customs should be acceptable to the Christian church. Most of the overzealous missionaries had arrived in China after the Boxer Uprising and had assumed some of the superior attitudes that the Catholics, diplomats, and businesspeople living in foreign concessions had affected. Some of them voiced the opinion that one factor contributing to the Boxer Uprising was that the old missionaries in the China Inland Mission had been too lax about adherence to the Christian doctrine. One young man argued that more discipline was needed in church teaching. The Reverend Halvor Ronning was personally criticized for allowing the use of the Chinese classics in his school of higher learning, as well as for associating freely with non-Christian Chinese, tolerating "ancestor worship," and attending "heathen ceremonies" like weddings and funerals. This was close to heresy! Ronning was infuriated by their fundamentalist attitudes and wrapped his fist around the cool piece of ancient jade in his pocket, trying to stay calm. The critics expressed the opinion that all Chinese customs were based on superstition and heathen beliefs and should therefore be abolished from the church and classrooms; and that no Chinese maxims, which were not in keeping with Christian law, should enter into school readings. "They are clearly the roots of evil and will put forth the evil stalk bearing the evil seed and thus spoil the harvest!" stated his accuser.

Halvor had no idea what the arrogant young missionary was trying to say, but he was deeply hurt by the attack. Rather than immediately voicing his opinion, he prepared a paper in his defense, which he read to his colleagues the next morning. He stressed that he felt it was impossible to apply foreign ideas to the conditions of a Chinese mission field and fail to recognize the existing Chinese customs. He shocked his self-righteous critics by asking, "Is it reasonable to come to China and claim that anything you are not accustomed to is not Christian, while thinking everything you are accustomed to, even though it originated in the most ancient Teutonic heathenism, should be imposed on the Chinese as Christian customs?"

Halvor went on to argue that all popular customs, whether Chinese or Western, are expressions of natural life, of the spirit of the time.

You seem to think that we early missionaries were, according to the standards of today, poorly prepared for our work. We came to share with the Chinese the unsearchable treasures in Christ, in all simplicity, and not to impose on them a certain system of theology and the white man's views and ways. To what extent church members may participate in so-called heathen customs without violating their conscience must be determined by the individual. If members of my congregation wish to pay respects to their ancestors that is their right. Most of us do the same but in different ways. In my mission I have but one rule in this matter: Christians may enjoy nature and respect ancient customs in so far as their communion with God remains unhindered by such enjoyment. I believe that the mission church in China, ever remembering her exalted character as the body of Christ, must bring the divine plan of salvation to the Chinese. Not westerners, but the Chinese themselves must bring the gospel of Christ to China under the conditions that already exist or not at all.

Halvor felt that Christian fundamentalism had no place in China and would only lead to misunderstanding and more trouble. Reverend Ronning was a pacifist, and his main concern was to avoid revolution through peaceful reform, education of the youth, and modernization of China within the system.

Before leaving, the three Fancheng missionaries climbed Radiant Hill—now called Coal Hill—overlooking Peking and the Imperial Palace. They picnicked in the forest near the historic pine tree where the last Ming emperor had attempted to save face by hanging himself. A refreshingly cool breeze was blowing from the Gobi. Halvor had suggested they take a look inside the Gate of Heavenly Peace but was discouraged when Sen Li-fu told him that any unauthorized person caught entering the gates of the Forbidden City would be doomed to the lingering "death of a thousand cuts": tied to a cross, slowly flayed, and then beheaded.

The Forbidden City was a supreme example of spiritual symbolism and metaphysical elements combined with architecture. Before the Allied Powers sacked the city, its seventy major buildings, all constructed in conformity with aesthetic rules and a series of geometrical and astronomical calculations considered to be "in harmony with the cosmic order," held a magnificent collection of nearly one million pieces of rare art. The main buildings and gardens are still the same. The grounds are divided into two main parts: Three Big Halls, where affairs of state were conducted, and the Imperial Gardens and Six East and West Palaces, where the emperor, his wives, concubines, children, servants, and eunuchs lived.

What Halvor was forbidden to see at the time is now open to the public. One enters through the Meridian Gate, where the emperors once reviewed their victorious armies. Then, crossing over the Golden River, an ornamental stream winding under marble moon bridges, one arrives at the Gate of Supreme Harmony. It presides majestically in a vast courtyard guarded by gigantic bronze lions. Once through the Gate, more marble terraces and courtyards greet the eye. In the center of it all stands the Great Hall of Supreme Harmony, where the golden Dragon Throne, guarded by two cloisonné cranes, stands in all its splendor in "the center of the world." It was here where the Imperial edicts were announced, war and peace declared, new years, birthdays, and weddings celebrated, and the ceremonial life of the empire conducted. Beyond are two more throne rooms: the Hall of Middle Harmony and the Hall of Preserving Harmony. On the stairway behind this hall lies the incredible Imperial Way. Over this marble carpet of clouds and dragons, the emperor in his sedan chair was carried by bearers walking on the steps on each side of the dragon pavement. It leads one into the courtyard before the crimson walls and the Gate of Heavenly Purity that divides the three ceremonial palaces from the Three Rear Halls, in the Imperial living quarters.

Halvor found it hard to believe that the hedonistic empress dowager had been reinstated on the Dragon Throne surrounded by geomancers, opium sots, eunuchs, effete scholars, and other parasites. The Manchu court was cut off from their Chinese subjects, seemingly oblivious to the crop failures, famine, floods, and droughts that brought misery and death to millions of Chinese every year.

December 14, 1906. Dearest Hannah: We have seen this once great city of Peking and I am longing to return. The conference is over. Some think I am a heretic. Maybe I am. Dearest one, I will hurry back. Tell the children that to our great excitement, we saw a long camel caravan walking, almost gliding, by the city wall in a calm, steady and rhythmic pace, perhaps coming from the Silk Road. The two-humped camels are among the most intriguing creatures on this earth. China is in the midst of turmoil but the camels remain poised and peaceful, almost majestic, as they lift their gangly legs with huge padded paws and place them softly on the ground. They don't seem to be burdened, as I am, by the follies of mankind or even the heavy bulging bags joined by ropes strung between their humps. As we peered up at the camels some would glance disdainfully down at us. I was riveted by their mysterious eyes: glowing black holes that seemed to hold the secrets of the universe . . . Tell the children that camels are "fungchu" animals: meaning they can walk long distances without food because they eat huge amounts at one time and store it in their stomachs . . . You would love them, Hannah! . . . I don't know where they were coming from or where they are going. But I know I am coming back to you. Your loving husband Halvor.

24

The Old Silk Road

If any place deserves to be haunted, it is the Old Silk Road. For amid the ruins of ancient Buddhist cities, once strung like prayer beads across the forbidding terrain of Central Asia, there have occurred more mysterious happenings, rich pageantry, magical rituals, sinister intrigue, heroic battles, and cruel massacres than the imagination can encompass.

—AUDREY RONNING TOPPING, 2010

Before Halvor left Peking, he met with an old friend, the Swedish archaeologist, explorer, and cartographer Sven Hedin, at the Grand Hotel des Wagon-Lits. Hedin was preparing for another expedition in search of the ruins of the legendary lost Buddhist cities along the Old Silk Road. He had first met Halvor in 1896 in Fancheng while mapping the interior provinces of China. Hedin had sought the advice of the veteran missionary because he was familiar with the terrain in Hubei Province. While both men sported stylish brush mustaches and dressed in Chinese clothes, Hedin, in horn-rimmed spectacles, looked more like a scholar than an explorer. His five-foot, four-inch frame barely reached Halvor's shoulders, but he would prove to have the endurance of a giant.

They walked the streets of Fancheng in search of local storytellers who, for a price, would tell legends about the lost cities. The tales had been handed down by word of mouth, told and retold for centuries. Like stars that emit beams light-years after they cease to exist, the lost cities, once strung like Buddhist prayer beads along what was then called the Emperor's Route, have sparked the imagination of mankind for millennia. The storytellers told of haunted cities vanquished by ruthless armies and left to be buried with their monumental Buddhist art beneath the shifting "singing sands" of the Gobi and the dreaded Taklamakan, the Desert of No Return.

The Old Silk Road became the first trans-Asian highway to link the two superpowers of the world—Imperial China and the Roman Empire. It was actually not a single road, but a network of trails twisting like silken ribbons through seven thousand miles of the most exotic and treacherous terrain on earth. Although some 360 once-thriving cities along the trade route have long since disappeared, the snow-tipped sentinels of Tian Shan, the Heavenly Mountains, still bear witness to the triumphs and tragedies of eternal China.

The road began in Chang'an, now Xi'an, where Eurasian and Chinese merchants loaded precious silks, jewels, and luxury goods, along with their families and households, onto the mile-long caravans of covered wagons pulled by camels, horses, yaks, oxen, mules, and donkeys, to begin the trek West. The caravans rested at the caravanserais, strategically situated at intervals of from one to three days' march along the route. These oasis towns evolved into great Buddhist cities complete with gold-encrusted palaces, elaborate temples, and monasteries filled with monumental works of art depicting the life of the Buddha.

The Emperor's Route achieved its greatest glory in the tenth century, during the golden age of the mid–Tang Dynasty (AD 618–907). By then, the Roman Empire had fallen, and Italy, Spain, and northern Europe were controlled by Germanic tribes. Although the Buddhist civilization experienced periods of peace, the history of the Old Silk Road was violent and cruel. For centuries, the cities had survived attacks by feuding nomadic tribes and competing Central Eurasian empires, but the death knell sounded for Buddhist civilization when the Uighur ruler of Kashgar converted to Islam in the tenth century. The Arab cavalry swept through Central Asia on a mission of rape and pillage, systematically wiping out whole populations. Rivers were diverted, irrigation channels cut off, people starved, cities burned. Most of Central Asia became Moslem and has remained so to this day.

After the Moslem invasion came Genghis Khan and his Golden Horde. By 1211, the Mongol chief, on his way to carving out the largest empire on earth, had unified Mongolia and begun the conquest that devastated Central Asia. The Mongols destroyed any city, Buddhist or Moslem, that refused to join his armies or pay due respect. Migrations of whole populations began and continued for centuries. No one has recorded the full horror of those years, but when Hedin and other foreign archaeologists discovered the ruins of the vanished cities some eight hundred years later, they told of the desert strewn with so many human bones that travelers piled them up as trail markers.

Although the desert sands hid what remained of the cities, the storytellers in the streets of China, along with books and operas, kept the incredible story alive. The storytellers warned that the ruined cities were haunted by hungry ghosts and evil spirits. Many men had ventured into the Gobi Desert in search of treasure, but few returned. The deadly burans (sandstorms) clogged the orifices and strangled men and animals. Many starved or were driven mad. Marco Polo, who passed along the edge of the Taklamakan in 1291, wrote about howling ghosts. By the time he journeyed back to Venice, after twenty years in the Imperial Court of Kublai Khan in Peking, the ruins of most of the Buddhist cities had been buried in the desert. The Silk Road was officially abandoned during the late Ming Dynasty (1368–1644). But some camel caravans still trudged along the overland trade routes until the sea trade took over. By the time Halvor and Hedin arrived in China, the lost cities had become legend.

The possibility of ancient relics buried beneath a sea of sand was irresistible to the Swedish explorer. He determined to find the ruins, if indeed they existed. In 1896, Hedin set forth with a camel caravan on his quest. After losing six camels and almost dying of thirst and starvation, he miraculously survived to try again. Two years later, on his second trip, he came upon the fabled ruins of Kharakhoto (the Black City) in Khotan and realized that he had found the remains of the long-lost Buddhist civilization that the old storytellers had described to him and Halvor.

According to the story, the Black City was once the magnificent capital of the Xixia Empire. It was a crucial trading center and a place of Buddhist scholarship on the edge of the Gobi Desert. Like most of the cities, it was a huge fortress surrounded by high stone walls, The Tangut inhabitants were ethnically Tibetans, and devout Lama Buddhists. Genghis Khan, on his way with his thundering tribe to conquer the largest land empire in the world, requested that the Tibetan king, a High Lama, join his Mongol hordes. The king refused. The Great Khan avenged the insult by destroying Kharakhoto and everyone in it.

After Hedin announced his discovery of the ruins, many international archaeologists arrived seeking the legendary treasure. In 1908, a Russian colonel, Petr Koslov, arrived on the scene. He later wrote: "The walls of the town are covered in sand, in some places so deeply that it is impossible to walk up the slope to enter the fortress." No one ever found the treasure, but the Russian carted away a wealth of relics and documents to St. Petersburg that are still on exhibit in the Hermitage. The colonel established a new field of study—"Tangut Culture and Xixia Language Studies"—so the mythical city lives on through scholarship and studies.

According to Halvor, Hedin had discovered the ancient city by following in the footsteps of the Buddhist monk Fa Xian, who had visited the Kingdom of Khotan in AD 299 and left a crude map. He was the first to describe the cities and the splendor of the king's monastery that took eighty years to build: "It [the monastery] is ornamentally carved and overlaid with gold and silver, suitably finished with the seven precocities: gold, silver, lapis lazuli, crystal, ruby, emeralds and coral. Behind the pagoda is a Hall of the Buddha splendidly decorated in gilt . . . The apartments for priests are decorated beyond expression for words." The remains that Hedin found two thousand years later seem well described by the Tang Dynasty poet Du Fu (AD 712–770):

THE CHARIOTS GO FORTH TO WAR

> Have you not seen at far Jing Hai,
> By the waters of Kharakhoto
> How the heaped skulls and bones of slaughtered men
> Lie bleaching in the sun?
> Their ancient ghosts hear our own ghosts weep
> And cry and lament in turn;
> The heavens grow dark with great storm clouds,
> And the specters wail in the rain.

In Peking, Halvor bid farewell to Hedin, who was preparing to leave on another expedition.

December 16, 1907. Dearest Hannah: I am about to leave Peking and come back to you. The convention was disappointing but I had a memorable afternoon with our friend Sven Hedin who is here loading provisions on a camel caravan for his third major expedition. This one is to Persia and Tibet in search of the source of the Indus River . . . Carl and Sven and I picnicked on Fragrant Hill overlooking the Forbidden City where the Empress Dowager and her Manchu court are living in seclusion after their return from exile . . . Not too long ago we thought the Emperor would make some reforms but now he is broken and weak, some say here in Peking that he is debauched with opium. I can't believe it. We think the "Old Buddha" is tormenting him. The Emperor is a tool of the Dowager because he is still considered the embodiment of the "Son of Heaven" and as "Supreme Intercessor" of his people. He is the central figure in all sacred ceremonies such the Winter and Summer Solstice Ceremony. Then the Emperor is carried in a yellow sedan chair by sixteen bearers to the "Temple of Heaven" to pray for bountiful harvests. Only the Emperor, by reason of his divine descent, is believed fit to ascend the Altar of Heaven and under the sky perform the ancient rituals of sacrifices to the Supreme Being. The circular marble altar is one of the few remaining relics of the original Chinese monotheistic faith that God is every-where, invisible but all-seeing. This was a belief widely held in Asia before the gods were personified and their idols enshrined in temples. As far as I know, no foreigner has ever witnessed the Emperor's Solstice ceremony and only a few Chinese.

Before the ceremony notices are sent to the Legations warning foreigners not to approach or even attempt to look upon the procession. Chinese are ordered to stay indoors and close their shutters. Anyone stepping on the road when the Imperial retinue is passing is automatically sentenced to death by strangulation. Oh when I think of the ancient superstitions and cruel punishments I am more convinced than ever that education is the only way for China to survive.

Peking is still in shambles from the Siege of Peking. The Old Buddha has charmed the foreign diplomats by giving tea parties for their wives. No one seems to remember that during the uprising she tried to kill them all. She even invited some who looted her Imperial Palace. The history of China is beyond my understanding. But I am more determined than ever to help them reform through Christ and peace, not violence and revolution.

One day we walked from the Tartar City, where the Manchus reside in luxury, over Beggar's Bridge into the Chinese city. The bridge lived up to its name, it was thronged with beggars. When they spotted us they clamored around, displaying horrible mutilations, some self-inflicted, in a pathetic effort to gain pity. Hell could not be worse than this. No wonder the Chinese are ready to revolt. Tell the children that Papa will be home for Christmas. I pray for you continually. Blessings. Your loving husband. Halvor.

25

The Last Years

FACING DEATH

Unreal!
Unreal are both creation
And destruction,
And man's body
Is illusion and a dream.

It is the house
Where for a space
Sojourn his heart and mind;
But seek not there
For man's real self—
It does not dwell therein.
—ZU MING,
  SUI DYNASTY (AD 581–618)

Come back in sleep
    For in life
Where thou art not
We find none like thee.
—HALVOR RONNING, 1908

When Halvor arrived home from Peking, he was shocked to find Hannah seriously ill. Her beautiful countenance did not convey her condition. Her gentle features without sharpness or creases were still given more to expressing joy, love, and tenderness. Only her eyes betrayed her pain. She harbored a lingering fear of death that she had tried to conceal from Halvor. But it was revealed in a letter to her mother: *My precious Mamma—Oh it was nice to hear from you. I do not write as often as I should and feel badly about it—but if I don't feel well enough to write at night I neglect it. I seem to get weaker every day, but Dr. Himle cannot find the mysterious cause of this. I cannot climb the stairs once as my heart throbs and flutters. It is from loss of blood since I gave birth—so at least it is not the heart. But anyway an anxious feeling takes hold of me once in a while as if death were near— and it may be—but I must leave that to God. Life is precious to me, I have eight pairs of hands to hold me to my life, my husband and seven children, and then there is my work—yet unfinished—and my dear friends. Mother of mine—beloved mamma—if we don't meet again in this world we shall meet in Heaven. Have no fear.* The letter ended with a revealing apology: *Excuse the pencil but I cannot bear the noise of the pen scratching on paper.*

The "mysterious cause" was later found to be Asian sprue, a painful and weakening illness resulting from a vitamin B and iron deficiency that slowly saps the white corpuscles. It struck many foreign women in China, but at that time, like scurvy, the cause was unknown and there was no cure. Hannah may have recovered had it not been for the exhaustion and dehydration caused by the famine. Dr. Himle recommended a trip to the mountains, or better still to leave China altogether. This, however, seemed to be unacceptable to Hannah. Early in January 1907, Halvor decided to take Hannah by boat upriver to Tze Ho and then up the mountain, by sedan chair, to the inspiring scenery and invigorating air of Ming Mang. One of the new missionaries, Miss Anna Lee, went along as nurse.

Halvor worked hard to make the boat comfortable. He installed a stove and a soft litter chair so Hannah could be moved on deck into the sunshine. They sailed up the Han River for several days, and each day Hannah grew stronger. Halvor was filled with hope when they anchored offshore at Tze Ho, but while they were preparing to continue up the mountain in sedan chairs, a messenger arrived from Fancheng with terrible news. Chester had come down with diphtheria.

Hannah wanted to return immediately, but Halvor insisted they continue. In another one of those strange coincidences that changed the history of our family, however, the decision was suddenly taken out of their hands. If the storm had not come, Chester would have almost certainly died, and I would not be recording these events. The sky blackened over the mountains, rain came in torrents, and the sedan-chair bearers refused to carry them up the slippery mountain path. There were no inns for shelter. They were forced to take a tender back to the boat. While Halvor was maneuvering their boat into a sheltered place, they hit a rock, the icy water came pouring in, and the boat began to sink. Fortunately the water was only up to Halvor's chest, so he was able to carry Hannah ashore and wade back for Anna Lee. The bearers carried the shivering women to a shelter, where they spent the night. Halvor built a fire, and the next morning he rented a boat. They sailed downriver with the swift current and reached home that evening. Adrenalin made Hannah remarkably strong. When she saw Chester struggling for breath, she insisted that Dr. Himle perform a tracheotomy. The operation kept Chester alive, but he remained delirious with fever. Himle said there was nothing more to be done; it was now up to God. Hannah took over and, with a force that amazed all, spent the next ten days and nights praying and nursing her son back to health. Chester recovered completely. Hannah had brought her son back to life. Halvor was again filled with hope. He felt that Hannah's great efforts and her prayers had rescued their son. But at what price? She suffered a relapse and soon lay fevered and chilled, too sick to move. Halvor kept vigil, whispering words of encouragement. He was still convinced she would recover, but Hannah knew the end was near. She tried to reconcile her husband and children to this, telling them gently that God would soon take her, that it was God's will. Halvor refused to believe it and assured the children that their mother would get well again if they had faith and prayed enough. Chester, then twelve, was filled with guilt. He prayed constantly. His father paced back and forth on the balcony outside their mother's bedroom crying aloud to God to have mercy and save his beloved wife. The children huddled in their beds, reassuring each other through tears that God could not refuse the prayers of such a good man.

Hannah Rorem Ronning died on February 9, 1907. Halvor poured out his grief in letters to Nils, who sought to safeguard his brother's privacy. In a deed that fills me, as the family recorder, with deep regret, he took it upon himself to destroy almost all the letters that Halvor wrote about Hannah's illness and death, just as he destroyed the letters that Halvor wrote to him about his sister Thea's death. Later, in explanation, Nils wrote: *Rev. Ronning expressed deep and growing concern in regard to his wife's health. He was steeling his heart for the worst. I shall not quote from his letters; they are too intimate, too sacred.*

Alice Landahl, who had married Carl after Thea died, was at Hannah's deathbed and wrote an article that was later published in the *Haugianeran*, the mission journal.

> Every day the children gathered around her bed while she gave motherly advice to each one of them. In between, Nelius read portions of the Bible and the oldest ones prayed and sang her favorite songs, but their mother did not rally. Hannah soothingly implored her husband to reconcile himself to the inevitable. He finally . . . yielded to God's will and

cried: "Thy will be done." Then he told his dear wife that she could go in peace. "We are all willing to give you up if God wants you, even though the parting will be more bitter than death."

Just before she died, she spoke to us with a clear strong voice to tell us how God had revealed himself to her in such a merciful and wonderful way that she was fully resigned to his will, and all anxiety for herself and her own left her fully. I will never forget her last, touching words: "I am so glad you have all come," she told us with a weak smile. "I want to tell you what an unusual experience that God has given me. It is wonderful! There are no words to describe it. I have like Paul been in Seventh Heaven and seen unutterable things. I saw Jesus in all his glory and he came so near to me. I just rejoiced in His nearness. I couldn't believe that such a poor human being as myself could contain such grace and holiness. O my dears! God has been so good to me. He fills me with joy and peace—it is so blessed and sweet to rest in Him. When they prayed and anointed me, the Lord did such a remarkable thing for me. He came right to me and His Love poured over my whole being. I could feel it go right through me. All my pain left. Since then I have rested so sweetly. I have endured pain. I know what it is to suffer. But the Lord took it away in the blink of an eye.

"Oh I am so fortunate! And I love all of you so much. I have never loved the Chinese like I do now. When we come near to God we learn to love. The nearer we come to God the nearer we come to each other. There is no difference. We are all one in Christ."

In her last hour she repeated this over and over. It was her last message: "The nearer we come to God the nearer we come to each other. There is no difference. We are all one in Christ."

Before she lost consciousness she looked up with a quick glance in her dimming eyes and joyfully called out, "Oh! Now you come so quickly Lord Jesus, so quickly, so quickly."

Halvor sat with one hand over her cold hand and the other on her forehead. As her spirit left her body he poured out his heart in prayer, whispering words of farewell and promising to meet again. It was a holy time. We knew that beyond Hannah's ravaged face was a soul as pure as the driven snow. Halvor saw her as he always had and always would—his beautiful, beloved Hannah full of song and laughter and an expansive, loving heart.

After his mother died, Nelius, fourteen years old, read the last two chapters in Revelation in a soft but strong voice. When he had read the fourth verse in the twenty-first chapter, he looked up at us with a smile and said: "Just think of it, no more pain. Mamma is in glory."

That evening [February 9, 1907] some of us gathered in Ronnings' room. The tears flowed easily and then Nelius spoke up. "Do not cry, I know Mama would not like it. She asked us not to cry because she was only going home to Jesus."

Many years later, Chester told me with tears in his eyes that at that time he had questioned the faith of his father for the first time. God had not answered his father's prayers. Chester felt guilty. Nelius, who kept his mother's unquestioning faith, would be the first in the family to join his mother.

The arrangements for Hannah's funeral evoked criticism from Christian fundamentalist missionaries. The services were attended not only by missionaries from various Protestant and Catholic churches, but also Chinese of many faiths including Buddhists, Confucian scholars, Daoists, Ancestor Worshipers, and Moslems. Hannah's body was dressed in her bridal gown and laid to rest in a simple Chinese coffin. Halvor planned everything meticulously. The church was decorated in black and white (white being the color of mourning in China). Green tree boughs with black and white ribbons were hung on the doors. The entrance to the church and the pathway to the Christian cemetery were strewn with boughs and flanked with white flags with a black border and various emblems in Norwegian and Chinese. White cloths were procured for the schoolchildren and the Christians to wrap around their heads as a symbol of sorrow. For the non-Christians, there were black and white paper flowers and white bands on which Halvor had written Hannah Ronning's name, date of death, and a message: "Till we meet again."

The church and schoolyard were overflowing with friends and admirers. The missionary choir sang "Nearer My God to Thee" followed by Chinese songs. Sen Li-fu gave a short talk in Chinese urging all to follow Mrs. Ronning's example so they could meet her in heaven. After the blessing, a procession was formed. The schoolchildren sang as they walked in front, carrying small American flags. Then came the coffin borne by Chinese followed by Reverends Ronning and Landahl, the Ronning children, other missionaries, the Chinese Christians, and finally the Chinese of other faiths, and the common people of Hsiangyang.

Reverend Trygstad conducted the "Committal" in Norwegian, followed by Reverend Landahl and Reverend Sen Li-fu, who spoke in Chinese, thanking everyone on behalf of the Ronning family for their sympathy and help. Alice Landahl wrote:

> The burial was deeply gripping and heartfelt. Though it lasted a half day it was the most quiet and festive burial ever seen out here. There was no screaming or wailing as at Chinese funerals. And glad we were! Even the large crowd of onlookers was unusually quiet and deeply stirred.
>
> What could be a more appropriate tribute to Mrs. Ronning's life than the beginning of an awakening and deeper spiritual life?
>
> I am certain that our sister who is dead still speaks to many. Nearer to God, nearer to each other is the message that goes to the heart. Her life was a sweet Christian influence to both the Chinese and the missionaries, which will continue to live.

The day after the funeral, Nelius and Chester sailed down the Han River with their father on a *hong chuan,* an open sailing junk with a small red cabin, to the Dabie Mountains, where Halvor selected a white marble stone from the quarry for a tombstone. An open Bible was carved at the pinnacle. The inscription Halvor carved in the stone was clearly visible six generations later:

MASTER AT THY WORD

HANNAH RONNING

Born ROREM

November 6, 1871

Home

Radcliff, Iowa. U.S.A.

Arrived in

China December 1, 1891

Gone Before Us

February 9, 1907

On the base, Halvor hand-carved the Norwegian words *Pao jen syn* (Till We Meet Anon).

On the back of a photograph of Hannah in an oval frame that Grandfather kept near him for the rest of his life, and that I now cherish, he had written:

Come back in sleep,

For in life

Where thou art not
We find none like thee.

Hannah was only thirty-six years old when she died, but she had lived the equivalent of many lives. Her love and fascination for China was passed on to her descendants, many of whom have made pilgrimages to Fancheng to pay their respects where her tombstone still stands in the old cemetery (now part of the schoolyard) near Reverend Ronning's church. She had established the first girls' school in Hubei and opened the first orphanage and medical clinic in Fancheng. In 1971, when I accompanied my father, Chester, and my siblings to Fancheng, I asked the headmaster of the school why they kept the tomb of a Christian missionary in the Communist schoolyard. He replied, "Because she was a revolutionary, too." One hundred and two years after her death, I returned again with my daughter Karen and her son, Hannah's great-great-grandson Torin Ronning Cone, to pay respects to both Thea and Hannah. During the Cultural Revolution in the 1960s the Bible had been knocked off her tombstone. I showed the headmaster a photo of the original tombstone, and he promised to replace it.

Halvor to Nils: *October 3, 1907. Life must go on. All my plans [for an independent church] have been upset. May God's chastening hand humble me and make me a better servant of His. Had a call from Radcliff, Iowa to be Minister in their church, but have returned it. I would rather be free from churches and work for the cause of missions, spiritual awakening and union of all the Norwegian Lutheran church bodies. Wouldn't that be a wonderful work? No, no I am but dust and ashes. I suppose people will say that I am a fanatic, but fanatics have their mission in life too. My first duty is towards my motherless children. I will take them to Canada next spring. It is going to be a strenuous trip. I have made arrangement for the house in Bardo to be ready by the time we get there. I have already acquired twenty head of cattle for the boys to round up. Nelius and Chester left to attend school in America. They are brave boys but my heart is breaking. May God give me strength.*

26

The End of the Imperial Qing Dynasty

Looking back upon the memories of these last fifty years, I perceive how calamities from within and aggression from without have come upon us in relentless succession, and that my life has never enjoyed a moment's respite from anxiety.

—EMPRESS DOWAGER CIXI, NOVEMBER 15, 1908

THE HUNDRED NAMES

From break of day
Till sunset glow
I toil.
I dig my well.
I plow my field,
And earn my food
And drink.
What care I
Who rules the land
If I
Am left in peace?

—UNKNOWN POET (2300 BC)

The crumbling Manchu Era completely collapsed three years after the death of the empress dowager. The Imperial dynastic system, founded by the first Emperor Qin Shihuang in 221 BC, had governed China for 2,200 years. The Manchus had ruled for 268 years. The empress dowager reigned behind the Brocade Curtain from the birth of her son until her death at the age of seventy-three. She made little use, if any, of her absolute powers to enhance the well-being of her nation. The Qing Dynasty at its height had produced a number of brilliant and benevolent emperors, such as Qianlong, but the empress dowager brought it to ruin with her selfishness, arrogance, greed, and disastrous manipulation of foreign policy. She died of dysentery a day after the violent death of her nephew, Emperor Guangxu, whom she had betrayed and kept imprisoned for ten years.

The official records stated that the emperor died of smallpox. It was rumored at the time, however, that the dowager was so afraid he would outlive her and besmirch her name that she ordered her chief eunuch, Cobbler's Wax Li Lianying, to poison him. Since the day before the young emperor died, the dowager had named a three-year-old child, Pu Yi (the "Last Emperor"), to replace him on the Dragon Throne, it seems clear that she plotted his death. Pu Yi's father, the Second Prince Chun, was appointed regent. It was no secret that the emperor had been physically ill and depressed for some time. But a Dr. Chu, who practiced Western medicine and cared for the emperor shortly before his death, held that the circumstances of his death had no connection with his illness.* The doctor reported that when he saw Guangxu three days before he died, the emperor was writhing in agony as if he had been poisoned by arsenic: "He could not sleep, he could not urinate, his heart beat grew faster, his face burned purple, and his tongue had turned yellow." When the dowager visited the emperor on his deathbed, he was unable to speak, but in one last gesture of defiance he scribbled out a terrible curse upon his tormentor.

To the very end, the dowager lived up to her reputation as a ruthless psychopath divorced from reality. Ambitious and forceful, she loved money, power, and intrigue. She pitched Chinese against Chinese, barbarians against barbarians, and blamed others for her crimes. She was more interested in punishments than rewards. She had been in power for thirty-nine years when she encouraged the Boxer Uprising against the foreigners.

Her demise began when she suffered a stroke that left the right side of her face paralyzed. Her mouth drooped, her face twitched, and her body was bloated from eating the rich foods her doctors had advised against. On November 15, she attended a fancy-dress picnic to celebrate her seventy-third birthday. The thirteenth Dalai Lama had come from Tibet accompanied by three hundred lesser lamas and a force of soldiers herding eight hundred camels, five hundred horses, and uncounted mules to pay his respects to the empress. The Old Buddha indulged her gluttonous appetite by consuming a large portion of crabapples and whipped cream and immediately suffered acute stomach pain. She fainted, but as she was borne back to the palace she mustered enough strength to dictate a final proclamation. "Looking back upon the memories of these last fifty

*Marina Warner, *The Dragon Empress: Life and Times of Tz'u Hsi Empress Dowager of China, 1835–1908* (London: Vintage, 1972), 261.

years," she declared, "I perceive how calamities from within and aggression from without have come upon us in relentless succession, and that my life has never enjoyed a moment's respite from anxiety."*

In accordance with Imperial ritual, Cixi's corpse was anointed with the oil of the acanthus flower and swathed as if in a cocoon in the Robes of Longevity embroidered with gold-wrapped silk thread and spun peacock feathers. The embroideries depicted scenes of a celestial paradise: curling clouds and the phoenix (sign of the empress) floating above a sea of waves where the Eight Jewels (pearls, coins, rhinoceros horns, musical stones, books, leaves, lozenges, and scrolls) appear. Mythical creatures, bats, cranes, and a myriad of immortality symbols were stitched around the edges.

Born in November 1835, the empress died on November 15, 1908, at the Hour of the Goat (between 1:00 and 3:00 p.m.). Her stunningly elaborate funeral unfolded in stark contrast to the simplicity of Hannah's funeral. It took the court astrologer a year to find the most auspicious day and hour for the event. Finally, after a three-day banquet for the court officials, her embalmed body, all orifices protected from the evil spirits by the insertion of ceremonial jade, was carried out of the Forbidden City by eighty-four bearers in a jeweled, four-poster catafalque for entombment in a mausoleum in the Eastern Qing Tombs. The coffin was accompanied by a mile-long procession, which to the Western eye looked like a cross between a coronation and a circus. Hundreds of mandarins in resplendent robes walked beneath umbrellas followed by thousands of eunuchs in white mourning robes. Then came the Dalai Lama, draped in a golden robe, sitting high in a glistening sedan chair at the head of a procession of red-robed lamas with high yellow hats beating gongs. Buddhist monks robed in saffron, their heads shaven to expose the nine sacred scars, marched before a caravan of the red-tasseled Bactrian camels, bearing platforms of musicians playing doleful music followed by garlanded horses drawing cartloads of professional mourners and wailing relatives. Finally came the Manchu cavalrymen in full regalia, banners flying, escorting wagons filled with objects made of colored paper: money, clothing, life-size statues of warriors, foot-soldiers, and attendants, three splendid chariots with curtains of yellow silk, emblazoned with dragons and phoenixes—all to be burned so as to materialize with the empress in her next life.

The royal procession took four days to reach the tombs, where, on November 9, 1909, at precisely 7:00 a.m., the empress dowager's body was sealed in the

---

*Bland and Backhouse, *China under the Empress Dowager*, 468–89.

royal vaulted tomb beside the remains of her husband, the Emperor Xianfeng, who had chosen her as a concubine of the third rank more than a half century earlier when she was a young girl of the Yehenara clan. Hers was to be the last Imperial funeral. It cost the already bankrupt nation 1.5 million taels, a third of what was spent on the emperor's funeral. The Empress Dowager Cixi was the last Manchu monarch of any consequence, although the influence of her reign extended to 1911, the year of Sun Yat-sen's Republican Revolution.

With the empress dowager's death, the Manchu court degenerated into a swamp of petty nepotism and clique rivalries fighting for power. As the last Imperial dynasty crumbled, the Warlord Era began. The Manchu tombs were broken into and robbed of their treasures. Horrid tales were told in whispers of the mutilation of the entombed body of the empress dowager. Some of her jewels were later emblazoned on the hats of powerful warlords.

PART III

SETTLING

in

CANADA

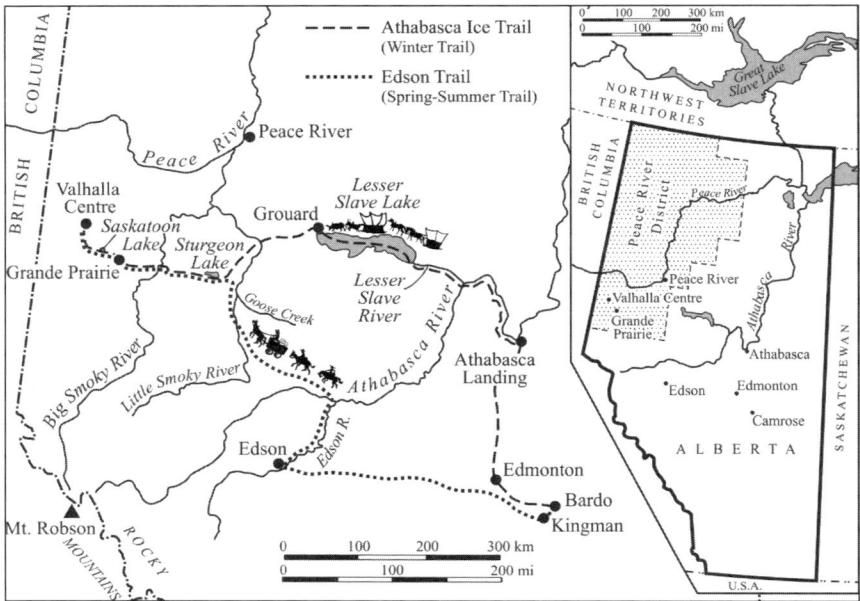

The Peace River District and Environs, Alberta

Map by Mary Lee Eggart

27

New Frontiers

I longed to go home to China where the people were friendly and did not regard me as
a foreign devil.

—CHESTER RONNING, AGE THIRTEEN, 1907

The Ronning children were devastated by the passing of their mother. Nelius
was thirteen, Chester twelve, Almah nine, Talbert six, Harold and Hazel four,
and Victoria only two years old. Halvor's concern now was for his children,
and he first gave thought to the education of his two eldest sons. He decided
to send them to live with their mother's sister Julia and her husband, Albert
Amundson, who owned a farm near Radcliff, Iowa. Chester and Nelius would
attend a Western school for the first time. At their parents' school, they had
studied Chinese culture, mathematics, and the Bible, and they spoke Chinese,
Norwegian, and English fluently. They knew virtually nothing, however, about
American customs and history. They had grown up with Chinese friends and had
absorbed the respectful attitudes and courtesies common to Chinese scholars.
Chester would later recall that he had felt there was no difference between him
and the Chinese except for his blue eyes. Both boys were tall for their ages with
handsome Nordic features.

At the public school in Radcliff, Iowa, Nelius was admitted into eighth grade
and Chester into seventh. On his first day of school, the teacher asked Chester
to write about the journey from China. With the title "I AM IT" printed in bold
capital letters on the cover of his school scribbler, he wrote this account:

*After Papa made arrangements for my brother and me to leave China, I began to
make preparations for our long journey to America. We started on April 1, 1907, with
Papa and Nelius in a Chinese junk and sailed down the Han River. In eight days we
arrived in Hankow, 400 miles from our home.*

*We did not spend much time in Hankow, the very same evening we went aboard
the* Malee, *a German Steamer. After a few days sailing down the Yangtze we arrived
in Shanghai. We spent a week there. We only had Chinese clothes, so Father had a
tailor make some foreign clothes for us. We wore our new suits and overcoats and fine*

looking hats when we boarded the S.S. Mongolia, a large ocean liner. As we were wav-
ing good-bye to Father from the deck, my new hat blew off and I helplessly watched it
*sailing back to China with my heart.**

In a few days we were in Nagasaki Japan and went ashore and bought some things.
In the evening we went aboard again and started our journey. In a day or two our ship
was wrecked on a rock. It nearly capsized. We were shipwrecked people in life boats
for one whole day and one long night. The next morning we got back on the ship and
sailed off again.

The boys' adjustment to life in Iowa was not easy. Chester wrote later in his
memoir: *In the Radcliff Public School, we were lost—utter strangers and completely*
ignorant of the ways of Americans. We soon noted, however, that the boys wore caps,
not hats, which helped me get over the pain of losing my only hat. We were daily
subjected to the questionable honor of a great deal of attention, and during the first
recess were treated to a chant of greeting in which all the natives joined: "Ching Chong
Chinaman eat dead rats; chew them up like ginger snaps."

We said nothing to our aunt about the reception. That night my pillow was wet
with an uncontrollable stream of silent tears, and I longed to go home to China where
the people were friendly and did not regard me as a foreigner.

It was not until my brother and I learned how to ride the range like cowboys,
round up cattle and drive a team of horses to cultivate corn on Uncle Albert's farm that
we were finally accepted by Radcliff's school community. We continued, however, to
clam up completely whenever the teacher asked questions about China.

In 1908, Halvor brought his five younger children from China to Bardo in
Alberta, Canada, where Chester and Nelius joined them after a year in Radcliff.
The farmers in Alberta all knew about the Ronnings. Many had contributed to
his China mission. They were met by Hannah's closest brother, Tom, and his
wife, Alice, who had emigrated from Iowa, as well as the Anton Horte family,
who had come from Minnesota with their five children. The youngest daughter,
Inga Marie, would become my mother. The Hortes had known the Ronnings
in Telemark, Norway. Anton Horte, my future maternal grandfather, was a tall,

---

*Chester never forgot his hat. Almost seventy years later, he wrote in his *Memoir of China in Revolu-*
tion: "When my father left us on the deck of the Pacific Mail SS *Mongolia* and was on his way back
to the Bund in Shanghai, we stood sadly waving to him on the tender. A gust of wind suddenly
blew my brand-new hat into the yellow waters of the Yangtze. To this day, whenever I am hatless I
still see that beautiful hat tossed like an egg-shell floating downstream headed for the Yellow Sea."
Asked on occasion why he was going to China, Dad would sometimes reply: "To get my hat."

striking man with twinkling blue eyes and a bright-red beard. He had suggested that his oldest daughter, Gunhilde, a beautiful thirty-six-year-old schoolteacher, become a governess for the Ronning children. Halvor accepted gratefully. Little Victoria ran at once into Gunhilde's arms as if she had always belonged there. All the children fell in love with their governess, and five years later she married their father, Halvor.

Chester and Nelius were overjoyed to be reunited with the family. They moved into a large, white frame house on 250 acres of rich prairie land in Bardo, one of the first rural Norse settlements in Canada. It was named after the location in Norway from which the founders of the settlement had come. The Ronnings prospered on their farm. Halvor became pastor of the local church with a large parish. He also traveled around Canada and the United States as an evangelist, preaching and raising funds for his school in China and for a Lutheran college in Camrose, a flourishing town twenty-eight miles south of Bardo.

Soon after arriving in Bardo, Halvor contacted the Honorable Frank Oliver, the prominent politician whom he had met in Calgary, to remind him that he had promised to make the whole family Canadians in exchange for his vote in the upcoming election. Oliver fulfilled his promise, arranging a naturalization ceremony that took only a few minutes. Changing nationalities did not prove easy for Nelius and Chester, however. They had to adjust to a new school much as they had in Iowa, but in Bardo their new Canadian schoolmates dubbed them stupid Americans as well as dumb Chinese.

In Iowa the boys had come to consider themselves loyal Americans. Chester later wrote: *We did not want to leave good old Uncle Sam to live under a petticoat government. The Canadian boys called us Yanks. As Americans we learned that we had thrown off the yoke of British monarchy and won all the battles of the Revolutionary War as well as those of 1812. In Canada we were informed that Canada and England had won all the battles of the War of 1812. In the United States, pro-British Americans were labeled "rebels" and had been driven out of the country. In Canada they were respected as "United Empire Loyalists."*

Almost every day after school, the Yanks and Canadians refought the War of 1812 with snowballs. Even though they were now joined by their nine-year-old brother Talbert, the Ronnings were, as Chester recalled, *greatly outnumbered and always snowed under . . . Our adjustment to the opposite views was painful but thorough. Eventually we were completely subverted, and I have never for a moment regretted my father's acceptance of the Honorable Frank Oliver's invitation to become a Canadian citizen.*

Chester was outgoing and, like his father, good-natured with a keen sense of humor. He soon gained a reputation as a storyteller and was often asked in school to read the essays he wrote about China to the class. After school he told his friends stories of his adventures in China and also related Chinese legends he had heard from the cook. No one believed his stories, so, like Marco Polo, when he was asked to admit he was exaggerating he would say, "I have only told half the story."

One school essay entitled "Chinese School" was particularly amusing to his Canadian friends. He was asked to read it aloud, which he did with gestures.

In a Chinese school they study loud, they sing their lessons out till they know them. It makes an awful noise. Then they go to the teacher and turn their backs to him and recite. While they are reciting they wiggle their backs and jump up and down and if they don't know the words the teacher spanks them and makes them do it again. If they do not behave well, the teacher will make them kneel down and take them up by the ears or if that doesn't cure them he makes them kneel down again and puts a bowl of boiling water on their heads, and if they move it will fall off and burn them. In China they start school about 5 o'clock in the morning. They have no clocks but they guess at it. All the pupils must be there before the teacher or they will get licked till they jump.

28

Vikings Go Forth

It has often been said that wherever there is a new frontier, Norsemen will be found. In the settlement of the Canadian Northwest, Halvor Ronning was amongst the vanguard.

—OLAF ANDERSON, 1914

After five years in Bardo, now happily married to Gunhilde, the wandering missionary seemed to have finally found a home. Halvor was forty-six years old, healthy and handsome with a shock of graying hair. His family was comfortably settled on a flourishing farm, with the younger children enrolled in the local school and Chester and Nelius attending the Camrose Lutheran College. But within a few months of the wedding, Halvor succumbed to his innate Viking wanderlust and decided to explore an undeveloped part of the Peace River District in northwest Alberta. He said it would be the realization of a vision he had cherished since leaving China. In *The Gospel at Work*, Halvor wrote:

As a modern fairy tale it must be considered that I, as an elderly missionary and minister, took my large family and traveled over four hundred miles through a vast wilderness to found a Norwegian settlement in Valhalla in the Peace River district.

That it was the Lord who called me I never doubted. As Abraham was commanded to get out of his country and go unto a land the Lord would show him, sounded in my heart an inner call to me.

Often on my visits to new settlements I was grieved that our Norwegian people seeking new land had neither church nor government to guide them. It was difficult to organize congregations which might become self-supporting. Then I began to think about the Peace River district where there would be grand opportunities. Strangely enough, the decision to go there was formed in my mind before I knew of it . . . As I looked at our beautiful home in Bardo, which I had been dreaming about as my sunset home, I asked myself: Are you willing to leave this home and start a home mission work in the Peace River district? I decided to make a trip to investigate conditions.

Halvor shared the land fever that was afflicting many Canadians at the time. In 1911, when the gold rush was on in the American West, he read an official announcement stating that all Canadian troops who had fought in the Boer War could purchase homesteads of 320 acres each in the Peace River District with the South African scrip that had been issued to them. The Boer veterans were also free, if they chose, to sell the scrip with the land rights. Halvor thought the Peace River District would be an ideal place for the new Norse immigrants from the United States and Norway to settle. The problem was that the only way to get to the district in the far northwest was to travel over old Indian trails through nearly impassable wild country. To Halvor, however, the distance or the difficulty getting there mattered not. This was the kind of challenge, like going to China, that he found irresistible.

Halvor was so certain he would find the Peace River District to be the place of his dreams that he bought South African scrip from a veteran sufficient to pay for two homesteads, totaling 640 acres. He told his congregation that he was making the trip to the Peace River District to fix the exact location of the "Viking Valhalla" that he dreamed of establishing. He assured them that it would remind them of Norway.

On September 12, 1912, Halvor set forth with his new wife, Gunhilde, her brother Olaf Horte, and friends Ole Forseth and John Johnson. Chester and Nelius were in college, and the younger children were left in Bardo with their Uncle Tom and Aunt Alice. The new Canadian pioneers, with horses and wagons, took the Canadian National Railway via Edmonton to Edson, where the Indian trail began. On September 16, the Ronnings began their daring journey four hundred miles north to Grande Prairie. Halvor drove a covered lumber wagon packed with provisions and pulled by a team of sturdy white Clydesdale draft horses. Gunhilde rode behind in a fairly comfortable double buggy hitched to high-stepping, purebred Hackney horses driven by her brother Olaf. The others followed on horseback. They set forth boldly on a warm spring morning and soon found that the farther north they traveled, the more difficult the trail became. Halvor insisted, however, that compared to the cart tracks in China it was easy going. He felt in his element, more so because he didn't have to worry about Boxers intent on killing "foreign devils" attacking his wagon train, and he was relieved to find that the North American Indians were friendly.

The rivers presented the greatest challenge: there were no bridges. Crossing the wider, swifter rivers such as the Edson, the Little Smoky, the Berland, and the treacherous Athabasca was a formidable undertaking that Gunhilde found very frightening. Halvor would drive the wagon down the steep riverbanks and onto wooden ferryboats called scows that were attached by rope pulleys to overhead steel cables anchored to posts on both banks. When a scow was fully loaded, the ferry handlers would guide it across the river by pulling on the ropes. On the other side, the horses had to struggle up the steep, muddy banks. Fearful of sliding backward, Gunhilde would get out and climb the riverbank to lighten the load in her buggy.

The most dangerous obstacles on the trail were the bottomless bogs called "muskegs." These quicksand holes could be safely crossed only on "corduroyed" platforms constructed of poles laid crosswise over heavy logs. Halvor noted that great care had to be taken to avoid loosening the platform poles: *Near each muskeg we came across the pitiful sight of dead horses and oxen that had broken their legs when the poles were loosened by too heavy loads or had been carelessly left by impatient drivers. We passed twelve dead horses and met several defeated homesteaders whose wagons had broken down. They warned us to turn back because the road was flooded and impassable, but my experiences in China stood me in good stead.* Olaf, an expert horseman, rode ahead and made certain that each muskeg platform was secure for horses. In two weeks, the wagon train arrived in Grande Prairie, a town at the southern edge of the Peace River District, where Halvor conducted the first Norwegian Lutheran service to be held in the district. But Halvor did not find the nearby land suitable as a site for the large colony he envisioned. Reading in the land surveyor's notes that land with excellent soil and luxuriant grass could be found farther to the northeast, he decided to press on. While Gunhilde remained in Grande Prairie, Halvor and Olaf left on horseback to ride through uncharted territory in search of the better land.

In several places, Halvor wrote, *we had to dismount and lead our horses. The next day at sunset we reached our destination . . . a fine open plain with wide, sweeping slopes. We knew this was our place. The whole landscape looked like an immense park. The grass was abundant. There was running water and fine timber. Small wonder we called it Valhalla, the home of the gods.*

When it became dark we turned homeward. Soon it began to rain and then to snow. We lost our direction and rode around in a wide circle, coming back to where we had started. The wind rose to a gale and I lost my hat. We crawled on hands and knees in the darkness but could not find it. Time and again we had to shout to one another so as not to drift apart. Wet, frozen, hungry and sleepy we arrived back in Grande Prairie at three in the morning.

The next day Gunhilde felt better and went along to see the new kingdom. We brought all our belongings. We had to ford streams and travel zigzag where it was open and dry. I went ahead and cut down the trees in our way. We covered only 15 miles the first day. It was extremely difficult to force our way through the heavy brush. In the evening we reached Valhalla.

On October 22, Halvor went to the land office, filed land claims on four homesteads for his four sons, and then, with Gunhilde, turned homeward.

On the way back to Bardo we ran into a terrible snowstorm. We had to break the ice to reach the ferry to take us across the Athabasca River. The horses were nervous as the water was up to their chests. How the horses were able to climb up on the ferry and pull the wagon after them, I never could understand. Mrs. Ronning sat in the wagon. When we had gone some distance on the ferry, our heroic horses again had to plunge into the water to reach the other shore. We had to go ahead, and ahead we went.

On our way we saw twelve dead horses. We wept. They had either starved to death or been driven to death by cruel and stupid people not worthy of them. Coming back to Edson we shipped our horses and wagons ahead and arrived in Bardo after an absence of six weeks. The children were overjoyed to see us.

In Bardo, Halvor resumed his duties as church pastor, but he was restless and began to travel as an evangelist to other churches in Canada and the United States. Meeting hundreds of young students from Norway who hoped to settle in Canada, Halvor spread the word about land available for settlement in the Peace River District.

The next spring, Halvor announced to his congregation that he intended to return to the Peace River District with his family to establish a settlement he envisioned as a "haven for Norsemen." He invited all who were willing to risk the difficult journey and join him in founding the settlement.

Halvor was undeterred by the fact that there were no roads to the Peace River District that could be used by homesteaders traveling in wagon trains carrying all their possessions and supplies. Fur traders and other hardy frontiersmen who ventured into the New Territories used "long boats" in summer on the rivers. Studying maps of the terrain, Halvor determined that the only way the home-steaders could make the journey in their covered wagons was to go over the Athabasca Ice Trail. The risky trail could be used only in the dead of winter when the ice was frozen solid.

The Ice Trail started at Athabasca Landing, about one hundred miles north of Edmonton, which could be reached by railway. From there, the trail extended on the frozen Athabasca River in ever-winding curves to the mouth of one of its many tributaries, the Lesser Slave River flowing from the Lesser Slave Lake. The trail then went westward close to the south shore leading to Grouard before turning southwest to Sturgeon Lake. There both the Hudson's Bay Company and Revillon Freres had set up fur trading posts at various Indian reservations where the settlers would be able to get supplies. From there, the trail went west past Hay Camp across Big Smoky River to Grande Prairie, where Halvor planned to visit the land office and buy more land. From the start at Athabasca Landing, the Ice Trail was said to be some 350 miles to Grande Prairie. Halvor estimated that it was one hundred miles shorter than the overland Edson Trail that Chester and Nelius would take in the spring to join them.

Determined to make the journey whatever the risks, Halvor sold his prosperous farm in Bardo for cash to buy provisions. The following February he set off with Gunhilde, her brother Olaf, and a few close friends. This time they brought with them the five youngest children— Almah, Talbert, Harold, Hazel, and little Victoria. Nelius and Chester would follow when their college semester ended in the spring.

Weather would be the determining factor in their venture. Would the ice of the trail be sufficiently frozen to bear the weight of their wagons? They sallied forth in a unique caravan of horse-drawn sleds. Olaf Horte drove one team; John Johnson drove an abandoned caboose "rescued" from a Canadian Pacific passenger train, mounted on bobsleds, that Halvor turned into the sleeping quarters for the family. He painted it bright red, and Gunhilde furnished it with beds, some fine Chinese furniture, beautiful carpets, two lacquer chests filled with clothing, a stove, a rocking chair where she could rock Lilly Victoria to sleep, and Hannah's treasured piano. Matt Knutson drove the ox team, and Ingebret Voekve and Halvor each drove sleds with a load of provisions for a whole year, including a fifteen-inch brush-breaking plow, snowshoes, and skies. Besides the horses, they had three cows, some chickens, two turkeys, and two geese that became such beloved pets of the children that no one dared eat them.

Halvor recorded the journey in his logbook:

Mar. 4. In the evening it grew rapidly colder, the thermometer registering 30 degrees below zero, and a heavy snowstorm set in. One of the cows got lost and I skied off to find him, almost getting lost myself. It is easy to get lost in the white snow without a compass, but we both survived. We had to put heavy quilts on the cows and double blankets and oil cloths on the horses. We slept in the caboose. In the morning Mrs. Ronning had a white nose, frozen stiff, and I had frozen all the toes of one foot. We quickly rubbed our frozen parts with snow until they came burning back to life.

Mar. 7. As we approached Slave River it got so mild that the snow melted and the rain poured down. It seemed impossible to go ahead and impossible to turn back.

Many other land seekers had joined us, by now there were in all forty teams with sleds. We were in a dangerous situation. If the ice on the river and lakes melted we could go no further. People almost went wild, cried and wept. Others swore and upbraided those of us, especially me, who had led them into this terrible country. I realized my responsibility and took my refuge with the Almighty and prayed as I had never prayed before, except in China, that the rain might cease and we might proceed on our way. The men listened, scowling, until I was through, then they opened the door and looked out. The ground was white and the snow poured down! We all wept. My heart was filled with gratitude and praise.

Mar. 15. Slave Lake was covered with snow and ice. The horses and oxen had been shod and made fine progress. It took us four days to cross the lake, but then we had fairly smooth going. However, on a steep hill Matt Knutson could not hold back the oxen. The poor beasts panicked and plunged down at full gallop. The whole load overturned. Matt was buried under miscellaneous articles on the top of the load but emerged in short order draped with a chicken crate about his neck. The birds made a fearful racket. On the same hill Olaf Horte slid from his perch on top of the load and fell between the horses. We thought he had been crushed under the steel runners, but to our wonder he kept on rolling around and around in front of the runners, and then with a sudden twist of the body landed beside the load with the reins in his hands. Pretty well done! That evening while we were warming up around the camp fire Matt walked into the circle with the chicken crate around his neck and we all laughed until the tears rolled down our cheeks.

The evening before Easter Day we arrived at Grande Prairie. Hurrah! But in the afternoon it grew so warm that the horses were unable to pull the sleds with their heavy loads any further. We had to hitch two teams to the caboose. We had about five miles left before we would reach "Happy Valley." We had previously been promised that we might stop there. We arrived at ten o'clock in the evening. The house was full of people. Two families had arrived earlier. We got water and feed for our horses and cattle. We heard that Olaf Horte had gone two miles further west. We too, went there.

On Easter Day we had service. I preached in my every-day clothes. As the weather had grown colder, we fetched our sleds. On the 24th of March we reached our land at last. Had to shovel away two feet of snow, put up our tent and place the mattresses on the frozen ground. It was a hard trip for the children. They hated to get up in the cold morning.

During the next days, on the site of what would be Halvor's dream settlement, the travelers set up several canvas tents shaped like Mongolian yurts, with wooden floors, octagonal walls lined with colorful Hudson's Bay blankets, and canvas domes with a hole for the chimney. They lived in these tents while building log houses.

The Ronnings all loved music, and when Halvor discovered that the piano had been shaken badly out of tune on the trip, he sent an urgent message to Chester in Camrose telling him to learn how to tune a piano before he joined them that summer. Chester, steeped as he was in filial piety, could not refuse, even though he had no piano. He enrolled in a correspondence course, later claiming to be the only person in the world who had learned to tune a piano without a piano. He had, however, been blessed with perfect pitch and claimed he could hear the music in his head. He received a beautiful diploma with a gold stamp and a red ribbon, which he rolled up carefully with a kit containing a tuning hammer, mutes, and extra steel piano strings and packed with the provisions he and Nelius planned to take on their trip up the Edson Trail to join the family.

29

Three Greenhorns on the Edson Trail

On the third day, after cutting through thick bush, we came to the 27-mile stopping place run by a Swedish proprietor. He prepared a meal of tough roast pork and watery potatoes, but we were so hungry we devoured it all. After the meal the host got out his fiddle and insisted we sing for our supper in Chinese, so we sang "Cho-shih Wode Duzi Tung" but did not tell him that it meant "How My Belly Aches."

—CHESTER RONNING, 1913

As soon as their semester at Camrose Lutheran College was over, Nelius and Chester hurried to Uncle Tom Rorem's home in Bardo, where Tom had kept horses and equipment for their expedition up the Edson Trail to join the rest of the family in Valhalla. They set out from Bardo in May 1913. Nelius was nineteen and Chester seventeen, both having grown into tall, strapping young men. Chester, at six foot three, had outgrown his father by one inch. They were accompanied by their stepmother's sixteen-year-old brother, Harry, who sported a halo of dark hair curling around a smiling face. Nelius was the serious one who often found himself in the role of the straight man for Chester's practical jokes. Harry enjoyed the jokes, but he scowled in frustration when the Ronning boys spoke to each other in Chinese.

Their pioneer journey turned out to be an extraordinary adventure. In his late eighties, Chester still remembered every detail of the trip and wrote an unpublished account entitled "Three Greenhorns on the Edson Trail," which is the source for this story.

Nelius and I hitched our spirited ponies to a sturdy democrat [a type of wagon] with all our worldly goods and a generous helping of grubstake from Aunt Alice. We led a saddled, half Cayuse, half Percheron mare, too large for the harnesses we had. We drove to Kingman, the nearest railway town, in a comfortable seat on the democrat with excellent springs. We considered ourselves to be very lucky to have this fine equipment riding. We rode along at a fast trot.

At the Kingman train station, they loaded the horses and all their equipment onto one large freight car to ride to the beginning of the trail in Edson. *Our four horses, including Harry's, were tied to a feed trough at the very front of the car. The bales of hay were stacked neatly at the back with the bags of oats. We left a narrow space at the back where one could take a snooze unobserved. The democrat occupied the space directly in front of the hay with wheels tied so it would not roll. The seat could accommodate all three of us but we chose to sit in the middle of the freight car to view the scenery out of the open doors on both sides of the car where we had arranged a bale of hay as a table where we could explore the grub.*

In Edson, when Nelius and Chester were hitching the horses and talking Chinese, they attracted the attention of some cowboys who recognized them as greenhorns. Nelius and Harry were packing the wagon, which was hitched to a team of lively Indian ponies named Lucy and Sailor. Chester was saddling a young mare named Daisy, who was to lead a packhorse named Dick, a tough dark-bay Cayuse gelding.

We were soon surrounded by a score of local yokels making crude remarks at our expense. We went about our work ignoring them for good reason, they outnumbered us ten-to-one. Being brought up in Old Imperial China, we had learned it was unwise to reply in kind to strange people especially when they outnumbered you. When we were ready to leave, a rugged cowboy sauntered over; "Hey China boy, you crazy? No one goes over the Edson Trail at this time of year except on foot!"

I was struggling to secure the pack load of blankets and clothes on Dick with a rope. The cowboy pushed me aside. "Here, let me show you how to tie the diamond hitch."

I did not have the ghost of a notion what he was talking about, but we watched in amazement as the cowboy formed a knot resembling a baseball diamond and hitched the stuff into a tight, well-balanced pack. Suddenly the wily cowboy slung a bag of our precious oats on his right shoulder, worth its weight in diamonds to us. Piling insult upon injury, he dragged a bale of our hay with his left hand, which was worth at least its weight in gold to us. He was wildly applauded by the crowd of ruffians who followed him. The cowboy took a bow. We were starting out for Valhalla but did not even have the Viking courage to prevent a diamond hitcher from collecting an exorbitant fee for his instructions. My horse Dick was alarmed by the attention and looked ready to cross the Heavenly Mountains in China. I found in due course that he was too miserable to cross even a shallow river.

The greenhorns thus began their trip amid a chorus of jeers, with Harry riding in the democrat, Nelius walking beside, and Chester riding Daisy and leading Dick. Before midday they arrived at the Edson River. After probing its depth, Nelius climbed into the democrat with Harry and drove across. The water came up to the wagon seat. Then Chester, riding Daisy, led Dick into the river, but the packhorse suddenly screamed and lay down in the middle of the river. Harry yelled to Chester to loosen the rope as Dick's head was going underwater. Chester dismounted in midstream and, trying to keep his head above water, loosened the diamond hitch. He was finally able to drag all the soaked blankets and bags of clothing off the poor beast. Dick struggled to his feet. Chester carried the wet stuff piece by piece to shore, and the boys rung it all out and hung it up to dry. They built a fire to warm up. Chester shot a fat rabbit with his .22 for dinner, and Harry prepared it for the frying pan.

We were starving. Harry cut us each a thick slice of homemade bread and Nelius divided the choicest cuts of rabbit. Almost simultaneously we ravenously took bites of the meat of the land which we had decided to live off of during our expedition up the Edson Trail. Equally simultaneously, we looked into each other's eyes and spat out the evil-tasting rabbit. He had lived on bitter spruce trees and tasted even worse. Pretending to be undaunted, we spread the bread with our precious butter and ate it while swearing Chinese vengeance on the diamond hitcher. We fed the horses more than the amount we had allocated for them. Dick was rewarded for solving his problem by resting in a tributary of the Athabasca River threatening suicide.

Their first rest was at the 27-mile stopping house, where they paid by singing for their supper. In the midst of the second song, they suddenly heard the terrifying shriek of a pig in distress. The Swede went for a lantern and his rifle. The boys followed him out in time to see an enormous grizzly bear carrying a fat pig over the pigsty. Two shots missed, and the bear disappeared into the night with the squealing pig. The next day was spent nervously looking around for the grizzly, and indeed they spotted one at the edge of a plateau looking down at them. They clutched their single-shot .22-gauge rifles that they knew would be useless against such a huge bear but proceeded with the comforting thought that the grizzly had a belly full of pork. A few days later, as they were approaching the 35-mile stopping place, which was the highest point on the trail, with a magnificent view of Athabasca Valley, they saw smoke rising from a chimney and decided to investigate. Nelius rapped at the door, and who should open it but the diamond-hitch cowboy himself. *Ai ya! He was as astonished as we were and made an effort to close the door, but Nelius pushed it open. The diamond hitch cowboy was alone this time, and the greenhorns had been emboldened by our experiences on the rough journey. Nelius smiled wickedly and told him we had come for lunch and to fetch back the hay and oats he had "borrowed." Outnumbered, the cowboy began preparing lunch with unaccustomed humility. During lunch, we made the cowboy extremely nervous by scowling at him and discussing in Chinese what punishments we should bestow on him. After considering water torture and the "death of a thousand cuts," we settled for large second helpings of mashed potatoes. Then we unhitched the horses, allowing them to eat as much of the cowboy's hay as they wished to consume. As the cowboy had no oats to repay us, we piled more of his hay on top of our wagon load. As we were leaving I poked the cowpoke playfully in the stomach and shouted, "Take a bow." The startled cowboy did so and to make sure we would leave happy he told us we were better pioneers than most people from the "outside."* The three greenhorns swaggered off toward Break Neck Hill.

At the edge of the river basin they caught up with an Englishman sitting in a lumber wagon piled dangerously high with his chattels and chickens, contemplating the steep trail down. He had started out the previous autumn but had been forced to spend the winter at a stopping place. They soon discovered why his progress had been so slow. Nelius asked him if he intended to block his wheels with a pole to slow him down, and he replied it wasn't necessary. Halfway down, at a sharp turn, the Englishman's horses were unable to hold his wagon back, and it went straight over the steep hill. Its contents spilled out and rolled down. Nelius and Chester ran down to help, but they slipped in the mud and went tumbling down with hens cackling and flapping all about them. The rest of the day was spent catching chickens and repairing the broken wagon. The lone traveler was pretty shaken up, so Chester offered him the only medicine they had—a spoonful of horse liniment labeled "good for man or beast." The Englishman wisely declined. The boys blocked the wheels of their democrat with wooden poles and proceeded down cautiously. They drove with the Englishman until evening, when they reached the next stopping place. When the proprietor asked how they had fared on the trail, the Englishman replied, "Oh, we got down all right, but all in a heap."

The next morning the boys and the Englishman crossed the Athabasca River on two flat ferries and continued to the 75-mile stopping place near Sturgeon, which was called the "Rabbit Kingdom." All harnesses had to be hung at least seven feet off the ground if one expected to find more than the metal parts the next morning. At night the ground was alive with nibbling rabbits. In fifteen minutes, the pioneers shot enough rabbits to keep them in food for the next few days. This was fortunate because the next stopping place, run by an old man, had just been raided by bears and all his supplies had been eaten.

Bears were not their only concern. Curious wolves surrounded their camps. The boys found that the wolves were not as fierce as their reputations and that they stayed away as long as the boys kept the campfires going, which meant sleeping in shifts. The greatest dangers lay in traversing the treacherous terrain. In the woods south of Rat Lake, their Indian pony, Sailor, slipped into a mud spring. The boys quickly unhitched him so the other horse, Lucy, would not be dragged into the quicksand with him. The more Sailor struggled, the deeper he sank, until only his head remained above the mud. Finally, they got a rope around his neck attached to Daisy's saddle horn, but Daisy kept sliding back. Then Chester remembered that in China he had read in a magazine called *American Boy* that a horse could pull as much weight with his tail as with the rest of its body. They decided to take a chance. They tied one rope to Daisy's tail and another rope from her saddle horn to Dick's tail and finally one to Lucy's tail. Then the three boys and four horses pulled with all the force they could muster. There was a sucking sound as if the mud was trying to vacuum the horse back into its deadly depths and then a loud pop as Sailor was released from certain suffocation in the mud. They did not need to tie the horses anymore since after dark the horses, afraid of wolves, stayed as close to the boys and the fire as they could get. An extremely close relationship developed between the boys and their horses. The horses found their own breakfast every morning and then would nuzzle the boys awake if they slept too long.

A few days later the boys came upon a burned-out area. They were soon covered with flying soot. With no wildlife to be seen, they began to wonder where the next meal would come from. As they discussed the situation, they saw a man stumbling down the trail toward them. "Have you boys got anything to drink?" he asked desperately. They offered him water but after a swig, he said, "Haven't you got anything in a bottle?" Chester suddenly remembered the horse liniment, "good for man or beast." Before he could get out a teaspoon, the man growled, "Give it to me!" He grabbed the bottle and drank the whole thing without stopping. Then he began to shriek, clutched his throat, and passed out. He looked dead. Chester was sure he would be hanged for murder.

The boys decided to put him on the wagon, dead or alive, haul him to Sturgeon, and give themselves up to the local sheriff. But suddenly the man stood up, belched loudly, and shook hands with each one of them, repeating over and over, "Thank you, boys, that was the best drink I ever had!" He refused their offer to join them and lurched off.

That was the beginning of the toughest day. The boys and horses were covered with soot, and the air and their nostrils were full of smoke. Chester wondered if hungry ghosts and evil spirits were haunting the Edson Trail. They made unsalted rice gruel with the last of their water and with the soot gritting in their teeth, but no one dared to complain. At sundown they camped by a small stream, but even the horses would not drink water so full of soot. There was no grass for feed. It was cold. There were no spruce bows for their beds so they slept in the soft, black ashes, wondering if they had descended into one of the eight Buddhist hells.

The horses nudged them up with the sun to get on their way. They hoped to reach Sturgeon Lake. The thought of water, grass, and food kept their spirits high. The horses, smelling water, increased their gait. When the boys saw green trees in the distance and then the blue Sturgeon Lake, they burst out singing, "Oh Canada, glorious and green!"

"Never," said Chester many years later, "have I appreciated and been so ecstatic about the celestial, green trees of Canada, and I have never gotten over that love."

The boys stopped at a fur trading post, the Revillon Freres, west of a Hudson's Bay post, and knocked at the door. A trapper opened up, took one look, handed them a bar of soap, and pointed to the lake. They ran to the water, unhitched the horses, stripped off their clothing, and all seven of them, boys and horses, jumped gleefully in the water, which was indeed "good for man or beast."

The next morning they proceeded north along the edge of Sturgeon Lake. Approaching the bridge over Goose Creek, they came upon hundreds of Navajo Indians, men, women, and children on both sides of the water laughing as they caught fish by the dozens. The boys were amazed to see the waters of the small river churning with thousands upon thousands of pike and pickerel rushing upstream to spawn. They had come upon the annual Indian fishing festival. The Navajos invited them to participate in the fun. The boys dug out their fishing gear and spent the afternoon catching fish. In the evening they sat around the fire with their new Indian friends feasting on fish and cornbread. It was the beginning of a deep friendship and sympathy that the boys developed for the Indians of the Peace River District.

At the next trading post, Hay Camp, they traded fish for butter and salt and hay for the horses. The hardest part of the trail was behind them. In a few days they ferried across Big Smoky River and stopped in Grande Prairie to file the land claims as their father had advised them to do. Then they headed west toward Lake Saskatoon. In the distance stood the ice-capped Rocky Mountains topped by Mount Robson. At the lake they were met by Harry's older brother, Chris Horte, who had come to guide them to their new home in Valhalla.

Halvor had been expecting his sons for three days. When he finally saw them through his binoculars he threw up his arms and shouted, "Here they come!" He ran with great strides to greet them. The whole family followed. Overwhelmed, the tough guys who had tracked over deadly muskegs and quicksand holes, braved bears and wolves, endured hunger and desperate thirst were reduced to tears. The younger brothers, Talbert and Harold, climbed up with Chester on the faithful horse Daisy. Their father and the girls climbed into the democrat and rode triumphantly to their new tent home, where sister Almah and stepmother Gunhilde welcomed them. The boys fed, curried, and petted their courageous horses before indulging in a homecoming turkey feast. After dinner, Chester carefully unwrapped his tuning hammer, and while his siblings watched with awe, he tuned the piano. Then, with exaggerated flourish, he played their fa-vorite tunes from *Sankey's Songs and Solos.* The children had all inherited their mother's resonant voice and love of music. They felt Hannah's spirit with them as their joyful songs echoed through Valhalla Valley—"There Is Sunshine in My Soul Today."

The three greenhorns were now accepted as seasoned pioneers. They were as proud of their achievement as were the Norsemen in finding the New World.

30

Valhalla Homestead

THE HAPPY FARMER

All the long night
The rain patterned down
On the thick, thatched eaves
Of my cabin.

This night, on ten times
Ten thousand farms
It has stirred the rice seed
To new life.

When the warm sun comes up
I shoulder my hoe
And go blithely forth
To my field

And I sing a song as I go,
Of the blue, blue sky,
And the water that shines
So green.
—CE NAN, QING DYNASTY (1644–1911)

The Ronning family devoted the next months to clearing the land and settling into the homesteads. On Sundays, Reverend Ronning donned his high starched collar and adjusted his worn black cravat as the children, dressed in their Sunday best, watched in awe. Talbert would proudly help his father into his thirty-year-old Prince Edward suit coat, which had become just a bit snug. Then, putting on his Hamburg, the preacher would mount Daisy and ride like a cowboy a mile south to the tent serving temporarily as the Lutheran church. The boys followed on horseback while their stepmother and the children rode in the buggy drawn by the same team of high-stepping Clydesdales that had pulled them up the Athabasca Ice Trail to Valhalla. Reverend Ronning's sermons to his growing congregation were dramatic and inspiring. Afterward, coffee and Norwegian pastries were served. Halvor wondered if the settlers came to hear the word of God or to eat Mrs. Ronning's cookies.

Halvor was a man of many seasons. On weekdays, he wore overalls and worked with his sons like a lumberjack. The boys were amazed at how quickly and frequently their father would change character. Halvor had chosen a building site for their new home that was both scenic and practical. It was shielded from the strong north wind by a half circle of aspen trees. There was a winding creek in a valley just to the east, which was dammed in several places by beavers. The boys arched Chinese-style moon bridges over the stick-and-earth dams. Eight miles west, Halvor found a grove of tall spruce trees that would make excellent logs for the two-story house he had designed. Eager to fell the first log, he ceremoniously selected a majestic tree close to the edge of the forest. He deftly chopped a horizontal V-shaped cut on the side of the tree facing the direction in which he wanted it to fall. Then he showed Chester how to cut it with a two-handled, crosscut saw. When the tree began to topple, the lumberjacks shouted "timber!" and jumped back to watch the noble spruce crash. Chester drove a team of oxen named Charley and Bright, whom he treated like house pets although they weighed together almost four tons. He hitched them to a chain to snake the logs out of the woods to a loading platform hitched to a rig. After felling a few more trees, they headed home to begin building their house. Other homesteaders, newly arrived from Norway, came to help. Some of them were builders, expert in the use of the eighteen-inch-wide broadax. They trimmed the sides of each log to make them the same width and in erecting the cabin carefully fitted the corners to form right angles without any overlapping. In a few months, the Ronnings moved into a comfortable, four-bedroom log house with a shingled roof, a porch, and an attic resembling an upside-down Viking ship. It was large enough to store the treasures that Halvor had brought from China. It was the only frontier house furnished with Chinese carpets, carved lacquer chests, and a well-tuned piano.

Talbert and Harold were soon old enough to join their father and older brothers in the clearing of the land and planting crops while Gunhilde and the girls—Almah, Hazel, and Victory—cared for the animals, milked the cows, gathered eggs, grew garden vegetables, and made flour, butter, cheese, and, on Sundays, ice cream. The boys sheared the sheep and the girls carded the wool with steel brushes until it was fine enough to be spun on spinning wheels and knit into clothing. They worked from sunrise to sunset, and the farm was soon self-sufficient. Halvor acquired fine horses, and the boys spent much of their time in the saddle riding the range and hunting for food. Their main meat was wild fowl, rabbit, and an occasional moose or deer, but for weeks in the winter there was nothing but rabbit. Gunhilde learned to cook rabbit in all manner of ways, and no one dared complain. One evening, however, after a hard day's work and facing yet another rabbit on the table, father Ronning managed to transform the dour faces of his children into smiles by digressing from his usual Grace:

> Father, we thank Thee—
> For rabbit roasted and rabbit fried,
> For rabbit cooked and rabbit dried,
> For rabbit young and rabbit old,
> For rabbit hot and rabbit cold,
> For rabbit tender and rabbit tough
> We thank thee Lord that we have enough.

The challenge now for the Ronnings was to clear all the land they could in fulfillment of their official homestead filings. With little rest, they cut the trees with axes, cleared shrubs with hoes, and broke the rich, black loam soil with plows pulled by six horses or four oxen. They cleared an average of about two acres a day and in three summers broke a total of 210 acres, enough to "prove-up" three homesteads. The challenge met, Nelius and Chester braved the Edson Trail once again, returning to Edmonton to study at the University of Alberta.

The Egg Lake Trail

After their first year at the university, Nelius and Chester began their return to Valhalla aboard the Edmonton, Dunegan & British Columbia Railroad. They left the train at Culp, a small town that was little more than a construction encampment of canvas tents for railroad workers. Several tents had flashy signs announcing accommodation for travelers. Chester chose to stay at the Royal Hotel. The fee was one dollar each if they would share a double bed.

In his memoir Chester later wrote: *Sitting on the bed, as there was no other furniture in the Royal suite, we were suddenly interrupted by the appearance of two giggling, painted girls waving their arms and advancing upon us. We grabbed our suitcases and rushed out of the tent leaving our precious dollars behind. We were lucky that no one saw the preacher's sons in the canvas house of ill repute. We headed for Watino, another tent city with more imperial hotels. Four of the tents were saloons with player pianos blazing music at double "ff" in different keys. The conglomerate result was excruciatingly painful.*

In Watino, we stayed in an old trapper's log cabin that had no floor. We made a comfortable bed of fragrant spruce boughs. Before going to bed we could not keep our eyes off the wild activity on Watino's main street. A woman ran out of one of the saloons. Two drunken men pursued her. She outran them which was actually unnecessary as they tumbled and fell fighting each other. Then she let herself be caught by a younger man, judging by his slow speed. They were attacked by several other men and women all screaming and fighting in a mad scramble. Two Mounties showed up and separated them. One man was hauled away. The turmoil in the streets continued.

Neither the wild people nor the saloon keepers who catered to the railroaders were local Canadian homesteaders. Most of them were American construction workers and professional "camp followers" who exploited the workers. This was the Wild West. Carrying our suitcases almost on the run down the nine miles from Culp had exhausted us. Nelius and I slept soundly in the old trapper's shack despite the impossibility of closing the door. There was none.

Early the next morning, the boys hired an Indian with pack ponies who for ten dollars would carry their baggage around Egg Lake to a railroad bunkhouse a dozen miles or more on the trail to Spirit River while they took a shorter route on foot. The Indian warned them to carefully follow trees that were blazed with slashes on the trunks: "Never leave a blazed tree before you have sighted another blaze and never walk out of sight of the next blaze."

Setting out on foot, the boys found that the trail winding through the woods was under shallow water. As they pressed on, the water on the trail became deeper. Before long, Chester and Nelius were knee-deep in water. In some places they sank into clinging mud. They found it easier to walk barefooted. Chester wrote:

Off went our shoes and socks. When the water was chest-deep, we tried swimming with our clothes on. That was even tougher. Fortunately, the water became shallower as we approached the next blaze. For 13 long miles, tough miles, our feet did not step on dry ground. The next time we found the water chest-deep, we took off all of our wet clothes, twisted them as dry as we could, and tied them on top of our heads.

Then we swam stark naked until we could wade again. We made better time that way and we had more fun.

We had the waters of Egg Lake Trail all to ourselves except for millions of frogs who kept up a continuous chorus of musical chirping.

Chester described vividly how they found a dry spot atop fallen trees where they drank water with cupped hands and devoured sandwiches that they had kept dry by carrying them atop their heads. *It was like finding a diamond in a desert of sand. Here was a most suitable place to celebrate our gourmet lunch. Each sandwich had two fat eggs between two thick slices of buttered bread. They were the most beautiful sandwiches we had ever seen.*

For the next four hours, they plodded on from tree blaze to tree blaze, often waist-deep in water before they came upon the railroad bunkhouse on the shore of Egg Lake. *When at last our feet met the solid ground, we shouted "Hurrah for Valhalla!" and ran full speed ahead to the bunk house. The front door was open and there were our bags.*

At dawn, as they resumed hiking on an old wagon trail, the boys were finally rewarded for their courage and determination. *We decided to sit down on a fallen log for a short rest. All of a sudden, we gazed at a team and a democrat, coming at a fast trot from the west. There was Father and Harold driving Sailor and Lucy. We dropped our bags and jumped into the democrat before it stopped. We almost wept before we shouted, laughed, and hugged them in great excitement.*

Chester Falls in Love

Although Halvor's wife, Gunhilde, and her three brothers had arrived in Valhalla in 1912, her parents and youngest sister, Inga Marie (who was to become my mother) did not arrive until 1915. Inga was a tall, beautiful young woman with long dark curls, hazel eyes that turned green in the sunshine, and a sweet mouth with a pronounced cupid's bow. For Chester it was love at first sight. Yet, because Inga was the youngest sister of his stepmother, who was twenty years older, and ostensibly his aunt, it was rather awkward for him to pursue Inga.

Chester: *In Valhalla I fell in love with Inga Marie Horte. She loved horses and owned a fine palomino mare named Flory. I sometimes wondered if she would have accepted me for "better or for worse" if I had not won a bet we made about Flory's first colt, a five-year-old gelding named Pet who was so wild that no one had been able to ride him.*

One day, Inga dared Chester to ride the unbroken bronco. "Foolishly," Chester would later comment, "I accepted," but he accepted on the condition that if he succeeded, she would become his girlfriend. Confident that Chester could not break her horse, she laughed and agreed.

The next day, Chester secretly rounded up the wild horses and isolated the spirited buckskin in their Montana-style corral, roped him, put a half-hitch over his nose to prevent him from bucking, and rode him bareback. He repeated this on three different days until he felt that if he could ride Pet bareback, it would be a "cinch" to ride him with bridle, saddle, and spurs. He set a date with Inga to watch as he broke her horse.

It was no "cinch." Pet resented the curb bit, which I held too tightly, and finally reared so high that he fell over backwards. Inga screamed wildly while I managed to scramble unceremoniously out from under Pet. Fortunately, I got to my feet before the horse did and jumped into the saddle as he was getting up. This time I let him have his head, spurred him into a dead gallop, banked him from side to side and knowing I could not stop him, headed straight towards the foot of a soggy old straw stack just out of Inga's view. There Pet was forced to slow down when he sank knee deep in the muddy, soaked straw. The poor horse was all a-lather when I reached down to pat him. When he calmed down I rode slowly back to claim my "win." Inga came running to meet us and I was already planning the wedding.

By 1916, when the Edmonton, Dunegan & British Columbia Railroad reached Grande Prairie, hundreds of land-hungry homesteaders had come to Valhalla. About two miles southeast of the Ronnings' homestead, a Lutheran church, a general store, and a grain elevator were built on a site that Halvor named Valhalla Centre. A school was opened, and Halvor appointed Nelius as teacher. When Nelius left to resume studies at the University of Alberta, the school board asked his father to find another teacher. Without hesitation, he replied: "Please don't worry. Chester is a born teacher." But Chester wanted to become a rancher. Having been raised in the Chinese tradition of filial piety, however, he felt he had no choice. After one term of nonpaid teaching, he decided that if teaching was to be his destiny, he should be properly prepared, and he went off to Camrose Normal School to study for his teaching certificate. Nelius received his bachelor's degree from the University of Alberta just after World War I broke out.

War

Both Chester and Nelius had planned to return to China. The war changed their lives. Reverend Ronning was an ardent pacifist, but when Nelius and Chester were called into the army in April 1918, he gave them his blessing. The patriotic young men rode forty-five miles on horseback in one night to Grande Prairie to join the military service. Nelius joined the Royal Flying Corps and was stationed in Toronto. Chester joined the Royal Canadian Engineers as a sapper. At Fort Osborne in Winnipeg, he was assigned to picking up refuse. "I felt like a Chinese beggar," he complained. A week later he asked to be transferred to the Royal Flying Corps as a cadet pilot. He earned his wings flying the recently invented single-propeller, double-winged plane dubbed "Death Crates."

When he returned to Valhalla on leave, he immediately rode to the Horte home to ask Inga's father's permission to marry his daughter. Anthon Horte had known Halvor's father in Telemark when he was a church sexton and owned a sawmill in the Bo Valley. In 1889, Anthon and his wife, Ingrid, moved from the village of Horte in Telemark to the United States with their three sons, Chris, Thor, and Olaf. They settled on a homestead near Nielsville, Minnesota, where Harry and Inga were born.

Chester found Inga's father fixing the roof of his house. *I sat in the saddle,* wrote Chester in his book, *looking up with the sunlight blinding my eyes, trying to see the dignified, red-bearded Sexton nailing shingles. I removed my army hat and somehow I stammered my way through the formula I had carefully prepared and rehearsed. He put down his hammer and with a kind smile said that he had wondered if I had the courage. Then he gave his permission, making it clear that it was only because he trusted the choice of his youngest daughter.*

Chester galloped back to tell Inga and, with his stepmother Gunhilde as chaperone, they hitched the horses to the buggy and drove to Grande Prairie to get a marriage license. Reverend Ronning performed the wedding ceremony attended by family and close friends. Chester stood tall in his army uniform, and Inga, who had cut her hair in a fashionable short bob, wore a stunning ankle-length dress of white lace. As they were about to retire into the second log house recently built by Halvor, the young people of Valhalla surprised them with an old-fashioned shivaree, raucously banging on pots, kettles, and dishpans until they were invited in by Mrs. Gunhilde Ronning to a feast she had prepared. The next day, the newlyweds went to Edmonton, where Inga enrolled in Alberta College. After a short honeymoon, Chester reported for duty in the Royal Flying Corps in Fort Osborne, Winnipeg.

At Fort Osborne, Chester flew the open-cockpit fighter planes. On his first solo flight, with his mind in Edmonton with his bride, he was suddenly jolted back to reality. Spinning his first loop above a cemetery near the airfield, he saw his safety strap hanging straight down—he had forgotten to fasten it. Only centrifugal force saved him from joining his ancestors. The war ended before he had to test his skills in combat over Germany.

After the Armistice, Chester and Inga moved to Edmonton, where he taught high school. After the birth of their first child, Sylvia Hannah, he completed his courses in education at the University of Minnesota. Although Chester and Inga never returned to live in Valhalla, Reverend Ronning and Gunhilde continued to live there for the rest of their lives.

In 1943, Halvor wrote: *Now, after 30 years we can hardly recognize the place. Valhalla Centre is a small village a short distance from our home (two miles) within easy walking distance. There are several stores with a post office, a primary school and a high school and a large cooperative creamery. We have a beautiful church with a fine parsonage, both paid for. There are four more Norwegian Lutheran congregations with fine churches in the Valhalla district and some preaching places. I was not the regular pastor at Valhalla, but having my home there, I often helped with the preaching. I began work at Dawson Creek, British Columbia, where we have a minister and a beautiful church. The field extends into the Peace River Block in British Columbia and is one of the largest Norwegian settlements in Western Canada.*

I am determined to return to China but not sure in which capacity. If my decision is not in accordance with God's plan, He will block my pathway and turn me into the path which He has ordained for me to travel.

—FROM THE LAST LETTER OF NELIUS RONNING, MAY 20, 1920

Nelius stayed with Chester's family in Edmonton while he was studying for his master's degree in geology at the University of Alberta and working as a field assistant in a survey expedition under Dr. J. Allen. Their most important discovery was the fossilized skeleton of a huge dinosaur (Albertosaurus) that Nelius found in Alberta's Red River Valley. After a lengthy excavation, the fossil was presented to the Museum of Natural History in New York, where it was displayed in the entrance hall before being moved to the Hall of Dinosaurs in the 1970s.

Nelius had reached a decisive point in his life. He had offers to go to Burma as a geologist for a British mining firm or to go to China for the Canadian YMCA. The Young People's League of America had asked him to represent them as their missionary in China and offered to pay his way at their seminary. He wrote to his father: *I must say that the offer came to me like "a bolt from the blue." I have been carefully considering the matter for over a month.*

In May 1920, Nelius was selected as one of four assistant geologists to go with Allen E. Cameron, a geologist for the Imperial Oil Company, Edmonton, to make surveys along the shores of Great Slave Lake, unexplored territory some eight hundred miles north of Edmonton in the wilderness of the Northwest Territories. The Department of Geology gave him a pair of gold cuff links as a parting gift. He was to be paid $150 per month and expenses, money he needed to continue his studies. Before leaving on the expedition on May 20, he wrote:

My Beloved Folks: The view from the hill as we approached the Peace River Valley was grand. Twilight was just coming on and only the shadowy outlines of the farther banks were visible. The tranquil Peace River reflected the remaining light like a ribbon of shining silver. Looking up the river I saw the confluence of the two mighty streams, the Peace and the Big Smoky, a beautiful scene. Numerous islands divide the strong and glassy current below the juncture. Still thinking about my offers.

Nelius was last seen on August 12, 1920. He and his companion, J. C. Mac-Dougall, had set off in their canoe to survey Great Slave Lake. The sky was ominous, but the young men felt they couldn't upset the plan that had been so carefully worked out by the Imperial Oil Company. They were to be picked up at a given point along the lake by Allen Cameron in his launch. The ice-cold lake is known for its sudden and violent storms. First one and then another storm raged in great fury before Cameron set off on August 19 to pick up the young explorers. But Nelius and MacDougall had disappeared. A week later, Cameron found the canoe, and after continued searching, MacDougall's body was found. It was speculated that MacDougall had clung to the canoe while Nelius, the stronger swimmer, went for help. Neither could have possibly survived the glacial waters for more than ten minutes. A telegram was sent to Halvor reporting that Nelius was missing. Bearing a second telegram from Cameron, Olaf Horte came upon Halvor in his parson's coat striding back and forth before his house like a caged lion. Before opening the telegram, which contained word that the canoe and MacDougall's body had been found, Halvor looked up to the heavens with tears in his eyes and whispered, "My boy has joined his mother in glory."

Halvor searched for Nelius along the shores of Great Slave Lake off and on for fifteen years before meeting an Indian brave who said he had found Nelius's body downstream from the canoe. He had recognized Nelius as one of the boys who had been fishing with them years earlier in Goose Creek. Not knowing who to contact, the Indians had buried him respectfully in their cemetery. He took Reverend Ronning to the grave in the Indian reservation. His resting place had been carefully cared for, covered with wildflowers, and enclosed by a white picket fence. Grandfather decided not to bring his son's body to the church cemetery in Valhalla but to leave him with his Indian friends in the vast wilderness he loved so well. Nelius's Uncle Nils wrote his epitaph:

Summers and winters have come and gone. In summer the grave is covered by beautiful wild flowers; in winter by the soft, comforting snow, while at night the silent stars keep their vigil and the winds sing their eternal requiem.

The thought of Nelius, the Beloved, comes to us as a benediction after prayer. His memory, his presence, will be an abiding blessing to all who know him, and there are many of us who know that his departure has meant a deepening of the spiritual awareness and an increasing spiritual power.

His friend Shi Gun-ching wrote from Fancheng, China: "When I was only a boy I had the privilege to live with him. His parents had much love for others and Nelius followed in their footsteps and became a man with great love and sympathy. He has always been kind and considerate . . . We heard of Nelius' graduation from college and when we heard that he was soon coming back to Fancheng, it filled our hearts with much joy, but when we received the news of his sudden death, it made our hearts heavy. The whole congregation here mourns his loss. I myself looked upon Nelius as a dear friend and I feel the loss more than I can express in words . . . We rejoice to know that he is in His Father's Home, safe at home. God's way is the best, although so often we cannot understand His dealings with us."

The Ronning family in Bardo, Alberta, just before leaving for the Peace River District, 1912. *From left:* Nelius, Almah (*standing*), Hazel, Rev. Halvor Ronning, Harold, Talbert (*standing*), Victoria, and Chester.
Ronning Family Archive

The Ronnings building the first two-story log house in Valhalla Centre, 1913. Chester is standing on a load of logs he just brought in; Halvor is on the roof in his preacher's hat. This home is now an Alberta Provincial Historical Site.
Ronning Family Archive

Valhalla, 1917: Inga Horte, who would marry Chester in 1918.
Ronning Family Archive

Chester bidding farewell to his father as he prepares to return to China, 1921, while brothers Harold and Talbert look on.
Ronning Family Archive

Chester upon his return to China in 1922, on a lion at the Summer Palace in Peking.
Ronning Family Archive

Trackers harnessed by bamboo cables to the top of the mast pull Chester and Inga's houseboat through the rapids on the way to Fancheng.
Ronning Family Archive, photograph by Chester Ronning

Graduating class of the mission school at Fancheng, 1926. Chester, with mustache, is seated in the front row with associate principal Tung Tse-pei, at his right.
Ronning Family Archive

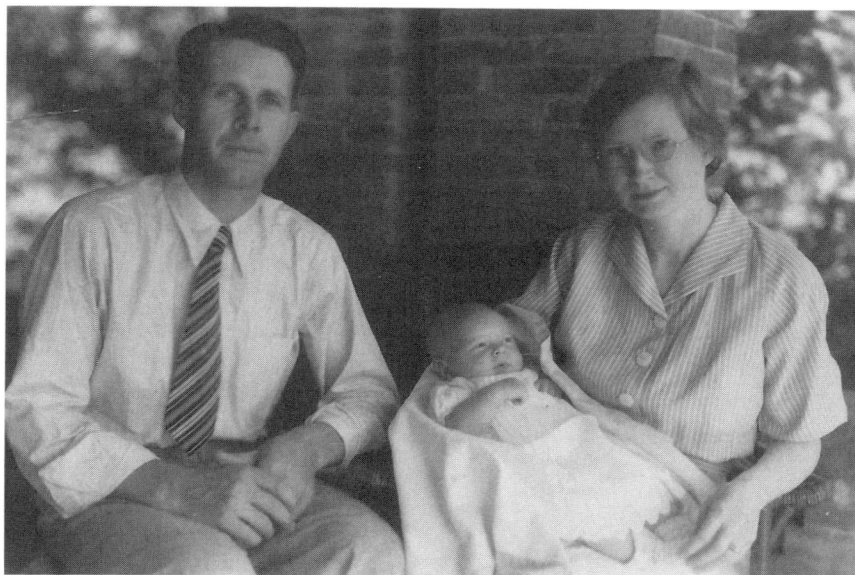

Talbert and wife Ella with their son Halvor (named after his grandfather), born in China, 1932.
Ronning Family Archive

Chungking, wartime capital on the banks of the Yangtze River, in Sichuan Province. This was Chester's first diplomatic post with the Canadian embassy in 1945. *Ronning Family Archive, photograph by Audrey R. Topping (1971)*

Chester Ronning, squadron leader and director of the Royal
Canadian Air Force intelligence unit, 1944. Because he could
read and write Chinese and read Japanese, Chester was able to
assist in breaking the Japanese code during World War II.
Ronning Family Archive

Generalissimo and Madame Chiang
Kai-shek in their mountain villa in
Kuling, 1946.
*Photograph by Carl Mydans, taken during
Chester Ronning's visit; used by permission*

Audrey with local
children in Peking in
1966, writing what
would become the
New York Times cover
story "Through Darkest
Red China." After
her departure, the
Chinese government
dropped the "Bamboo
Curtain" and allowed
no Westerners in again
until 1971.
*Ronning Family Archive,
photograph by Audrey
R. Topping (timed self-
photo)*

Mao's "Little Red Book" was in every hand when China reopened its borders to Western visitors in 1971.
Ronning Family Archive, photograph by Audrey R. Topping

China's Premier Zhou Enlai (*right*) welcomes his old friend, Canadian ambassador Chester Ronning, in the Great Hall of the People, 1971. They met in the Hubei Room, named after the province where Chester was born. Ronning's fluent Chinese made the interpreter unnecessary.
Ronning Family Archive, photograph by Audrey R. Topping

1975: Vice Premier Li Xiannian; Audrey; Ye Jianying; Chester; Zhou Enlai's successor and later Paramount Leader, Deng Xiaoping; Audrey's daughter Susan Topping; and Premier Zhou Enlai.
Ronning Family Archive, Zhou Enlai's photographer, name unknown

Audrey riding with Kazaks on the Old Silk Road while on assignment for the *New York Times* and *National Geographic Magazine*, 1975.
Ronning Family Archive, photograph by Lesley Topping

1975: Audrey was the first Western journalist to report the spectacular discovery of the terracotta warriors buried in 210 BC to guard the tomb of China's first emperor, Qin Shihuang.

Photograph courtesy of Huang Hua, former Chinese ambassador to Canada

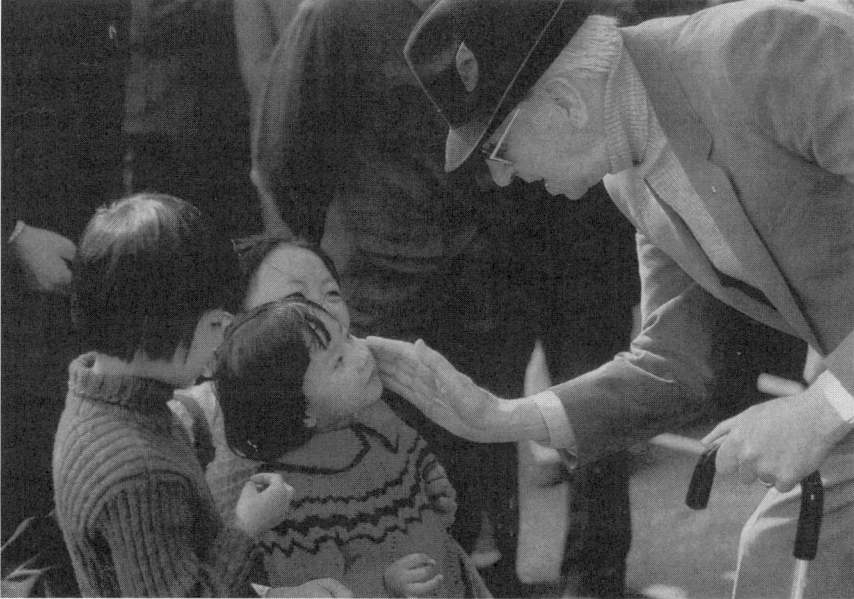

1984: Chester Ronning, known as "Venerable Teacher" in Fancheng, greets children at the elementary school he attended as a child. The school was founded by his mother Hannah and is on the same campus as the Hung Wen School of Higher Learning, founded by his father. Chester was headmaster and teacher from 1923 to 1927. *Ronning Family Archive, photograph by Audrey R. Topping*

Photo of the Topping family taken almost one hundred years after the 1899 photo of Hannah and Halvor with children in Hankow (first photo insert). Some family members are wearing the original Chinese robes once worn by Audrey's parents and grandparents.
Ronning Family Archive

PART IV

CHESTER
RETURNS
TO
CHINA

In the Footsteps of Halvor, 1921

Though I'm sad unto death,
The tears refuse to come,
And my long-drawn sighs
Are changed to joyous song.
The flowers in the courtyard
Spread their colors to the sun
Can I forever grieve and sorrow
When spring calls loud and long?
—SUI FUREN, SUI DYNASTY (AD 581–618)

Chester was devastated by the death of Nelius. His life had been entwined with that of his beloved older brother since birth. Father Halvor was comforted by his complete faith in the afterlife, telling his children that God works in mysterious ways beyond our understanding. Yet Chester felt broken, as if part of him had died with his brother. And he felt guilty for surviving. Why Nelius? Why Mother? He had depended upon Nelius to always be there to laugh with him, sing, play, and share their secret languages. Only Nelius understood the complex, multidimensional nature of his character formed by early immersion and nurturing in China, Norway, the United States, and Canada, societies with diverse ideologies, cultures, and religions. There was now a vacancy in his life that would never be filled, and he would have to learn to bear it.

Reverend Ronning, who had been counting on his oldest son to continue the family's missionary work in China, now looked to Chester to fulfill his dreams by nurturing the mission schools that he and his beloved Hannah had founded in Fancheng. Halvor did not need to persuade his son. The moment Chester heard that his brother had been lost in Great Slave Lake, he knew his own life would be changed forever. Although Chester had recently graduated with a degree in education from the University of Minnesota and had been offered a lucrative position teaching high school physics in Minneapolis, he now felt duty-bound to return to China.

Chester's wife, Inga, was not enthusiastic about his return to China. She was an accomplished pianist and absorbed in her study of music theory. Daughter Sylvia was only five years old. They were happy in their home in Edmonton, and Inga felt uneasy about venturing into a troubled land on the other side of the world. But she loved Chester, and even as she protested, she knew she would yield to his stronger will.

Chester never claimed to feel the religious "call" that had motivated his parents and Nelius. He was driven more by a desire to help educate Chinese students than to convert them to Christianity. Like his father, he felt that education for the ordinary Chinese was the essential factor in China's modernization.

Their journey to China did not begin propitiously. The family set forth on the *Empress of Australia*, but on the third day the steamer developed engine trouble. The ship returned to Vancouver, where they transferred to the old *Empress of China*. Inga was not surprised: Chester seemed destined to follow in the footsteps of his father.

In Shanghai they transferred to a Jardine, Matheson & Co. riverboat to steam up the Yangtze River to the British Concession in Hankow, where his parents had been married and where Nelius had been born. They purchased tickets to ride on the recently finished railway from Hankow to Peking. But when Chester learned that the trains through Henan Province were being attacked by soldier-brigands of feuding warlords and scores of passengers had been killed, he decided to sail back to Nanking and take the luxurious *Blue Express* that hurried along the coastal plain via Tientsin to Peking (at that time called Peip'ing). Inga was delighted. Chester kept the reports of the murders on the railroad from her. The food on the *Blue Express* was good, and the views from the diner of the walled villages, mysterious distant pagodas, and emerald-green rice paddies were more picturesque than she had imagined. Eight miles from Peking, they crossed a spidery steel trestle spanning the Yungting River, where Chester pointed out the white marble arches of the Marco Polo Bridge, so named because in the thirteenth century Polo had stood on the bridge and written in his famous *Travels*: "Its length is three hundred paces, and its width eight paces; so that ten mounted men can, without inconvenience ride abreast." It also became a strategic point for the defense of northern China when, in 1937, the Japanese declared war on China. From the window, the landscapes of eternal China looked so peaceful that Inga was inspired to paint. Unfortunately, she would soon learn that eternal China looked far better from a distance.

The plan was to spend a year in Peking learning Mandarin at the North China Union Language School before continuing on to Fancheng. The school had been founded in 1910 by missionary William B. Pettus to teach Chinese to missionaries and later military men, diplomats, and journalists. Although Chester spoke the Hubei dialect he had learned as a child, he needed to learn to speak, read, and write classical Mandarin if he was to become headmaster of a high school (called a "middle school" in China). The school also gave Inga the chance to learn the language. On arrival in Peking, they were not aware that political events within the country were evolving toward the violent upheaval that would become known as the Great Revolution.

Peking was an overwhelming cultural change for Inga from the life she had known in Alberta, a young, peaceful, and sparsely settled land that had become a province of Canada only ten years earlier. Peking, in contrast, had a rich and tumultuous history dating back three thousand years. Except for two brief interludes when the southern city of Nanking had served as the capital, Peking had reigned as China's capital for seven hundred years. Inga wrote to her sister Gunhilde: *Walls, walls, walls, nothing but walls is my first impression of Peking. Some walls curtain away the squalor of dirty courtyards and wretched homes. Some walls deprive one of glimpses into the gracious gardens of the wealthy. But the fact that the walls hide the unknown, always lends scope to the imagination.*

Chester had left Imperial China in 1907 as a boy and now returned in 1921 as an adult to the newly established Republic of China. The world had changed enormously during the interim under the impact of World War I, the Bolshevik Revolution in Russia, and the fall of the two-thousand-year-old Imperial dynastic system in China. Chester soon learned details of the power struggle that was in progress in China among the warlords who dominated various regions of the country. The Chinese people were not only battling for the right to their own destiny against foreign domination, but also were struggling to cope with the corrupt and repressive systems prevalent in this Warlord Period.

In 1911, following the fall of the Manchu Dynasty, Dr. Sun Yat-sen, whose democratic reforms Halvor and Chester admired, became the provisional president of the republic. Two months later, however, he was forced to resign in favor of Yuan Shikai, who controlled the army. In 1913, as opposition developed to Yuan's dictatorial rule, Sun led a revolt against his regime. The coup was aborted when supporters in Hankow gave away the plot by mistakenly exploding a bomb a week before the planned uprising. Sun fled to Japan seeking political asylum, leaving Yuan in control as president. Sun would return to China in 1917 to work politically and militarily to further the democratic revolution against the warlords. After his death in 1925, he was recognized by both the Nationalist (Kuomintang) and Communist parties as the father of the Chinese republic.

Yuan was the sinister mandarin who, in 1898, had betrayed Emperor Guangxu during the Hundred Days of Reform in collaboration with the empress dowager. The real emperor was imprisoned, and at his death in 1908, Pu Yi (the "Last Emperor"), a three-year-old, was placed on the Dragon Throne. He was allowed to abdicate in 1912, four years after the dowager died. Yuan Shikai then attempted to place himself on the throne and ordered the mint to put his profile on millions of silver dollars. In 1914, during World War I, when Chester and Nelius were half a world away serving in the Canadian armed forces, Japan entered the war on the side of the Allies. It was a self-serving move. Japan sent its naval vessels carrying troops into the Yellow Sea, and they occupied the Chinese coastal province of Shandong, which had been held by Germany as an extraterritorial concession. The Chinese were outraged and demanded its unconditional return. Instead, Japan presented President Yuan Shikai with the infamous Twenty-One Demands, which effectively would have put Japan in economic and administrative control of China. China was pressured not only to ratify Japanese sovereignty over Shandong, but also to grant trade, rail, and industrial concessions in Inner Mongolia, Manchuria, and the Yangtze Valley, lease Port Arthur and Dairen (today's Dalian) for ninety-nine years, and agree not to contract concessions or negotiate loans with any other power without Japan's consent. Finally, China was asked to accept Japanese military, political, and financial advisors and joint Japanese control of schools, police, and arsenals.

Yuan Shikai yielded to the demands in exchange for Japanese loans, which he intended to use to consolidate his power. When his maneuvers were exposed, a storm of indignation swept through China. Yuan, now apparently senile, ignored the public outcry and declared himself emperor, placing himself on the Imperial Dragon Throne as the founder of a new dynasty. To control the provinces, Yuan appointed military commanders in each province who exercised both military and civil power. They were his most trusted army officers. But when he proclaimed himself emperor, his commanders' opposition mounted rapidly. It was the onset of the chaos of the Warlord Period. Three months later, Yuan was forced to resign. In 1916, he formally decreed the end of the Qing Dynasty, although it was effectively already dead. When the self-appointed emperor died shortly after, it was rumored that arsenic had been slipped into his bird's nest soup.

After World War I, when the results of the Paris Peace Conference became known, the Chinese people became disillusioned with the United States. Initially, the United States supported Peking in its insistence that Shandong Province be returned to its sovereignty. But when Japan threatened to withdraw from the League of Nations, President Woodrow Wilson yielded. Japan was granted control of the former German extraterritorial concession.

When university students in Peking, already outraged by imposition on China of the unequal treaties, learned of this humiliating capitulation, they rose up in an unprecedented protest that became known as the May Fourth Movement, which the Chinese proudly mark to this day. On May 4, 1919, thousands of students assembled in Tiananmen Square and paraded through the streets shouting, "Down with traitors." They cajoled merchants into boycotting Japanese goods. The protests spread to other principal cities. Students in Halvor Ronning's school in Fancheng joined the protests. Tung Tse-pei and Shi Gun-ching, who had learned English from Chester and Nelius by reading the American Declaration of Independence and had become ardent supporters of Sun Yat-sen's democracy movement, were leaders in a protest march. When they discovered that the straw hats that were part of the school uniform were made in Japan, they tossed them away and replaced them with white cloth caps. The widespread campaign to destroy Japan's market in China lasted nearly a year and seemed to have some effect. Three Chinese officials, denounced by the students for their role in the Shandong negotiations, were dismissed by the Peking government. The Chinese delegation in Paris refused to sign the Peace Treaty. Shandong was returned to Chinese control in 1922.

Peking

In 1922, when the Ronnings arrived, the streets of Peking were thronged with the soldiers of the warlords, some with great cutlasses strapped to their backs. Chester was never certain who among the warlords was in control of the capital. When Sylvia asked questions about the armed men on the streets, her mother told her that some were good and some were bad. Sun Chuanfang (a.k.a. the "Nanking Warlord") was "bad," and General Feng Yuxiang (the "Christian General") was "good."

Chester wrote: *Dear Father: We arrived safely. Many changes have occurred in the past fourteen years since our family left China. The war has changed the balance of power. The French and British suffered greatly during the war, and their influence in the Far East is on the wane. The British lack the manpower to keep their far-flung empire. The Germans have been knocked out of China by war; the Russians have been driven out by the Bolshevik Revolution. Peking is filled with destitute White Russian refugees who have fled across Siberia and into China. The whole country has fallen prey to the private armies of hundreds of warlords. The super warlords are swallowing the smaller ones. The Peking Government has been reduced to a ridiculous sham. Parliament is little more than a political football in a deadly struggle among the most powerful duchuns; the provincial military governors have turned warlords hoping to grab the Mandate of Heaven. Inga and Sylvia are afraid of the soldiers on the streets. Most are from the defeated armies who have banded together and survive by ruthlessly looting the peasants and villagers. The warlords and foreign powers cannot suppress Chinese nationalism forever. The handwriting is on the wall. The revolution is beginning. The blood of martyrs is the seed of the Church.*

Peking fell under control of the most powerful warlord of the North, Zhang Zuolin. His photograph was in the newspaper, and information about him circulated among officials and in the streets. He was small and delicate in physique, but his cunning had earned him the nickname "Mukden Tiger." Reputedly a descendant of the traditional red-bearded bandits of Manchuria, he lived in a fabled palace in Manchuria that was filled with black teak furniture, silken carpets, precious jades, and porcelains. On his black satin skullcap he wore a spectacular pearl that he claimed was the largest in the world. To hold power, the Mukden Tiger was forced to share his domains with the Japanese in the Manchu capital of Mukden (today's Shenyang), where the Japanese maintained their headquarters for administering the industrial centers that China had been forced to surrender in Manchuria.

The Mukden Tiger had seized power from another warlord, Marshal Wu Peifu (the "Jade Marshal"), a Confucian scholar turned soldier who, unlike the other warlords, paid his men their full salary on time and consequently had a loyal army. He was regarded by the diplomatic corps as the strong man China needed. Between battles, Wu lived like a Confucian gentleman. He studied the classics, practiced calligraphy, wrote poetry, and like Li Bo and other famous Chinese poets, engaged in serious drinking. The struggle for control of North China swirled mainly around these two marshals.

In September 1922, a third warlord, General Feng Yuxiang, who had an army of thirty thousand men, arrived in Peking from Shanxi Province. The students at the Language School heard stories that General Feng was providing his soldiers the advantages of education, industrial training, instruction in sanitation, and, incredibly, the opportunity to hear the message of Christianity. Feng Yuxiang, it was said, had converted to Christianity and was known as the "Christian General." Chester decided to investigate the reports. One morning he rode alone on horseback to the warlord's army encampment on a plain on the outskirts of Peking. From the crest of a hill, he saw rows and rows of gray tents. A long column of gray-clad soldiers were marching with military precision. Chester was stunned to hear a great chorus singing, accompanied by the sound of men tramping. They were marching in time to a familiar Christian hymn. A huge, sturdy man in a gray uniform was leading the march. When he noticed the foreigner on horseback watching from the hill, he called a halt and came to greet him. It was General Feng himself. When Chester introduced himself, the general took him to a private room and had his batman bring tea.

When the general learned that Chester's parents had been missionaries in Hubei during the Boxer Uprising, he broke down and with tears in his eyes confessed that as a young private in Yuan Shikai's army he had witnessed the Boxers massacre the missionaries and their children at Paotingfu. The courage displayed by the missionaries had impressed him deeply, and the memory of the horrible killings had remained in his mind forever.

It had happened on the afternoon of Saturday, June 30, 1900, he said, and he claimed the empress dowager was chiefly responsible. She had issued a proclamation urging the Boxers to exterminate all foreign devils. According to Feng, about twenty Boxers were led by a local Boxer named Zhu Duzi, who had been presented with a badge of distinction giving him official sanction by the empress to kill the foreigners and all Chinese Christians. Zhu was known as a bad character and was accompanied by a crowd of thieves and robbers to whom he promised loot. He had spread rumors that the missionaries intended to kidnap their children. The mob beat the old gatekeeper to death, piled stubble against the west gate of the Presbyterian compound, and set it afire. Then they looted the hospital, the church, and three of the missionaries' homes before burning them to the ground. Two Chinese gatekeepers, some loyal servants, two old women, and some children were killed and thrown into the well.

Chester listened in shock as the warlord told him that the soldiers were under orders to do nothing to stop the murders. Feng had stood on a grave mound and watched in horror. He saw one missionary try to talk reason from a window in the main house but to no avail. In a last desperate stand, the missionaries attempted to hold the Boxers at bay with one rifle, two revolvers, and a shot gun. The leading Boxer, Zhu Duzi, was killed and ten others wounded.

The frenzied mob set the house on fire. Feng saw a woman with a baby in her arms confront the mob, pleading with them to spare the life of her child. She offered them jewels and silver, but they showed no mercy. Through the smoke and flames he saw a man holding his two small boys by their hands. Suddenly the boys dashed for the door and ran outside to escape the flames. The helpless children were slashed to death and their bodies thrown in the cistern. The foreigners in the house all perished in the inferno. About twenty Chinese who had chosen to remain with the missionaries were tortured and killed. One tried to kill himself by jumping into the well but was pulled out, taken to the city, and tortured all night in an effort to secure evidence against the missionaries. The man died rather than betray the missionaries.

Chester was stunned to hear this eyewitness account of the massacre about which he had heard from his parents. General Feng explained to Chester that the soldiers had been trained and brainwashed to be cruel and that he himself had been a man of fierce, uncontrollable temper, cruel to his family and his men. For the next eleven years he had been tormented by his inability to save the foreigners. Then, in 1911, when stationed as a major in Peking, he attended a meeting led by a missionary named Dr. Mott. Chester knew of the compelling voice of Dr. Mott, and he could not bring himself to hate Feng Yuxiang. He could see that the man was truly repentant. His dominating personality remained, but his selfish, unbridled nature had been replaced by a kindness and thoughtfulness that made him a well-beloved commander. He was the only warlord making an effort to reform the military in China. He told Chester that he believed soldiers should have spiritual guidance as well as food and clothing. He wanted all his men to convert to Christianity and be baptized. Chester was amused by the innovative way the general solved that issue: he lined up his troops and sprayed them with a fire hose. In this way, his soldiers were anointed Christians whether they liked it or not. His men were forbidden to drink or smoke opium and marched to songs with words like "We must not gamble or visit whores, we must not drink or smoke." Chester had a fleeting thought that the general might be the hope of a New China.

In Peking, the Ronnings rented a gracious, Chinese-style house in the Beizongbu Alleyway (hutong) near the Legation Quarter in the Manchu district. They shared a walled-in compound with Colonel and Mrs. Joseph W. Stilwell and their children, who occupied the house that stood across the cobblestone courtyard with a goldfish pond and a water well with a hand pump. Stilwell and Chester were classmates in the advanced class, which required them to master three thousand Chinese characters. They soon became close friends with the codirectors, missionary William Bacon Pettus and John Leighton Stuart, whom Chester would meet again when they were both diplomats in Nanking. Chester and Stilwell both studied Chinese history, religion, economics, and current affairs. Stilwell was the U.S. Army's first Chinese-language officer. Chester later recalled that he found Stilwell *extremely bright and curious about everything Chinese. He was unusually adept at the language although he spoke with a flat, American accent.* The two men continued to have much in common during their subsequent careers.

Later in the 1940s, both Stilwell and Chester were assigned to China on related missions. In 1942, during the war with Japan, Stilwell, then a major general, became the commander of American and Chinese forces in the China-Burma-India Theater. Dubbed "Vinegar Joe," he was regarded as the best field commander in the American army. He was later recalled by President Franklin Roosevelt because he had quarreled with Chiang Kai-shek, objecting to, among other things, the Nationalist leader's actions in diverting his troops from operations against the Japanese to his civil war against Mao Zedong's Communist forces. After the war, Mao's People's Republic erected the Stilwell Museum in Chongqing (rendered as Chungking in the Nationalist era) in his honor. In the war against Japan, Squadron Leader Ronning served as director of the Intelligence Discrimination Unit of the Royal Canadian Air Force. His knowledge of written Chinese characters, similar to those of the Japanese language, enabled the unit to break the Japanese military code, a key factor in the victory over Japan in the Pacific. In 1945, with the end of the war, Chester entered the diplomatic service and was stationed as minister-counselor at the Canadian embassy in Chungking, Chiang Kai-shek's wartime capital. He worked there with President Harry Truman's envoy, General George C. Marshall, in the failed effort to end the civil war between Chiang and Mao. In his honor, a Chester Ronning Museum was built in Fancheng, his birthplace.

Back in 1921, Inga enrolled in the beginner's class of the Language School, where she hoped to learn seven hundred characters and speak ordinary Chinese by the end of the year. She would have made faster progress if her husband had not made such fun of her attempts to speak the language. At lunch after her first lesson Chester offered her some rice, and she proudly thanked him in Chinese: "*xie xie.*" Chester burst out laughing.

"You must be careful to use the correct tone," he said. "You just said 'shoes.' Thanks, but I have shoes."

"No, I said thanks, thanks," said Inga. "Can't you understand Chinese?"

"But you used the second, rising tone meaning 'shoes.' The first, high flat tone means 'to rest,' the third falling and then rising tone is 'blood,' and the fourth falling tone is 'thanks.'"

Inga was quick to adapt, and despite her initial misgivings, she came to love Peking. Despite the struggles of the warlords that spilled into the streets, the Ronnings would remember that period as one of the happiest times of their lives. They explored the ancient landmarks. The gates to the Forbidden City had been closed since the fall of the Qing, and the famous Imperial Gardens were used by the various warlords as stables for their horses. But they were able to visit the undisturbed Temple of Heaven. Chester gathered information in the teahouses near the Temple by chatting with old-timers who displayed their pet crickets in jars and talking mynah birds in bamboo cages. Inga and Sylvia whispered to each other at each end of the Whispering Wall. One morning they took the train to the Great Wall and rode donkeys along the top.

While picnicking with friends in the Western Hills, Sylvia learned to fly kites shaped like butterflies and climbed over the huge stone statues of animals and mandarins standing guard along the Sacred Way leading to the Ming Tombs. The city was usually peaceful except for the intrusion of the sounds of distant sporadic fighting.

Sylvia was entranced by the Manchu ladies, who only came out in late afternoon wearing their embroidered shoes and elaborate headdresses. When a Manchu man met a Manchu woman, they both curtsied to each other by bending the left knee and placing their folded hands on the right knee. Sylvia soon began imitating them to the delight of onlookers.

During this tumultuous and chaotic time in China, the Manchus, no longer in power, were experiencing difficult circumstances. They were not employed simply because they were not accustomed to common labor. In their days as rulers of Imperial China, they had received official pensions and were expected to shun ordinary work. This had gone on for nearly three hundred years. Many became teachers but had never learned to properly tie their own shoes. Highly talented Manchu scholars, artists, and poets, such as the cousin of the last emperor, Prince Pu Ru (Pu Xinyu), did private tutoring. The prince, a descendant of the Imperial Aisin-Gioro family, is generally acknowledged to be the last Chinese literati painter of the twentieth century. One of his accomplished students was Dora Fugh Lee, who later wrote a beautifully illustrated book about her famous teacher. Pu Ru's profound quote reveals the essence of Chinese painting: "Chinese painting basically relies on line and brushwork. The brush I use is the same one I use for calligraphy. A good painting needs balance, that is, brushwork and line should be balanced by washes and color. The brushwork is the structure, the bone of a painting; the washes and color are the flesh."*

Inga's heart went out to these once wealthy, proud, and spoiled aristocrats who seemed doomed to pay for the sins of their fathers. Many survived only by pawning their jewelry and fancy robes at unfair prices to pay for food. For others, opium was the only refuge. Some of the most powerful warlords, such as the Mukden Tiger, were descendants of Manchu Bannermen.

The three big competing warlords staged their most bloody battles within a few miles of Peking. The Ronnings could hear the boom of cannon and see flashes of artillery fire at night. When fighting erupted, the city gates would be closed, sometimes for weeks, and when they reopened, no one knew which warlord was in power. In 1922, Marshal Wu Peifu and the Christian general Feng Yuxiang joined forces against the Mukden Tiger. One evening the sound of fighting came so close that stray artillery shells landed in the street close to the alleyway where the Ronnings and the Stilwells lived. Both Chester and Joe happened to be at the American legation at the time. Inga hid under the dining room table with Sylvia and the two Stilwell children while Mrs. Stilwell ran next door to telephone the American legation that they were under attack. She was outraged when the clerk advised her to go home and sit tight until the fighting passed. When it was over, Wu and Feng were in control of Peking. The defeated Mukden Tiger retreated to Manchuria to make ready for the next battle. Although the Christian General disapproved of Wu's heavy wine drinking, they banded together to control the north. General Feng ordered four of his most trusted men to guard the Ronnings' compound.

At this time, two young Communist Party leaders, Mao Zedong and Zhou Enlai, who were destined to reshape China, had arrived upon the political scene. Sixty-three years later, during Chester's last visit to China at the age of ninety, when someone asked his "propitious age," he would amuse and confuse them with the reply, "I am two years younger than Mao Zedong and four years older than Zhou Enlai." More than a joke, his remark reflected his deep involvement with the two men over the succeeding years.

Mao Zedong, born in 1892, was the brilliant son of a middle-class peasant and a graduate of the Hunan Normal School. Unable to afford higher education,

*Dora Fugh Lee, *Pu Xinyu: A Manchu Prince Who Embodied Chinese Culture* (n.p., n.d.).

he worked at Peking University as a library assistant to a well-known Marxist scholar, Li Dazhao, and was greatly influenced by the older man's ideology. When the May Fourth Movement began, Mao returned to Hunan and launched a magazine that advocated "democracy and a new culture." The publication aroused the wrath of the local warlord, and Mao fled back to Peking. Mao's mentor, Li Dazhao, stimulated his interest in Marxism and introduced him to the revolutionary appeal of the *Communist Manifesto*. In July 1921, the Chinese Communist Party was formally established, with Chen Duxiu as secretary general. Mao, together along with Dong Biwu, from Chester's Hubei Province, and ten others were charter members. Mao eventually became the revolutionary leader and chairman of the Communist Party.

Zhou Enlai was born four years after Chester, on March 5, 1898, into a mandarin family with declining fortunes in Jiangsu Province. Homeschooled in the Chinese classics as a youth by his adoptive mother, Zhou moved to Mukden in northeast China, where he attended the Western-style Dongguan Model Academy. After moving to Tientsin, he enrolled in the Nankai Middle School, headed by Zhang Boling, one of the most important Chinese educators of the twentieth century. His teaching methods of "high discipline" and a "strict moral code" attracted many students who later became prominent in Chinese public life. Like many young Chinese, Zhou traveled to Japan to further his education, and upon his return he enrolled at Nankai University, where he graduated at the top of his class. Arrested during the 1919 May Fourth Movement for student agitation, Zhou was imprisoned for six months in a windowless cell with sixteen other students. Released after staging a hunger strike yet incensed by harsh police treatment, Zhou once again left China, this time for France, where he studied and made ready for revolution. He joined the Chinese Communist Youth Corps, which set up branches of the Chinese Communist Party abroad. When Mao Zedong succeeded in establishing the People's Republic of China in 1949, Zhou served as foreign minister and premier in close collaboration with Mao.

Zhou Enlai was to become one of Chester's closest lifelong friends. Chester was at the conference table in Chungking in 1945 with Zhou Enlai during General George C. Marshall's failed attempt to avoid a Chinese civil war. Later, he worked in close association with Zhou Enlai at the Geneva Conference in 1954 that determined the future of Indochina.

After graduation from the Language School, the Ronning family prepared for their return journey to the Fancheng mission.

33

The Grand Canal

THE GRAND CANAL

The waters of the Grand Canal
Flow blue as the sky,
And the east wind sighs
In the willow trees
—WANG ZHIHUAN,
TANG DYNASTY (AD 618–907)

The Ronnings embarked on a historic route home to Fancheng. The plan was to sail from Peking to the southern capital of Nanking along the famous Grand Canal, which connects the Yellow River to the Yangtze, an engineering accomplishment comparable to the Great Wall. They would then sail up the Yangtze to Hankow and continue up the Han River to Fancheng.

The Ronnings boarded a comfortable houseboat, which was named *Little Red* after the first ship to sail down the full one-thousand-mile length of the Grand Canal. The canal was completed during the Sui Dynasty (AD 581–618) in about three years by the joining, without the use of machinery, of rivers and small canals by Emperor Yang. His father, a prime minister of the Northern Zhou Dynasty (AD 577–588), the last of the northern dynasties, had seized power from his own king. Like Emperor Qin Shihuang, he conquered the other kingdoms, reuniting the country. In AD 581, the prime minister mounted the throne himself as the first emperor of the Sui Dynasty. Not long afterward he was poisoned by his son, who usurped the throne and thus earned the sobriquet "Yang the Shady."

When the Ronnings reached the garden city of Soochow, which Europeans called the Venice of the East, they spent two days walking the narrow streets lined with white houses with black-tile roofs, separated by canals and joined by moon bridges. Historical records describe Yang the Shady as an eccentric, ruthless Legalist with a saving strain of Daoism. He ruled only a short time but managed to build not only the Grand Canal but also vast palaces. To build the

Grand Canal, he dragooned every able-bodied man over fifteen years of age into hard labor on the project. Any man's attempt at evasion was met with severe punishments for him and his whole family. Heavy taxes were levied, and every group of five families was obliged to send a woman, young boy, or old man to help serve food to the 3.6 million conscripts laboring on the canal under the control of fifty thousand soldiers. The monumental work, like the Great Wall, caused unspeakable suffering and death. The emperor, however, was delighted at the miraculous construction he had wrought. He celebrated the completion with one of the richest and most spectacular imperial pageants in the history of China. Fifty lavish dragon boats were ordered as tribute from the famous ship-builders of the Yangtze River Valley. The emperor's boat, called *Little Red* because red was a symbol of good luck, was 45 feet high and 2,000 feet long with four decks. On the upper decks were two magnificent reception halls, the East and West Halls, and a luxurious throne room that stood in the center of a miniature palace. On the lower decks were 120 royal cabins decorated with gold and jade, for his retinue.

Historian Tsui Chi, in *A Short History of Chinese Civilization*, describes the magnificent pageant:

> The Empress had a barge to herself in similar style named Flying Yellow Dragon. A series of nine barges following these had the name Floating Landscapes, and the imagination is left to picture their appearance. The rest of the fifty brought up the rear—Shimmering Light, Crimson Bird, White Tiger, Seven Stars, Flying Feathers, Green Sheldrake, and a host more, every one as gorgeously adorned as the wit of man could devise, and manned by diplomats and merchants, monks and nuns, princes and princesses, the imperial concubines, ministers and officials.
>
> Thousands of men, dressed in silk, drew the barges along with ropes, while hundreds of young girls, specially chosen for their beauty, mingled with the barge men and pulled on brightly colored cords. Lambs frisked beside them to add to the charm. On both sides of the canal stood rows of willow trees.
>
> When the fleet started out at last, it stretched over the waters of the canal for nearly a thousand li. Horsemen galloped along both banks, waving their banners, and the onlookers crowding the way were dazzled at the array and the splendor. After the fleet had passed, perfumes lingered on the air for tens of miles.

Such was the caprice of an emperor!

The canal is still used today (though not quite as splendidly). For more than a thousand years, before railroads and highways, it was the main communication system for trade and cultural exchange between northern and southern China. It was also the main cause of the downfall of the "Shady" Emperor and the Sui Dynasty. Exorbitant taxes to pay for the Grand Canal and foolish military expeditions led by the emperor laid such burdens on the people that they rose in rebellion. Yang the Shady was murdered in his Guangling Palace by a furious mob. Yet the canal he built at such enormous human cost did prove to be a boon to the development of China.

The three Ronnings disembarked from *Little Red* on the Grand Canal at Chinkiang, where they boarded a junk to continue up the Yangtze to Nanking and Hankow. The last leg of their journey up the Han River to Fancheng had nightmarish aspects that Chester would describe in a letter of November 24, 1923, to his father in Valhalla:

Dear Father: Our trip up the Han River from Hankow had its variations from the daily routine and its excitements. We were in a "peizi" [houseboat] with a guard of eight soldiers in another junk to protect us from the robbers but they were not much better themselves. One night we landed only 10 miles from where pirates had robbed some 50 boats which we caught up with the following day. The river was quite swift and our boat got tangled up with several others and went whirling down the stream with everyone shouting and no one doing a thing to save the situation. We catapulted down several li in great excitement and one boat nearly tipped before we banged the shore and the laopans [captains] managed to anchor. We finally got disentangled. Sylvia thought it was fun but Inga was rather upset.

Another day, while anchored for dinner, some boats which were out of control in the swift current came crashing into us. The soldiers went after the man who had nearly crushed our boat and we found out later that they squeezed 8,000 cash out of him although the damage they did was to our property not theirs. The same day I shot a big goose as we had to supply our own food but it drifted down river and another boat picked it up. The soldiers forced the sailors to give it up. But by that time Inga did not feel like eating it so the soldiers had a feast. I caught another fish for us.

The last days we had good sailing winds and came steaming up stream to Fancheng. We found the people here very excited over the fact that the robbers were not far away and were heading for the city. It came as a surprise to us as we had had no news during the 15 days on the river. We learned about it from some foreign missionaries from Laohokow who had fled to Fancheng to escape from a great robber

*band menacing their mission. They were living on house boats ready to flee at a mo-
ment's notice. We had to live on our boat almost a week after we arrived.*

*When it was safe we came marching up through Kung Kwan men, past Shi Tze Kai
(I still remembered the old way) right up to our old Mission Gate, which looked just
the same except that the paint is different. Here the old men and women remembered
me and came in flocks to welcome us.*

*We came into the front yard of the old place. The house looked smaller than I
expected. It looked old and worn out. The yard was still pretty but it was all very sad,
everything looked so deserted. My brothers and sisters, Nelius, Almah, Talbert, Harold, Hazel and Lily were not to be seen anywhere. Papa was not in the office. Mama
was not there. Liu se fu and Tung se fu were not in the kitchen. Trung Yahr I saw a
few days later. We walked in, through the long hall which seemed narrower now. The
room was smaller too. Our wonderful old sitting room with the red velvet couch and
Mama's painted mirrors was used as a store room, dusty and gloomy. I could see the
twin Christmas trees, the bright lights, the happy comrades, Papa reading the Christmas text, Mama putting packages under the tree. All of a sudden it brightened up.
The old memories came in floods. I could see Mama seated at the organ and hear the
strains of "Silver threads among the gold." Upstairs we saw the old school room where
I had diphtheria, where we had the fire which I fled from so rapidly one morning.
Then across the hall I could see old Kungma putting Harold and Hazel to bed. In the
middle room I remembered how far it used to seem to the parents' bed when the nights
were dark. In the large bed room I remembered the children who knelt at evening
prayers by a loving mother's knees. The book was in her lap, she had just finished the
evening story. Across the hall it was difficult to go. I felt that I must tread softly. When I
came in the whole scene which had been burned into my memory came back. The last
evening, that Saturday night when we saw the gates of Heaven open and our sainted
mother enter, and the last message "Rermere Gud, remer hverandre," came to mind
vividly and the tears began to flow. Later we stood at her last resting place on earth.
Inga and I stood there with bowed heads in silence. Holy memories, which had almost
become a dream, were real again. Your beloved son, Chester*

34

Return to Fancheng, 1923

A SONG

Is it only today
That we said farewell?
The lamp shines bright—
But it lights up
An empty room.
—POETESS ZI YE,
JIN DYNASTY (AD 265–420)

Chester was accorded a great welcome in Fancheng. Observing his emotional reception, Inga was moved to a deeper understanding of Chester's profound attachment to his Chinese friends. Among those who warmly welcomed him was Tung Tse-pei, who had led the revolutionary cell in Halvor's school, Chester's adopted brother Peter, now a teacher, and his former playmates Shi Gun-ching and Li Shih. They talked joyfully about the old days when they had chased paddy chickens (frogs) in the rice paddies, and Chester learned what had befallen them during his absence.

The boyhood friends that Chester had left behind were now full-grown men. Tse-pei's large, luminous eyes were the same, but his appearance had changed dramatically: like the others, he had at last cut off the hated queue. Like his Chinese friends, Chester had also changed in appearance: his wavy hair was darker, and he stood six feet three inches tall. Tse-pei looked up at him and laughed. He pointed to Chester's mustache and called him Lao Houzi (Old Whiskers), Halvor's old nickname among the students. Tse-pei had accepted Chester's early offer to become the associate principal. He had obtained a Western-style degree at Cheeloo University in Hsinan (today's Xinan), Shandong, and continued his revolutionary activities. He participated in the Wuhan uprising of 1911 and in the May Fourth Movement. In spite of his modern ideas and the fact that he loved another woman, Tse-pei had capitulated to patriarchal tradition and married the girl he had been betrothed to as a child. He later told Chester that he felt compelled to save face for both families and keep the girl from disgrace, but he soon learned that his bride was as much against the marriage as he was, and the union was never consummated.

Chester found that the intellectuals of China were even more active than before and had a deeper political and social consciousness. They had been humiliated by the unequal treaties and disillusioned by the failure of the United States to oppose the sellout of Shandong Province to Japan at the Paris Peace Conference. This disillusionment spurred distrust of their politicians and the warlords.

The chaotic warlord struggles were still in progress, and terror and pillaging by the warlord armies were a continuing nightmare for the population of Hubei Province. The Chinese saying that "bandits and soldiers are breathed from the same nostril" now seemed particularly apt. The warlords squeezed the peasants mercilessly by increasing the existing taxes and inventing dozens of new ones. They robbed the peasants of their possessions and conscripted their labor. The Chinese warlords, like the Manchu Bannermen, seized mainly young men. Almost every day Chester saw, as his father had, men and boys roped together and being led off by soldiers to act as baggage coolies and servants for the warlord troops. These unfortunate young men received no pay and often never returned to their families. Although there were some respectable warlords, Chester thought most were unsavory and acted as if they were above the law. Their armies looted at will. Their usual method of raiding a village was to surround it before dawn and fire shots to intimidate the people, steal everything they could find, and then, often, set fire to the village.

December 1923. . . . The large band of robbers, probably hungry soldiers from the warlord's army, has been defeated now and they are on their way westwards so we are living in peace again. The poor Chinese who lived in the district where the robbers pass, have suffered terribly. What the foreigners suffer is nothing in comparison. The other night my old friend "Hsi Tutze," an evangelist 25 miles up north, told us awful tales of the happenings of that place during the robber occupation of two days. They carried off everything in the town. The only thing in his house which was not broken was a picture of our family that Father had hung so high on the walls that no one else could reach it.

It was not long before Chester saw the evidence of the pillaging of the bandit warlords firsthand. Two notorious bandit leaders, Lao Yangren (Old Foreigner) and Bailang (White Wolf), were vying for power in the Fancheng area and conducted frequent raids on the towns. One night Chester was awakened by the gatekeeper with news that White Wolf had occupied Tsaoyang (today's Chaoyang), a city forty-five miles from Fancheng. Two missionaries, the Reverend and Mrs. Kilen, had been shot and left to die. Mrs. Kilen, the daughter of former missionaries, had been one of Chester's childhood friends. Chester went immediately to appeal for help from an embryo warlord, an enemy of White Wolf, who had temporary control of the twin cities Fancheng and Hsiangyang. The warlord assigned one of his lieutenants and a squad of twenty soldiers to go with Chester. Against the pleas of Inga, who was expecting another child, Chester and the soldiers loaded into a Model-T Ford one-ton truck on which a rickety wooden body had been built, and set forth. He sat with the troops in the rear on wooden planks, which served as seats. *The driver*, Chester wrote later, *had little experience but lots of nerve. He pulled the accelerator down as far as it would go and kept his hand on it while he guided the vehicle over the rough, winding narrow road with the other. The truck rattled, bumped and twisted. Each soldier sat holding his rifle between his knees with fixed bayonets.*

After they had crossed a tributary of the Han on a barge and entered White Wolf's territory, the lieutenant told Chester to join him in the front cab because the sight of a foreigner might cause them trouble. *The headlights penetrated the darkness with two long cones of light which lit up the countryside. On the eastern horizon a reddish glow appeared, and gradually the whole sky reflected the fire of burning villages. Still not a sign of life. We thundered past burning houses on both sides of the road, black smoke curling above leaping tongues of fire as we passed through the center of larger villages. If there were bandits, they remained discreetly silent. Our headlights had warned them. It was uncomfortably hot as we dashed through narrow streets past livid flames. Not a word was uttered. The driver had nerves of steel. He turned and twisted the old Model-T through crooked streets dodging fires on both sides. Sometimes it appeared as if we were about to crash into a wall of fire. The driver never for a moment lifted his heavy hand from the little lever, and we finally came out in an open area between the burning villages and the city of Tsaoyang.*

At the city gate, they learned that the injured missionaries had already been taken by Chinese friends to a hospital. There was nothing more Chester could do. An old Chinese warned Chester that the bandits, who camped north of the city, were expected to return any time and would kill the foreigners on sight. The lieutenant turned the truck around immediately and, without imbibing as much as a drop of tea, returned the way they came. The villages were still smoldering. Chester saw a few dazed peasants wandering like lost specters among the ruins.

He knew that hundreds of innocent people had been killed or had lost their possessions during that terrible night. He was filled with anger and frustration and became more devoted than ever to do what he could to help the Chinese revolutionaries who were committed to ending the chaos stemming from the senseless efforts of warlords to capture the Mandate of Heaven.

When Chester returned home, he learned that Reverend Kilen had died but his wife had survived. Inga had been awake all night worrying about Chester. The constant turmoil reduced her to living in a state of fear. Unlike Chester's family, she was not drawn to this land of horror and beauty. She longed to return to Canada and the security of her own family. If it had not been for her love of Chester, she would have at once taken a boat home. The day after Chester came home, she suffered her first miscarriage.

By 1924, China was engulfed in the prolonged warlord warfare. Sun Yat-sen repudiated the impotent Peking regime and proclaimed his program of the Three Principles of the People. When Sun's appeals for support from the United States and Great Britain were ignored, he turned to Moscow, whose agents in China had been urging him to collaborate with the newly formed USSR. In the hope of uniting all revolutionaries, Dr. Sun invited the Chinese Communist Party (CCP) to cooperate with the Kuomintang (KMT) in a united alliance. They agreed to join forces to end warlord rule, unify the country, and end imperialism. A year earlier, in 1923, in preparation for a military expedition against the Peking government, Sun Yat-sen had sent Chiang Kai-shek to lead a politico-military mission to Moscow. The Russians, in turn, sent Michael Borodin to be a personal advisor to Dr. Sun and some forty others to advise the Nationalists on how to re-model the KMT on the pattern of the Communist Party of the Soviet Union. On Chiang's return, a military academy was established at Whampoa near Canton, with Comintern (Communist International) funding and Soviet advisors. A sign in gilt characters over the entrance read: "He who seeks place or riches need not enter here." Chiang was appointed head of the academy, and in line with the new Kuomintang-Communist alliance, Zhou Enlai became his deputy political commissar in charge of indoctrinating the revolutionary army and preparing for the Northern Expedition, a military drive against the most powerful warlords in central China and the Peking government.

The year 1925 was a very memorable one for Chester. He was saddened by the death of Sun Yat-sen, who died of liver cancer just after accepting an invitation from the warlords Mukden Tiger and Wu Peifu, in power in Peking, to join a conference on "reorganization" for national union. But fate interfered. Sun spent his last hours at the home of his friend Wellington Koo and was attended by his wife, Soong Ch'ing-ling; his son, Sun Fo; and his closest aide, Wang Ching-wei. His last words were "Peace . . . Struggle . . . Save China." The whole nation mourned him. Chester was saddened and shocked by the news. The students in the middle school in Fancheng swore to carry on the principles of Sun.

At his death, Sun left four lieutenants in a precarious state of collective leadership, one of whom was Chiang Kai-shek, who later became his successor. Chiang was installed on July 9 as supreme commander of the Nationalist armies. Sun's son, Sun Fo, held his father's picture aloft as Chiang received his new command.

In May 1924, the Ronnings were filled with joy at the birth of their first son. Chester wrote to his father in Valhalla: *Hallaluya! On May 13 a baby boy was born to us. We have named him Alton Nelius. He is strong and healthy. Inga has been disturbed by the unrest here but she is well and so happy now with our son. Sylvia is glad to have a playmate. We are blessed and will soon move into the new house.*

When Inga returned from the mission hospital with the baby, they moved into a new, two-story stone house with a balcony that Chester, with the Chinese workmen, had built just opposite the old home Halvor had built. Inga had furnished it tastefully with Chinese antiques and a red Western-style sofa that made her feel more at home, but there was no peace. One night, the Ronnings were awakened by a loud banging on their door. Chester grabbed the shotgun he kept beside his bed and a wooden chair with the other hand to use as a shield, and went to the top of the stairs.

"What do you want?" he shouted.

A deep sonorous voice shouted in Chinese, "I am the Lord thy God, open the door."

"Go away!" yelled Chester. "Leave us alone."

"How can you repudiate the Lord? I am Jesus Christ. Let me in."

Inga was convinced that the speaker had come to kill them, but Chester assured her that he was only a crazy man, yet wondered how he got in the gate. The shouting and banging went on until Chester, hoping the man was alone, ran down the stairs, opened the door, and, swinging a chair in front of him, chased the man, who continued shouting that he was Jesus. The mission gate was open and the gatekeeper gone. The next morning, old Lao confessed that he had left his post to visit a woman in the town. They never found out who the character was, but the incident left Inga fearful and more eager than ever to return home.

In early 1926, the Kuomintang held its second convention in Canton and Sun's Revolutionary Government was converted into the Nationalist Government. Mao Zedong, Zhou Enlai, and other leading Communists were given important roles in the new regime. On February 26, the Nationalist Coalition Government declared war on the warlords in Peking, branding them as arch agents of foreign imperialism.

Chiang Kai-shek personally spearheaded the drive across the rice-bowl country from Ch'angsha in Hunan to the tri-city area of Wuhan in Hubei. His forces made the eight-hundred-mile trek, almost half of the way by foot, in record time, and all along the route they were welcomed by the people. One of his officers, reporting on the August offensive, said: "Our forces proved vastly superior owing to their relatively greater political consciousness . . . This was evident from the very beginning when, during our advance into new territories, the population manifested no fear but greeted us with open arms."* By September, although Wu Peifu still held on in Peking, the warlord-held cities of Hankow and Hanyang had surrendered, and after forty days of heavy fighting, Wuch'ang fell.

In Fancheng and at places in the interior of China, Sun Yat-sen's followers were uneasy about the Kuomintang-Communist alliance. In a prophetic letter to his father, Chester wrote: *We have just heard fearful news, there was a student demonstration on March 18 before Government House in Peking and over forty students were massacred by the warlord's police. It is hard to believe they could sink to such loathsome barbarism. The warlords are fearful of the new KMT-CCP (Nationalist and Communist) alliance. We are all wondering how long before the Communists and Nationalists clash. Chiang Kai-shek is moving to consolidate his power in Canton by striking against the Communists and Soviet advisors. Without the guidance of Dr. Sun, we fear there may be serious trouble.*

In Chester's Hung Wen Middle School, the students and the staff—with the exception of one old scholar who taught Chinese classics—were all supporters of the Northern Expedition. Some of the students had joined the troops. On weekends, the teachers and students of the mission school, together with students of the government schools of the twin cities, visited the villages in teams to organize the illiterate peasants. They taught them how to read the basic ideographs, enabling them to read newspapers and pamphlets written in *putonghua* (the common, spoken language).

Describing the campaign, Chester wrote to his father: *My friend and associate*

*John McCook Roots, "The Canton Idea," Asia, April 1927, 39.

principal, Tung Tse-pei, has predicted that millions upon millions of Chinese will die in the struggle before the people reach the promised land envisioned by the revolutionaries. Let us pray that the price will not be too high but I doubt that many realize just how great a revolution is needed to free China from the ancient traditions which hold them in such a firm grip. Tung sometimes refers to Mao Zedong's policy of organizing peasants as the soundest way of getting revolution started. First, the peasants must become literate so they can organize their own struggle against the warlords. I know you have always been a pacifist but I hope, my dear Father, that you understand why we are doing this.

Communist political agents in Hunan had already organized some two million peasants into associations to rise against the landlords. Mao Zedong described the movement as colossal and predicted: "In a very short time, in China's central, southern, and northern provinces, several hundred million peasants will rise like a tornado or tempest . . . They will break all trammels that now bind them and rush forward along the road to liberation."

The student revolutionary movement also extended to action against foreign powers, especially Britain and Japan, in charging that they were destroying village industries by imposing their products on China. Chester described a related incident in his memoir:

August 2, 1926. One day when I was conducting a class of forty young men, a student opened the door, walked in and whispered something to the boy next to the door. He in turn passed something on to the chap sitting next to him. Some message was passed from ear to ear until the whole class knew something which I did not. A few minutes later the whole class rose and walked silently out into the hall. I followed them, wondering if this was some expression of anti-foreign feeling being directed against me, since I was the only foreigner. But the halls were filled with all of the several hundred students, and they walked silently out of the school. I joined the other teachers. If they knew what was going on they said nothing. We followed the students down the street to the city gate facing the Han River. From the gate we saw hundreds of students coming out of the gates of Hsiangyang . . . They boarded junks going upstream and forcibly seized all foreign kerosene and tobacco. They stacked it in piles, drove holes in the kerosene tins, and set fire to it. The flames leaped into the sky with a frightening roar and the students all cheered wildly. It all ended peacefully but Inga and the children were very frightened by all the noise and the flames. I believe this is going on all over the province. It is all part of the campaign throughout China against Japan and Great Britain.

Inga heard the explosions and saw the flames from the balcony. She was eight months' pregnant again and afraid for her two children and unborn baby. Chester took the family to a nearby mountain resort called Hai Shan, where his father had built a summerhouse for the mission and where Inga could have the baby in peace.

On September 16, 1926, my older sister Bernice Ingrid was born in Hai Shan. Everyone called her Mei Mei (little sister), which we spelled "Meme," and the name stuck for her entire life. Eight decades later, in 2008, when I visited Hai Shan with my husband, daughter Karen, her son Torin, and our adopted Chinese son, Peter Liu, our hosts proudly showed us around the old house that Grandfather Halvor had built in 1904. It was filled with historic photos of our family; over the bed in one room was a sign that read, "Mei Mei was born here." (The place is now a tourist attraction.)

Inga's delivery was not easy, but she recovered quickly. In a few weeks, Chester was elated to see his beautiful wife looking well again. She had always made him feel so strong, so needed. They both loved nature, and the mountain air was invigorating. In the early mornings, they rode horses out to view the spectacular scenery. Halvor had chosen a choice area to build the mountain house overlooking the valley. Inga's hair had grown long again and curled gently around her face. Her flawless skin, so carefully protected from the sun, glowed with happiness, and her long-lashed, green eyes sparkled with pride as she clasped her new baby to her breast. It took so little to make Inga happy; she was a natural optimist. Chester was grateful that she had agreed to come to China, but he suffered great pangs of guilt over the turmoil to which she was exposed.

When Meme was a month old, Chester hired sedan chairs to carry the family down the steep mountain path to catch a boat back to Fancheng. About halfway down, one of the bearers carrying Inga and Meme asked the baby's age. When she told him one month, the man looked horrified and yelled something to the other bearers. Ai ya! They all stopped dead. Although they were in the middle of a stream, they lowered the sedan chairs into the cold water and backed away. When Chester asked what was the matter, they explained that they could not move a baby under three months old since up to that age it had no soul and the wrath of the gods would surely come upon them. No amount of persuasion or bribery could change their minds. They refused to carry the baby and began to move down the mountain, leaving the Ronnings stranded. There was no way the family could make it alone down the narrow, treacherous path with a child and two babies plus their belongings.

Chester ran after them. "Wait, wait," he called. "You are right! But foreigners are different. Yes, it may be true that Chinese babies don't get their souls until they are three months old, but, you see, we are from Canada, across the sea, on the other side of the world. It takes only one month for Canadian babies to get their soul."

The bearers stopped and began conversing among themselves. "Why is this so?" they asked suspiciously.

Chester had to think fast. "Because the Celestial Kingdom has a longer history and the people here are more civilized than those in the younger nations. It is only logical that it would take longer to make a more sophisticated Chinese soul."

This seemed to please the bearers. They decided to proceed with their passengers. "It is only logical," they mumbled as they loaded the inferior Canadians back into the sedan chairs. "Only logical!"

35

Narrow Escape, 1927

REGRETS

The plum blossoms
Have fallen from the trees
And vanished quite;
The wind has flung the flowers
Of the willow
Far and wide.

The springtime of my years
Has vanished too,
And no friend remains
To answer my call.
—POETESS ZI YE,
    JIN DYNASTY (AD 265–420)

At the end of 1926, Chiang Kai-shek, aware of the growing power of the left-wing labor unions in Shanghai and secretly fearing the Communists were growing too powerful there, decided to make a push down the Yangtze River to the coastal metropolis to oust the dominating warlord, Sun Chuanfang, and take control of the city, rather than moving north to topple the Mukden Tiger, Zhang Zuolin, in Peking. In Shanghai, Zhou Enlai had organized an uprising of union workers against the ruling warlord. The presence of foreign powers in Shanghai would also pose special problems for Chiang if he were to take control. There were numerous foreign concessions in the city, some twenty-two thousand foreign troops stationed there, and more than forty foreign warships anchored in the harbor. Hundreds of foreign merchant ships were constantly docking in the harbor unloading goods for sale in China.

For the battle with Chiang's troops, the Mukden Tiger ordered new planes and guns, but his grand design miscarried. The other top warlords refused to accept his command. Instead, the warlords began to battle among themselves, resulting in an eruption of violence virtually all over China.

Amid the chaos, the American and British consuls ordered the Ronnings and other missionaries in the interior to evacuate immediately. British gunboats were sent up the Han River to rescue the foreigners. The Ronnings, however, could not leave with the others. Inga had contracted scarlet fever, and the whole family was quarantined. Even worse, she had to bind her breasts and wean the baby. Meme was put on powdered milk and cared for by a kind Chinese amah while her mother went into isolation. This was a terrible experience for Inga and the children, and when I was a child in Canada I heard the story frequently. By the time Mother was well enough to travel, conditions were so chaotic that they were unable to find *laopans* brave enough to take foreigners downriver. The Chinese boatmen feared attacks from the bands of soldiers, stragglers from the armies of defeated warlords, who had turned into river pirates as a means of survival. In the lower reaches of the winding Han River there were innumerable S-turns where the pirates could hide in small boats called *huazi* and attack the junks. The pirates would massacre all on board and make off with the cargo. The danger of attack was far worse when there were strong headwinds, giving the lumbering junks little chance of escaping the swifter pirate boats.

The Ronnings joined a small group of American missionaries who had not left on the gunboats. Altogether they needed four junks, but they could not find even one captain willing to risk the river journey. Finally Chester and a Chinese friend, Chang Hua-t'ang, walked ten miles downriver from Fancheng to the mouth of the Beihe (North River), where some sturdy junks called *bianzi*, from Henan, were anchored. There they found a *laopan* ready to make a bargain. Chester soon discovered why the man was so confident.

Hanging on the wall of the junk's cabin was an assortment of weapons: long-handled broadswords of the type Chester had seen as a child when he had by chance witnessed an execution, and long spears that he recognized as the "magic spears" used by the Hongqiang hui (Red Spear Society), who were affiliated with the Boxers. The captain explained that he was a commander of the society, which had been resurrected, and that the other Henan *bianzi* captains were also members. He claimed that the Red Spears would defy the bandits who were driving the junks off the rivers of Henan and Hubei. For the right price, they would take the missionaries down the river. Chester hired four junks and asked the captain to cover the weapons with straw mats so Inga and the children would not see them. The Ronnings again bade their farewells to their Chinese friends and, like Halvor and Hannah during the Boxer Uprising, disguised themselves as Chinese peasants and rode in mule carts the eight miles along the banks of the river to the boats in the hope of making their escape.

They had difficulty getting their tall Nordic frames through the door to the cabin in the bulkhead. The roof was so low they could hardly stand up. There were some rough blankets on the floor for Sylvia and Alton and a wicker basket for baby Meme, then five months old. Inga was so relieved to be leaving China that she was grateful for any accommodation. Fortunately, she was not aware of what lay ahead.

On the second day out, about a mile from the walled city of Chunghsiang, strong headwinds forced the boats to stop. For protection against the pirates, they anchored with a large fleet of other junks. The captain told the missionaries to stay hidden while the crew went to eat. When the sun set and the sailors did not return, Chester got suspicious. He saw a circle of burning torches on the riverbank and heard ominous noises. He suggested to fellow missionaries Reverends Klyve and Palmer Anderson that they investigate.

On the riverbank, heads covered, they approached through the shadows until they saw a ring of spectators. Within the circle, about fifty men stood in a row about ten feet apart. They were dressed in black tunics with red bands around their heads and wide crimson girdles, similar to the Boxers' attire. Each man held a burning incense stick under his nose and was inhaling the fumes with loud gasps. Soon, one by one, the men began to sway, fall over, and thrash around on the ground as if in a seizure. When this happened, several Red Spear men ran from the edge of the circle waving their execution swords and shouting. They began slashing wildly at the sand around the man who had fainted and kept it up until the victim stopped struggling and lay unconscious. At first, Chester thought he was witnessing another execution but then realized the sword wielders were keeping evil spirits from possessing the unconscious man. Finally, all the inhalers except one had collapsed on the ground. A hush fell over the crowd when the last man standing, who appeared to be in a trance, was lifted up by three *laopan* and placed in a chair on top of a square table. Then they knelt in the sand before him and began to ask questions about the river pirates and the journey ahead. They obviously thought he had oracle powers. The captain of the Ronnings' junk asked how long the headwinds would last. The oracle began to vibrate like a G-string on a base viol. The reply came in a loud voice: "The spirits of the wind and water are angry. No ship can sail against the wind. As long as there are foreigners on the boats, the headwinds will not stop!" Chester and friends dared not wait to hear the rest. They ran back to the junks. By the time they arrived, they could hear the chilling cries of the mob in the distance, "*sha yang guizi!*"(kill the foreign devils!). Chester urged the others to stay calm and with trumped-up bravado assured them that he would *jiangli* (talk reason) with the Chinese. "In the meantime," he said, "pray like never before for a change in the wind."

When the sailors, some armed with swords, came close to the junk, Chester, like the stories told about his father, jumped on top of the cabin and stood erect before the mainmast. A stone whizzed by his ear, but he stood his ground. Inga had discovered the spears on the wall of the cabin and prepared herself to fight to the death. The shouting was coming closer: "Kill! Kill!" Eight-year-old Sylvia hugged Alton and put her hands over his ears (forty years later, she claimed she could still hear the yells ringing in her ears).

Chester raised his arms to the heavens and shouted to the mob to be reasonable. The frenzied junkmen paid no attention and began throwing globs of mud. Suddenly Chester realized that the wind was no longer in his face. He spit on the palms of his hand and held them to the wind. The one facing north dried first. Miraculously the wind from downriver had turned. "Spit on your hands!" he shouted in a mighty voice in the local dialect. "Hold them to the winds! The headwinds are now behind us!" The surprised junkmen recognized the gesture and did the same. Then a wild shout arose that Chester later understated as "most pleasant to my ears": "*xunfeng huiliao!*" (favorable winds have arrived), they cried.

The crisis was over. Chester knelt on the deck and gave thanks to the Lord before he crawled down into the cabin to comfort his family. Inga was still holding the spear, pale and trembling. He told her she looked magnificent, that there had really been nothing to worry about because he was convinced that their *laopan* would not have lost face by harming them after boasting that, as a leader of the Red Spears, he would take them to safety. Inga was not convinced, but the incident renewed her confidence in Chester's ability to get them home safely.

At cock's crow the next morning, the usual time to *kaitou* (break journey), the crew rocked the long scull-oars back and forth on their fulcrums to ease the boat out into the main stream. But the danger was far from over. At Shayang, about halfway to Hankow, the junks met several battered boats coming upriver. They had been fired on by pirates. Sails were torn, and corpses still lay on the bloodied decks. The captain refused to continue downriver. The missionaries were stranded. After a day docked in Shayang, Chester went to send word of their predicament to the British consulate in Hankow. Inga and the children were to remain hidden while Chester and Palmer Anderson went to the cable office. On the way back, a gang of hostile students followed them. Not wanting to lead the mob to the junks, they ducked into a teahouse and calmly ordered jasmine tea to give the appearance of inner peace and tranquility. The students followed them.

"Look at the foreign devils!" they shouted: "Destroy them! Down with imperialism!"

On impulse, Chester jumped onto the table and shouted back, "You are absolutely right! Down with foreign imperialists! Let us destroy them!"

The amazed students fell silent and gawked at this blue-eyed giant who looked like a Westerner but spoke a local dialect. Chester waved his long arms like a performer in a Chinese opera: "That is exactly why I want to go down the Han River to the Yangtze and cross the Pacific Ocean to my home beyond the seas. I will attack imperialism from our side and you must attack imperialism from your side and together we will surely crush it!" He slammed a tight fist against the palm of his left hand and grinned broadly.

The mood of the crowd changed in a flash. Here was a blue-eyed foreign devil who sounded like a true "lump of mud." "That's right," yelled Chester, "I am just a lump of mud like you are!" (This became a phrase he used often to identify himself with the locals.) The students laughed, escorted him back to the boat, and wished the missionaries favorable winds on their mission to fight imperialism.

In the meantime, Inga, not understanding the commotion on the docks, sat trembling in the hold with the children and swore that if she ever got out of China she would never, ever return. When Chester finally came below, smiling and exhilarated by the incident, he could not understand why his wife was so upset.

When they reached Hankow, they found the great industrial city in a fever of fresh revolutionary activity. On January 1, 1927, the Revolutionary government had moved from Canton to Hankow and was dominated by left-wing Nationalists. They included Sun Fo, Sun Yat-sen's son; Foreign Minister Eugene Chen; and Soong Ch'ing-ling, Dr. Sun's beautiful widow, sister of Madam Chiang Kai-shek and of T. V. Soong, one of the wealthiest businessmen in China. Comintern advisor Michael Borodin had become the power behind the Nationalist leadership. The Nationalist forces had occupied the British concession after a clash between the British bluejackets and Chinese civilians. Most of the foreigners had been evacuated. Madam Soong Ch'ing-ling invited the Ronnings to stay with her in the former British legation. She would meet Chester again in Peking after the Communists triumphed in the Civil War.

There was still sporadic fighting all over the city. Inga and the children never left the compound. Chester went out secretly to meet his friend and associate teacher Tung Tse-pei, who warned him that a day of reckoning was imminent between the Kuomintang's right-wing generals under Chiang and their Communist counterparts. He advised Chester to get out while he could, rightly predicting that Chiang would betray the Communists and wage a full-scale war against them. He said Communists were already being secretly killed in Hankow. Tung planned to return to Fancheng to warn the student leaders. Chester and Tung, sworn blood brothers, embraced for the last time. (It was not until Chester returned to China eighteen years later, in 1945, that he learned to his great sorrow that Tung Tse-pei had never arrived in Fancheng. He had been captured by Kuomintang agents and executed in the cruelest way.)

While in Hankow, waiting for a gunship to take them down the Yangtze to Shanghai, Chester received a request to become principal of the Camrose Lutheran College in Alberta. He accepted the offer but wondered if he would ever get there.

In mid-March, the Ronning family was offered space on an American warship commanded by a young Lieutenant Olds. The gunboat was headed down the Yangtze to Nanking and Shanghai, where the Ronnings planned to board an ocean liner to Canada. En route, Commander Olds received an urgent radiogram from J. K. Davis, the American consul in Nanking, asking for help. It read: "S.O.S. British and Japanese consulates were attacked and the consuls killed. Cold-blooded murder of one American missionary and the attempted murder of many others by Nationalist soldiers. Police warn we will all be destroyed."

Lieutenant Olds's gunboat arrived in Nanking harbor on March 24, 1927, the same day the Nationalist troops had occupied the city and unexpectedly unleashed a day of terrorism against the foreigners. The soldiers were rampaging through the city killing foreigners. Six people, including the vice president of Nanking University, John E. Williams, had been killed. Many of the foreigners, including Pearl Buck and the wife of a Catholic missionary, hid in the homes of Chinese friends. Others were saved by the American and British gunboats shelling the southern part of Nanking to prevent the troops from attacking the foreigners. Eventually more than seven thousand foreigners took refuge in Socony Hill, the Standard Oil property, and many in the foreign concessions were forced to escape over the city wall. The Ronnings witnessed the events from the deck of their gunboat. Some escapees climbed down the outside of the thirty-foot-high city wall on ropes and the weaker ones were lowered in baskets to be taken by rafts to a Jardine Matheson steamer. The Ronnings transferred from the gunboat to the steamer, where Chester and Inga helped to pull the refugees onto the deck and tend to their rope burns. Baby Meme had been the youngest passenger on the gunboat.

The Ronnings' escape from Nanking in 1927 was followed by even deeper trouble when they continued downriver to Shanghai on the Jardine Matheson steamer. They arrived shortly after the purge of the Communists in the city ordered by Generalissimo Chiang Kai-shek. A year earlier, the Communists and Nationalists had agreed to join in the Northern Expedition, the military campaign whose main objective was to end the rule of local warlords and unify China under a Kuomintang banner. Shanghai was still held by the warlord Sun Chuanfang. Skirmishes between the warlord troops and union worker squads were erupting in the harbor area when their ship anchored. Passengers were forced to lie facedown in the passageways between cabins to avoid stray bullets coming through portholes. The streets of Shanghai were filled with the worker squads who had been armed and mobilized by Zhou Enlai, in preparation to facilitate the liberation of the city from warlord rule by Chiang's advancing Northern Expeditionary Force. Both KMT and Communists agents had been sent earlier into the city to organize the laborers. Although they were poorly armed, the worker squads outwitted the warlord's troops by employing such stratagems as setting off strings of firecrackers in empty gasoline tanks to simulate the sound of machine-gun fire. The squads did not harm foreigners. Chester managed to take his family by rickshaw to the Cathay Hotel, on the Bund, where they had to wait two weeks to get an ocean liner to Canada.

While the Ronning family was in the Cathay Hotel, Chiang Kai-shek betrayed the Communists. Instead of marching peacefully into the city to join forces with his Communist allies, Chiang Kai-shek's forces came in with their guns blazing, not against the warlord forces as promised, but against the Communists.

Earlier, on April 12, 1927, Chiang had arrived in Shanghai harbor by gunboat and made contact with bankers and foreign-backed political leaders. They warned him that he must break with Zhou Enlai or forfeit their support. Chiang knew he could not control the city without the help of international bankers and owners of commercial establishments to whom communism was anathema. He made a decision that years later would cost him the Mandate of Heaven. Instead of joining Zhou Enlai's workers in keeping with the agreement,

Chiang commanded his expeditionary forces to seize all left-wing strongholds and shoot every armed worker on sight. Chiang's forces were joined by the police of the French Concession and agents of the Green Gang, the Shanghai Mafia, who controlled the rackets. Zhou's labor union squads were taken by surprise. Outnumbered and ill-equipped, they were slaughtered by the hundreds by their presumed allies. From the windows of their hotel room overlooking the Bund along the Huangpu River, the Ronnings could see the people dying in the streets, hear the shooting, and the cries of agony. The fighting lasted for two days and two nights. When Chester ventured out in search of powdered milk for the children, he was horrified to see bodies hanging from the trees along the Bund. Hundreds of corpses lay like rag dolls in the streets, and the gutters literally ran with blood. Armed troops paraded in the streets and raided homes in search of anyone connected with the left wing. Thus began the massacre of the Communists, not only in Shanghai but all over China. The bloodbath lasted a full year (1927–28). In Shanghai alone, upward of five thousand workers, party organizers, and anyone suspected of befriending a Communist were hunted down and often tortured and executed without trial. The Communist Party was decimated and the working-class movement shattered in most cities.

Fortunately for China, Zhou Enlai made a miraculous escape. During the first hours of the purge, he hid in the offices of Shanghai's major publishing house, the Commercial Press, escaping only moments before the KMT raided the building. Later, disguised as a curio dealer wearing a long silk gown and gold-rimmed spectacles, Zhou went underground with his two lieutenants, Luo Yinong and Zhao Shiyan. The curio shop became a front to track down traitors who informed on the whereabouts of Communists. Luo was caught by Nationalist agents and executed on April 21. Zhou Enlai was captured by General Bai Chongxi, thrown into prison, and told he would be executed at sunrise. Toward midnight he was awakened by a former Whampoa cadet. The soldier, at the risk of his own life, untied his former director and led him to the dark street while the sentries looked the other way. Although his picture was posted all over Shanghai, no one betrayed him. He escaped by sailing in a junk up the Yangtze River to Hankow and then on to Nanchang, where he was chosen by the Communist Party to lead a full-scale uprising against Chiang's Nationalist Party. His closest aide, Zhao Shiyan, was captured and executed on July 19.

In Hankow, the Kuomintang Central Executive Committee, in which the Nationalists and Communists had originally united to oust the warlords, branded Chiang a "counterrevolutionary, guilty of massacre of the people and oppression of the party." They adopted a resolution that expelled him from the Nationalist Party and dismissed him from all his posts. But Chiang was in command of the army, and in a move reminiscent of the self-named emperor Yuan Shikai, he responded by establishing his own Nationalist government in Nanking and making himself head of it. He made it "a crime punishable by death" to be a Communist or a member of any organization or union considered as such by his "purified" Kuomintang. It was the beginning of the Civil War between the forces of Chiang Kai-shek and Mao Zedong that would ultimately end in defeat of the Nationalists on the mainland in 1949.

The Ronnings were trapped in their hotel room for two weeks. Although Chester did his best to hide the horror from his family, Inga was aware of what was transpiring. They could hear the sporadic shooting and the rumble of the open trucks loaded with doomed revolutionaries making their sinister trips to the execution grounds in the suburb of Lunghua. Chester was sick at heart and felt that everything he had ever worked for in China was being destroyed. All his hopes for reforms in China had been blown to the winds, and there was nothing he could do about it. What made it worse was the knowledge that Chiang Kai-shek had attacked his Communist allies with the support of foreign intervention.

When the streets of Shanghai became safe for foreigners, Chester took his family to the waterfront, where they boarded a ship sailing to Vancouver. There, to Sylvia's delight, they took a Canadian Pacific train through the majestic Rocky Mountains. My father became president of the Camrose Lutheran College and became active in politics. He was elected to the Alberta legislature representing the United Farmers of Alberta (U.F.A.). In Camrose he purchased a small section of choice land just off the college campus and built a small house in a grove of blue spruce trees. I was born there on May 21, 1928. Six years later, my sister Kjeryn was born, and two years after that, brother Harmon joined the family. My mother said she would never, ever return to China. It took my father fifteen years to change her mind. In the meantime, Chester's younger brother Talbert continued in the footsteps of Halvor and Chester and went to China as a missionary. This was during the Japanese occupation of China.

36

Uncle Talbert

It is better to light a candle than to curse the darkness! That's why I am here as a missionary.

—REVEREND TALBERT RONNING, AN-K'ANG AIR BASE, CHINA, 1942

In 1931, three years after Chester and his family made their harrowing escape from Shanghai, his younger brother Talbert and his new wife, Ella, witnessed tumultuous events that became turning points in Chinese history.* While Talbert was the only child of Hannah and Halvor born in America, he spent most of his childhood in China and was fluent in the language. Talbert was tall and good-looking like his older brothers, Chester and Nelius. During World War I, when the brothers were serving in the Royal Canadian Air Force, Talbert graduated from St. Olaf College in Northfield, Minnesota. Following ordination at Luther Theological Seminary in St. Paul, Minnesota, he became a pastor in Madison, Minnesota. He married Ella Gryting, a lovely, somewhat innocent young woman with reddish curly hair and green eyes, and in Halvor and Hannah's footsteps, they went as missionaries to China.

By the time of their arrival, Generalissimo Chiang Kai-shek, having betrayed his Communist allies in the Shanghai debacle, had set up a Nationalist government in Nanking and was launching a series of so-called bandit-suppression campaigns to eliminate pockets of Communist resistance in the provinces. In October 1934, the Communist Red Army, the forerunner of the People's Liberation Army, began a trek on foot and horseback that was to last a whole year and take them to the loess caves of the Yan'an Valley in mountainous North Shaanxi. The epic Long March was, in fact, a series of marches in which a number of Communist armies moved westward to escape encirclement by the overwhelmingly larger and better-armed forces of Chiang Kai-shek. The lead column was that of the First Front Army led by Mao Zedong and Zhou Enlai. While Mao's forces were tramping westward from Jiangxi Province, traversing some six

*This chapter is based on a narrative account that Talbert later wrote for me. Direct quotes are italicized.

thousand circuitous miles through eleven provinces, over snowy mountains and raging rivers, swamps and forests, while suffering constant harassment by Nationalist forces, many observers assumed that Chiang Kai-shek had won the Civil War. Only about seven thousand ragged remnants of the original one hundred thousand troops of Mao's band reached Yan'an at the end of October 1935. Mao established his headquarters and rallied his scattered supporters to prepare the counteroffensive that would culminate victoriously with the triumphant establishment in Peking of the People's Republic of China on October 1, 1949. But, in the 1930s and early 1940s, when Yan'an was still blockaded by Nationalist forces, the possibility of such a victory seemed extremely remote for the Communists. This was the China that Talbert and Ella encountered on arrival.

In the Shanghai turnabout, Chester had witnessed Generalissimo Chiang Kai-shek's transformation from crusader against the warlords to an utterly ruthless opportunist intent on achieving supreme power. Chester was shocked by Chiang's ongoing policy of exterminating the Communists. It was a policy that took countless lives both in the so-called bandit-suppression campaigns and in the "white terror" in the urban areas during which suspected Communists or sympathizers were executed. Chester could not accept the view, as Talbert and other missionaries did, that Chiang was an upright Christian leader. In 1931, on the insistence of Chiang's fiancée, the beautiful, American-educated Soong Mei-ling, Chiang joined the Methodist Church. While Chiang professed Christian piety, his policies indicated that he remained essentially a warlord and authoritarian Confucian. Madame Chiang Kai-shek, however, in her efforts to win support for the Nationalist cause, particularly among Americans, spread the word that the Generalissimo was a pious Christian who read the Bible daily. In Chester's view, this cloak of Christianity was only a maneuver to throw dust in the eyes of foreigners.

While Chiang was pursuing the Communists, the Japanese Imperial Army in 1931 had occupied Manchuria and closed in on North China. On July 7, 1937, Talbert was vacationing on Kikung Shan (Rooster Mountain) with his family when the news came that the Japanese had clashed with the Chinese and seized the famous marble-columned Marco Polo Bridge, twenty-five miles southwest of Peking. This marked the onset of the Second Sino-Japanese War (Talbert's parents had witnessed the first in 1894–95), which would continue until the Allied victory in 1945. The day after the bridge incident, the American embassy cabled all missionaries to leave the interior of China. Talbert found himself facing the same dilemma that his father and brother had faced before him: to flee or not to flee.

Talbert decided that Ella and their baby son, Halvor, would remain on

Rooster Mountain while he returned to his mission in Sinyeh in northeastern Henan Province and tried to find a means of leaving China. He boarded a
crowded freight train north to the road junction at Hsuchang, where he found
that the government had commandeered all buses and even mules. He was able
to hire a kind Chinese man willing to pull a wooden cart bearing his luggage
while he walked alongside in the unremitting heavy rain. He walked for twelve
days on muddy roads to his mission station, and along the way he passed thousands of soldiers on the march, wearing rude sandals, bearing heavy packs and
weapons, staggering along in the intense August heat. Many had collapsed and
lay at the roadside. Talbert was moved to write that he was inspired by their
courage. He had seen Chinese soldiers in both victory and defeat: *I was challenged. Am I willing to give my life for God as they do for their country? A Chinese
soldier is a peasant, forced into the army who has suffered drought, flood, hunger and
bandits in peacetime. War to a peasant is no worse than peace.*

Upon reaching the Sinyeh Mission and putting things in order there, he
left for Rooster Mountain to retrieve Ella and their baby. He rode his bicycle,
the main form of transportation for many foreigners at that time, on the path
alongside the railroad track. En route he stayed one night with a family of the
Lutheran Brotherhood, who warned him that soldiers had just clashed with bandits on the road ahead. But the next morning, Talbert pressed on through the
mountains. *I passed the body of a bandit hung on a tree. His stomach had been sliced
open and his insides were hanging out.*

At Rooster Mountain, Talbert gathered up Ella and the baby, intending to
return at once to the Sinyeh Mission, but they were delayed by heavy rains.
While waiting for a break in the weather, Talbert visited a large American-owned
tobacco factory that had been turned into a hospital for wounded soldiers. The
company motto still hung on the wall: "A cigarette in the mouth of every Chinaman!" Each hospital bed was made up with a couple of boards over two saw-
horses, with a thin mat and a blanket.

Talbert, in an effort to comfort the wounded, jumped on a box and shouted
in Chinese: *"Soldiers of China, I congratulate you for your sacrifice for your country.
I see you have been wounded in battle. Some have lost an arm or a leg, and you have
shed blood for your country."*

*With one accord, they shouted back in an obviously rehearsed reply: "It was our
duty. The enemy is taking our land, mistreating our women, carrying off our children
to Japan, old men are being killed. If we ever get well, we are going back to fight."
Such was the pathetic, almost dog-like loyalty of the illiterate Chinese soldiers toward
their officers. They ask nothing more than three bowls of rice a day and are willing to*

die for a man who feeds them. It was largely this spirit of loyalty and toughness that restored military morale after each defeat and gave them the strength to carry on the fight against the Japanese atrocities that were occurring all over China.

When the roads dried we were able to continue our journey. We got an old truck and climbed on top of the luggage with a crowd of Chinese passengers and reached the Norwegian Mission the next day. Then we took rickshaws for 40 miles to our station in Sinyeh.

Talbert recorded the intense suffering of the Chinese people during this period. He described how Nationalist soldiers seized young men on the streets, tied them together, and marched them off for service in the army without notifying their families. One disgruntled soldier told him how the general of his unit got ten dollars to make clothes for each soldier, but had pajama-like suits made for three dollars and pocketed the rest. This was typical of the corruption that weakened Chiang Kai-shek's forces and later enabled the highly indoctrinated Communist troops to achieve victories over the better-armed Nationalist troops.

In 1938, as Talbert and his family were desperately seeking a way out of embattled China, the Japanese began to heavily bomb targets in the interior as their troops moved westward. The family managed to make their way to Hankow, still held by the Nationalists, where they found that the Shanghai and Nanking ports on the Yangtze River had fallen to the Japanese. Talbert decided to take the train south to Hong Kong, but while they waited at the train depot, Japanese planes made bombing runs over Hankow. The Ronnings hid in nearby woods and watched as anti-aircraft guns opened fire and Chinese fighter planes rose to attack the bombers. *Several planes were hit. We saw planes falling in explosions and pilots bailing out. The firing of cannons so close by was extremely shocking to Halvor, in my arms, who was not yet two years old.*

The Ronnings reached Hong Kong, where they boarded a ship for home. Recalling their escape from Hankow to Hong Kong, Talbert wrote that the bombing at the railway depot had a lasting effect on baby Halvor. When they returned to St. Paul, some boys ignited firecrackers in a tin can in fun, making a loud explosion. The child disappeared and was later found under the grand piano shaking in fright. *Just think of the terrible fear suffered by the Chinese children with no escape!*

Talbert Returns to China at War

In 1940, the war in China was still raging. The Japanese had occupied the Yangtze River Valley, and Chiang Kai-shek had moved his capital from Nanking up the Yangtze River inland to Chungking, in the nearly impenetrable Sichuan Province. It was the year before the Japanese attack on December 7 on Pearl Harbor. Despite the widespread fighting in China, Talbert and two fellow missionaries, Reverends Albert Anderson and Kristopher Twedt, were called upon by the Foreign Mission Board to return to China. The board had received word that Chinese Christians were being attacked by the Japanese and were pleading for shelter and protection from American missionaries. The United States was not yet at war with Japan, but the risk for Talbert and his fellow missionaries would nevertheless be considerable since the Japanese were handling all Westerners roughly and were not respecting the extraterritorial rights of the foreign Christian missions. Talbert did not hesitate. Chester, then a squadron leader in the Royal Canadian Air Force, advised him not to go. His father, Halvor, left the decision to his son. Talbert later wrote: *Many friends said I was crazy. Maybe they were right. The Bible says, "Go . . . and lo, I am with you always!" Matt. 28:18–20.* He left his never-complaining wife, Ella, four-year-old Halvor, and six-week-old Julian at home and did not return until Julian's fifth birthday.

When the missionaries arrived in Shanghai, it was largely under Japanese control, but the Japanese were still bombing sections of resistance. They stayed at the China Inland Mission in the Chapei District. *That night we slept in the basement of the church and were suddenly awakened by the sound of an exploding shell and the cry of a child. I grabbed a lantern and ran out to find the child. The next minute another shell exploded through the roof of the church and landed in my bed, but, thank God, I wasn't in it.*

Talbert and Albert Anderson were determined to get to Kwei-te in Henan in Free China, where the Lutheran Free Church had a mission that was being harassed by the Japanese. *When things looked peaceful we started out with our carts and bicycles. We ran into a troop of Japanese soldiers gathering scrap iron from the poor Chinese, even taking their iron cooking woks. Before we realized it, we were surrounded. Now what? "What are you carrying?" "Christian literature, medicine, no guns, no opium." "Where are you going?" This was before Pearl Harbor so Americans were fairly safe. We were held for an hour before they waved us on. We finally reached an Inland Mission with a large American flag spread on the roof. My room was on the ground floor. While I was shaving next morning I heard the roar of planes and stepped out to look. The sky seemed filled with planes in perfect formation like Canada geese flying in the sky. I grabbed a quilt and pulled it over my head and the next second, BOOM! The glass window came tumbling in over my head. Three bombs landed in the mission compound. Two nurses were sleeping upstairs. Amazingly no one was hurt. All the servants fled, with hundreds of people trying to get out of town and across the river.*

In several instances, the boats were loaded and the boatman called "No More!" But some frantic person would jump in the boat causing it to tip over and the people were thrown in the river. Few could swim. Then the planes would circle back to strafe the multitude on the water and on the sandbanks. The pilots flew so low I could almost see the whites of their evil eyes. The water was filled with blood. Our number one servant was thrown in the water. He told us, "I could not swim but prayed to God for help!" I don't understand how he reached the bank across the river. I thought of how God had helped the Israelites across the waters. So I thanked God.

Talbert's problems would only worsen, but he felt he had been given a unique opportunity to serve as a missionary.

The next day the Japanese bombed Nanyang where we were heading. We saw the dark clouds of smoke. Nine planes came flying directly toward us. Three on each side of the road. We ran to the ditches. The planes roared over our heads spitting bullets. I thought this was the end. My first thought was for Ella, Halvor and Julian. "Lord take care of my family! Lord save my soul! Forgive me all my sins!"

Many refugees were dead. The terrified and wounded came running to us. "What shall we do?" All I could do was shout in Chinese, "Listen, listen to the good news, Jesus Christ descended to earth to save you and me" . . . and then I quoted Matt. 10:28. Do not fear. Those who kill the body but cannot kill the soul . . . for everyone who calls upon the name of the Lord will be saved. Rom.10:1. Many fell on their knees. The bombers circled back. We prepared for the worst. I began to sing loudly "Jesus Loves Me, This I know" in Chinese. The planes destroyed a bridge only a hundred yards from us and then flew off. What an opportunity to witness for the Lord!

When the sky was clear, the refugees rose from their hiding places in the fields and ditches and began walking down the road again. Not knowing where to go, many followed the two foreigners—who were also puzzled as to what to do. There were no inns to provide shelter and no food available to buy. Talbert saw some smoke coming out of a house and found a woman making millet gruel.

"May we buy some food? Do you have a bowl and chopsticks?"

She gave him a bowl and dipped some gruel into it. He found an ox cart to sit upon and lifted the bowl to his mouth. The crowd gathered around. Some Chinese soldiers walked by and one said, "Peace, Pastor. How can you eat that millet gruel? That is food for beggars."

Talbert answered, "When a man is hungry, he can eat a beggar's food." The crowd reluctantly agreed, and everyone feasted on the beggar's food for which Talbert had paid his last penny.

After resting a few days, Albert Anderson and Talbert rode their bicycles to the mission in Sinyeh. As they approached the city, they heard the church bell ringing. Albert got off his bicycle and removed his hat, to thank God that the Chinese were welcoming them back. Then they saw people fleeing from the city. The church bell that once called them to worship was now being used as an air raid warning.

After Pearl Harbor

Before December 7, 1941, the American missionaries felt tolerably safe carrying on the mission work of sheltering hundreds of Chinese Christians, especially women, from Japanese atrocities. But after Pearl Harbor, the Americans were in constant danger and sought ways to escape, especially since their presence now was endangering Chinese Christians. Three of the missionaries in Talbert's mission were captured by the Japanese: Marie Anderson and Martha Kulberg died in prison. Reverend Hans Nesse survived but died shortly after his release at the end of the war.

In January 1942, to coordinate operations against the Japanese on the Asian mainland, President Franklin D. Roosevelt, in agreement with Britain, appointed General Joseph Stilwell as theater commander for China-Burma-India. Stilwell was to command American troops and also Chinese Nationalist divisions in agreement with Generalissimo Chiang Kai-shek. His principal mission, which he eventually accomplished, was the opening of the Japanese-held Burma Road, the principal overland supply route from India to Free China. The Burma Road supplemented the transport by air over the Hump (the Himalayan Mountains) linking India to China. However, problems arose thereafter between Stilwell and Chiang over operations against Japanese advancing into the interior of China. Stilwell regarded Chiang's strategy as inept, and he protested his use of troops to blockade areas held by his political opponents, the Communists, rather than deploying them against the Japanese. As relations between Chiang and Stilwell worsened, President Roosevelt recalled the American commander in October 1944.

Talbert's mission was not far from a vital American air base established in Laohokow in a Nationalist-controlled area of Hubei. He was often called upon to help the airmen as an interpreter with the Chinese troops who were working with the Americans, and the commander of the base asked Talbert to serve as a temporary chaplain there. Talbert later wrote: *Once, a fighter plane crashed near my station. The pilot had been shot in the leg. He bailed out and was bleeding to death. The superstitious natives were afraid to touch him. I came too late to stop the bleeding.*

I picked him up in my jeep. He softly prayed the Lord's Prayer with me but he died on the way to the makeshift hospital. I drove on with tears in my eyes. War is hell! I felt helpless but was thankful to be of some comfort. Another time I helped pick up the body of a young pilot whose plane had run out of fuel. He bailed out but his parachute did not open.

Three huge Super Fortresses returning from a bombing mission to Japan were brought down by Japanese fighter planes near my mission field. I saw one burst into flames. The airmen bailed out but five of them lost their lives. Two others broke their legs on landing. They did not know whether they had landed in Jap-occupied or free China. If in occupied territory they would have been captured, tortured and killed because the Japanese told their captives, "You bombed our cities and do not deserve to live." When the airmen saw me, they realized they were free. They hugged me. I took 12 men to our station. Chang Shih-fu, our cook . . . soon had a meal for them . . . How thankful were these American flyers to have landed safely and found help.

Talbert had been ordered to leave China, but there was no way out, and the missionaries were without funds. Dr. Daniel Nelson—an old missionary and a colleague of Talbert's father, Halvor, in Hankow—along with Lutheran World Action bought an airplane named *St. Paul* to help evacuate the missionaries. Then Reverend Halvor Ronning and Dr. Nelson had another brilliant idea. The large American C-46 transport planes that brought supplies from India over the Hump returned to the base carrying sand bags for ballast. Dr. Nelson approached the military, asking, "Why not take missionaries back as ballast instead of sand bags?" It worked. Halvor sent word to his son to come home ASAP, as a sand bag if necessary. But, perhaps for the first time, the filial son disobeyed his father and arranged for 150 missionaries, not including himself, to be evacuated from the main headquarters of the Norwegian mission. Only six missionaries were left behind: Talbert; his friend Reverend Anderson from Fancheng; and four men from the Norwegian mission.

At daybreak, Talbert and Anderson rode their bicycles to the mission in T'enghsien where Talbert and Ella had lived. When they tried to get out of the city, *the gates were closed because the Japs were coming. I went to the Mandarin and he said that they would fight the Japs but if they could not hold them back they had plans to flee west to the mountains and I could come with them. I decided to try to get to the airport and pleaded with him to open the gates and let me go. He told me I could go at my own risk and opened the gate. I was strong and my legs were in good shape and though heavily loaded, I rode at a brisk pace, fleeing for my life. I had 40 miles to go. After about 10 miles the gears in the back gave out and I couldn't ride the bike, so I just walked along wheeling the bike beside me . . .*

After going on my way, I heard an Army truck but did not know if it was Chinese or American. It was coming my way. I knew they were not allowed to pick up civilians. But without a second thought, I stood in the middle of the road and waved my foreign helmet. To my surprise they screeched to a stop rather than run over me. "I am fleeing from the Japs and my bike has broken down. Please help me!"

The Americans were hauling empty gasoline barrels back to the airbase. They threw my bike in the back of the truck and me with it . . . Suddenly we reached the top of the hill overlooking Laohokow and the American air base just outside the city. Large clouds of smoke were rising into the sky and hundreds of refugees were fleeing. Some recognized me. The driver thundered ahead. Well, I arrived at the airport just before the Japs. The Americans were destroying everything before fleeing. Blowing up ammunition and gasoline. A transport plane had arrived loaded with gas. Another plane ran into its tail and damaged it. The Americans blew it up, hence all the black smoke. I was met by two officers. One was a doctor. I asked him if it was convenient I would be thankful if there was a place on the last plane for me. Otherwise I would flee into the hills with the Chinese. The second man, the intelligence officer named Lovet said, "Missionary, come here! What information do you have about the position of the Japs?" I told him the cavalry was right behind me. Perhaps an hour. "Then if you help us as an interpreter we will give you a ride out."

The Chinese soldiers who were pumping gas to refuel the transport planes were tired and hungry and afraid. The Americans were rude to them. I asked for food for them and told them that the Americans were helping to fight the battle against the Japs. It was important now to help save what they could. I convinced them to pump gas for the planes. It was getting dark. I lined them up in two rows with lanterns so the planes could see the runway to take off.

Finally there was one plane left. The wrecking crew of about a dozen Chinese threw my bike into the baggage department and helped me into the plane. They gave me a parachute and wished me luck. Off we went. The plane flew very high, lest it be caught by Japanese fighter planes. The next air base at An-K'ang was 150 air miles and the descent was rapid. The plane was not pressurized in the baggage department. My head and ears seemed about to burst. When we landed, I could barely hear.

When I tumbled out with the baggage I was surrounded by American soldiers who shouted, "What in hell are you doing in this God forsaken country?"

"What are you doing here?" I retorted.

"We were conscripted to fight for our country. We risk our lives for these bloody Chinese who are to protect our bases, but they run when the Japs come and leave us in the lurch. We can't trust them."

To this outburst I responded, "Well, I too am a soldier. I was called by my church to leave my family to come out here. 'It is better to light a candle than to curse the darkness!' That is why I am here as a missionary. I understand you soldiers. While you were stationed in Laohokow I was called upon several times to help some Americans who paid the supreme sacrifice. I too am a soldier, a soldier of the cross. I am willing, if need be, to give my life for the cause of God and country."

The chaplain at An-K'ang was on sick leave so I was again asked to fill in.

There followed a painful episode. When Talbert and the American airmen got word that President Roosevelt had recalled the very popular General Stilwell because of his disagreements with Chiang Kai-shek, they were terribly distressed. They had admired the courage of "Vinegar Joe," who personally had led the troops who opened the Burma Road. When President Roosevelt died suddenly on April 12, 1945, Talbert was asked to lead the memorial service. He attributed the sparse attendance at the service to the soldiers' disappointment over Roosevelt's recall of Stilwell.

A month later, Talbert flew from An-K'ang air base as ballast in a transport plane to Chungking, the city on the Yangtze where Generalissimo Chiang Kai-shek had established his wartime capital. The Japanese were finding it difficult to capture the city because the only approach was extremely difficult, blocked by the narrow canyons of the Three Great Gorges of the Yangtze River. To open this route, the Japanese were bombing its defenses almost daily. Fearing the bombing, thousands of Chinese lived in caves honeycombed into the mountainsides the city was built on. In May 1939, Chungking had almost been destroyed by one of the most disastrous single bombing raids, at that time, in military history. Twenty-seven Japanese planes had arrived without any air-raid warning when schools were in session and the streets thronged with people, dropping 108 bombs that killed or wounded 3,750. Talbert took refuge in one of the caves. During a halt in the raids, he flew south to Kunming in Yunnan Province aboard one of General Claire Chennault's Flying Tiger transport planes. From there he flew over the Hump, homeward bound. One day soon, his brother Chester would make the same hazardous flight in the opposite direction, on his way to serving as a diplomat at the Canadian embassy in Chungking. After five years of missionary service in China, Talbert surprised his family by arriving home in time for his son Julian's fifth birthday party. Talbert later became pastor of a Lutheran church in Chicago.

37

Camrose and Valhalla

But since I have read your verse
    'Tis easy to guess the rest,—
Because in the hearts of the children
    There is neither East nor West.
—RUDYARD KIPLING, "TO JAMES WHITCOMB RILEY" (1890)

After their escape from China in 1927, Chester and Inga settled in the town of Camrose, in the lake district of Alberta, with their three children, Sylvia and the China-born Alton and Meme. I was born shortly after they arrived, and the family was completed with the birth of my sister Kjeryn and brother Harmon. Father accepted the position he had been offered unexpectedly while waiting in Hankow for a gunboat down the Yangtze en route home. After their long journey from Shanghai to Vancouver, they took a train to Camrose, where Chester became president and professor of mathematics at Camrose Lutheran College. Another source of pride for him was the distinction he enjoyed as the conductor of the college choir, which was later invited to perform in New York's Carnegie Hall.

In Camrose, the Ronning family never really escaped the China stamp. Kjeryn was nicknamed "Chinka" and is still called that by friends today. Brother Alton was "Chink." He was big and tough and wrestled other kids who dared to tease him with the ditty:

Chiny Chinky Chinaman,
Sitting on a fence,
Trying to make a dollar
Out of fifty cents.

But our Chinese ties also brought compensation. We received gifts of candied ginger and fresh litchi nuts from Dad's Chinese friends who ran the York Cafe, the only Chinese restaurant in town.

Growing up in the small town of Camrose was like living in an extended family. We knew everybody who lived there. I still can recall the names of my class-mates and teachers in elementary school. We lived in a small house on the edge of the college campus furnished with Chinese rosewood tables, Tientsin rugs, and ancient scrolls given to us by Grandfather. Across the road was an enchanted forest where we kids played Tarzan. Alton informed us proudly that beyond the woods lay China, where he was born. We created our own games and had heard our parents talk so much about China that we sometimes played "Chinese and Missionaries" instead of "Cowboys and Indians." Just beyond our backyard was a ski hill. Summers were sunny, but winters were harsh and toughened us up. By Halloween we had plenty of ammunition for snowball fights. We sometimes endured temperatures of forty degrees below zero, when we could see our breath freeze. Then Mother would bundle scarves over our faces and propel us out the door to run the fifteen minutes to school. We would race to the top of the hill and toboggan down the snow-covered slope across a frozen creek and partway up a far slope from which we dashed to the school door, where teachers waited to rub snow on any white frozen spots found on our cheeks. Skating on the creek and skiing were our favorite sports. When I was ten years old, I won third prize in a downhill slalom competition, which made me late for supper at six—a cardinal sin in our house. When I told Dad I came in third he forgave me, and I spent the rest of the week fearing that he would find out there had been only three in the race. The best skiers were the four Servold boys who lived next door. Not able to afford skis, they made their own from the staves of pickle barrels. Jens became famous in Camrose when, during a jumping exhibition, he lost one ski while jumping off the high scaffold and landed safely on the other. Irvin was an Olympic skier, and Clarence put Camrose on the map by becoming a three-time Canadian cross-country champion.

While the Lutheran church was our religious and social center, our parents encouraged us to be free thinkers and, if need be, to challenge what was preached. It was reflective of what Dad's missionary father, Halvor, had taught him. There were times, while walking home after listening to the Sunday sermon, Dad would say: "Don't believe everything you hear. Use your own head." While encouraging us to think independently, our parents provided useful home-spun advice. Mom wouldn't tolerate regrets: "Yesterday is gone, tomorrow never comes, today is the day we live." Often, Dad would say, "Nothing is impossible." To amuse ourselves at the dinner table, we would conjure up instances of the impossible, trying to prove him wrong. To keep us quiet, he made us chew thirty-two times before swallowing. Growing up in Camrose helped prepare me for the

CAMROSE AND VALHALLA ✻ 295

challenges I later faced as a journalist in turbulent China and other struggling countries.

My fondest memories as a child were of our family visits to Grandpa's farm in Valhalla every summer. Dad would drive our new Model T five hundred miles north of Edmonton on a narrow dirt road that had replaced the Edson Trail. Mom sat in front with Kjeryn in the middle and baby Harmon in her lap. Sylvia, Alton, Meme, and I squeezed into the backseat, and our heroic collie dog Shep rode on the fender. A grub box of provisions was in the trunk with the spare tire, and a green tent with poles was secured on top of the car. No complaints were tolerated, so we sang all the way to Valhalla. We were required to identify all the trees. It usually took us about a week to get there, depending on the weather. The most frightening part was crossing the rivers on a scow or ferry. When it rained, we usually got stuck in the muddy gumbo and had to get a local farmer to pull us out with a team of horses. At night we pitched the tent or found a cabin. Grandfather was always waiting for us with all sorts of uncles and aunts and cousins.

The summers in Valhalla are short but sunny, and the wheat and profusion of wildflowers grow so fast one can almost see and hear them stretching upward to the mighty canopy of blue. I have never beheld a lovelier landscape than those wide, sweeping slopes and large fields of grain taller than us kids. Far to the west, the purple outline of the Rocky Mountains was visible, dividing Alberta from British Columbia. At night the stars shine brilliantly and the northern lights wave across the sky in a prism of spectacular colors. Grandpa, who had learned his building skills in China, built two houses. The kids stayed in the two-story log cabin with the spooky attic full of Chinese treasures, while the adults re- laxed in a commodious, white stucco frame house. I thought it was the most beautiful "palace" I had ever seen, with Chinese carpets, a piano, upholstered Chesterfields, and a Ming Dynasty rosewood (*huanghua li*) dining table, with the Ronning name carved in Chinese characters on the back of the chairs. Grandpa's farm was self-sufficient. A generator supplied electricity for lights, and we had the rare luxury of running water and indoor bathrooms. The house was heated with a coal furnace in the basement. We had great fun taking saunas in his Finnish bathhouse with an iron stove, where we made steam by throwing water from the artesian well onto round, hot rocks. Behind the house was a forest in a sweet-smelling valley with a winding brook. We kids would pitch a tent and feel like explorers. Grandfather loved animals. He taught us to ride horses bareback. Alton, Meme, and I would all ride together on Lady, a swayback strawberry roan, to Uncle Ole's general store, where, with pretend money made from the silver paper of Wrigley's spearmint gum, we could buy candy. We helped to milk the cows. Every cow responded to her own name. One of them, Agnus, became the subject of many a Norse tale because she would kick the milk pail over until someone sang to her. At least that's how Grandpa taught us to sing the Norwegian national anthem. Both his large stucco house and the pioneer log cabin, the first one built in Valhalla, were later designated by Alberta as Provincial Heritage Sites. The Norse settlement he established in Valhalla Centre in the Peace River District is now a thriving hamlet.

During the Depression in 1932, Dad became as deeply concerned about the welfare of the Alberta farmers as he had been about the downtrodden peasants of China. He was nominated as a candidate of the Cooperative Commonwealth Federation (CCF), in a by-election for the Legislative Assembly of Alberta. Sylvia and Alton, then teenagers, were conscripted to plaster compelling photos of Dad on telephone poles with captions reading: "VOTE FOR CHESTER RONNING . . . A Man of the People."

Not long after he launched his campaign, Dad was told by a supporter that a very damaging whispering campaign about him was being circulated throughout the constituency and that if it wasn't countered, he had no chance of winning the election. "What part of my dark past has been discovered?" he asked. The supporter said: "They say you were born in China and that your mother was unable to give you milk, and that cow's milk was not available in China. The worst part is they say that since you were brought up on milk of a Chinese wet nurse, you must be partly Chinese." No election was going to make Chester deny his gratitude to the kind Chinese woman who had saved his life in infancy. "Well, according to that logic," he replied, "I might have absorbed some of the traditional Chinese wisdom of the great philosophers, which should make me the best possible representative of the Camrose constituency." His supporter looked puzzled. "Well, then," said Dad, "why don't we start a whispering campaign about my opponents?"

"What do you know about them?"

"I have it on fairly good authority that they were brought up on cow's milk, but I wouldn't go so far as to imply they are full of . . ."

He told that story implying the bovine upbringing of his opponents at every public meeting to appreciative audiences. He won that election. But, as Dad told us in all modesty, "I was thrown out on my ear in the next round. The electorate must have decided that I had not acquired the sagacity of the Chinese sages after all."

Our family life took on unexpected new directions after the outbreak of World War II. My brother Alton, despite Mom's expressed apprehension, joined the Royal Canadian Air Force, and at age seventeen he became the youngest pilot in the RCAF. Dad rejoined the air force as head of the RCAF Intelligence Discrimination Unit, and the family moved to Canada's capital city in Ottawa, Ontario. Employing Chester's understanding of Japanese and Chinese written characters in their cryptanalysis of Japanese communications, Chester's intelligence unit was able to intercept enemy military communications and gain vital information that helped Allied forces to mount effective strikes against the enemy throughout the Pacific combat zone.

His work was so secret that we never knew what Dad was doing until the war was over. Years later he told us his story. With tears in his eyes, he said: "I felt deep sorrow for the Japanese soldiers I had to kill. Working in Ottawa, I was able to pinpoint Japanese bases on Guam and other Pacific islands as targets for American and Canadian bombers."

When Dad retired from the RCAF, the Department of External Affairs asked him to join the diplomatic staff of the Canadian embassy in Chungking. My mother, looking back on the harsh life they had endured in China, was understandably reluctant to go back, although Dad assured her that life in the diplomatic service would be easier than life as teachers in a missionary school. Meme and I, as teenagers eager for adventure, were thrilled. We coerced Kjeryn and Harmon to side with us. By then, Sylvia, a teacher, and Alton, a wing commander and test pilot in the RCAF, were married and settled in their own homes. Mom finally yielded, and Dad informed the undersecretary of state that he would go on the condition that the family would join him and that he would be free to try it for one year before committing to a career in diplomacy. Chester could not anticipate that he and his family were heading back into China just as the country was plunging into one of the most violent political and military upheavals in its history, or that he would serve for another two decades in the diplomatic service, rising to become Canada's top ambassadorial expert on Asia and a major player in the international negotiations that would reshape the continent.

You do not understand the actual conditions here because you come from a totally different background.

—ZHOU ENLAI TO CANADIAN AMBASSADOR VICTOR ODLUM, 1945

Chester was assigned to Chungking with the senior rank of first secretary, under Ambassador Victor Odlum. The two of them, with the military attaché, Brigadier Bostock, made up the entire diplomatic staff of the newly established embassy.

In early November 1945, Chester left Ottawa for Chungking. Transportation from Ottawa to Chungking could only be provided by the armed services, and Chester was expected to make his own arrangements. He spent seventy hours in the air and fifteen days traveling a fifteen-thousand-mile route. From Montreal to Cairo he flew aboard an RCAF Liberator bomber, a five-day trip with stops in the Azores, Rabat, and Malta. After a week's delay in Egypt, he obtained passage on an Empire Flying Boat to Karachi. That trip took four days, with stops at the Dead Sea, Lake Habbaniyah and Basra in Iraq, Bahrain, and Fort Sharjah in what is now the United Arab Emirates. In Karachi he was treated like a maharaja as a guest of the prime minister of Sind before taking another Flying Boat to Calcutta, with stops at Rajahmundry and Allahabad. From Calcutta he flew in the same plane over the Himalayas, taking in a view of Mount Everest, to Kunming, the base of the Flying Tigers in Yunnan, China, where General Claire Chennault's fighters, bombers, and transports had engaged in operations against the Japanese. One of Chennault's small transports took him to Chungking, landing on the narrow, tricky airstrip of an island in the Yangtze River. He was then driven through the mountainous terrain to the embassy on Fairy Grotto Street by Lao Chu, the embassy chauffeur who had been a driver on the Burma Road, the wartime link from India to Free China.

Ambassador Odlum, a former army general, welcomed him at the door with a firm military handshake and a salute. The formidable walled-in embassy building was impressive, but the interior was not a pleasant surprise to Chester. Instead of living quarters with all the luxuries he had promised the family, he was escorted into an unheated bedroom without hot water. After bathing in four inches of warm water poured from two buckets into the large marble tub, he lay down on a rock-hard bed. He was jarred awake by the sound of a monkey gong, familiar from childhood days. The number-one boy, Liao, explained that the general had given strict orders to summon everyone to dinner twenty minutes before seven and that there would be another gong in five minutes. When Dad said that the gong was used only by monkey trainers, Liao replied, "We know that, but the ambassador doesn't, and he wouldn't believe it if I told him." Liao added that there would be a similar "monkey" warning before breakfast, served at seven sharp, and lunch, served at one. Chester, in cahoots with the servants, never enlightened the ambassador.

In the first of his circular letters to family members, Chester wrote: *The entire embassy staff, that is all three of us, sat down sharply at seven and Number One Boy served a splendid dinner. After dinner I congratulated the cook and retired to my room to watch the night life of Fairy Grotto. It was not long before I learned that the mud walls of the embassy had been penetrated by a complex system of tunnels with openings into every room. Chungking rats occupied the building and were in open competition with the human inhabitants for anything edible . . . including me.*

Growing up in a missionary family, Chester had acquired sensitivity to Chinese attitudes and culture that made him a highly effective and respected diplomat in China. In December 1945, eighteen years after he and his family had been forced to leave China by Nationalist military operations, Chester, in top hat and black tie and tails, ceremoniously presented his diplomatic credentials to the triumphant warlord, Generalissimo Chiang Kai-shek. Their meeting was cordial despite Chester's known reservations about Chiang's dictatorial rule. The following week he made the required diplomatic courtesy calls on leading Chinese figures, including the banker H. H. Kung, who had acquired an enormous fortune in questionable business deals by exploiting his family connections with the Chiang Kai-shek family.

On January 2, 1946, Chester wrote home: *I must tell you about my visit to the famous or notorious, H. H. Kung, depending on your point of view. He is the husband of one of Mme Chiang Kai-shek's sisters and finance minister. He lives in a palatial suburban mansion on top of one of Chungking's many miniature mountains. Lao Chu parked our car outside the gate, and I handed my card to the gate keeper. A young secretary accompanied me to a commodious house decorated with huge porcelain vases and beautiful Tientsin rugs. After excellent Lung-Ching tea I was escorted by two secretaries through the garden, where the dwarfed and twisted spring plum blossoms were in full bloom, filling the air with sweet fragrance. In the second residence, which was even more luxurious than the first, I was seated in the drawing room, where I was served scented tea . . . The room was done in blue with a cozy fireplace. A servant brought another brand of tea, which must have been "his tea." Dr. Kung came in dressed in a long satin fur-lined robe over which he wore a black satin Ma Kua, the old-fashioned wide-sleeved short jacket designed for equestrians.*

One could not help being impressed by this old-style Chinese gentleman. I could not dislike him, despite all the stories about his financial wheeling and dealing. In spite of his six years of American education at Oberlin and Yale he preferred to speak in Chinese. He had an amiable personality. Most of his conversation was an explanation of why he was no longer in the thick of things. He has been superseded by his ambitious brother-in-law Dr. T. V. Soong.

Old H. H. was truly a Chinese gentleman of the old order. Can China afford them today? I must agree with the communists—No! China must be modernized to end the misery, poverty, corruption and skullduggery suffered by the masses who sustained this luxury and culture for the wealthy, privileged few. China can no longer afford old H. H. Kungs! But the time may come again.

Shortly after his arrival, General George C. Marshall asked Chester to act as an advisor and interpreter in the peace talks between the Nationalists and Communists, which Marshall was mediating in Chiang Kai-shek's headquarters in an attempt to form a coalition government and avoid the renewal of the Civil War. In August 1937, a "United Front" agreement for joint action against the Japanese invaders, with Chiang Kai-shek in command, had been signed. This was at the time when Talbert was fleeing on his bicycle from the Japanese, whom, he observed, were engaged in battling Communist guerrillas who had infiltrated behind their lines. However, the United Front agreement broke down repeatedly in subsequent years with mutual recriminations. Mao Zedong accused Chiang of utilizing Communist troops for operations against the Japanese while reserving Nationalist forces to consolidate his own power. The final breakdown in the United Front came in January 1941 with the New Fourth Army incident. Chiang had ordered the Red Army's New Fourth Army to transfer from south of the Yangtze River to the northern shore. While the Communist troops were crossing the Yangtze River, they came under Nationalist attack. Most of the Communist troops were killed and the survivors disarmed. For the remainder of the war with Japan, the Communists stood their ground defiantly in the face of blockade by Nationalist troops. Full-scale civil war was renewed after Japan surrendered.

In Chungking, after months of meetings, Chester wrote that he had hopes for peace: *A "Committee of Three" consisting of three Generals, George Marshall as mediator on behalf of the United States, Chang Chih-chung for the Nationalists, and Zhou Enlai for the Communists, have reached an agreement on a cease-fire ending all hostilities. The Marshall Mission, working quietly and without the fanfare of Ambassador Hurley's efforts, appears to have been successful.*

The American ambassador, Patrick J. Hurley, an ardent supporter of Chiang Kai-shek, had made a futile solo effort at arranging a peace agreement. He traveled to Yan'an for talks with Mao Zedong, and after returning to Chungking for talks with Chiang, professed to have been tricked when his effort failed.

During the peace negotiations, Chester and Zhou Enlai became friendly and had numerous personal conversations in Chinese about conditions in China. Zhou related details of his 1927 escape from Shanghai after Chiang Kai-shek, scrapping his political alliance with the CCP, had engaged in a wholesale massacre of the Communists, who had been allied with the Nationalists in battling the warlords during the Northern Expedition. Zhou was able to join the scattered Communist forces in the field. He and Mao Zedong thereafter led the Long March to the Yan'an stronghold in mountainous Shaanxi. Zhou's left arm was paralyzed after he was thrown from his horse during the march, but otherwise he remained in vigorous condition. Zhou was amused when Chester told him how his brother Talbert had traveled around China on a bicycle dodging the Japanese. The two men developed an enduring friendship and a partnership in international negotiations that later helped to better relations between China and the Western nations. In the early 1970s, after he retired from the diplomatic service and was free to visit the People's Republic of China, Chester made three visits to China at Zhou's invitation and was one of the last foreigners to see the premier before his untimely death from cancer in 1976.

From Chungking, Chester kept the family informed regularly by letters sent out in the Canadian embassy's diplomatic bag.

Dearest Inga and children: Last night the Ambassador and I were dinner guests of Zhou Enlai and his brilliant wife, Deng Yingchao, who with her husband, had played a key role in the Long March. Listening to her talk one would never suspect that this cultivated, modest person could have endured the grueling hardships of the 1927 massacre that we witnessed in Shanghai and the terrible Long March which lasted a whole year.

We had a hai-shen, sea slug feast with t'ien-chi, paddie chicken [frogs' legs]. Zhou is a handsome man with a sculpturesque head and bushy black eyebrows. His pitch-black hair has a wave, which is very unusual in China. His argument is forceful and logical, his earnestness convincing, his enthusiasm contagious. He is completely unpretentious. In his conversation, he is direct and almost blunt. He said rightly to the Ambassador two or three times: "You do not understand the actual conditions here because you come from a totally different background."

Conditions in Chungking are pretty grim. Oh how it drizzles and fogs up! I have not caught even a glimpse of the sun so far. The people of China are changing their attitude and way of thinking. One senses an undercurrent which surfaces in the most unpredictable ways. The Chinese are desperately attempting to modernize against the tremendous momentum of the oldest traditions, which continue to swallow even the most ardent revolutionaries.

On April 18, Chester wrote: *General Marshall returned to Chungking after a visit to Washington for consultations with President Truman. The situation, especially in Manchuria, has deteriorated seriously during his absence. To Marshall's dismay he found that the truce agreement and cease-fire he had arranged in January was no longer in effect and fighting had resumed. The American journalists here have failed to communicate the real story that Chiang Kai-shek is losing popular support and that a communist victory is inevitable.*

In November, the peace negotiations collapsed, and Mao Zedong recalled Zhou Enlai to Yan'an. Chiang's Kuomintang Party (KMT) had reneged on an agreement reached earlier for a constitutional framework that would have provided for a degree of autonomy for the provinces, thus assuring the Communists continued political domination in the areas that they currently held. Chiang also refused to pull Nationalist troops back to the positions of January 13, 1946, specified under the terms of the cease-fire negotiated by Marshall. The breaking point had been the Nationalist seizure of Kalgan, a key Communist position in northwest China on the Communist supply corridor to their forces in Manchuria.

A further complication was the agreement negotiated by President Truman, under pressure from the China lobby in the United States, to sell war surplus material to the Nationalists at a fraction of their procurement price. The Communist leadership pointed to the agreement as proof of unilateral American support of the Nationalists. It was a disruption in Mao's relations with the United States that was not patched up until President Richard Nixon went to China in 1972. Earlier, Mao had voiced publicly his hopes for an understanding with the United States, saying that he was ready to form a coalition government since China must have a long period of peace to rebuild the economy. He was looking for trade and economic assistance from the United States. A *White Paper* reviewing the Chungking negotiations published later by the State Department commented: "With respect to the United States military aid programs, General Marshall was placed in the untenable position of mediating on the one hand between two Chinese groups while on the other hand the United States government was continuing to supply arms and ammunition to one of the groups, namely the Nationalist Government."

With the end of peace negotiations, the Generalissimo had decided to move his capital back to Nanking and called upon all the diplomatic missions to follow his government. Chester remained in Chungking to pack up the embassy equipment for transport down the Yangtze River to Nanking. He used the time to collect Chinese antiques and socialize with old friends. One was the so-called Christian General who had witnessed the massacre of the missionaries during the Boxer Uprising before he was converted.

April 30. . . . A few nights ago I had a most interesting experience. I was the only foreigner invited to a farewell dinner given in honor of the famous "Christian General," Feng Yuxiang, whom, you will remember we met in Peking in 1923. He remembered me and said that when he learned I was in Chungking he had asked our host to invite me. He is about to leave for the US to study water conservancy and hydroelectric projects to start similar projects on the Yellow River. Cynics say that he has more experience with water than anyone else in China, having baptized thousands upon thousands of his troops using fire-hoses to ensure total immersion. When Feng talks, everyone listens. He speaks simply and directly in the common language without ostentation. I remember him as a most colorful character since the day I first met him at the Nan Yuan parade grounds just south of Peking.

It did not take me long to realize that all the guests were anti–Chiang Kai-shek. They were of the opinion that Chiang feared that General Marshall would insist upon a Presidential election if a coalition was established. It was speculated that the Christian Generalissimo Chiang was getting the Christian General Feng out of China because he knew Feng would win. Hence the pretext of sending him to study water in the US.

In May 1946, Chester made arrangements to travel with the Christian General to Nanking on the same river steamer. Chester went to Chungking's river port to inspect the vessel, the SS *Ming Pen*. The ship had been sunk by a single Japanese bomb the previous year, but was said to have been repaired, floated, and ready for inspection. Chester was accompanied by an agent of the Ming Sung Company, which had built the ship. He was astonished when he saw the vessel, whose bow seemed to be reaching for the sky while her stern hung low in the water. Dad asked how passengers could be safeguarded from sliding down the deck and piling up at the stern. The man replied that twelve locomotives would be loaded on board to level the ship in the water. The Christian General's adjutant felt he could not let his boss risk the Yangtze rapids in such a contraption. Ronning, however, felt he had no choice as Canada was building ships for the Ming Sung Company, and he could hardly show a lack of confidence in the firm. The ambassador remained in Chungking while Chester left to establish a Canadian embassy in Nanking.

Aboard the tilted ship, Chester sailed from Chungking down the Yangtze through the then untamed Three Great Gorges: *The Yangtze churned and boiled, plunged and twisted. The turbulent waters shook the patched up* Ming Pen *as we raced headlong towards dreaded Wind Box Gorge which, as the Chinese say, was cut through the mountains by a furious blast of wind from the nostrils of wizard Wu Tzu, and is kept open by the "eternal wind." As we hurtled downstream through the 3000-foot-high solid cliffs, the gorge rapidly narrowed to a slit through which we could barely see the sky. We seemed trapped, heading for a crash into the sheer rock that closed the passage. A jangle of bells urged the pilot to make "full steam astern" and the speed was miraculously checked.*

Chester spent the next month buying embassy land for Canada in Nanking.

February 26. . . . During the past month I have done more negotiating than necessary to get an international treaty ready to sign—with the result we now have a house for us and one for our Chancery. Last night I was a guest of the famous General Ho Ying-ch'in, who is head of the Nationalist Army. He is more feared than anyone in China except the Generalissimo. The night before I dined with the Mayor of Nanking. The food was superb, the mayor being Cantonese. In China everyone knows that "for food there is no better place under Heaven than Canton."

As chargé d'affaires, with Military Attaché Brigadier Bostok at his side, Chester proudly raised the Canadian flag on the grounds of the Canadian embassy.

March 7, 1946. . . . The Canadian flag flies in Nanking. It was raised for the first time today in the hope it would stand for friendly relations between China and Canada. The pole man put on a worthy exhibition. Pausing half-way up, he hung by his feet and one hand while tapping his chest with the other and gasped for breath. Finally he threaded the pulley and with the rope in his teeth made an astonishingly rapid descent. As he was about to collect his fee, who should appear but his wife. She pocketed the fee and departed.

Chester was soon to see firsthand that suspected Communists were still being hunted and that punishments in China had not changed since his father, Halvor, had witnessed their cruelty in Imperial times. In March, an American named Douglas Dakota had crashed on a rock ridge near the top of Purple Mountain, and the crew of four Americans, who were slated to be sent home, had been killed instantly. Chester went with some American pilots to view the remains of the aircraft: *The plane had exploded and was scattered all over the top of the mountain. Only the tail remained as a mute marker of the tragedy.* Not far from the site of the plane was a small block house. Chester climbed on top to get a better view and noticed a small hole in the roof. Looking down, he saw the face of a tortured man looking up at him. To his great astonishment, he saw four Chinese with their hands tied behind their backs with barbed wire that cut into their swollen flesh. The men stood in complete silence. Chester immediately found some Chinese guards and demanded the meaning of this cruel treatment.

One guard informed me that two Red Army spies had been trying to destroy the wireless installations on the mountain top. "But you have four people in there," I said. He replied, "Yes, you see one of the two got away, and we took his relatives from a village in the valley." I asked if they had destroyed much equipment. The answer was, "No, we caught one before they did any damage." I asked if they had had a trial. The guard said, "No, not before we get the one who ran away." When I protested, the guards walked off. There was nothing I could do to stop the insanity. CHINA IS A POLICE STATE.

Nanking is known as one of the three "furnaces of China," the others being Chungking and Canton. In August, the foreigners and wealthy Chinese would go to Kuling on the Lu Shan Mountain to escape the intolerable heat of the plain. When Ambassador Odlum returned, he and Chester were invited to spend ten days as guests of Generalissimo and Madame Chiang Kai-shek in their spacious villa on Kuling. The other guests, in another villa, were General George and Mrs. Marshall.

August 22. . . . The Ambassador and I flew to Kiukiang where we were met by the Generalissimo's brand-new private car . . . a fifteen-mile drive through villages at the foot of the mountain brought us to the end of the road where sedan chairs with four bearers each were waiting. After tea we climbed 3,500 feet to the rim of the mountain before reaching the mountain pass which is Kuling. The author of Lost Horizon *must have gotten his inspiration from Kuling, as no place could be more like the original Shangri-la. It is enchanting. In the evening light, it has an air of mystery. Luxurious vegetation, splendid trees, rushing mountain torrents, rocks and caves, summer cottages of stone, and Gothic churches make Kuling a wonderful resort. Clouds touched the top of the mountain. We were escorted to the house assigned to us.*

At five the next afternoon we were taken to the main reception room. The Gen-

eralissimo was in uniform. He stood to greet us and shake hands. He has a pleasant winning smile. He looked young and alert but seemed definitely nervous. When he listens to what is being said, he keeps up a continuous "Hm, hm, hm, ha, ha, ha, hah."

Suddenly Mme Chiang walked in followed by a beautiful Alsatian dog. We stood up. The Generalissimo was called away and she took his place, the conversation continuing in English. She is a very impressive woman. She speaks English with an Eastern American accent. When the Generalissimo returned, she acted as interpreter, speaking to him with a Shanghai accent although her Mandarin is perfect. She is quite bitter about the Communists, and her eyes flashed as she denounced them. Her handsome dog lay at her feet, it was obvious that she loved dogs . . . Every evening we were all dinner guests, usually in the garden, where the food was prepared in an outdoor oven. When the Generalissimo found out I had been a cowboy in Canada, he offered me his white Arab horse to ride. He said the horse needed the exercise. I happily accepted.

Chester and Mme. Chiang became quite friendly. She talked about how much she missed her friends in America, where she had attended Wellesley College. One of her best friends had been Iphigene Ochs (later Mrs. Arthur Sulzberger), whose father founded the *New York Times*. Mme. Chiang had recently been on a fund-raising trip to the United States and told Chester of her concern about the unjust criticism incurred because on an overnight visit to the White House she had brought her own silk sheets. She said that she brought the sheets not because American sheets weren't good enough, but because she was allergic to the soap they were washed in. On one occasion she came to Chester's villa in a state of great distress. She tearfully confided to him that she had quarreled with her husband and he had lost his temper and shot her dog. She quoted the Tang dynasty poet Du Mu: "To kill the rider, shoot his horse." Chester was sworn to secrecy and never mentioned it again. It was a sad end to the mountain vacation.

When Chester returned to Nanking, he found that he had to report a critical worsening of conditions to the Canadian government. Fighting had intensified in the Civil War, particularly in Manchuria, and a crisis had developed in relations between the Communists and the United States, reducing any gains that General Marshall had been able to bring about. In personal letters home, Chester wrote:

August 30. The US has sold $100 million worth of war surplus equipment to Chiang at bargain prices . . . [T]he Communists issued a statement bitterly attacking the American policy of supporting the Nationalists and interfering in the internal affairs of China . . . Communist strength continues to grow in Manchuria.

October 30. My Dearest Inga: General Odlum has returned to Canada and I am in charge of the Embassy as Chargé d'Affaires once again. It has been so lonely here. I am longing to see you and the children and am anxiously awaiting your arrival in Shanghai next month.

39

Chester's Family Arrives in War-Torn Nanking

Over Chungshan swept a storm, headlong
Our mighty army, a million strong, has crossed the Great River.
The City, a tiger crouching, a dragon curling, outshines its ancient glories.
In heroic triumph heaven and earth have been overturned.
With power and to spare we must pursue the tottering foe.
And not ape Hsiang Yu the conqueror seeking idle fame . . .
—MAO ZEDONG, APRIL 1949

Culture Shock

In December 1946, while my father, as chargé d'affaires, was establishing the first Canadian embassy in Chiang Kai-shek's capital of Nanking, I was sailing to China with my mother, sisters Meme and Kjeryn, and brother Harmon on a converted troopship, the SS *Marine Lynx*. I was eighteen and had just graduated with my nineteen-year-old sister, Meme, from Camrose Lutheran College. Meme and I were like twins and shared everything. We had heard so much about the arrival of my grandparents and parents that when we docked in Shanghai we both experienced déjà vu. We went through a similar hassle with ragged coolies fighting to carry our baggage. I began to understand the culture shock that my grandmother, who had celebrated her twentieth birthday while crossing the Pacific on the SS *Oceanic*, must have experienced on arrival in China. The only visible change in the scene was that the giant portrait of Queen Victoria on the clock tower of the Customs Building had been replaced by one of Generalissimo Chiang Kai-shek.

On January 3, 1947, from the Canadian embassy in Nanking, I wrote the first of many letters to my sister and brother still in Canada.

Dear Sylvia and Alton:

Well, here I am in China at last, I can hardly believe it. Hey, Alton, you were right! It looks just like Grandpa's attic! The Marine Lynx *sailed from San Francisco trailed by thousands of colored streamers flying in the wind. They played "Sentimental Jour-*

ney" over the loudspeaker, and Meme and I sang along as we sailed under the Golden Gate. When the sun was setting the Pacific looked calm, but it did not last long. That night we were awakened by a choppy sea. The Captain said there was an earthquake in Japan. On Christmas day the ocean was a mass of huge swells and he warned that we were on the edge of a typhoon. Mass panic. All portholes were battened down. The ship rocked, rolled, pitched and trembled. We put on life jackets and hung onto the sides of the double-decker berths originally installed for accommodating troops and listened to the waves thundering over the top deck. Dishes, baggage, chairs and people were falling all over the place. I didn't get seasick but I can't say that for the rest of the family. We were two days late arriving in Shanghai.

When the sun came up on Dec. 31st our whole family was standing on the deck of our battered battleship as we sailed up through the murky yellow waters of the Whangpoo River. It looked just like Grandpa said it would. We were surrounded by all types of Chinese junks with patched sails and sampans dangerously overloaded with people and animals. Dad was the first to come on board. Oh how good it was to see him again. Mom almost cried. He gave us all big hugs. He looked as strong and handsome as ever, only his wavy brown hair was touched with gray. What a reception we got in Shanghai. WOW! Everyone had come to welcome us, of course. A horde of coolies came running up with their rickshaws. While Dad was trying to keep us all together, a sneaky fellow grabbed Kjeryn's shoulder bag and ran off. Harmon spotted him and yelled "Stop thief!" Dad raced after him followed by the whole family. When he saw the tribe of foreign devils racing after him, he threw the bag in the air and disappeared into the crowds of onlookers, who were howling with laughter.

We loaded into pedicabs and dodged through the heavy traffic towards the Cathay Hotel. There is quite an anti-American feeling here now. All over the buildings in Shanghai we saw posters in English reading: "G.I.'s go back where you came from." "Go away you monsters." "We want the rapid withdrawal of all American forces." When we arrived at the Cathay Hotel Dad doled out a mere 6,000 Chinese yuan to each coolie. You should have seen Harmon's face. I miss you. Love Audrey

We were as appalled by the poverty on the streets as we were amazed by the luxury of the hotel. We were transported into a totally different world. Crystal chandeliers lit the long red-carpeted corridors. There were more bowing servants in white gowns than guests. It was New Year's Eve 1946. We celebrated our reunion with a twelve-course Chinese feast replete with caviar and champagne.

January 15, 1947
Hi Sylvia:

Here we are in Nanking. I can't believe it!

On New Year's Day we boarded an overnight train to Nanking. The station in

Shanghai was crammed with more people than have ever been seen in Camrose. They stood goggle-eyed staring at us. Harmon had the time of his life making funny faces and showing off, as usual. When we got in the train, the people stood gaping outside the windows at Harmon. I guess he thought it was his duty to amuse them so he proceeded to go through all sorts of contortions. They thought he was a big joke. I guess he was the best show on the road.

We traveled with wealthy Chinese in a special first-class compartment with sleeping berths and an adjoining dining room. The only other passenger accommodations were third-class cars packed with Chinese who slept sitting up on wooden benches and ate hard-boiled eggs and noodles. There is no second-class in China. Only the haves and have-nots. On the way we passed many villages consisting of small adobe or straw huts. Goats, fat black pigs, donkeys and chickens wandered in the front yards. The Chinese children ride the long-horned water-buffalo to herd the ducks. On the train Meme, trying to be polite, offered a Chinese man a stick of gum. He looked at it curiously for a while, then chewed it a bit and swallowed it. He must have thought that foreigners ate funny food.

In Nanking, Col. Bostock, the Canadian Military Attaché, met us at the station. We pushed our way thru the people, a troop of soldiers were sleeping out on the platform and inside the floor and tables were covered with sleeping people. We piled into the flashy Embassy car flying a Canadian flag and drove through the streets crowded with people pulling loaded wagons along with horses and ox-carts and cars. We stopped at a high stone wall topped with barbed-wire and cut glass. Our chauffeur, Lao Dru, honked the horn three times and two servants opened the iron gate to a large stone mansion. Two more servants in white gowns and smiling faces lit firecrackers to chase away the evil spirits. The house has large spacious rooms furnished with stuffed furniture and rosewood tables but the beds are really hard. One side of the house is all glass doors, upstairs and down, leading out to a terrace with a bird bath and a large garden with a swing and slide for the kids. Service is great here. I think all you lazy people would really enjoy it. There's the 1st boy, 2nd boy, the amah, cook, the gardener and chauffeur and two guards. I don't know if they are to keep us in or keep the thieves out. Dad gave Meme and me some silk brocade to make suitable dresses for diplomatic receptions, Kjeryn got a teapot and four cups edged with gold gilt, and Harmon got a hunting dog. I guess it'll take Meme and me a while to fit into diplomatic circles. 1st boy Lao is teaching us Chinese manners.

Dad had done his best to make the old stone mansion livable. It was beautifully furnished but was so cold in winter that we slept in our fur coats longing for our small cozy home in Camrose. The house had been occupied by a Japanese general during the monstrous Rape of Nanking in late 1937 and 1938. Nanking in its entirety bore no resemblance to any working capital city. Large sections were still in shambles, scarred when the Japanese stormed the city in December 1937. Streets were jammed with refugees from the north, where Civil War battles were raging. Many lived in makeshift shelters put together from scraps of cardboard boxes and corrugated tin left over from the construction of barracks for the Joint U.S. Military Advisory Group (JUSMAG), sent to China to train Chiang Kai-shek's troops to fight the Communists. Nanking was encircled by twenty-seven miles of high, wide walls built with monster bricks in the form of a medieval fortress. On our first Sunday, Dad took the family for a walk along the top of the city wall to show us the area where, back in 1927, he had helped rescue the foreigners escaping over the wall from the attacking Nationalist troops. It was not a pleasant outing. When Meme and I peered over the edge of the wall, we were shocked to see the bodies of two dead babies lying below. There was nothing we could do. It was too late. I thought of the devotion and courage of my grandmother, who had rescued infant girls and raised them in her orphanage. She was right in saying her work was but "a thimble in the ocean." Now, a half century later, female infanticide was still being practiced.

Dear Sylvia: We're lucky to have a little heat in our house, most of the houses don't have any at all. In fact we are lucky to have a house. Nanking is on the banks of the Yangtze River. Thousands live in makeshift houses. Whole families live in rows and rows of straw hovels no bigger than barrels. The ragged, filthy little children go around in the cold weather with no shoes, picking anything they can find for firewood and food. Some of the conditions are horrible; I can't begin to tell you. Most of the people living in such places are refugees or ones that couldn't get their homes back after the war. The Japanese too occupied their houses and when the Chinese army drove out the Japs, they occupied the houses leaving thousands homeless. Some became beggars, many are old sick persons. At least the missionaries tried to do something for the poor Chinese but the diplomats can do nothing but talk. The American Military keeps sending arms to Chiang Kai-shek's Nationalist forces against the advice of most diplomats, including Dad.

Once settled, Kjeryn and Harmon attended the Anglo-American school for children of diplomats, and Meme and I took part-time work with the JUSMAG in China. We rode to military headquarters in a Women's Army Corps (WAC) bus. I became a newscaster and disk jockey for the American Armed Forces Radio Station and attended Nanking University. I was the only foreigner in the school choir. I rode to school in a rickshaw pulled by a strong young fellow named Liu, who became my friend and self-appointed bodyguard.

Almost every morning on the way to school I pass corpses lying on the road, some covered with straw or sacking, of refugees who have starved or frozen to death during the night. No Chinese dares to take the responsibility of disposing of the dead for fear they will be obliged, in keeping with Chinese tradition, to pay for the burial. The bodies are left to be tossed into garbage carts pulled by the hated Japanese prisoners of war wearing green uniforms and white gauze masks. My loyal rickshaw puller shoos off the beggars who harass me. I am just as distressed by the deplorable conditions of horses, donkeys, stray dogs and other animals suffering from lack of food and the cruel treatment. The Chinese are cruel to animals. It breaks my heart. They beat their donkeys without mercy and sell their chickens alive. They treat each other cruelly too. The beggars in filthy clothes have sores all over them. Old and feeble rickshaw men, eyes watering, stand in the streets in the bitter cold, wearing torn clothing, feet wrapped in rags. The rich careen along the roads in luxury cars, honking at the starving refugees and fleeing animals.

One day Meme and I went outside the West Gate and met a woman selling colored stones in water which she called "Live Rocks." She said they could give birth to other stones. So we bought two. Now we have six. What do you think of that?

Nanking University

My fellow students at Nanking University were mostly sons and daughters of elite Nationalist officials who were deeply concerned about the well-being of their country. Many felt frustrated and trapped between the extremist right-wing dictatorship of Chiang Kai-shek and the Communist totalitarianism of Mao Zedong. They angrily opposed American intervention in the Civil War in support of Chiang Kai-shek, who advocated democracy for China but acted like a military dictator and refused to negotiate with the Communists to stop the fighting. Student leaders were urging the students to demonstrate against the government. After classes at Nanking University, my rickshaw boy pulled me to the Armed Forces Radio Station at American military headquarters to broadcast the latest news and play popular music on request for the American GIs.

Nanking, March 1947

Dear Sylvia: In spite of an order from Chiang Kai-shek, my fellow students in Nanking University staged a demonstration. It is rumored that the Generalissimo was so enraged at this disregard of his personal warning that he was ready to order the troops to use machine guns on the students but was persuaded by Premier Chang Chun not to take the drastic action.

Meme and I were coming home from work in the big army bus when we ran into the demonstration and couldn't go any farther. To us it appeared that the students had a large percentage of merchants and other people behind them. Crowds were hand-clapping on the sidewalks. The students were quite prepared for brutality on the part of the police and they had Red Cross Squads and even a truck with stretchers, but this truck was not allowed through by the police. When we were stopped, we could see the truckloads of students and students walking behind carrying banners and cheering; they were also distributing leaflets to the crowd. I recognized and waved to some of my fellow students and wanted to join them but the bus driver, a burly American army sergeant, cursed me and locked the door. A student handed him a pamphlet through the window. It was an extract, in Chinese, from a Chinese poem first published in the Yenching University News in Peking which showed the attitude of the students. Dad translated it for me when we got home.

> *Speaking of Democracy*
>
> *Life is bitter; life is cruel*
> *Take a look at China and the "people's rule."*
> *THEY Say:*
> *You plow the fields in heat and rain,*
> *I build the barns and reap the grain*
> *You place the brick and lay the tile*
> *But I move in and live in style*
> *All the young and strong must conscripts be*
> *To shoulder guns and fight for ME.*
> *You thick-skinned workers, rough and green*
> *Are nothing but a "live machine"*
> *I skin you and eat you*
> *I strip you and beat you*
> *And if my orders you resist*
> *You are a god-dam Communist!*

When the parade started from Nanking University, armed policemen tried to stop the students but they broke through the police cordon. When they reached the middle part of the city, on Kuo Fu Lu, where we met them on their way to the People's Political Council to protest the war, they were met by the police and gen-darmes armed with sticks, stones and bayonets. Armed Cavalry soldiers on horses were standing ready too. We could easily see that there would be trouble and we had been warned to stay away from demonstrations, so the driver took a detour home. The next day we heard the reports that a number of students were killed or injured. The Garrison Commander has "outlawed" student processions and the secret police are arresting any who talk "opposition" to the government. About 50 students have been arrested in midnight raids so far. Yesterday as I was leaving class for home three car-loads of garrison troops tried to break into the university by the front gates which were defended by the students. At last the gendarmes broke through the back fence and charged the campus. We avoided what might have been a serious clash by sitting down quietly and starting a sing-song. We sang for an hour while the troops cooled their heels. I was in good voice and the only foreign student singing along, so I made many good friends.

What I didn't know was that some of my friendships would last a lifetime.

My professor of historiography at Nanking University was Dr. M. Searle Bates, a distinguished historian with an aura of deep sadness about him. I soon found out why. He was one of the few foreigners, among them Tillman Durdin of the *New York Times* and A. T. Steele of the *Chicago Daily News*, who had actually witnessed the Japanese atrocities during the Rape of Nanking. More than one hundred thousand captured Chinese soldiers and civilians—some estimates are far higher—had been slaughtered. Many thousands of women were raped or otherwise violated by the Japanese soldiers. Dr. Bates had circulated a letter written on Christmas Eve 1937 detailing the story of the crime and horror perpetrated by the Japanese troops in Nanking. I found it secreted in a brown envelope in my father's desk. Dr. Bates wrote of the Japanese: *This is such a story as seems to be almost unbelievable, a story of the degradations of a horde of degraded criminals of incredible bestiality, who have been, and now are, working their will unrestrained on a peaceful, kindly, law-abiding people.*

In a preface to his letter, he said: *What I am about to relate is anything but a pleasant story. I cannot recommend anyone without a strong stomach to read it . . . I cannot rest until I have told it, and unfortunately, I am one of the very few who are in a position to tell it.* He concluded with a question and an expression of hope. *What of the future? The future is anything but bright, but the Chinese have an unsurpassed capacity for suffering and endurance, besides their many other good qualities and right must triumph in the end.*

The letter had been written ten years before I came upon it. But the shock of the Japanese atrocities he described is too deep to write about. The aftermath of the war still hung over Nanking like a black cloud. We felt our house was haunted. Iron gates sealed each stairway. The Japanese general who had lived there likely installed them to guard against assassination attempts. The rattle of machine-gun fire from a Nationalist army training ground nearby was a constant reminder of the immense tragedy that had befallen the city.

Hi Sylvia and Alton:

We had a bit of excitement last night. There is a Chinese Nationalist army camp right across the street from our walled-in mansion. We hear them marching and shooting every day but lately they've been doing a lot of extra practice at night. We hear rumors about Communists in the vicinity. We know they are getting closer. Well, about 1:30 this morning we heard some explosions and bangs and numerous smaller shots like strings of firecrackers. When you're half-asleep you imagine all sorts of things. I thought the Communists had come and were attacking the camp. Dad came in our room and said they were probably shooting at looters. Then, from the window, we saw a red blaze in the sky. WOW! There was a rip-roaring fire across the street. A large building was up in flames; it was a store room for small-arm ammunition. The soldiers were screaming. Dad ordered the servants to get out the fire hose in case the matting we had around our house to keep the sun off caught fire. We all went out to watch the blaze except Meme. She just covered her head and slept through the whole thing.

The people for blocks around came running in a weird array of night attire. The ammunition building exploded and burned to the ground and the fire began to spread our way. But just in the nick of time, the American fire engines came hooting down the street, sending people flying all over. They finally got the fire under control. When there was no more danger of it spreading, what should come clanging down the street but the Chinese fire engines, with their cow bells ringing, whizzing along at about five miles an hour. The firemen were yelling like mad for the people to get out of the way, when all the time the latecomers were streaking past them. I have never heard such a racket in all my life . . . WOW!! Kjeryn and I laughed so hard Dad had to scold us. He said the excitement was over and herded us back to bed with strict orders to go back to sleep. After a while I felt I might be missing something so I sneaked down to look over our iron gate—and who should I see in my place, but Pop. Ha! When I got upstairs Meme turned over and grunted, "What the dickens are you doing out of bed?"

Boredom was never a problem in Nanking. In the evenings, our family and other diplomats would attend lavish embassy National Day celebrations and government receptions. The receptions were sometimes hosted by the Generalissimo himself in his splendid uniform with rows of medals and the beautiful Madame Chiang Kai-shek wearing stunning embroidered brocade robes with sleeves large enough to tuck her white Pekinese dog in. Few talked openly about the military reverses the Nationalists were suffering and the advance of the Communists toward the city. Dad alluded to the scene as "Nero fiddling while Rome burns."

Meme and I often attended formal diplomatic parties. One evening, after dancing in our pink chiffon gowns at the Siamese Ball with such diplomats as Count Jean de Lipkovsky, a charming third secretary at the French embassy, Meme and I were offered a ride home by a Nationalist government official in his limousine. The streets were crowded with refugees, some of whom had green mouths from eating grass. I exclaimed to the official: "Oh, it must be terrible for you to see the suffering of your people." He replied haughtily, "What people? We don't consider them people!" It was enough to convince me that revolution was inevitable.

Shortly before we arrived in Nanking, Dad closed a land purchase for the Canadian embassy. It was a fine site on high land where four prefabricated lumber houses imported from Canada were to be constructed; one for the Chancery, three for staff residences, plus brick buildings for servant quarters. After six months in the Chinese haunted stone house, we were delighted to move into a wooden Canadian house, complete with a tennis court and swimming pool. During the building, it was found that the site had once been a cemetery, necessitating the removal of some four hundred old and long-forgotten graves.

Top Arrives in Nanking

We had just moved into our new embassy home when something happened that would change my world. At a dinner party given by the American military attaché in the JUSMAG's officers' club, I met Seymour Topping, a young correspondent of the International News Service who had recently been transferred to Nanking from a base in Peking from which he had covered the Civil War in North China and Manchuria for six months. He had arrived in Peking in September 1946, at the age of twenty-six, still wearing the uniform of an army captain, to take up a job as a foreign correspondent covering the Civil War. How could he foresee that he was destined to marry me and become a member of the Ronning family? Topping was on a troopship bound for Leyte in the Philippines when the atomic bombs were dropped on Japan. Then an infantry lieutenant, he celebrated with his fellow infantrymen aboard the SS *Letitia Lykes*. The infantrymen onboard had been earmarked for a possible invasion of Japan. Hiroshima relieved doubts of their own survival if they had landed on the shores of Japan.

At the end of the war, after service in the Philippines, he flew to Peking, fulfilling a long-held dream of becoming a correspondent in China. In his memoir, *On the Front Lines of the Cold War,* he writes: "Within days of my arrival, decked out in an ill-fitting pinstriped suit with massive shoulder pads made by the Chinese tailor, I was swapping gossip with other correspondents at the bar of the elegant Peking Club and lunching with sources in the diplomatic community."

When not reporting on the battlefields, Top, as friends called him from childhood days, took Mandarin lessons at the same Peking Language School that General Joseph Stilwell and my parents had attended forty-four years earlier. He developed a working knowledge of the language. While in Peking, he had already undertaken extraordinary assignments for a young reporter. He had flown to Kalgan in North China to interview General Fu Tso-yi, a top Nationalist general who had just captured the Communist-held city. The conquest had dealt a severe blow to the Communists, who were still holding peace talks involving my father and Zhou Enlai in Chungking. After accepting the surrender of the city by the Japanese occupiers in 1945, the Communists had transformed Kalgan into a major communications center and established a fine university. In taking the city, the Nationalists had partially blocked the vital corridor to Communist-held areas in Manchuria. General Fu welcomed Top and put on a show with a ride past his famed cavalry units, which were mounted on the same type of rugged Mongolian ponies that the dreaded Mongol hordes of Genghis Khan had ridden in the conquests of Asia and Eastern Europe. The use of these Mongolian ponies in the drive on Kalgan may have been the last time in history that mounted cavalry was employed in a major military operation.

In November 1946, Top flew to Mao's headquarters in the caves of Yan'an, where he met with top Communist leaders, including General Zhu De and Liu Shaoqi, who ranked just after Mao in the leadership hierarchy. One evening at dinner with Zhu De, the army chief, Top was told about the collapse of the Chungking peace talks, which Chester had been monitoring. He also heard bitter complaints about President Truman's sale of surplus war goods to the Nationalists.

After our first meeting in Nanking at the officers' club, we danced the evening away. The next morning a coolie arrived with a rickshaw full of red roses and a scribbled note from Top asking me for a date. How could I refuse? It was the beginning of a passionate, whirlwind courtship. Meme and Mother let me know that among my suitors, Top was their favorite. The fact that he was Jewish and I was Lutheran was noted but never became an issue. Top soon became a family favorite and was invited to join us playing Chinese checkers. He even kept his cool when I asked him to shake hands with my pet monkey. Dad soon became one of Top's important sources. In spite of our busy lives, we managed to enjoy all the romantic places in Nanking: boating on Lotus Lake, picnicking near Murphy's Pagoda, strolling by the ancient elephants on the Sacred Way to the first Ming Tomb, and climbing the one thousand steps to Sun Yat-sen's mausoleum. We were madly in love and captivated by China. One evening as we sipped white wine on top of Purple Mountain overlooking Sun Yat-sen's blue and white mausoleum, Top offered me a diamond engagement ring. Sixty-three years later, I am still wearing it.

About the same time, Meme had fallen in love with a handsome American naval officer, David Westlein, and they were married by the last American ambassador in Nationalist China, Dr. Leighton Stuart. One of the guests at Meme's wedding was Admiral Olds, the same gunboat captain who had rescued the Ronning family in 1927 when Meme was five months old. My younger sister Kjeryn and I were bridesmaids, wearing shimmering silver brocade. Our gowns and Meme's spectacular wedding dress were created by Madame Chiang Kai-shek's tailor, whom she had graciously offered. I thought Meme was the most beautiful bride in the world. It was a huge event attended by Nationalist leaders, the full diplomatic corps, and journalists, including *New York Times* correspondent Hank Lieberman with his fiancé, Ambassador Stuart's secretary, Kay Martin. Some of the guests, like the bride, had also survived the Nanking Massacre. It was the first time I saw my father cry.

Inflation

I continued my work at the American Armed Forces Radio Station, but as a Canadian I was classified as a local and paid in Chinese yuan rather than U.S. dollars. I thus understood firsthand the frustration of the Chinese as they saw their money devaluing by the minute. Savings stashed away by Chinese had become virtually worthless. On payday I would take my paycheck and a large suitcase to the Chinese bank to be filled with stacks of million-dollar bills recently printed in the Central Reserve Bank of China, adorned with a picture of Sun Yat-sen and marked $1,000,000. Then, feeling like a tycoon, I would run to the American Bank across the street to exchange my millions for about US $80 to $90, depending on how fast I could run. By August 19, 1948, the official exchange rate had rocketed to US $1 for 12 million Chinese yuan. In December, the government, in a frantic effort to stabilize the economy, issued permits to purchase gold bars for a fraction of the black-market rate. The banks became jammed with frenzied citizens desperate to buy the gold before their holdings of paper currency became worthless. In the mad stampede that ensued, dozens of people were crushed to death. Armed gendarmes finally cordoned off the banks. The people soon learned that the offer to sell the bars was phony: The great bulk of the gold reserve together with priceless ancient relics gathered from the museums throughout China and loaded on 108 ships had already been transferred to Formosa (Taiwan), where Chiang Kai-shek intended to take refuge with his government. The new "gold yuan" was plummeting, and the Chinese people were being fleeced again.

Evacuation

As Communist troops advanced on Nanking, an evacuation of dependents of foreign diplomats began. Dad, then minister-counselor of the embassy, was asked by External Affairs to remain in Nanking as chargé d'affaires. To pacify Mom, he agreed to stay on the condition that he would later be posted as ambassador to Norway. Top remained to cover the fall of the capital to the Communists but planned to meet me in Canada soon. On the morning of November 23, 1948, I was evacuated with my mother, Harmon, and Kjeryn in an Australian Air Force transport to Japan. Meme and her husband, David, had already left for South Africa, where David joined the Naval Attaché Office. A week before the Canadian dependents were evacuated, eight hundred American officers and enlisted men had been ordered to withdraw overnight by the Joint Chiefs of Staff in Washington because they believed the American military advisors could no longer serve a useful purpose and that Nanking would soon be in Communist hands. Upon leaving, in a statement on his relations with Chiang Kai-shek, the Nationalist supreme commander, General David Barr, stated: "No battle has been lost since my arrival due to the lack of ammunition or equipment. Their military debacles in my opinion can all be attributed to the world's worst leadership."

We went to Japan, where we took a train that passed by the ghastly remains of bombed-out Hiroshima to Tokyo. A month later, we sailed from Yokohama, enduring another stormy Christmas on a Norwegian freighter en route to Vancouver. I continued my education at the University of British Columbia (UBC).

We had arrived in Canada at a time when McCarthyism was taking hold in the United States. At UBC, my professor of Chinese history, an American citizen, was one of those who had fled to Canada after being accused of being pro-Communist and then being dismissed from the University of California. The unrestrained fear of communism had spread to Canada and was evident on the campus. I soon learned that many people only hear what they want to hear. When I told Canadian students and others who asked about conditions in China that Mao Zedong's Communist armies were obviously winning the Civil War, some looked at me suspiciously and labeled me a "Pinko." I eagerly awaited the promised reunion with Top. I soon received word of Top in a strange way.

Top Covers the Decisive Battle of the Huai-Hai

In December 1948, one of the largest battles in history, involving more than a million troops, was about to take place on the vast Huaipei Plain north of Nanking. Top was determined to become the first Western reporter with the Communist armies as they advanced on Nanking. With a pocket full of silver dollars given to him by Chester, Top traveled north on a Nationalist troop train to Pengpu on the Huai River. On New Year's Day, he crossed the Nationalist lines and made his way northward on foot toward the battle area, but he was intercepted by Communist guerrillas. He was moved by stages on foot and horseback to Communist headquarters and confined under guard in a wooden hut. What transpired thereafter is told in the prologue he wrote for his memoir:

> The artillery thundered through the night but now at dawn fell silent. It was January 7, 1949. I lay awake beneath the cotton blanket atop the sacks of grain in the Chinese peasant hut listening, wondering what the silence portended. Then I groped in the darkness toward the doorway but retreated when I came face to face with a soldier, his carbine leveled. I was a prisoner of the People's Liberation Army (PLA), held in a hut near the battlefield where 130,000 of Chiang Kai-shek's troops were encircled by 300,000 of Mao Zedong's forces. I would soon learn that the abrupt halt in the gunfire meant that the trapped Nationalists had surrendered. It was the end of the Battle of the Huai-Hai. In running engagements across the frozen Huaipei Plain of Central China, Chiang Kai-shek had in sixty-five days lost more than a half million of his troops. Mao Zedong's triumph in the decades-long Civil War had thus become a certainty.
>
> A correspondent for the Associated Press, I had ventured across the Nationalist front lines into the no-man's-land of the Huaipei Plain bent on reaching Mao's headquarters, to seek an interview and cover the ad-

vance of his armies on Nanking, Chiang Kai-shek's capital. Intercepted by Communist guerrillas, I was led on foot and horseback to the hut on the edge of the battlefield, put under guard, my typewriter and camera confiscated. On that morning when the gunfire ceased, the Communist political commissar who had interrogated me upon my arrival two days earlier reentered the hut. "We ask you to return," he said. "The horses are outside the door." When I protested, demanding to know the outcome of my request for an interview with Mao Zedong, the commissar shook his head impatiently and stalked out. I paced the hut and in frustration beat my fist against a stack of grain stalks. So, Mao would not receive me. The victor was no longer talking to Americans.

That was the defining moment for me in the tumultuous years of 1946–80 when I covered the East-West struggle in Asia and Eastern Europe. Mao's victory in the Battle of the Huai-Hai marked the onset of an era in which East Asia would be engulfed in war, revolution, and genocide. Tens of millions would die in China, Korea, Indochina, and Indonesia in wars, political purges, and sectarian violence. The United States would suffer in the region its worst military and political defeats.

In the meantime, shortly after Christmas, I was walking with a friend on a rainy night in Vancouver when I noticed a wet *Vancouver Sun* lying on the sidewalk with a headline about China with a byline by Seymour Topping. I picked it up and noticed a box on the front page: "Perhaps the loneliest man in the world this Christmas is Associated Press correspondent Seymour Topping, who is in a Jesuit Monastery behind Communist lines in China." It was by Harold Milks, the AP man in Nanking who had spoken to Top on the single telephone line out of Pengpu before he crossed the lines and had written the dispatch.

The Communist advance reached the banks of the Yangtze River opposite Nanking in the early morning of April 23, 1949. Top was awakened in the AP compound by explosions on the Nanking waterfront. He jumped into his open army jeep and drove to the river port, which was ablaze with torched buildings and exploding fuel dumps. The Nationalist garrison had abandoned the city, and the municipal police had fled with them. Thousands of Nationalist soldiers and refugees fleeing south filled the streets. The Judicial Yuan was in flames. Top picked up Bill Kuan of Agence France-Presse, his close colleague, and they drove toward the Northwest Gate hoping to meet the Communist troops. Top later wrote:

It was 3:20 A.M. Suddenly, I heard a shout in Chinese of "halt," and I stopped. From shrubbery on the sides of the boulevard, two soldiers with rifles aimed at us converged on the jeep. "Who are you and what are you doing?" one of the soldiers said, beaming a flashlight on us. Kuan replied: "I am a correspondent of the French news agency, and he is from the American Associated Press." Shining his flashlight on my face and examining me intently, the soldier exclaimed: "American, American!" Then he said: "Do you know who we are? We are the soldiers of the People's Liberation Army." They were men of Chen Yi's army, the point on the first column into Nanking. We were about a mile and a half from the Northwest Gate. The soldiers asked us to follow and led us to an infantry officer leading a column of troops into the city. The soldiers, sweating under full packs and carrying heavy weapons, looked exhausted . . . The infantry officer questioned Kuan and me and then impatiently ordered us back into the city. Gratefully, I drove quickly back up Chungshan Road past the burning Judicial Yuan to the telegraph office, where Kuan and I flipped a coin to determine who would file first. Kuan won and sent a three-word flash: "Reds Take Nanking." My own tightly written sixty-five-word dispatch followed. Immediately after the transmission of my bulletin, Communist troops severed the cable landline between Nanking and Shanghai. When Kuan's dispatch reached the Agence France-Presse desk in Paris, the editors waited for additional details, which did not come until morning when the radio transmission resumed. The delay denied Kuan a world beat and bestowed it on me. My own dispatch went out immediately on the AP wires.

At daybreak Top picked up my father at the Canadian embassy and drove with him to the Northwest Gate. Chester later wrote in his memoir: *Top came early to pick me up. He had been chasing around all night reporting the news, while I had been watching the spectacular artillery duel north of the river from the top of the Canadian Embassy residence. We rushed off in his jeep, anxious to see the triumphant entry. Top and I stood on that memorable day just inside the Northwest Gate watching thousands of battle-weary Communist troops in their padded yellow uniforms and flat peaked caps marching into the city. They sat down in orderly lines on their bed rolls along the sidewalks, with rifles tilted over their shoulders and singing revolutionary songs. People brought them tea. Nationalist army stragglers passed by unmolested.*

What we saw was not the triumphant entry of a conquering army with fanfare and firecrackers that had characterized the entry into Nanking a century ago, of an army of angry and ignorant peasants of the Taiping Rebellion, fired by visions of a "kingdom of heavenly peace." The peasants in the army we saw were literate and disciplined. They had come not to rule and exploit like the war lords but to liberate the people from China's ancient, multitudinous evils and the never-ending cruelty of man's inhumanity to man. This was most unconventional in China's armies.

On October 1, 1949, Mao Zedong stood atop the Gate of Heavenly Peace in Peking to announce the establishment of the People's Republic of China and reestablished Peking as the capital. After the departure of American Ambassador Stuart from Nanking earlier in August, the former capital shriveled as a news center. The Nationalists then announced that they would relax the coastal blockade to permit the wartime troop transport the *General W. H. Gordon* to pick up foreigners in Shanghai. Top later recalled how the Shanghai customs officials who had worked under the Nationalists passed him through whispering friendly remarks: "A Communist officer watching over the proceedings saw that I was declaring books. He stuck a hand into my trunk and came up with the grass woven paperback copy of Mao Zedong's *On Coalition Government*. . . . . 'Where did you get this?' the Communist exclaimed in Chinese. 'In Yenan in 1946,' I replied. The officer looked at me intently, ordered my trunk closed, and waved me and my baggage past the guards without further formalities."

Top came to Canada, and I turned in my books. Unlike Meme's lavish wedding in Nanking, we had a simple ceremony in my sister Sylvia's home in Camrose. I had impulsively bought a beautiful bridal gown for sixty dollars from a shop window in Vancouver, and it happened to fit perfectly. Kjeryn looked gorgeous in the same bridesmaid's dress that I had worn at Meme's wedding. Harmon was the ring bearer. Mom was upset because shortly before graduating from UBC, I was running off with the "Wandering Jew," as she laughingly called Top. However, she rose to the occasion and gave us a lovely reception with red wine for us and red grape juice for the Lutheran teetotaler Reverend Vinge, who, to our amusement, took the wrong glass.

Dad could not attend the wedding. He remained in Nanking for another two years. After the Communist occupation, Chester became the doyen of the diplomatic corp. Communist officials had decided to speak to the diplomats only in Chinese, and Chester was the only one among the foreign envoys who spoke the language fluently and had the essential background in Chinese affairs. During this period, he became one of the foremost advocates of Western diplomatic recognition of the People's Republic of China. The stand he took was never forgotten by Zhou Enlai and other officials of the new government. Chester saw an opportunity to influence the policies of the Maoist regime through the prompt opening of diplomatic relations. When Canada decided in June 1950 to enter into diplomatic relations, Chester was designated the first Canadian ambassador to the People's Republic. However, with the eruption of the Korean War later that month, Ottawa scrubbed the plan and instructed Chester to close the embassy. He returned to Canada to head the Far Eastern Division of the Department of External Affairs. Later, Ottawa honored the promise they had once made on the condition that he stay on in China, and my mother's wish came true: Chester served as the Canadian ambassador to Norway and Iceland, then as high commissioner to India, Ceylon, and Nepal. He wouldn't return to China for twenty years. On April 21, 1971, he accepted a long-standing invitation from Premier Zhou Enlai, and I accompanied him back to the People's Republic of China.

40

Audrey and Top

If you love me as I love you
We'll play the game and win it too.
—RUDYARD KIPLING, "AN OLD SONG"

Seventeen years would pass before Top and I would return to mainland China. Yet in the interim, as journalists covering the Cold War, we remained directly involved or in close touch with the tumultuous events there. I offer glimpses here of what transpired in those intervening years in the life of a journalist family traveling a turbulent world and of the extraordinary turn of events when Chester, on behalf of the American and Canadian governments, undertook secret negotiations aimed at ending the American war in Vietnam.

After our marriage in Camrose in November 1949, we flew to New York, where Top's family held a fancy reception for us before we flew to Hong Kong. The AP had assigned Top to open a bureau in Peking, but when the Maoist government barred all American correspondents from entering China, we stayed on in Hong Kong. Top reported on the Communist advances on the mainland as they mopped up the remaining Nationalist strongholds in the west and south. He was the last correspondent to visit Hainan Island off the South China coast just before the Communists in a fleet of junks landed and overran it, leaving only Formosa in Nationalist hands.

With no China visas in view, we flew to Saigon (today's Ho Chi Minh City) in February 1950, where Top was slated to spend a month reporting on the French Indochina War. But after President Truman initiated direct American involvement in the Indochina War by pledging aid to the French colonial military forces, our stay stretched to two years. Top opened the AP bureau and became the first American correspondent to be stationed in Indochina. Our first child, Susan, was born in a French military hospital. As I was being wheeled into a delivery room where wounded French soldiers were treated, I could hear gunfire. French artillery was covering an outpost under attack by Ho Chi Minh's Viet Minh guerrillas.

Assignment to London followed, where for the next four years Top covered the diplomatic beat and the 1954 Geneva Conference on Indochina and Korea. Two more daughters, Karen and Lesley, were born two years apart in Queen Mary's Nursing Home on Hampstead Heath. I also had a front seat at the spectacular coronation of Queen Elizabeth II. I studied sculpture at the Slade School of Art and used my toddlers as models. I was delighted when two of my terracotta portraits of children were exhibited at the Royal Institute Gallery.

All our children seemed fated to grow up amid the tensions of the Cold War. In 1956, we were assigned to divided, isolated West Berlin, where a fourth daughter, Robin, was born in an American military hospital. The city was divided into sectors and then threatened by Soviet Premier Nikita Khrushchev, who was seeking to oust the United States, Britain, and France from their sectors in the city. Susan and Karen entered first grade at the Anglo-American school. From the window they could see tanks of the American garrison rolling by to respond to Soviet pressures on the city's lifeline routes to West Germany. The school was guarded by American sentries with rifles slung over their shoulders. After the first day of school, Karen refused to return, crying, "Mom, if I am a bad girl, the soldiers will shoot me!" She felt more secure after I introduced her to a friendly American soldier.

During home leave in 1959, Top left the AP for the *New York Times*. After a year in New York, Top was assigned to Moscow as bureau chief for the *Times*. We lived in the Soviet Union for three years, 1960 to 1963.

In Moscow, we were in close touch with developments in China. Shortly after our arrival, one of the most momentous developments in world politics began to unfold. On June 12, an editorial in *Pravda*, the official newspaper of the Soviet Communist Party, denounced unidentified "revisionists and sectarians." It was the first hint in the Soviet press of the veiled ideological polemics in progress between Moscow and Peking. They were harbingers of a dispute between Russia and China whose implications would alter the balance of power in the world. The Western nations would no longer be dealing with a monolithic Communist bloc. By 1969, the Sino-Soviet split brought on clashes on the Siberian border between Soviet and Chinese troops. The Soviets withdrew all support of the Chinese Communists. Fearing a Soviet nuclear strike, the Chinese initiated construction of a nationwide system of air-raid shelters. When Chester and I visited China in 1971, we saw widespread evidence of these shelters, even in the rice paddies. Zhou Enlai informed us that all of China could go underground in five minutes. Mao Zedong eventually reached out for new foreign support by mending relations with the United States as embodied in the Shanghai Communiqué entered into during President Nixon's historic journey to China in 1972.

On November 23, 1960, Top was astounded when his story of the Sino-Soviet split was passed unmarked through the green curtain masking the Soviet censorship bureau in Moscow's cable office. The Russians had decided for the first time to allow the ideological dispute to be made public. The next morning the story led the front page of the *Times*.

I began working as a freelance photojournalist, but my toughest job was to feed our four children. The next big story was when Yuri Gagarin became the first cosmonaut to blast into space in a 10,395-pound spacecraft named *Vostok* (East) *I*. The first official word of the flight came over Moscow Radio: "Russia has successfully launched a man into space!" That afternoon I was standing with the children on Prospect Mira (Peace Street) in a long queue of women waiting to buy potatoes and onions when two planes flew low, dropping pamphlets. They extolled the superiority of Russian technology and claimed proof that there was no heaven because Gagarin had looked into space and commented, "I don't see any God up here." At that time, religion was forbidden in the Soviet Union, but skepticism was written on the faces of the babushkas who picked up the leaflets.

When the next cosmonaut, Gherman S. Titov, made a safe landing after orbiting the earth seventeen times, I was standing in line again. This was not unusual because, unlike the American diplomats, who could buy food in the American commissary, journalists lived off the Russian economy. I had six mouths to feed, and fresh food was very scarce in this land of superior technology. This time the pamphlets claimed that Titov had spent twenty-five hours and seventeen minutes searching the heavens in *Vostok II*, again without seeing God. There was an audible grumbling among the shoppers while they wrapped up their groceries in the antireligious proclamations and stuffed them in their homemade string bags.

The next man to orbit the earth was the American John Glenn. Once again I was standing in queue with the neighborhood ladies, but there were no pamphlets to distract us from socializing. I told them about John Glenn. They looked doubtful until I added, "Guess what? He saw God." This caused a great deal of hilarity as they passed the message along and pushed me to the head of the line.

The Russian censors had forbidden foreign photographers to take pictures without special permission, but during our hours of waiting in line, the women let me take photos freely while the police turned their backs. I was able to publish sixteen illustrated stories (four covers) about life in Russia in the *New York Times Magazine*. The ladies also helped me practice my Russian and tried not to let me know they thought I was pretty stupid because my children aged two, four, six, and nine spoke it better than I did. Susan and Karen were among the first American children to attend Russian schools and after the first year were soon talking like their Russian classmates.

Five years later, when we had settled in Scarsdale, New York, Susan and Karen attended Scarsdale High School and Susan wrote this article for the *New York Times:*

January 11, 1967. During our academic lives my sister Karen and I have attended schools in London, West Berlin, Moscow, Hong Kong, Taiwan and Bonn. Now we are attending school in our own country. Each school has been an adventure in itself . . . When I told my best friend in America that I was leaving for Russia, she comfortably informed me that that Russians cut foreigners' heads off. Being 9 years old I believed her and consequently lived a life of terror until I actually met some Russians. When my sister and I finally entered the Russian school, I realized the only way my head was going to fall would be from working too hard.

In 1962, during the Cuban missile crisis, we, like the Muscovites, lived in fear of an exchange of missiles between our two countries. On November 7, the forty-fifth anniversary of the Bolshevik Revolution, we were invited with diplomats and other correspondents to a reception in the Kremlin's Georgian Hall soon after the Cuban missile crisis had effectively ended with an agreement between Khrushchev and President Kennedy. While reaching for more caviar, I found myself across the food-laden table from Premier Nikita Khrushchev downing vodka with his deputy Leonid Brezhnev. Khrushchev smiled and raised his glass, "Nasdrovia" (your health). Although journalists had been told to surrender their cameras at the door, I pulled my hidden Leica M2 out of my evening bag and focused on him. He waved away the converging KGB agents and kept smiling. I got my pictures. The Soviet premier then beckoned Top and me to his side of the table and told us how relieved he was and that we had been "dangerously close" to a thermonuclear war. The Russians and Americans continued the conciliatory celebration with toasts to American President Kennedy and Soviet Premier Khrushchev, who, at the last minute, had decided to remove the missiles. Next day my portraits of Khrushchev appeared on the front page of the *New York Times.* My male competitors were not pleased.

Chester's Secret Mission to Hanoi

From 1963 to 1966, we were assigned to Hong Kong, where Top served as chief correspondent for Southeast Asia, devoting most of his time to covering the

Vietnam War. Top and I had been living in Hong Kong for three years when, in February 1966, my father, then a vigorous seventy-one, paid us an unexpected visit. Canadian Prime Minister Lester Pearson had recalled him from retirement to undertake a secret mission, code-named "Small-Bridge," to Hanoi, the capital of North Vietnam. He had retired only several months earlier as high commissioner to India, where as a close friend of both Prime Minister Pandit Nehru of India and China's Premier Zhou Enlai, he had been a key intermediary in defusing the dispute between China and India over rival claims to the border territory of Aksai Chin. Chester's mission was to visit Hanoi to explore what was needed to bring the United States and North Vietnam into negotiations for an end to the Vietnam War. He carried a letter from Lester Pearson to President Ho Chi Minh urging peace talks.

En route to North Vietnam, he visited us in Hong Kong, where we were living in a high-rise apartment building overlooking Repulse Bay with the four children, three cats, and Charlie, a white Australian cockatoo that I had rescued, for eighty Hong Kong dollars, from a cruel peddler on Cat Street. Charlie, like most parrots, was an accomplished mimic and had learned to swear in Chinese like the peddler who had been abusing him. The parrot was soon calling us all by name and acting like a member of the family. When Dad walked into our home, he was startled to hear Charlie screech the Chinese insult, "*Ni wangba dan!*" (You turtle's egg!). Dad and Charlie soon became best of friends. Before the day was out he was calling Dad "Grandpaw" just like the other children and perching on Dad's head to let him know who was at the top of the pecking order in our house. It occurred to me that Charlie and Chester had much in common: For example, Chinese was their first language. Both threw themselves with gusto and enthusiasm into whatever they did—from cracking nuts to negotiating problems of state. They thrived on excitement and shared a basic philosophy of life. When I asked Dad what was his secret of longevity, he replied, "Participation in life!" Obviously Charlie agreed with this.

A severe typhoon struck the day before Dad was to fly to Hanoi via Vientiane, the capital of Laos, on his mission. Mudslides wiped out hundreds of homes and killed hundreds of Chinese in the Wanchai District of Hong Kong. The roads to Kai Tak airstrip, a ribbon reclaimed from the sea that jutted into the middle of Fragrant Harbor, were blocked. By late afternoon, the debris had been cleared, but the *New York Times*'s car had disappeared in a landslide. However, our loyal cook, Chin, drove Chester to the airport in his old Volvo. Dad arrived at Hanoi in time and entered immediately into four days of talks with Premier Pham Van Dong and other leaders. He returned elated to Ottawa, believing he had achieved a breakthrough and found a basis for negotiation. The North Vietnamese had dropped a number of preconditions for talks and insisted on only one: The United States must immediately and unconditionally halt all bombing of North Vietnam.

In June 1966, en route back to Hanoi bearing an American reply to the North Vietnamese terms for negotiation, Dad stopped over again in Hong Kong. The moment he entered our apartment, Charlie yelled, "Hello, Grandpaw!" Dad did not share with us the contents of the American reply, but he seemed disappointed. The bombing of North Vietnam had not stopped.

The day after he left for North Vietnam, I was unexpectedly granted a visa to the People's Republic of China. Since American correspondents were being denied visas, I had applied as a Canadian housewife without stating in my application that I had lived in Nationalist China and that my husband was an American journalist. I quietly lined up a freelance assignment with the New York Times and became one of the first Western journalists to venture into China on the eve of the historic Cultural Revolution.

Looking somewhat worried and a bit envious, Top kissed me good-bye at the train station in Kowloon. Draped in cameras, I boarded the British "Nine Dragon Train" that snaked through the New Territories to Lo Wu on the Chinese border. Then, with some trepidation, I walked alone, carrying my cameras, across the bridge over the Sham Chun River to China. Red flags were flying in the wind. Two soldiers with bayoneted rifles slung over their shoulders escorted me down a covered walk hung with portraits of Mao Zedong and huge posters hailing socialism and denouncing American imperialism. A grim-looking official met me and asked if I had any precious stones, books, opium, lottery tickets, or live pigeons (which, I assumed, he thought I might use to send out messages). Then he thumbed through my Canadian passport, which contained four visas to Taiwan. He scowled. Didn't I know it was enemy territory? In my rusty Chinese, I explained that Taiwan was not Canada's enemy and that I had visited two of my children who were attending school there. He disappeared, and I assumed my trip was over. But then he returned with a red wax crayon and deftly struck out the Taiwan visas. Take that, Taiwan! Then a woman customs inspector asked, "How many rolls of film?"

"About sixty."

"You are only allowed thirty-six." She walked away and returned with an elderly gentleman who spoke English. He asked why I needed so much film.

This is it, I thought. They know I'm a journalist. I forced a smile. "China is such a beautiful country," I said. "I want to take photos to show my children." I waited for the unmasking.

"Any sons?"

"Yes, one. His name is Charlie."

He smiled. "You will have to pay 10 yuan each for the extra rolls."

I tried to look as miserable as possible. "Well, I don't need them that much."

"As a special favor we will let you take them all. Welcome to the People's Republic of China." Then to the accompaniment of "The Song of the Mother-land" blaring from loudspeakers, I boarded a punctual, spotlessly clean train and continued my journey. Patriotic music blasted through the train compartment until, applying a little trick I had picked up in the Soviet Union, I found a button hidden under the tea table and switched it off.

As I looked out on the picturesque countryside, I reflected on my odd circumstances. Here I was in Mao's China; daughters Susan and Karen were in Chiang Kai-shek's Taiwan; my father was in North Vietnam; and my husband was in South Vietnam covering the war. Lesley and Robin were enjoying British amenities in Hong Kong. In Canton, I was joined by a pleasant English-speaking guide, a Miss Lu, and we continued on a seventeen-day journey to coastal cities. In Nanking, where I had lived for two years, a handsome young Chinese met me at the train station and asked if I recognized him. I did.

It was Teng Chi, a former classmate and member of the choir at Nanking University. He was the son of a Nationalist official, but, like many students of elite families, he had turned to the Communists. Teng offered to meet me secretly and show me around Nanking but asked me not to tell Miss Lu or other officials. At the Metropole Hotel, I was given an hour's briefing by city officials, who assured me that China was in fine shape and told me they were building a bridge over the Yangtze River according to Mao Zedong's theory of dialectical materialism. I requested a visit to the university, but they refused.

One day, I slipped out to join Teng Chi when Miss Lu was napping after lunch. Driving around, I hardly recognized Nanking. The city had been cleaned up. Millions of planted trees, mostly Lombardy poplars, had brought down the temperature, and there were no beggars or opium addicts on the streets. We drove to our old Canadian embassy compound and knocked on the gate. The sullen gatekeeper refused to open up until I insisted that it was my house and that I was the daughter of Ronning Lao Fuzi. He smiled and escorted us around while asking about Dad. I was disappointed to find our house and grounds in sad disrepair. Teng and I drove to our old haunts and climbed the belltower overlooking the Nanking University campus, which was strangely empty. I later learned that Guang Yaming, the rector, had been purged because of his "ignoble and villainous conspiracy to suppress the revolutionary movement of the university." Teng warned me that militant antiforeign Red Guards unleashed by a Cultural Revolution were demonstrating in the streets. He urged me to return to Hong Kong rather than take the train to Peking. If I had known that a violent upheaval of historic proportions was under way, I might have turned back.

Meanwhile, back in Hong Kong, studying Chinese media and Allied intelligence reports, Top reported that what had been dubbed the Cultural Revolution was essentially a power struggle. Mao had denounced Liu Shaoqi, the chief of state, and Deng Xiaoping, the Communist Party general secretary. At an earlier Central Committee meeting, Mao's power had been reduced in response to his failed economic policies, such as the Great Leap Forward, which had cost the lives of millions of peasants. Mao was now seeking to regain power. His wife, Jiang Qing, was leading the ideological counteroffensive, which she called the Cultural Revolution, with the help of Shanghai radicals later dubbed the Gang of Four. Mao had called upon university students to demonstrate as Red Guards and smash his opponents' party cells throughout the country.

On arrival in Peking, I found the city in pandemonium. The streets were crowded with demonstrators wearing the red armbands of the Red Guards, marching, banging drums and gongs, fists in the air as they shouted slogans calling for elimination of old habits, customs, culture, and ideas, which Lin Biao, Mao's deputy, had characterized as the "Four Olds," along with "decadent Western influence." I checked into the Peking Hotel, just east of the Forbidden City, opposite Tiananmen Square, and asked for a front room with a balcony, not mentioning that I wanted to photograph the scene below. The street was no place for a tall blonde. I was given a small room in the back.

In the Peking Hotel I learned the importance of connections in China. Assuming that the hotel phones were tapped, I decided to phone my father in Hanoi, hoping it might influence the managers. I knew that the best hotel in Hanoi was the Metropole, so from a phone in the hallway I asked the hotel operator to connect me. Fortunately, the operator at the Metropole spoke English. I asked to speak to Ambassador Chester Ronning. She said he had just left. "This is his daughter in Peking," I said. "My father is there on a special mission, so please call your leader, Uncle Ho Chi Minh, and ask him where Chester Ronning is."

"Yes, madam. I will call you back in fifteen minutes."

Fifteen minutes later I was called to the phone. She had located Dad in conference. He was as amazed as I was that I had found him. I told him I was in
Peking, and he said he couldn't talk now but would see me in Hong Kong. He
asked only one question: "How is Charlie doing? Say hello from Grandpaw."

The Chinese must have thought this was a secret code. I had just returned to
my room when there was a knock on the door and an extremely polite attendant
was pleased to inform me that a front room had become available. He escorted
me to a spacious room with a view from the balcony. I had a unique photo opportunity to shoot the chaos on Chang'an Boulevard. The next morning Miss Lu
and I visited the Great Wall. Red flags were flying over the parapets and armed
soldiers were marching alongtop of the monumental construction that stretches
like the backbone of a dragon some 3,800 miles across the vast expanse of northern China. I was the only tourist.

The next day my guide abandoned me, and I found myself stranded in riotous
Peking. My dilemma was solved by a remarkable coincidence. One evening I
heard a louder than usual commotion and looked over the balcony to see hundreds of students running up Chang'an. Like most journalists in search of a story,
my curiosity overcame good sense; I grabbed my camera and followed them to a
side street called Taichichang. We headed toward a massive Russian-style building with floodlights illuminating huge portraits of Mao, Lenin, Stalin, and Marx.
It was the Communist Party headquarters, and several officials in gray Mao suits
were standing on the steps shouting slogans and urging the young Red Guards
to sweep away the "Four Olds." They were shouting back "Long Live Chairman
Mao" with upraised fists. I climbed up on the first rung of a wrought-iron fence
to take photos. When I stepped down I was surrounded by hostile students. I
couldn't get away; my back was already against the wall. Two of them, shouting
curses, tried to grab my camera, which I refused to surrender. At that point I
heard a voice shouting, "Audrey! Audrey!" I looked across the street and saw, on
the steps of the International Club, an old friend from my Nanking days: Colonel
Jacques Guillermaz, the French military attaché. He yelled, "Audrey! Audrey,
run!" While the Red Guards were staring at the foreigner on the adjacent steps,
I ran to the safe side. I threw my arms around Jacques and cried, "Oh Jacques !
A million thanks! What are you doing here?" "Audrey," said Jacques, taking off
his monocle and raising his heavy eyebrows, "don't you think I should be the one
asking you that question?"

After drinks at the International Club, I asked Jacques if he would send out my film in the French diplomatic bag since the Chinese did not know I was a journalist for the *New York Times* and might confiscate my film. "Audrey," said Jacques with a sigh, "the Chinese know exactly who you are and what you are doing. You are not hard to follow in China. You don't exactly blend in with the scenery, *n'est pas?*"

With the help of the colonel, I managed to get passage on a plane south to Canton, where I boarded a train for Hong Kong. The train was filled with free-riding and dangerously exuberant Red Guards. It was impossible to keep a low profile. I was soon the center of attention. Many wanted to practice their English. When they learned my middle name was Ronning, it evoked high hilarity. "Aiya!" one yelled. "We have an American Ronning dog of Imperialism." I laughed and waved my Canadian passport, shouting in Chinese: "I am a Canadian." At the border, the customs officers were so eager to get rid of me that they never asked about my film. I had arrived the day before all hell broke loose in China and the bamboo curtain was slammed shut once again. China was closed to foreign journalists while the Cultural Revolution raged on for another five years (and continued underground for still another five). My illustrated article was published as a cover story of the *New York Times Magazine* with the title "Through Darkest Red China."

In the meantime, as my father was returning from his second visit to Hanoi in June, Top, who was in Vientiane covering the war in Laos, arranged to meet Chester in Bangkok on his way back to Ottawa. At a secluded table in the balcony restaurant of the Oriental Hotel, Chester related to Top for the first time the details of the "Small-Bridge" secret mission. When Chester returned from his first trip to Hanoi with the offer to negotiate an end to the war if the United States stopped the bombing of North Vietnam unconditionally, President Johnson rejected it and stipulated that there would be no halt unless Hanoi reciprocated by terminating its assistance to the National Liberation Front in South Vietnam. Specifically, the United States was demanding that the North Vietnamese desist from supplying the Vietcong with weapons and fighters. Chester returned to Hanoi convinced that the North Vietnamese would not agree to this counterproposal, and he was not surprised when the North Vietnamese flatly rejected it. Chester's only gain was Hanoi's agreement to keep a channel open. Upon arrival in Ottawa, he informed Washington of Hanoi's position and almost immediately, the U.S. Air Force carried out a previously planned massive air strike on oil depots in the Hanoi-Haiphong area. The bombing continued intermittently for two years until President Johnson finally accepted terms similar to those that Chester had brought back from Hanoi. During that interval, tens of thousands of American and Vietnamese were killed in the war.

Return to the New China

In 1971, prior to the visit of Henry Kissinger to China to prepare for the arrival of President Nixon in 1972, Chester accepted the long-standing invitation from Zhou Enlai to visit China, and sister Sylvia and I jumped at the chance to accompany him. We flew to Shanghai. The familiar portrait of Mao Zedong had replaced Chiang Kai-shek on the clock tower of the Customs Building on the Bund, and its bronze bells, once chiming like London's Big Ben, now rang out "The East Is Red" every half hour. Everyone seemed to be carrying the "Little Red Book" of Mao's quotations.

The biggest visual change in Peking was the tragic disappearance of the historic city wall, which had been torn down during the Cultural Revolution and its bricks used to build houses. Only a few of the towering monumental city gates remained. We were escorted proudly to view the new subway, whose palatial underground stations had been constructed beneath the old city wall. It was free, and people were riding around for the fun of it.

On May Day, Premier Zhou Enlai invited us to dinner in the Great Hall of the People. When our car arrived, he was waiting outside, looking strikingly handsome in his neat gray tunic suit bearing a small Mao button reading "Serve the People." As the old friends embraced, Zhou said, "Chester, I will never forget what you did for me in Geneva." He was referring to an incident that happened in April 1954 at the Geneva Conference at which, following the defeat of the French colonialists in Indochina, Vietnam was divided.

At the opening reception, Chester, as head of the Canadian delegation, entered the ceremonial hall directly behind U.S. Secretary of State John Foster Dulles (who, incidentally, like Chester, was the son of a Protestant minister). Zhou Enlai, his counterpart in the Chinese delegation, happened to be standing near the entrance to the hall. The United States and China had not yet established diplomatic relations, and there was no contact between the two delegations. Nevertheless, Zhou courteously extended his hand in greeting. As other delegates looked on, Dulles ignored Zhou's outstretched hand and strode away. Shocked, Chester hastened forward, grasped Zhou's hand and greeted him warmly in Chinese, thus mitigating the insult and the loss of face. Zhou never forgave the Dulles snub, nor did he forget Chester's compensating gesture.

While the premier and Dad sipped tea and chatted, I sat transfixed by this man who at seventy-two years of age was governing China under Mao's general direction and was an active leader in world politics. I also marveled that this charming man of delicate features had survived the torturous Long March that brought the hard-pressed Red Army to safe haven in Yan'an. After dinner, Dad stood on a rostrum atop the Gate of Heavenly Peace with Chairman Mao Zedong and Zhou Enlai to view a fantastic fireworks display. Sylvia and I, enthralled, sat on benches below the Gate. Dad said afterward that the sight of hundreds of thousands of people gathered in Tiananmen Square imparted to him a sense of a new people's power. The Chinese Communists later spoke to us of the power of what they called "collective positive thinking." As an example, they told us that on one day during the building of the Yangtze River Bridge at Nanking, fifty thousand soldiers and civilian "volunteers" pitched in to assist the six thousand regular bridge workers in completion of the construction.

In New York, Top, then assistant managing editor at the *New York Times*, had applied at the Chinese consulate for a visa but received no reply. Then one day came a magical call from the consulate informing him that a visa was waiting. After the May Day celebration, Dad had asked Premier Zhou if he would grant a visa to his son-in-law, and Zhou readily agreed, though he did not say when we might expect Top's visa.

For the next month Dad, Sylvia, and I traveled by train, car, and boat on a seven-thousand-mile guided tour of China. The highlight of the trip was a visit to Fancheng, where my grandparents Halvor and Hannah had their mission and where Dad was born. From Hankou we took a train, and, looking out the window, Dad observed: "The walls and watch-towers are gone. In the old days the villages were clusters of mud huts. Every village had a tower as a look-out for robbers and looting soldiers."

We were met at Fancheng by hundreds of "old friends" and curious residents who had heard on the radio that the Ronnings were coming back. It had been fifty-four years since my parents' departure, but the white marble tombstones of Grandmother Hannah and Great-Aunt Thea were still standing on the grounds of the school Halvor had founded.

At the suggestion of Zhou Enlai, we also visited the historic garden city of Hangzhou. We soon found that this world-renowned statesman was a romantic at heart. The trappings of Old Cathay had survived almost untouched in Hangzhou. It had been a resort for the emperors for centuries and was still described by Chinese as "a paradise on earth." We were guests in a luxury hotel beside West

Lake. The deep-blue waters were dotted with moon bridges and pavilions. There was a Song Dynasty garden named Park of Orioles Singing in the Willows, a monastery known as Souls Retreat, Cave of the Morning Mist and Sunset Glow, the Pavilion of Calm Lake, and Autumn Moon. These were fantasies that Zhou wanted us to experience. The usual propaganda posters and martial music were absent.

On May 21, 1971, my birthday, a new guide, Yu Zhangjing, came to us in a state of excitement and asked Dad and me to come with him. But why? He just smiled. We drove to the airport, where a plane had just landed with a single passenger. To my surprise, it was Top. Happy Birthday! Top had no idea why he had been directed to Hangzhou. Zhou Enlai had secretly planned it all. Dad and Sylvia returned home, but Top and I went on to Peking, where we were invited to dinner with Zhou Enlai at the Great Hall of the People. We had a chance to drink a toast in maotai to thank him. Zhou granted an interview to Top in which, for the first time, he elaborated for publication the government's long-term policy for Taiwan. The island was to be united with the mainland by a policy of peaceful attraction. The policy remains in effect to this day.

In 1975, when Father, Meme, and I returned to China once again, we found ourselves plunged into a devastating imbroglio. We were doing research for a documentary later produced by the National Film Board of Canada. We had been invited to visit Premier Zhou Enlai but were told that he was in the hospital with cancer. Mao Zedong was also ill with Parkinson's disease and dementia. There was a power vacuum, and Mao's ambitious wife, Jiang Qing, and the Gang of Four were striking out ruthlessly to take power. Zhou Enlai stood in their way. The premier was the most popular leader in the country and still somewhat active, even from his hospital bed. We were not aware when we arrived that Zhou was seriously ill. When Dad asked to see him, we were told he was away and would see us when we returned from our scheduled filming trip. Three weeks later, upon our return to Peking, an old friend came to see us at the Peking Hotel. He looked shaken and, making sure no one saw him, handed Dad a note scribbled hastily in English on a bit of torn paper. It was from Zhou Enlai, asking Chester and me to come to the hospital immediately. We knew the hospital was only a ten-minute walk from the hotel. As we were leaving, we were stopped in the hallway by two burly hotel guards and escorted back to our suite. We tried again several times to leave the hotel, but we were stopped each time. Dad was furious. The next morning he said, "Let's just go!" We eluded the lobby guards and went quickly to a side entrance. As we were going out, two soldiers holding rifles with fixed bayonets stopped us. Dad protested and began to walk on, but the sentries blocked the way with pointed bayonets. They would not talk reason. There was nothing more we could do. Armed guards made sure we took our scheduled flight the next day. We left China depressed and deeply worried.

Premier Zhou died on January 8, 1976, at the age of seventy-eight. Like us, Huang Hua, his closest friend and associate (later foreign minister), and his wife, He Liliang, had been barred from seeing him. We believed that Jiang Qing had isolated Zhou and denied him the life-prolonging medication he needed. Mao died in September, and Jiang Qing was arrested with the Gang of Four after an attempted coup. Sentenced to death for her excesses during the Cultural Revolution, she committed suicide in a prison hospital where she had been previously confined for treatment of cancer.

It was a tragic ending to a remarkable era in which three generations of the Halvor Ronning family had sought during hardship years to make contributions to the well-being of the Chinese people. Our own family destiny was determined in the process. Since those years I have returned to China on many journalistic assignments, the latest in 2010, and witnessed the rise of the People's Republic to the status of a world economic superpower.

Except for influencing, even saving, some individuals in China, members of our family working as missionaries, teachers, diplomats, and journalists would never claim to have made a difference in the fate of China. But we do know that China has made a great difference in the destiny of our family. My grandparents and parents believed that change in a society starts with the individual. They attempted to transform, not the nature of man—for who can say what is the true nature of man?—but the attitudes and customs formed by centuries of authoritarian emperors and predominantly selfish thinking. As a family we have witnessed firsthand the transformation of China from a downtrodden and exploited country to a proud and prosperous country exploding with national confidence and hopefully heading toward a Chinese version of democracy. We also learned that true changes in the cyclical evolution of the ancient civilization of the Middle Kingdom can never be imposed from the outside.

In the end, eternal China will always go her own way.

I AM CONTENT WITH LIFE AND
AT PEACE WITH THE WORLD

Today I have wine,
Today I shall sing,
Today I shall drink my fill.

Anger and sorrow
are but wasted hours.
Let the cares of tomorrow
wait on tomorrow's sun.
—LUO YIN, FIVE DYNASTIES (AD 907–960)

My family's principal mission in life has been to promote peace and understanding between East and West.

Grandfather Halvor Nelius Ronning

After serving seventeen years as a missionary in China, Grandfather Halvor Ronning went to Canada and became a Canadian pioneer. He finally settled on his homestead in Valhalla Centre in the Peace River District, where he lived with his second wife, Gunhilde. But China was always on his mind. He converted the steep valley on his land in Canada into a Chinese scholar's garden with moon bridges cresting over the creek and Tai-ho rock gardens filled with a myriad of exotic flowers and blossoming trees. This summer paradise served as a new launching pad for Halvor, who continued to travel. From 1921 to 1933, Reverend Ronning served the church as an evangelist traveling around the nine districts of the Norwegian Lutheran Church of America. Grandfather's opposition to extremists and his outspoken acceptance of Chinese philosophy and cultural traditions made him a controversial figure in church circles. His brother Nils Ronning wrote the following about Halvor's ministry:

Though loyal to the organized church and supporting it to the best of his ability, my brother emphasizes the Third Article Church, the fellowship of believers, limited to no church body. Having met and associated with representatives of the different denominations, sects and Eastern religions and observing how God also blesses their efforts, he is tolerant and sympathetic toward them. He often said: "It would be just too bad if God saw His way clear to make use only of the Lutherans."

Some people who "belong" to a conservative party or church body said he was too liberal, too radical. He does, however, give very good reasons for the faith that is in him. In Norway, America, China and in Canada he has witnessed with indignation the arrogance, the callousness, the stupidity, yes, the cruelty of many of the privileged towards the underprivileged members of society. Rev. Ronning has always had a deep concern for souls. He had the native ability to win the confidence of all sorts of people. He is by nature a psychologist and can detect what hinders people from finding Christ or from yielding themselves to God. He has considerable experience in dealing with souls, not the least so in private conversations. He maintains that as a physician makes a thorough diagnosis before he operates or prescribes medicine or a good farmer carefully studies the soil before he decides what seed to plant, so a soul-winner must diagnose or study the persons he deals with.

In a report to a General Convention of the Norwegian Lutheran Church of America, Halvor expressed his concern about the future of the Church: *With pain and sorrow we must admit that all is not well with spiritual life in many congregations. Worldliness, sin and godlessness hold sway. Many of the unconverted church goers find their main comfort in the observation of the ceremonies alone.*

Dr. Martin Hegeland of the faculty at St. Olaf College wrote about his concerns:

It was with serious misgivings that President Boe and I considered the advisability of inviting the Rev. H. N. Ronning to speak at St. Olaf College. He belonged to the old school of evangelistic preachers and there were questions in our minds as to whether or not he could make an effective approach to modern student youth

He spoke twice a day at Chapel Services. This was different than a professor's formal lecture. He built his talks largely around illuminating and heart-gripping stories of human experiences of folly and wisdom, in the Far East and the American West which he had observed in his long and eventful life . . . Ronning possessed a good deal of dramatic power. He carried his audience from a hearty laugh one moment to a most sober, soul-searching self-analysis the next. His addresses were a panorama of struggles and triumphs, defeats and victories, in the lives of men and women he knew.

Reverend Alvin Snesrud, pastor of the Moreland Lutheran Church in Chicago wrote this about Ronning: "I saw the large number of young people who even at the stroke of midnight stood beside the door waiting to see him about their soul's condition. His presentation of the message was stirring to the depths, and the attendance increased every night. He had a way to win their confidence . . . He helped them through to see the glories of peace with God."

Reverend Ronning was particularly interested in troubled students in the institutions of higher learning who were, like his own sons, World War I veterans. Many were suffering from post-traumatic stress disorder (PTSD), then called "shell shock," and were seeking spiritual help. Because of the losses of his own loved ones and his experiences in China, Halvor understood their pain. One of his students was Reverend Morris Wee, Ph.D. pastor of Bethel Lutheran Church in Madison, Wisconsin, who later wrote: "Rev. Ronning's type of meeting had no appeal to me. I was depressed by the war. My roommate asked me to go so I reluctantly tagged along. The hall (seating some three hundred) was full. He spoke on the parable of the Prodigal Son. Before the speech was half over, I had the annoying awareness that there was a startling similarity to my life. Before the evening was over I knew that Rev. Ronning was speaking directly to me and about me . . . after midnight he answered my knock at his door and let me in to what was to be the single most important hour of my life. When he let me go, I was a child of God once more."

In June 1940, the fiftieth anniversary of the founding of the Norwegian Lutheran China Mission, St. Olaf College in Minnesota reluctantly conferred an honorary Doctor of Divinity (D.D.) on the Reverend H. N. Ronning. In the letter informing Ronning of the decision, Dr. L. W. Boe, president of St. Olaf College, wrote: "I know how you may feel personally and there are times when our friends have gone out of their way to express opposition to conferring honorary degrees on anyone. But it happens to be that is the only way in which a college can show its appreciation, and I hope you will accept the degree in the same spirit in which members of the Faculty want to give it."

In China, the Lutheran church Reverend Ronning built in Fancheng has the largest congregation in Xiangyang Prefecture. The school (Hung Wen) founded by Halvor and Hannah in 1894 has been replaced by many buildings on a large campus. It is now the largest middle and high school in Hubei Province. When, five generations later, in 2010, my husband and I visited the school with our daughter Karen, our adopted Chinese son, Peter, and our grandson Torin, we were greeted enthusiastically by the four thousand cheering students who now attend the Ronning School, causing my grandson to exclaim, "Hey, Grandma, in China you're a rock star!"

At the age of eighty-eight, Grandfather Halvor died in action. On March 1, 1950, while repairing the shingles on the roof of his three-story house on a rainy day, he slipped and fell to the ground. He never recovered. I remember exactly where I was when my grandfather died. I was asleep in a four-poster bed in a small French inn in Haiphong, in North Vietnam. Five months earlier, Top had been assigned by the Associated Press to cover the French-Indochina War and was traveling along the Vietnam-China frontier in a French Foreign Legion convoy on the Frontier Route Coloniale 4: The Rue de Mort (Road of Death). We planned to meet in the resort town of Hong Gay, on the beautiful Ha Long Bay at the terminus of the Rue de Mort.

In Hanoi I hired a reluctant taxi driver to take me by jeep 120 kilometers east to Haiphong, a strategic coastal city on the Gulf of Tonkin. There I would catch a rice boat to sail four miles down the winding Cam River to meet Top and continue our honeymoon in Hong Gay. French officials had sternly warned me from making the hazardous journey down the narrow river, which flowed through Viet Minh territory. They said the banks were patrolled by armed guards. Exasperated by my insistence, they pointed out that my blond hair would be an obvious target and they couldn't take the responsibility. I hadn't told them that I was four months' pregnant with our first child.

They were right, of course, but at that age I still felt immortal and had not yet developed a sense of consequence. That happened five months later when Susan was born in a French military hospital under artillery fire in Saigon. When I first held her in my arms, I suddenly realized I had to be responsible for my own actions. It was with some trepidation, however, that I checked into the old French inn in Haiphong. Cold and hungry, I ignored the cockroaches, pulled the comforter over my head, and fell into a deep sleep. Suddenly, around midnight, I awoke to see a vision of my grandfather in his Prince Albert coat standing in a cocoon-shaped mist at the foot of my bed. "Grandpa!" I exclaimed aloud. He stood for a moment with a peaceful smile on his face. Then he raised his hand and said in a clear voice—did he speak or just convey the thought?—"It's all right, Audrey. Everything will be all right." I thought I must be dreaming, but my apprehension was replaced by a warm feeling of confidence and courage. Then I heard some English voices in the next room, real voices sounding like Carl

Mydans, a *Life* photographer, and Wilson Fielder with *Time* magazine, who had come with Top and me from Saigon to Hanoi and had left on the same armed convoy with Top. I knocked on the door. Carl opened it. "Oh, Carl, it's really you! What are you doing here? Where's Top?"

After he got over the shock of finding me in this deserted inn, he explained that they had flown with Top in an old three-engine German Junker, dodging through cloudy mountain passes to Lang Son, a French Legion garrison near the Chinese border. From there they were escorted by a weapons carrier loaded with ten heavily armed Legionnaires, all German. When they turned off the road for Chi Ma, an outpost on the border, the lieutenant halted the jeep and said to them: "Gentlemen. You must now make a choice: either our jeep goes ahead on the road, which is often mined by the Viet Minh, or the Legionnaires go first in their truck. If we go first in the jeep and hit a mine, one or two of us may be killed or wounded, but the Legionnaires will be able to beat off the Viet Minh who will attack after the mine explodes. However, if the Legionnaires go first and their truck hits a mine, we probably will be overwhelmed and killed by the Viet Minh ambushers. Now take your choice—which goes first, our jeep or the truck." The three victims exchanged glances: Carl Mydans, a short, dynamic man, wise in the ways of war, who had distinguished himself covering World War II and was famous for his photos of General Douglas MacArthur wading ashore back to the Philippines; Wilson Fielder, the amiable young reporter for *Time,* newly based in Hong Kong; and my husband, Top. They elected to go ahead of the Legionnaires' truck in the jeep. They drove back to Lang Son that night, but just before the convoy took off, Carl and Wilson had received orders to go to Korea to cover the war. They were on the way to Korea when they ran into me in Haiphong. They told me that Top had set off with another convoy, but they had no idea what had happened to him. The convoy in front of them had been hit.

They looked at me strangely when I told them that my grandfather had just died and his apparition had appeared at my bedside to tell me everything was all right. Early the next morning, after failing to dissuade me from making the dangerous journey to meet Top in Hong Gay, Wilson and Carl took me to the river dock. Carl took photos of me boarding a native craft; it was about thirty feet long, with a gas motor, and loaded with bags of rice, sixteen Vietnamese, and a Frenchman with a submachine gun who was assigned to look after me and was not happy about it. He looked uneasily at my blond braids, slapped a conical hat on my head, and ordered me to hide behind the rice sacks. As the boat nosed through the narrow defiles for the next six hours, the Frenchman kept his gun trained on the cliffs towering above us. It was the last time I saw Wilson. He disappeared in Korea during the battle for Taejon, and his body was later found lying by a roadside.

When I arrived in Hong Gay, Top was nowhere to be found. I waited for three rainy days in another small French inn eating mostly bananas and fighting swarms of mosquitoes. Finally, Top walked in looking like Indiana Jones with a black beard. The vin rouge flowed freely that night. The sun came out and we had a wonderful two days boating around the amazing rock formations in the bay before returning to Saigon. There was a telegram waiting for me from my father who had been stranded in China because of the Korean War.

GREAT SADNESS STOP DEAR FATHER AND GRANDFATHER JOINED HIS ANCESTORS ON
MARCH 1 BLESSINGS COURAGE LOVE DAD

Grandfather Halvor left the following message:

GREETING TO MY CHILDREN AND MY CHILDREN'S CHILDREN ALL:

When I look back upon my long life, with its many and varied experiences, I see many faults and much weakness, and must wonder that God through His grace has been able to use such a weak instrument. I must say with Hudson Taylor: When God was looking for a man to begin the China Inland Mission, He could find no weaker person than myself, that His might be the Glory.

I want to share with you these three Scripture passages which are my daily stay and comfort:

Fear not, little flock, for it is your Father's pleasure to give you the kingdom. —Luke 12:32

And God is able to make all grace abound toward you; that ye, always having all sufficiency in all things, may abound in every good work. —2 Cor. 9:8

Be careful for nothing, but in everything by prayer and supplications with thanksgiving let your requests be made known to God. —Phil. 4:6.

God bless you, my dear children!

Your father forever,

Halvor Ronning

Inga Marie Horte Ronning

My mother, who had supported Dad through all his adventures, left this world in 1967 after a failed operation for diverticulitis. When Dad told me she was dying,

I left my family in Scarsdale to fly back to Camrose and be with her the last few days. My siblings Sylvia, Alton, Meme, Kjeryn, and Harmon congregated from all over the world and arrived in time to hold hands around her deathbed and tearfully wish her Godspeed on her eternal journey. She died with a smile on her still-beautiful face. It was October and the leaves were almost gone. Mother was a true artist but had little time to pursue her own talents. A week earlier she had won a prize for her oil painting of falling leaves.

I returned home in a state of depression. I felt that a part of me had died with my mother. Then another mysterious thing happened. Mom came to me in a dream so realistic that I still don't really know if I was hallucinating or not. She was wearing her favorite hat and sat on the foot of my bed. She looked at me with an expression of peace beyond understanding, touched my foot, and said the same thing as Grandfather: "It's all right, Audrey." Then she disappeared. I woke up feeling that everything in the universe was the way it was supposed to be. I still don't know what happened, but I do know the healing was real. Inga was loved by all who knew her. Her many descendants will never allow her memory to pass into the mists of time.

Chester Ronning: Three Last Wishes

Dad continued to travel, lecture, and write, but he was never quite the same after Mom died. He was a wise and gentle teacher, a man profoundly moved by the suffering of mankind with a passion to ease that suffering. Like his parents before him, he learned to love and respect the Chinese and their ancient civilization, but he lived rather than just preached Christianity.

Dad made four more adventurous trips back to China before his extraordinary zest for life and the fiery dynamism of his younger years were tempered with age, but he remained tender, compassionate, and more loving than ever. Shortly before his ninetieth birthday, during a family reunion in Camrose, Dad looked at his grown children with his deep, compassionate eyes, which I always believed could see right through me, and said wistfully, "I wish I could revisit my birthplace just once more before I kick the bucket." He laughed at himself for using such a euphemism. His eyes held a pensive look I had not seen before. "Would you like to come with me?" he asked. "I think I am too old to travel alone. You know, I am not as competent as I used to be." Speaking slowly, he explained that he had three wishes: to pay his respects to his mother's grave, to visit the temple caves of Dunhuang in Gansu Province in far western China that as a child the explorer Sven Hedin had told him about, and to journey to the Impregnable Pass Under Heaven at the western end of the Great Wall. These would not be easy wishes to fulfill. He was still the gutsiest old man I had ever encountered. Maybe it was possible. Why not? "Well, let's all go," I said.

Dad's eyes lit up with their old fire. "Good shot!" he said. Then he raised his silver cane and shouted "*Kai bu zou! Forward March!*" We were soon to hear him shouting this all over China.

A "red flag" limo and two Toyotas met us in Beijing and took us to a luxurious guest house that Dad immediately recognized as the home of the late Nationalist Generalissimo Chiang Kai-shek, whom the Communists had driven to Taiwan. The next day we were invited to a banquet in Dad's honor at the Great Hall of the People. Former foreign minister and friend Huang Hua welcomed us. "It is such an honor to have you back," he told Dad.

"Well," said Dad with the old twinkle in his eye, "I don't know if you are honoring me or not, because I noticed that you put me up in Chiang Kai-shek's old house." After a moment's hesitation, Huang Hua laughed heartily. "That's because you were a friend of both Chinas—old and new."

We soon started on our "three wishes" journey. Dad seemed to grow stronger every day. We flew to Dunhuang and took a chartered bus along the Old Silk Road. Our first stop was at the Mogao Grottoes—the Caves of the Thousand Buddhas—near Dunhuang, the largest treasure house of Buddhist art in China. We explored only 210 of the 492 temple caves, the oldest of which was hewn out in AD 366. The Gobi Desert was cold and haunting. We stopped by the crumbling walls of a lost city, where our guide said we could dig for lost treasure. When father wasn't looking, brother Alton buried some Canadian coins to mystify some future treasure hunter. Dad said, "Well, I'm going to find the pot of gold at the end of the rainbow."

Dad didn't find the end of the rainbow, but the next day, just before sunset, we arrived at the fortress at the end of the Great Wall and climbed the Gate of Enlightenment. There below us, the wall undulated over the sand dunes like a tired, jagged-spined dragon. Exhausted it should be: it had stretched in circuitous fashion over three thousand miles from Badaling Pass east of Peking, where in the 1920s Dad and Mom had ridden donkeys along the wall. We watched a lone camel disappear into the shimmer of a desert mirage as the sun slipped into the saffron mists.

To fulfill Dad's last wish we flew to Hankou and boarded a train to Fancheng, where Grandmother Hannah's descendants joined hands around her tombstone and tearfully paid our last respects. The next day, on the occasion of Dad's nine-tieth birthday, a noisy and joyous celebration was held. Most of the population stood outside the Grand Hall lighting firecrackers while friends and officials gathered around circular tables brimming with symbols of long life. The chef himself presented the last of sixteen indescribable courses: longevity noodles hanging a foot long from chopsticks held high. Tributes were made while maotai and rice wine flowed freely. Dad was deeply stirred. He amused his hosts with old Chinese rhyming riddles and made flowery toasts to his fellow provincials— *Hubei ren* in the local dialect, referring to himself again as "just an old lump of mud like the rest of you." "In heaven," he said, "is a wonderful nine-headed bird. On earth are the wonderful *Hubei ren.*"

Dad turned to me and said, "I wonder how in the world I remembered that." Then he became pensive.

"Are you all right?" I asked

"I was only thinking," he said softly, "of what has been and is no more."

He joined his worthy ancestors at the age of ninety. Friends from all over the world, including the Chinese ambassador to Canada, came to Camrose to attend his funeral on a cold, wintery day. Daddy was buried next to Mama. The ground was covered with powdered snow. Brother Harmon and I lay down and made angels with wings and frozen tears.

Chester's family received hundreds of condolence letters from many nations and from people of all religions who all had one thing in common: a love and respect for their friend Chester.

Tran Van Dinh, Vietnamese diplomat and author, wrote: "I believe he would have a joyful and interesting time in Heaven. He would pay his respects to the Emperor of Jade and his ancestors. He would look up his old friend Zhou Enlai and they would call on Buddha, Laozi, Confucius and over cups of lotus cosmic tea, would discuss the human condition on this earth."

Historian Arthur Schlesinger Jr.: "He nobly served the cause of rationality and peace in the world, and history will do him great justice."

Journalist Harrison Salisbury: "How curious the world will be without your father to make us laugh and make us understand what it is all really about; what is important and what is trivial."

Chester A. Ronning was awarded five honorary doctorates from various Canadian and American universities. He was designated an Officer of the Order of Canada, 1967, and Companion of the Order of Canada, 1972. In December 1984, he received the Order of Excellence from the Province of Alberta.

It is interesting to note this strange coincidence: My father was born in the heart of China on December 13, 1894, and died on the opposite side of the world, in the heart of Canada on December 31, 1984. Note the reversed numbers—this is considered a rare and propitious happening by the Chinese. I like to believe it was a sign that my father had completed the full circle in the mysterious and wondrous Wheel of Life. Let it be.

BIBLIOGRAPHY

Beckwith, Christopher I. *Empires of the Silk Road: A History of Central Asia from the Bronze Age to the Present*. Princeton: Princeton University Press, 2009.

Backhouse, E., and J. O. P. Bland. *Annals & Memoirs of the Court of Peking (from the 16th to the 20th Century)*. Boston: Houghton Mifflin, 1914.

Bland, J. O. P., and E. Backhouse. *China under the Empress Dowager: Being the History of the Life and Times of Tzu Hsi: Compiled from State Papers and the Private Diary of the Comptroller of Her Household*. New York: Houghton Mifflin, 1914.

Brackman, Arnold C. *The Prisoner of Peking*. New York: Van Nostrand Reinhold, 1980.

Chang, Iris. *The Rape of Nanking: The Forgotten Holocaust of World War II*. New York: Basic Books, 1997.

Chou Hsiang-kuang. *A History of Chinese Buddhism*. Allahabad, Upper Pradesh, India: Indo-Chinese Literature Publications, 1955.

Cohen, Paul A. *China and Christianity: The Missionary Movement and the Growth of Chinese Antiforeignism: 1860–1870*. Cambridge, Mass.: Harvard University Press, 1963.

———. *History in Three Keys: The Boxers as Event, Experience, and Myth*. New York: Columbia University Press, 1997.

Davies, John Paton, Jr. *China Hand: An Autobiography*. Philadelphia: University of Pennsylvania Press, 2012.

Dolin, Eric Jay. *When America First Met China: An Exotic History of Tea, Drugs, and Money in the Age of Sail*. New York: W. W. Norton & Co., 2012.

Durdin, Tilman, James Reston, Seymour Topping, Audrey Topping, and Frank Ching. *The New York Times Report from Red China*. New York: Avon, 1971.

Esherick, Joseph W. *The Origins of the Boxer Uprising*. Berkeley: University of California Press, 1987.

Fay, Peter Ward. *The Opium War, 1840–1842: Barbarians in the Celestial Empire in the Early Part of the Nineteenth Century and the War by Which They Forced Her Gates Ajar*. Chapel Hill: University of North Carolina Press, 1975.

Fleming, Peter. *The Siege at Peking*. New York: Harper and Brothers, 1959.

Frillman, Paul, and Graham Peck. *A Remembered Life*. Boston: Houghton Mifflin, 1968.

Gao Wenqian. *Zhou Enlai: The Last Perfect Revolutionary.* New York: Public Affairs, 2007.

Glover, Archibald E. *A Thousand Miles of Miracle in China: A Personal Record of God's Delivering Power from the Hands of the Imperial Boxers of Shan-si.* London: Pickering and Inglis, 1945.

Goodrich, Carrington L. *A Short History of the Chinese People.* New York: Harper, 1959.

Han Suyin. *The Crippled Tree: The Unforgettable Story of War and Revolution in China.* New York: Putnam, 1965.

———. *A Mortal Flower.* New York: Putnam, 1965.

Hart, Henry H. *Poems of the Hundred Names.* 3rd ed. Stanford: Stanford University Press, 1954.

Himle, Pastor Th., H. N. Ronning, A. O. Oppegard, and Trykt Hos. *Evangeliets Seier, 1891–1916.* Minneapolis: K. G. Holter, 1916. In Norwegian.

Hopkirk Peter. *Foreign Devils on the Silk Road: The Search for the Lost Cities and Treasures of Chinese Central Asia.* London: Murray, 1980.

Issacs, Harold R. *The Tragedy of the Chinese Revolution.* London: Secker and Warburg, 1938.

Ketler, Isaac C. *The Tragedy of Paotingfu: An Authentic Story of the Lives, Services and Sacrifices of the Presbyterian, Congregational and China Inland Missionaries Who Suffered Martyrdom at Paotingfu, China, June 30th and July 1, 1900.* New York: Fleming H. Revell, 1902.

Kissinger, Henry. *On China.* New York: Penguin, 2012.

Lawrence, Earl. *Yangtse Incident.* London: Harrap, 1950.

Lee, Dora Fugh. *Pu Xinyu—A Manchu Prince Who Embodied Chinese Culture.* N.p., n.d.

Luo Guanzhong. *Romance of the Three Kingdoms.* Translated by Moss Roberts. Beijing: Foreign Language Press, 1955.

Milton, David, and Nancy Milton. *The Wind Will Not Subside: Years in Revolutionary China, 1964–1969.* New York: Pantheon, 1975.

Mirsky, Jeannette. *Sir Auriel Stein: Archaeological Explorer.* Chicago: University of Chicago Press, 1977.

Peng, Mike. "A Study of Chinese History." Unpublished typescript.

Pruitt, Ida, and Lao T'ai-t'ai Ning. *A Daughter of Han: The Autobiography of a Chinese Working Woman.* Stanford: Stanford University Press, 1967.

Richard, Timothy. *Forty-Five Years in China: Reminiscences.* New York: Stokes, 1916.

Ronning, Chester. *A Memoir of China in Revolution: From the Boxer Rebellion to the People's Republic.* New York: Pantheon, 1974.

Ronning, Halvor N. *The Gospel at Work.* With N. N. Ronning. Minneapolis: N. N. Ronning, 1943.

Ronning, N. N. *The Boy from Telemark.* Minneapolis: The Friend, 1933.

———. *A Summer in Telemark.* Minneapolis: The Friend, 1930.

Roots, John McCook. "The Canton Idea." *Asia,* April 1927.

Sacks, Oliver. *Hallucinations.* New York: Knopf, 2012.

Schell, Orville. *"Watch Out for Foreign Guests": China Encounters the West.* New York: Pantheon, 1980.

Service, John S. *Lost Chance in China: The World War II Dispatches of John S. Service.* New York: Random House, 1974.

Sima Qian. *Records of the Grand Historian.* Translated by Burton Watson. New York: Columbia University Press, 1961.

Smith, Arthur Henderson. *China in Convulsion.* 2 vols. New York: Fleming H. Revell, 1901.

Snow, Edgar. *The Battle for Asia.* New York: Random House, 1941.

———. *Red Star over China.* New York: Vintage, 1971.

Snow, Edgar, and Lois Wheeler Snow. *Edgar Snow's China: A Personal Account of the Chinese Revolution.* New York: Random House, 1981.

Sokolsy, George E. "The Kuomintang." In *The China Yearbook, 1928,* edited by Henry Woodhead. London: Routledge, 1969.

Sullivan, Lawrence R. *Leadership and Authority in China, 1895–1976.* Lanham, Md.: Lexington Books, 2012.

Taylor, Dr. and Mrs. Howard. *Hudson Taylor's Spiritual Secret.* Chicago: Moody Press, 1989.

Teng Ssu-yu and John King Fairbank, eds. *China's Response to the West: A Documentary Survey.* Cambridge, U.K.: Cambridge University Press, 1954.

Tong, Hollington K. *China and the World Press.* N.p. [China?], 1948.

Topping, Audrey. *Charlie's World: The Improbable Adventures of a Hong Kong Cockatoo and His American Family.* New York: Earth Times Books, 2000.

———. *Dawn Wakes in the East.* New York: Harper and Row, 1973.

Topping, Seymour. *Journey between Two Chinas.* New York: Harper and Row, 1972.

———. *On the Front Lines of the Cold War: An American Correspondent's Journal from the Chinese Civil War to the Cuban Missile Crisis.* Baton Rouge: Louisiana State University Press, 2010.

Tsui Chi. *A Short History of Chinese Civilization*. New York: Putnam, 1943.

Tuchman, Barbara. *Stilwell and the American Experience in China, 1911–1945*. New York: Macmillan, 1971.

Walshe, W. Gilbert. *"Ways That Are Dark": Some Chapters on Chinese Etiquette and Social Procedure*. Shanghai: Kelly and Walsh, 1890.

Warner, Marina. *The Dragon Empress: Life and Times of Tz'u Hsi, Empress Dowager of China, 1835–1908*. London: Vintage, 1972.

Weale, B. L. Putnam. *Indiscreet Letters from Peking: Being the Notes of an Eye-Witness, Which Set Forth in Some Detail, from Day-to-Day, the Real Story of the Siege and Sack of a Distressed Capital in 1900—the Year of Great Tribulation*. New York: Dodd, Mead, 1907.

Westad, Odd Arne. *Restless Empire: China and the World since 1750*. New York: Basic Books, 2012.

Wilson, Dick. *The Long March, 1935: The Epic of Chinese Communism's Survival*. New York: Viking, 1971.

Wright, Mary. *The Last Stand of Chinese Conservatism: The T'ung-ch'ih Restoration, 1862–1874*. Stanford: Stanford University Press, 1962.

Yü Chün-fang. *Kuan-Yin: The Chinese Transformation of Avalokiteśvara*. New York: Columbia University Press, 2001.

Zou Rong. *The Revolutionary Army: A Chinese Nationalist Tract*. Translated by John Lust. Paris: Mouton, 1968.